REA: THE LEADER IN TEACHER CERTIFICATION PREP

PRAXIS II® SOCIAL STUDIES
Content Knowledge (0081)

TestWare® Edition

Jeanne M. Bowlan, M.A.
Elizabeth Upper Academy
Elizabeth, New Jersey

Research & Education Association
Visit our Educator Support Center: www.rea.com/teacher
Updates to the test and this book: www.rea.com/PRAXIS/ss0081.htm

Research & Education Association
61 Ethel Road West
Piscataway, New Jersey 08854
E-mail: info@rea.com

**PRAXIS II® Social Studies: Content Knowledge (0081)
with TestWare® on CD-ROM, 2nd Edition**

About Research & Education Association

Founded in 1959, Research & Education Association is dedicated to publishing the finest and most effective educational materials—including software, study guides, and test preps—for students in middle school, high school, college, graduate school, and beyond.

REA's Test Preparation series includes books and software for all academic levels in almost all disciplines. Research & Education Association publishes test preps for students who have not yet entered high school, as well as for high school students preparing to enter college. Students from countries around the world seeking to attend college in the United States will find the assistance they need in REA's publications. For college students seeking advanced degrees, REA publishes test preps for many major graduate school admission examinations in a wide variety of disciplines, including engineering, law, and medicine. Students at every level, in every field, with every ambition can find what they are looking for among REA's publications.

REA's practice tests are always based upon the most recently administered exams and include every type of question that you can expect on the actual exams.

REA's publications and educational materials are highly regarded and continually receive an unprecedented amount of praise from professionals, instructors, librarians, parents, and students. Our authors are as diverse as the fields represented in the books we publish. They are well-known in their respective disciplines and serve on the faculties of prestigious high schools, colleges, and universities throughout the United States and Canada.

Today, REA's wide-ranging catalog is a leading resource for teachers, students, and professionals.

We invite you to visit us at *www.rea.com* to find out how "REA is making the world smarter."

Acknowledgments

We would like to thank Larry Kling, Vice President, Editorial, for his editorial direction; Pam Weston, Vice President, Publishing, for setting the quality standards for production integrity and managing the publication to completion; John Cording, Vice President, Technology, for coordinating the design, development, and testing of REA's TestWare®; Diane Goldschmidt, Senior Editor, and Alice Leonard, Senior Editor, for pre-flight editorial review; Kathleen Casey, Senior Editor, for project management; Heena Patel, Technology Project Manager, for software testing; Christine Saul, Senior Graphic Artist, for cover design; and Maureen Mulligan, Graphic Artist, for post-production file mapping.

We also gratefully acknowledge Alison Minion for copyediting, Caragraphics for typesetting, the Editors of REA for proofreading, and Stephanie Reymann for indexing the manuscript.

About the Author

Jeanne M. Bowlan teaches social studies at the Upper Academy in Elizabeth, New Jersey. Ms. Bowlan earned her B.A. from Wells College and her M.A. in History from Rutgers, The State University of New Jersey. In her high school teaching career, Ms. Bowlan has taught Advanced Placement European History, United States History, Sociology, and Anthropology. Ms. Bowlan has also taught college courses in European History, Women's Studies, and Writing.

CONTENTS

CHAPTER 4
GOVERNMENT, CIVICS, AND POLITICAL SCIENCE   247

CHAPTER 5
GEOGRAPHY   285

CHAPTER 6
ECONOMICS   311

Contents

Introduction

ABOUT THIS BOOK AND TestWare®

If you're looking to secure certification as a secondary social studies teacher, many states and districts require the Praxis II Social Studies: Content Knowledge 0081 test (Praxis II 0081). Think of this book and the accompanying TestWare® as your toolkit to pass the test. It will help take the mystery and anxiety out of the testing process by equipping you not only with the nuts and bolts, but also, ultimately, with the confidence to succeed alongside your peers across the United States.

We at REA have put a lot of thought into this, and the result is a book that pulls together all the critical information you need to know to pass the test. Let us help you fill in the blanks—literally and figuratively! We will provide you with the touchstones that will allow you to do your very best come test day and beyond. In this guide, REA offers our customary in-depth, up-to-date, objective coverage, with test-specific modules devoted to targeted review and realistic practice exams, in printed form and on the enclosed TestWare® on CD-ROM, complete with the kind of detail that makes a difference when you're coming down the homestretch in your preparation. We also include a quick-view answer key and competency-categorized progress chart to enable you to pinpoint your strengths and weaknesses. We strongly recommend that you begin your preparation with the TestWare® tests, which provide timed conditions and instantaneous, accurate scoring.

Chapter 1

ABOUT THE PRAXIS SERIES

Praxis is Educational Testing Service's (ETS) shorthand for Professional Assessments for Beginning Teachers. The Praxis Series is a group of teacher-certification and licensing tests that ETS developed in concert with states across the nation. There are three categories of tests in the series: Praxis I, Praxis II, and Praxis III. Praxis I includes the paper-based Pre-Professional Skills Tests (PPST) and the Praxis I Computer-Based Tests (CBT). Both versions cover essentially the same subject matter. These exams measure basic reading, mathematics, and writing skills and are often a requirement for admission to a teacher education program.

Praxis II embraces Subject Assessment/Specialty Area Tests, of which the Praxis II Social Studies: Content Knowledge 0081 is a part. Most Praxis II examinations cover the subject matter that students typically study in teacher education courses such as language acquisition, school curriculum, methods of teaching, and other professional development courses. However, the Praxis II 0081 is expressly for prospective and practicing social studies teachers; it measures skills and knowledge in the areas of U.S. History, World History, Government/Civics/Political Science, Geography, Economics, and the additional behavioral sciences of Anthropology, Sociology, and Psychology.

Praxis III is different from the multiple-choice and essay tests typically used for assessment purposes. With this assessment, ETS-trained observers evaluate an instructor's performance in the classroom, using nationally validated criteria. The observers may videotape the lesson, and other teaching experts may critique the resulting tapes.

Who Takes the Test?

Most people who take the Praxis II Social Studies: Content Knowledge are seeking initial certification. Thirty-five states require the Praxis II 0081 and you should check with your state's education agency to determine which Praxis examination(s) you should take; the ETS Praxis website (*www.ets.org/praxis/*) and registration bulletin may also help you determine the tests you need for licensure.

When and Where Can I Take the Test?

ETS offers the Praxis II Social Studies: Content Knowledge test three times a year, usually mid-month in March, June, and November. Pre-registration is required for this test, so contact your district's administrative office for exact availability in your area.

How Do I Get More Information on the ETS Praxis Exams?

To receive information on upcoming administrations of any of the Praxis II Subject Assessments, consult the ETS registration bulletin or website, or contact ETS at:

Educational Testing Service
Teaching and Learning Division
P.O. Box 6051
Princeton, NJ 08541-6051
Phone: (609) 771-7395
Website: *www.ets.org/praxis*
E-mail: *www.ets.org/praxis/contact/email_praxis* (use the online
form)

Special accommodations are available for candidates who are visually impaired, hearing impaired, physically disabled, or specific learning disabled. For questions concerning disability services, contact:

ETS Disability Services: (609) 771-7780
TTY only: (609) 771-7714

Provisions are also available for examinees whose primary language is not English. The ETS registration bulletin and website include directions for those requesting such accommodations. You can also consult ETS with regard to available test sites; reporting test scores; requesting changes in tests, centers, and dates of test; purchasing additional score reports; retaking tests; and other basic facts.

Is There a Registration Fee?

To take a Praxis examination, you must pay a registration fee, which is payable by check, money order, or with American Express, Discover, MasterCard, or Visa credit cards. In certain cases, ETS offers fee waivers. The registration bulletin and website give qualifications for receiving this benefit and describe the application process. Cash is not accepted for payment.

Can I Retake the Test?

Some states, institutions, and associations limit the number of times you can retest. Contact your state or licensing authority to confirm their retest policies.

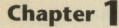

HOW TO USE THIS BOOK AND TestWare®

What Do I Study First?

Read over REA's subject reviews and suggestions for test taking. Take practice test 1 on the CD-ROM to determine your areas of weakness, and then restudy the material focusing on your specific problem areas. Studying the reviews thoroughly will reinforce the basic skills you will need to do well on the exams. Make sure to do the practice questions in this book so that you will be familiar with the format and procedures involved with taking the actual test.

When Should I Start Studying?

It is never too early to start studying; the earlier you begin, the more time you will have to sharpen your skills. Do not procrastinate! Cramming is not an effective way to study because it does not allow you the time needed to learn the test material.

FORMAT OF THE TEST

The Praxis II Social Studies: Content Knowledge test covers six major content areas and has 130 multiple-choice questions. You will have 2 hours to complete the exam.

Content Category	Approximate Number of Questions	Approximate Percentage of Exam
United States History	26	20%
World History	26	20%
Government/Civics/ Political Science	26	20%
Geography	19	15%
Economics	19	15%
Behavioral Sciences	13	10%

A number of the questions are interdisciplinary and reflect the complex relationship among the multiple fields of social studies. Approximately sixty-percent (60%) of the questions require recall, knowledge, and recognition; the remainder will require higher-order thinking. You will be asked to interpret material such as written passages, maps, charts, table, diagrams and photographs. Ten- to fifteen-percent of the multiple-choice questions will contain content covering the diverse experiences of people in the United States with regard to gender, culure, and/or race, and/or content relating to Latin America, Africa, Asia, or Oceania.

The multiple-choice questions assess a test-taker's knowledge of certain job-related skills and knowledge. Four choices are provided for each multiple-choice question; the options bear the letters A through D. The exams use four types of multiple-choice questions:

1. The Roman numeral multiple-choice question

2. The "Which of the following?" multiple-choice question

3. The complete-the-statement multiple-choice question

4. The multiple-choice question with qualifiers

The following sections describe each type of question and suggested strategies.

Roman Numeral Multiple-Choice Questions

Perhaps the most difficult of the types of multiple-choice questions is the Roman numeral question, because it allows for more than one correct answer. Strategy: Assess each answer before looking at the Roman numeral choices. Consider the following Roman numeral multiple-choice question:

Below is a partial list of signatories of the Declaration of Independence.

I. Ben Franklin
II. George Washington
III. John Hancock
IV. Thomas Jefferson
V. John Adams
VI. Samuel Adams

Of the combinations listed below, which NEVER served as commander-in-chief of the United States?

(A) I, III, VI

(B) II, IV, V

(C) IV, I, II,

(D) I, III, IV, V

In reviewing the questions, you should note that you may choose two or three answers by selecting (A), (B), (C), or (D). The correct answer is (A) because none of the three of signers ever served as president.

"Which of the Following?" Multiple-Choice Questions

In a "Which of the following?" question, one of the answers is correct among the various choices. **Strategy:** Form a sentence by replacing the first part of the question with each of the answer choices in turn, and then determine which of the resulting sentences is correct. Consider the following example:

Which of the following political ideologies advocated the rapid expansion of settlements in the western United States?

(A) Social Darwinism

(B) Temperance

(C) Imperialism

(D) Manifest destiny

Using the suggested technique, one would read:

(A) Social Darwinism advocated the rapid expansion of settlements in the western United States.

(B) Temperance advocated the rapid expansion of settlements in the western United States.

(C) Imperialism advocated the rapid expansion of settlements in the western United States.

(D) Manifest destiny advocated the rapid expansion of settlements in the western United States.

Read all of the options. By substituting the various choices into the sentence, the correct choice should become obvious if you think it through: (D) Manifest destiny. Social Darwinism (A) is the ideology that credits advances in a given society to the relative superiority of its members. The temperance movement was a *movement*, not an ideology as such, and it was concerned with the overuse of alcohol. Imperialism (C) was the basis of nineteenth-century colonism in Africa.

Not all "Which of the following?" multiple-choice questions are as straightforward and simple as the previous example. Consider the following multiple-choice question that requires reading a passage:

"Non-violence is the greatest force at the disposal of mankind. It is mightier than the mightiest weapon of destruction devised by the ingenuity of man...Non-cooperation is directed not against men but against measures. It is not directed against the Governors, but against the system they administer. The roots of non-cooperation lie not in hatred but in justice, if not in love."

Which of the following figures most likely made this statement?

    (A) Aurangzeb
    (B) Jinnah
    (C) Mohandas Ghandhi
    (D) Winston Churchill

The answer is (C) Mohandas Ghandhi, who worked to unite Muslims and Hindus as well as other factions in their bid for independence from the British through a program of nonviolent resistance. He advocated for non-violent civil disobedience and argued against Britain's plans to partition India.

Strategy: Underline key information as you read the question. For instance, as you read the question, you might underline or highlight the word and phrases such as *non-violence, non-cooperation* and *the system they administer*. By highlighting key words you can eliminate those people who do not fit the key concepts. The highlighting will thus save you time; saving time is helpful when you must answer 130 questions in two hours.

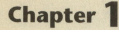

Complete-the-Statement Multiple-Choice Questions

The complete-the-statement multiple-choice question consists of an incomplete statement for which you must select the answer choice that will complete the statement correctly. Here is an example:

Enlightenment thinkers whose writings became popular in France were known as
(A) philosophes.
(B) arrogant.
(C) protestants.
(D) clerics.

The correct answer is (A), philosophes. With this type of question your strategy should be to eliminate answer choices you are certain to be wrong, thus reducing your choices.

Multiple-Choice Questions with Qualifiers

Some of the multiple-choice questions may contain qualifiers—words like *not*, *least*, and *except*. These added words make the test questions more difficult because rather than having to choose the best answer, as is usually the case, you must actually select the opposite. **Strategy:** Circle the qualifier. It is easy to forget to select the negative; circling the qualifier in the question stem is a flag. This will serve as a reminder as you are reading the question and especially if you must reread or check the answer at a later time. Now consider this question with a qualifier:

Which of the following is NOT a characteristic of Italian Renaissance humanism?

(A) Its foundation is in the study of the classics.
(B) Intellectual life was its focus.
(C) It was noticeable in the artistic accomplishments of the period.
(D) It was based on learning and understanding about what it means to be human.

You are looking for the exception in this question, so you want to compare each answer choice to the question to find which answer is not representative of Italian Renaissance humanism. Humanism is *not* learning and understanding, nor is it the study of being human, so (D) is the correct answer. Humanism was an intellectual movement based on the study of the classics. And, artistic accomplishments of the period did reflect the characteristics of the Renaissance.

New question formats will, at times, appear on the Praxis II Social Studies: Content Knowledge. If such a new-format question appears on the test you are taking—don't panic! You have the tools you need to succeed. Simply follow these steps:

1. Read the directions thoroughly.

2. Read the question carefully, as you would any other question.

3. Decide what you should be trying to determine.

4. Look for the details that will help you answer correctly.

You will receive answer sheets, similar to the ones in this volume, on which you will fill in your response: (A), (B), (C), or (D). As the previous example questions have shown, there are four options for each of the multiple-choice questions; questions with more than one correct answer may use Roman numerals. Individual test items require a variety of different thinking levels, ranging from simple recall to evaluation and problem solving.

You should spend less than a minute on each question on each of the practice tests—and on the real exams, of course. You have to answer 130 questions in two hours.

The reviews in this book will help you sharpen the basic skills needed to approach the exams and offer you strategies for attacking the questions. By using the reviews in conjunction with the practice tests, you will better prepare yourself for the actual tests. You have learned through your coursework and your practical experience in schools most of what you need to know to answer the questions on the test. In your classes, you gained the expertise to make important decisions about situations you will face in the classroom. The reviews in this book will help you fit the information you have acquired in practice into its specific testable category. Reviewing your class notes and textbooks along with systematic use of this book will give you an excellent springboard for passing the Praxis II Social Studies: Content Knowledge (0081) test.

SCORING

The number of raw points awarded on the Praxis II Social Studies 0081 is based on the number of correct answers given. Most Praxis examinations vary by edition, which means that each test has several variations that contain different questions. The different questions are intended to measure the same general types of knowledge or skills. However, there is no way to guarantee that the questions on all editions of the test will have the same degree of difficulty. To avoid penalizing test takers who answer more difficult questions, the initial scores are adjusted for difficulty by using a statistical process known as equating. To avoid confusion between the *adjusted* and *unadjusted* scores, ETS reports the *adjusted scores* on a score scale that makes them clearly different from the *unadjusted scores. Unadjusted scores* or "raw scores" are simply the number of questions answered correctly. *Adjusted scores*, which are equated to the scale ETS uses for reporting the scores are called "scaled scores." For each edition of a Praxis test, a "raw-to-scale conversion table" is used to translate raw to scaled scores. The easier the questions are on a test edition, the more questions must be answered correctly to earn a given scaled score.

PRAXIS Pointer

Don't make questions more difficult than they are—there are no "trick" questions or hidden meanings.

The college or university in which you are enrolled may set passing scores for the completion of your teacher education program and for graduation. Be sure to check the requirements in the catalogues or bulletins. You will also want to talk with your advisor. The passing scores for the Praxis II tests vary from state to state. To find out which of the Praxis II tests your state requires and what your state's set passing score is, contact your state's education department directly.

To gage how you are doing using our practice tests, if you score a 75% or above you can be assured that you passed the practice test.

Score Reporting

When Will I Receive My Examinee Score Report and in What Form Will It Be?

ETS mails test-score reports six weeks after the test date. There is an exception for computer-based tests and for the Praxis I PPST examinations. Score reports will list your current score and the highest score you have earned on each test you have taken over the last 10 years. Along with your score report, ETS will provide you with a booklet that offers details on your scores. For each test date, you may request that ETS send a copy of your scores to as many as three score recipients, provided that each institution or agency is eligible to receive the scores.

STUDYING FOR THE TEST

It is critical to your success that you study effectively. To that end, here are some tips to put you in the driver's seat on test day:

- Choose a time and place for studying that works best for you. Some people set aside a certain number of hours every morning to study; others may choose to study at night before retiring. Only you know what is most effective for you.

- Use your time wisely and be consistent. Work out a study routine and stick to it; don't let your personal schedule interfere. Remember, seven weeks of studying is a modest investment to put you on your chosen path.

- Don't cram the night before the test. You may have heard many amazing tales about effective cramming, but don't kid yourself: most of them are false, and the rest are about exceptional people who, by definition, aren't like most of us.

- When you take the practice tests, try to make your testing conditions as much like the actual test as possible. Turn off your television, radio, and telephone. Sit down at a quiet table free from distraction.

- As you complete the practice test, score your test and thoroughly review the explanations to the questions you answered incorrectly.

- Take notes on material you will want to go over again or research further.

- Keep track of your scores. By doing so, you will be able to gauge your progress and discover your strengths and weaknesses. You should carefully study the material relevant to your areas of difficulty. This will build your test-taking skills and your confidence!

STUDY SCHEDULE

The following study schedule allows for thorough preparation to pass the Praxis II Social Studies: Content Knowledge (0081) exam. This is a suggested seven-week course of study. However, you can condense this schedule if you are in a time crunch or expand it

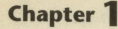

PRAXIS Pointer

Take the practice test under the same conditions you will take the actual test.

if you have more time. You may decide to use your weekends for study and preparation and go about your other business during the week. You may even want to record information and listen to it on your MP3 player or CD as you travel in your car. However you decide to

study, be sure to adhere to the structured schedule you devise.

WEEK	ACTIVITY
1	After reading the first chapter of this book to understand the format and content of the exam, you'll be taking the first practice test on CD-ROM. Our computerized tests are taken from the tests presented in this book. They provide a scored report which includes a score analysis chart indicating the percentage right in each category. This will help you pinpoint your strengths and weaknesses. Make sure you simulate real exam conditions when you take the practice test.
2	Review the explanations for the questions you missed, and review the appropriate chapter sections. Useful study techniques include highlighting key terms and information, taking notes as you review each section, and putting new terms and information on note cards to help retain the information.
3 and 4	Reread all your note cards, refresh your understanding of the exam's subareas and related skills, review your textbooks, and read over notes you took in your college classes. This is also the time to consider any other supplementary materials suggested by a counselor or your state education agency.
5	Begin to condense your notes and findings. A structured list of important facts and concepts, based on your note cards, college textbook, course notes, and this book's review chapters, will help you thoroughly review for the test. Review the answers and explanations for any questions you missed on the practice test.
6	Have someone quiz you using the note cards you created. Take the second practice test for your exam, adhering to the time limits and simulated test-day conditions.
7	Review your areas of weakness using all your study materials. This is a good time to retake the practice tests, if time allows.

THE DAY OF THE TEST

Before the Test

- Dress comfortably in layers. You do not want to be distracted by being too hot or too cold while you are taking the test.

- Check your registration ticket to verify your arrival time.

- Plan to arrive at the test center early. This will allow you to collect your thoughts and relax before the test; your early arrival will also spare you the anguish that comes with being late.

- Make sure to bring your admission ticket and two forms of identification with you, one of which must contain a recent photograph, your name, and your signature (e.g., a driver's license).

- Bring several sharpened No. 2 pencils with erasers. You will not want to waste time searching for a replacement pencil or pen if you break a pencil point or run out of ink while taking your test. The proctor will not provide pencils or pens at the test center.

- Wear a watch to the test center so you can apportion your testing time wisely. You may not, however, wear one that makes noise or that will otherwise disturb the other test takers.

- Leave all dictionaries, textbooks, notebooks, calculators, briefcases, and packages at home. You may not take these items into the test center.

- Do not eat or drink too much before the test. The proctor will not allow you to make up time you miss if you have to take a bathroom break. You will not be allowed to take materials with you, and you must secure permission before leaving the room.

During the Test

- Pace yourself. The Praxis II Social Studies: Content Knowledge is administered in one two-hour sitting with no breaks. Follow all of the rules and instructions that the test proctor gives you. Proctors will enforce these procedures to maintain test security. If you do not abide by the regulations, the proctor may dismiss you from the test and notify ETS to cancel your score.

- Listen closely as the test instructor provides the directions for completing the test. Follow the directions carefully. Be sure to *mark only one answer* per multiple-choice question, erase all unwanted answers and marks completely, and fill in the answers darkly and neatly. There is no penalty for guessing at an answer, so *do not leave any answer ovals blank.* Remember: a blank oval is just scored as wrong, but a guessed answer has a chance of being right!

- Do your best! Afterward, make notes about the multiple-choice questions you remember. You may not share this information with others, but you may find that the information proves useful on other exams that you take. Relax! Wait for that passing score to arrive.

United States History

PHYSICAL GEOGRAPHY OF NORTH AMERICA

North America is the northern of the two continents of the Western Hemisphere; it is joined to South America at the tip of Panama. It is virtually surrounded by the Artic, Atlantic, and Pacific oceans. North America, which includes Greenland, Central America, and most of the islands of the West Indies, has a total area of 9,360,000 square miles (24, 240,000 km²) and is exceeded in size only by Asia and Africa.

This New World, as it has been called, was unknown to Europeans until comparatively recent times. Although inhabited by indigenous peoples, North America has drawn migrants from all parts of the world, bringing with them a heritage of ideas and skills. North America is rich in mineral, water, and forest resources, and is a world center of agriculture and industry.

The **Northeast** has a varied geography of rivers, lakes, valleys, plateaus, and mountains. Bordered on the east by the Atlantic Ocean and on the west by the Ohio River and by Lake Erie and Lake Ontario, two of the five Great Lakes, this region's southern border is the boundary between Pennsylvania and Maryland. The coastal plain gradually narrows from south to north as the Appalachian Mountain range extends in a northeasterly direction, from Georgia into Maine. The Northeast possesses several major waterways, including the Delaware, Hudson, and Connecticut rivers. Vegetation in the northeast is mainly mixed and deciduous forests.

The **Southeast** contains the broad Atlantic Coastal Plain, which gradually widens from Maryland in a southwesterly direction until it meets the Gulf Coastal Plain on the edge of the Gulf of Mexico. The Appalachian and Blue Ridge Mountains are the highest elevations in the southeast. Many rivers irrigate this region, including the Potomac, James, Roanoke, Savannah, Chattahoochee, Mississippi and Red rivers. Vegetation in the southeast is primarily mixed forest between the Atlantic coast and the Appalachian Mountains and deciduous forest between the Appalachians and the Mississippi and Ohio Rivers.

The **Midwest** is bordered on the north by four of the Great Lakes: Lake Superior, Lake Michigan, Lake Huron, and Lake Erie. The region's eastern border is the Ohio and Mississippi rivers and the Rocky Mountains form its western border. The states of Kansas and Missouri are the southern border of the Midwest region. The main physical characteristics of this region are the Interior Plains and Great Plains. The major rivers in the Midwest include the Ohio, Illinois, Mississippi, Platte and Arkansas. The Midwest's vegetation is deciduous forest in its center, with mixed and evergreen forests in the extreme northern parts (Michigan, Wisconsin, and Minnesota). On the western side of the region, the vegetation changes to tall grass prairie and then short grass prairie closer to the Rocky Mountains.

The **Western** region rises out of the Great Plains, into the Rocky Mountains and then proceeds to the Pacific Ocean at a generally much higher altitude than in the rest of the United States. A large part of the **Southwest** is desert. The Sonoran and Painted Deserts are in Arizona while the Mojave Desert is in California. North of these deserts are the Colorado Plateau, which is surrounded by the Rocky Mountains, and the Great Basin, which lies between the Rocky Mountains and the Sierra Nevada mountain range. The Central Valley of California extends north to south between the Sierra Nevada Mountains and the Coast Ranges. North of the Great Basin, the Columbia Plateau lies between the Rocky Mountains and the Cascade Range in the states of Oregon and Washington. The major rivers in the West include the Pecos, Rio Grande, Colorado, Gila, Snake, Columbia, Sacramento, and San Joaquin. The vegetation in the west is a mix of evergreen forests and shrub in the mountain ranges, desert in most of Arizona, southeastern California, Nevada, and Utah. The valleys in California, Oregon and Washington have a mix of short grass prairie and mixed forest. The Continental Divide runs through the Rocky Mountains. Rivers to the west drain into the Pacific Ocean while those on the east drain into the Atlantic Ocean and the Gulf of Mexico.

Broad Climate Patterns of Each Major Region of North America

The **Northeast,** which includes New England and the Mid-Atlantic states, has a temperate climate that averages about 15 degrees colder in Maine than in Virginia in the winter and about 10 degrees warmer in Virginia than Maine in the summer. Summers in the southern part of the region are often humid with thunderstorms, while winters get colder and snowier the farther north one is.

The **Southeast,** which includes Alabama, Georgia, Tennessee, Florida and the Carolinas, has a mild and moist climate. While January average high temperatures range from 47 in the interior northern part of the region to 72 in Florida, summer average high temperatures in the entire region are in the low 90s. The summers in the southeast are quite hot and humid with plentiful rainfall, although usually in short, intense downpours rather than all day.

The **Southern region**, including Texas, Oklahoma, Arkansas, Mississippi, and Louisiana, has a hot and humid climate in the summer and mild winters. Average high temperatures in the region range from the low to high 90s, while average high temperatures in the winter have a wider range from 47 in Oklahoma City to 62 in New Orleans.

The **Midwest** is generally cold and dry in the winter and warm and humid in the summer; however, the most moisture is in the southeastern part. This region includes Ohio, Kentucky, Missouri, Illinois, Indiana, Iowa, Michigan, and Wisconsin. Winters in Michigan and Wisconsin are considerably colder and summers milder than in Kentucky and Missouri.

The **High Plains**, which include the Dakotas, Minnesota, Nebraska, and Kansas, have the coldest winters and mildest summers of any U. S. region. Generally, the climate is dry and very cold in the winter and dry and mildly warm in the summer.

The **Northwest** region includes Washington, Oregon, Idaho, Montana, and Wyoming. There is a noticeable difference between the coast and the interior climates in this region. Winters along the Pacific coast are cool and wet, whereas away from the coast winters are colder and drier, except for snow, which can be quite heavy in the high elevations. Summers in this region are generally dry and mild along the coast and warmer but still dry in the interior.

The **Southwest** is the driest climate in the country, although the California coast gets more precipitation than the interior areas and winter snows in the mountains can be quite heavy. Colorado, Utah, New Mexico, Arizona, Nevada, and California are the states in this region. Winters are generally mild, with the warmest being in the Arizona and California deserts. Summers range from mild in San Francisco (71°) to sizzling in Phoenix (105°) (http://weathereye.kgan.com/cadet/climate/climate.html).

Location of Main Geographic Features of the North American Continent

Rivers: Over 800 rivers cross the continental (lower 48) states. Most are small branches and/or tributaries of larger rivers. The U.S. Geological Survey, part of the Department of the Interior identifies the 32 largest rivers based on three characteristics: total length from source to mouth, area of basin (or watershed) drained by the stream, and the average rate of flow or discharge at the mouth of the river. Of the 32 largest rivers, 12 are tributaries to the other rivers on the list. The 20 largest rivers discharge directly into an ocean, sea, gulf, or bay. While the **Mississippi River,** which divides the country roughly into one-third to the east and two-thirds to the west, has the largest average discharge and drainage area, it is second to the **Missouri River** in length. The third and fourth largest rivers are the Yukon River in Alaska and the Rio Grande River, which runs through Colorado, New Mexico, and Texas. (Kammerer, J.C. 1990) http://pubs.water.usgs.gov/ofr87242

Lakes: The **Great Lakes** (**Superior**, **Michigan**, **Huron**, **Erie**, and **Ontario**) form a boundary between the United States and Canada. Minnesota, Wisconsin, Illinois, Michigan, Ohio, Pennsylvania, and New York all border on at least one of the Great Lakes. The **Great Salt Lake** in Utah while much smaller than any of the Great Lakes is the largest lake in the western United States.

Mountain Ranges: Five of the most prominent mountain ranges in North American are the **Appalachian Mountain Range**, **Cascade Range**, **Klamath Range**, **Rocky Mountain Range**, and the **Sierra Nevada Mountain Range**. Each of the mountain ranges is located in different regions of the United States and, therefore, each range is unique. The differences in vegetation pertain to the climate and elevation of the particular region. The composition of the mountain relates to the way it was geologically created— whether it be on a fault line, from a volcano, etc. Much of the mountainous region in the United States is in the western half of the country. The land in the Mid-west does not contain any ranges, but the East Coast has the Appalachian Range.

Plains: The Great Plains of North America is a roughly triangular area covering 1.4 million square miles that extends for about 2,400 miles from Alberta, Saskatchewan, and Manitoba southward through Texas into Mexico and approximately 1,000 miles from the foothills of the Rocky Mountains eastward to Indiana. Rainfall increases from west to east, resulting in different types of prairies, with the short grass prairie in the rain shadow of the Rockies, mixed-grass prairie in the central Great Plains, and tall grass prairie in the wetter eastern region. Today, these three prairie types largely correspond to the western rangelands, the wheat belt, and the corn/soybean area, respectively.

Deserts: Three of the four major deserts of North America are contained within a geological region called the **Basin and Range Province**, lying between the **Rocky Mountain Range** to the east and the **Sierra Nevada Mountain Range** to the west. The geological structures of these deserts are similar although the types of plant life found in each makes the region distinct.

The Great Basin region is a series of many basins, interrupted with mountain ranges produced by tilted and uplifted strata. The Great Basin Desert, the largest U. S. desert, covers an arid expanse of about 190,000 square miles and bordered by the Sierra Nevada Range on the west and the Rocky Mountains on the east, the Columbia Plateau to the north and the Mojave and **Sonoran** deserts to the south. Un-drained basins are also characteristic of the **Mojave** (bordering Arizona and California) and **Chihuahuan** (bordering Mexico, New Mexico and Texas) deserts. The **Sonoran Desert,** the hottest of the deserts, usually has hydraulic systems forming streams draining into the Gulf of California or the Pacific. There are also a few playas in the Sonoran Desert. One of these, called the **Salton Sea**, was filled by Colorado River flood waters in 1906 and remains full.

Alluvial fans are common in the Mojave Desert and the California portions of the Sonoran Desert. These are formed through geologic time where an arroyo or wash drains a mountain, depositing the detritus in a semicircle at the canyon's mouth.

In the Sonoran Desert, the linear ranges, usually formed by volcanic uplift, are often surrounded by a skirt of detritus—boulders, rocks, gravel, sand, soil—that has eroded from the mountain over time. Much of this has been washed down during torrential summer downpours. In the Southwest these detritus skirts, or pediments, are frequently called **bajadas**. The substrate is coarser, with larger rocks on the upper bajada and finer at the lower elevation.

Deep arroyos may cut through the bajadas. Special plants such as the Desert Ironwood and Canyon Bursage may grow along the arroyos, giving them the appearance of dry creeks.

The areas between the desert ranges have been filled with water-washed alluvium. This alluvium, or fine soil, produces the extensive flat spaces one usually associates with deserts. The water table may be high on the flatlands, and the drainage is often slow. Poorly drained patches and larger playas become alkaline through accumulation of soluble chemicals.

Desert streams and rivers are formed where there are grasslands, semiarid woodlands and forested uplands called watersheds. Like giant geological sponges, the upland watersheds collect and hold water throughout the year, releasing it slowly into the desert below. These desert streams with their riparian woodlands of cottonwoods, willows and other hydrophilic (water loving) plants were centers for abundant wildlife, as well as native peoples. However, abuse to the watersheds through overgrazing, timber cutting, mining and other modern activities has dried up many desert rivers. Also, much of the water table, once just below the desert floor, has been pumped lower and lower, and may now be hundreds of feet below the surface.

NATIVE AMERICAN PEOPLES

While historians disagree as to when the first Americans reached the Western Hemisphere, there is no disagreement as to where: the Bering Strait between Siberia and Alaska. Sometime between 15,000 and 30,000 years ago, people began migrating from Asia to North America across a land-bridge that formed as water receded. Several waves of migration occurred with the final one bringing the Inuit to North America in boats, since the Ice Age had ended and the seas had risen to cover the land-bridge.

The northernmost Native American culture that survives today is the **Inuit**. These people are maritime hunters, concentrating on seal and walrus. They live in the Arctic regions of North America.

The **Kwakiutl**, or Northwest Indians, were primarily salmon fishers. Thanks to the abundance of the region, the Kwakiutl lived in permanent villages stretching from northern California to southern Alaska.

Far to the south, the **Anasazi,** or cliff dwellers, settled east of the Grand Canyon in the Four Corners area, where the states of Utah, Colorado, New Mexico, and Arizona meet. The Anasazi dug vast apartment-like complexes into the mountain walls. In the dry climate of the southwest, the Anasazi population thrived thanks to building terraced fields irrigated by water collected on the mountains. Maize was the most important vegetable grown. The Anasazi also hunted animals. In the late 13th century, however, a drought severely reduced the Anasazi food supply. The Anasazi abandoned their cliff dwellings and migrated into other farming communities along the Rio Grande River. These communities, called **Pueblos** by the Spanish, also built interconnected apartment-like structures, but not in the sides of mountains. The Pueblo peoples are **matrilineal** and have strict community codes of behavior. The Pueblos are the oldest continuously occupied towns in the United States.

The **Plains Indians** were nomadic hunters and gatherers who lived in small communities. When the Ice Age ended, large mammals like the wooly mammoth died off. Plains Indians began to hunt bison instead. The herds of bison numbered in the millions before the Europeans arrived. Plains Indians developed sophisticated techniques for killing their prey, including deadly spear points and stampeding hundreds of bison over cliffs.

In the Mississippi River valley, the Mississippian culture arose during the tenth century C.E. Perhaps the most distinctive trait of this culture was the building of enormous mounds as temples, which has earned them the nickname, **Mound Builders**. Three developments facilitated the emergence of the Mississippian culture: the bow and arrow created by the Plains Indians was adopted east of the Mississippi River; a variety of maize was developed that grew well in the temperate climate of the region; and farmers began to use flint hoes, which were more productive than the sticks used previously. Mississippians lived in permanent settlements spread across the states of Ohio, Missouri, Alabama, Arkansas, Tennessee, and Georgia. The largest settlement was a city of more than 30,000 at **Cahokia**, near present-day St. Louis, Missouri. The Mississippian societies were complex hierarchical societies ruled by political chiefdoms and involved in extensive trade networks, craft specialization, and highly productive farming.

Like the Anasazi, the Mississippian culture reached its zenith in the 13th century and by the time the Europeans arrived; the Mississippian culture in the southeast had largely been replaced by less urban cultures, the largest of which were the **Cherokee.** During Andrew Jackson's presidency, the Cherokee were forced to move from their lands in present-day Tennessee to "Indian country" in present-day Oklahoma. Their journey is called the "Trail of Tears," which we will review in detail later in this chapter.

The **Iroquois** were one of the largest cultures living in the northeast, specifically in present-day upstate New York and Ontario, Canada. They were farmers who lived in matrilineal extended families. Success in cultivation led to population growth and, eventually, five Iroquois nations inhabited upstate New York. Historians believe that the Iroquois Confederacy united these five nations beginning in the 15th century. The **Iroquois Confederacy** was the most important and powerful Native American political alliance. It successfully ended generations of tribal warfare.

The **Seminoles** are a linguistically- and racially-diverse people who came to inhabit the Florida peninsula. The original native inhabitants were decimated by disease when the Spanish arrived in Florida. As the European population grew in the present-day states of Alabama, Georgia, and South Carolina, a group of Indians from the **Creek Confederacy** began moving into unoccupied lands in Florida in the early 1700s. They were joined by other Indian groups as well as by runaway slaves. After the **Creek War of 1813-1814**, even more Indians immigrated to Seminole territory in Florida.

EUROPEAN EXPLORATION AND COLONIZATION (1492–1763)

In 1492, **Christopher Columbus** was able to test his theory that one could reach Asia by sailing west from Europe thanks to the support of the Spanish monarchs, **King Ferdinand** and **Queen Isabella**. Columbus believed that the western ocean was much smaller than most people believed and thus theorized that a faster route to Asia might lie to the west rather than the eastern route around Africa that the Portuguese had pioneered. Both the Spanish and Portuguese were interested in finding quicker and cheaper routes to Asia than the centuries-old way through the Mediterranean Sea and then involving travel over land controlled by Muslims and Italians. Therefore, the impetus for exploration was twofold: economic and scientific curiosity.

In addition to economic motives, Catholics such as Columbus and his patrons, Ferdinand and Isabella, wished to bring new converts to their religion. Ferdinand and Isabella completed their unification of Spain as a Catholic country by defeating the Muslims in Granada just months before sending Columbus on his first voyage across the Atlantic. Once the Muslims were expelled, Ferdinand and Isabella ordered Jews to convert to Catholicism or leave Spain. Religion thus proved to be both a powerful cause and purpose of Spanish exploration.

The final motive for Spanish explorers was the fame that they could achieve if they were successful in claiming new lands for the crown. The abundance of gold and silver that natives displayed attracted more explorers hoping to find new sources of wealth for the crown as well as themselves. Between the drive to mine gold and silver and the desire to convert the natives to Catholicism, the Spanish established numerous permanent settlements and set up a system of governing based on viceroyalties. The Spanish forced Indians to work for them in a system known as **encomienda**—which was virtual slavery.

The earliest Spanish explorations and settlements were primarily in Central and South America. The first permanent settlement of Europeans in the present-day United States was not established until 1565 when the Spanish founded St. Augustine, Florida. It would be almost another 35 years before the Spanish established their first permanent settlement in the West in New Mexico in 1598. When Pueblo Indians revolted in 1690 and pushed the Spanish out of New Mexico temporarily, the first Spanish settlement in Texas was established. The Spanish had explored the coast of California since the mid-1500s but the first permanent settlement was not established until 1769 at San Diego.

Although both England and France sent explorers across the Atlantic Ocean, religious and political issues in Europe as well as their goal of finding a northern route to Asia, kept them from establishing permanent settlements in North America for almost a century after the Spanish had conquered much of Central and South America. Sponsored by the Spanish monarchy, **Ferdinand Magellan** had discovered the southern route to the Pacific Ocean and onward to India in 1519. France and England, initially, sought a northern route. Thus, the English sent Giovanni Caboto (better known in English as **John Cabot**) to North America in 1497. In 1583 and 1585, the English attempted to establish colonies in present-day Newfoundland, Canada, and on Roanoke Island, off the North Carolina coast. The first permanent English colony, however, was not established until 1607 at **Jamestown**, Virginia. The English king, James I, licensed two joint-stock companies to pursue organizing settlements in Virginia. The **Plymouth Company** and the **London Company** were backed by private investors to establish colonies in the land previously claimed for the English crown.

Meanwhile, the French had sent **Giovanni da Verrazano** in 1524 and **Jacques Cartier** in 1534 to find a northwest passage through North America into the Pacific Ocean. No passage was found and troubles at home, primarily the religious wars stemming from the Protestant Reformation, kept the French preoccupied until the 17th century when explorers such as **Champlain**, **Marquette**, **Joliet**, and **LaSalle** would claim lands for France drained by the St. Lawrence River in present-day Canada and the Mississippi River in what is now the United States. The French did not establish large settlements in North America since their two main interests were the fur trade, which allowed them to create luxury clothes for sale in Europe, and the conversion of the Indians to Catholicism. In general, the French had better relationships with the Indians than did either the Spanish or the English.

To conclude, the English and French at first pursued a northwestern route to Asia in order to compete with the Spanish who had discovered the way around South America and into the Pacific Ocean. In the end, the Spanish, English, and French contented themselves with the riches they found in their "new world." The Spanish exploited Indian labor in the *encomienda* system which made both the Spanish colonists as well as the Spanish monarchy very wealthy, for a time. The English used joint-stock companies to finance the risks associated with establishing permanent settlements. The French and Spanish sent fewer settlers than the English to establish colonies. Instead, they attempted to convert Indians both into subjects of their monarchs as well as into Catholics.

Table 2.1   Major European Explorers and the Region Explored

Country	Explorer	Region Explored
Spain	Columbus	Caribbean
	De Soto	southeastern United States
	Ponce de Leon	Florida
	Cabrilho	California Coast
	Coronado	southwestern United States
	Cabeza de Vaca	southwestern United States
	Cortes	Mexico

Country	Explorer	Region Explored
England	Cabot	Atlantic coast of Canada
	Hudson	Hudson Bay, Canada (Hudson also explored for the Dutch. On that trip he sailed along the Atlantic coast of Canada and the United States as far south as the Chesapeake Bay as well as up the Hudson River in present-day New York State.)
	Raleigh	founded the ill-fated Roanoke Island colony off the coast of North Carolina
France	Cartier	Northeastern Canada and the St. Lawrence River as far as Montreal
	Champlain	St. Lawrence River and the Great Lakes
	Marquette and Joliette	the Upper Mississippi River
	LaSalle	the lower Mississippi River and New Orleans

The exchange of foods, plants, animals, and diseases between the Europeans and Native Americans is known as the **Columbian Exchange.** Europeans introduced sugar, rice, and coffee to the Americas. Combined with native plants such as tobacco, cotton, vanilla, and chocolate, these foods changed the world as Europeans developed an insatiable taste or use for them and industries based on them sprang up. Europeans took corn and potatoes back to Europe where they became staple crops that fed people much better than the relatively low-producing wheat that had been the staple of people's diets.

Europeans brought horses, pigs, and cows. The horse was quickly adopted by Native Americans, especially in the Plains where they were used to great advantage in hunting bison. Native Americans who interacted with the English and French became increasingly dependent on the fur-and-hide trade. The disruption to established agricultural communities was severe in some cases as Indians abandoned their responsibilities to provide food in pursuit of the European goods they could barter for in exchange for the furs and hides. Moreover, Indian nations increasingly fought each other for possession of lands as they depleted a region's fur-bearing animals.

By 1800, the native population had declined by at least 70 percent. The consequences of interactions between Native Americans and Europeans were decidedly in the Europeans' favor. The Native American population was decimated by European diseases such as smallpox, influenza, and measles. The trade that did occur between natives and Europeans resulted in much vaster wealth for Europeans and created economic dependency among the Native Americans. Due to political and linguistic differences, Native Americans were severely hampered as they attempted to respond to the threat posed by the European colonists. Competition among Native American tribes for advantageous trading relationships with Europeans led to some tribes making alliances with one group of Europeans against another group, which, in turn, had its own native allies.

Colonial Culture, Society, Religion, Economy, and Political Institutions

Two groups of merchants gained charters from James I, Queen Elizabeth's successor. One group of merchants was based in London and received a charter to North America between what are now the Hudson and the Cape Fear rivers. The other was based in Plymouth and was granted the right to colonize in North America from the Potomac to the northern border of present-day Maine. They were called the **Virginia Company of London** and the **Virginia Company of Plymouth**, respectively. These were joint-stock companies, which raised their capital by the sale of shares of stock. Companies of this sort had already been used to finance and carry on English trade with Russia, Africa, and the Middle East. The Plymouth Company, in 1607, attempted to plant a colony in Maine, but after one winter the colonists became discouraged and returned to Britain. Thereafter, the Plymouth Company folded.

The English colonies along the Atlantic seaboard can be divided into three regions: Plantation or southern, New England, and Middle.

The Plantation Colonies: Virginia, Maryland, North Carolina, South Carolina, and Georgia

The **Virginia Company** was a joint-stock company whose primary goal was to make a profit. Religious motivation was much less important than in the founding of Maryland, Pennsylvania, Rhode Island, and Massachusetts. Most of the immigrants to the southern colonies were single men. Into the early 18th century, the ratio of men to women was 3:2. The **Virginia Company of London**, in 1607, sent out an expedition of three ships with 104 men to plant a colony some forty miles up the James River from Chesapeake

Bay. Like the river on which it was located, the new settlement was named **Jamestown** in honor of England's king. It became the first permanent English settlement in North America, but for a time it appeared to be going the way of the earlier attempts. During the early years of Jamestown, the majority of the settlers died of starvation, various diseases, or hostile action by Indians. Though new settlers continuously replaced the losses, the colony's survival remained in doubt for a number of years.

There were several reasons for these difficulties. The company owned the entire colony, and all members shared the profits regardless of how much or how little they worked; thus, there was a lack of incentive. Many of the settlers were "gentlemen," who considered themselves too good to work at growing the food the colony needed to survive. Others were simply unambitious and little inclined to work in any case. Furthermore, the settlers had come with the expectation of finding gold or other quick and easy riches and wasted much time looking for these while they should have been providing for their survival. For purposes of defense, the settlement had been sited on a peninsula formed by a bend in the river; but this low and swampy location proved to be a breeding ground for all sorts of diseases and, at high tide, even contaminated the settlers' drinking supply with sea water. To make matters worse, relations with Powhatan, the powerful local Indian chief, were at best uncertain and often openly hostile, with disastrous results for the colonists.

In 1608 and 1609 the dynamic and ruthless leadership of **John Smith** kept the colony from collapsing. Smith's rule was, "He who works not, eats not." After Smith returned to England in late 1609, the condition of the colony again became critical. In 1612, a Virginia resident named John Rolfe discovered that a superior strain of tobacco, native to the West Indies, could be grown in Virginia. There was a large market for this tobacco in Europe, and Rolfe's discovery gave Virginia a major cash crop. To secure more settlers and boost Virginia's shrinking labor force, the company moved to make immigration possible for Britain's poor, who were without economic opportunity at home or financial means to procure transportation to America. This was achieved by means of the indenture system, by which a poor worker's passage to America was paid by an American planter (or the company itself), who in exchange, was indentured to work for the planter (or the company) for a specified number of years. The system was open to abuse and often resulted in the mistreatment of the indentured servants. To control the workers thus shipped to Virginia, as well as the often lazy and unruly colonists already present, the company gave its governors in America dictatorial powers. Governors such as Lord De La Warr, Sir Thomas Gates, and Sir Thomas Dale made use of such powers, imposing a harsh rule.

The introduction of tobacco cultivation made the British colonies in the Chesapeake region economically viable. By the mid-1700s, tobacco was the most valuable cash crop produced in the Southern states. In order to make a profit with this labor-intensive crop, tobacco required a cheap labor source. At first, indentured servants played this role in the growth of the tobacco plantation system in Virginia and Maryland. They were the chief source of agricultural labor in both of these colonies before 1675. Planters in Virginia and Maryland used the "headright" system to encourage the importation of indentured servants. Whoever paid the passage of a laborer received the right to acquire 50 acres of land. Masters thus enjoyed the benefits of this system.

For such reasons, and its well-known reputation as a death trap, Virginia continued to attract inadequate numbers of immigrants. To solve this, a reform-minded faction within the company proposed a new approach, and under its leader, Edwin Sandys, made changes designed to attract more settlers. Colonists were promised the same rights they had in England. A representative assembly, the House of Burgesses, was founded in 1619—the first in America. Additionally, private ownership of land was instituted. Despite these reforms, Virginia's unhealthy reputation kept many Englishmen away. Large numbers of indentured servants were brought in, especially young, single men. The first Africans were brought to Virginia in 1619 but were treated as indentured servants rather than slaves. Virginia's Indian relations remained difficult. In 1622 an Indian massacre took the lives of 347 settlers. In 1644 the Indians struck again, massacring another 300 settlers. Shortly thereafter, the coastal Indians were subdued and no longer presented a serious threat.

Impressed by the potential profits from tobacco growing, **King James I** determined to have Virginia for himself. Using the high mortality and the 1622 massacre as a pretext, he revoked the London Company's charter in 1624 and made Virginia a royal colony. This pattern was followed throughout colonial history; both company colonies and proprietary colonies tended eventually to become royal colonies. Upon taking over Virginia, James revoked all political rights and the representative assembly—he did not believe in such things—but fifteen years later his son, Charles I, was forced, by constant pressure from the Virginians and the continuing need to attract more settlers, to restore these rights.

When the price of tobacco fell sharply in the late 1600s, the supply of English indentured servants declined. Small farmers, many of whom had immigrated as indentured servants, were hard-pressed to compete with large landowners when the profit margin for tobacco shrank. **The English Royal Africa Company** began importing slaves directly to North America; although slaves were expensive, they could be worked harder than indentured servants since they were not under a contract.

Laws governing slavery were piecemeal until 1705 when Virginia assembled all these kinds of laws into a **slave code**. As early as 1662 in the Virginia colony, children born to a slave mother were themselves slaves for life. Slave labor in colonial Virginia spread rapidly in the late seventeenth century, as Africans displaced White indentured servants in the tobacco fields. Slavery flourished because the cultivation of tobacco required inexpensive labor and by the early 1700s, slavery was legally established in all 13 colonies. Natural increase among the slave population provided a continuous source of unpaid labor for tobacco planters in the Chesapeake region, and later for rice and indigo planters in South Carolina. By 1750, approximately 80 percent of slaves were born in the colonies.

Unlike Virginia and the New England colonies, **Maryland** was founded not by a corporation, but by an individual proprietor. King Charles I gave **Lord Baltimore**, the land now known as Maryland. Lord Baltimore fully intended to profit from his land grant, but he also wanted to provide a haven for his fellow Roman Catholics. Maryland was a religiously tolerant colony from the beginning since the majority of immigrants were Protestants.

The **Carolinas** and **Georgia** were also proprietary colonies. The British king gave a group of philanthropists the charter for Georgia because the government wanted a buffer between the Spanish in Florida and the English colonists in South Carolina. The philanthropists wanted to establish a colony for debtors who could be released from English prisons and given a second chance in the colonies.

The **Massachusetts Bay Company** was organized by Puritans who wanted to escape political repression, religious restrictions, and an economic recession. In 1630, they established settlements in Boston and a few other towns. Puritans came to New England in family groups, which helped to stabilize the colony and to increase the population more quickly than was the case in the southern colonies. The Puritans typically lived in small villages surrounded by farmland.

The typical Puritan community was characterized by a close relationship between church and state. Under the leadership of Governor John Winthrop, the Puritans created a model Christian society with a strict code of moral conduct. For example, Puritans banned the theater. The Puritans' powerful sense of mission—to build an ideal Christian society is captured in this quote from Winthrop's famous sermon as the Puritans crossed the Atlantic Ocean in 1630:

> For we must consider that we shall be as a city upon a hill. The eyes of all people are upon us. So that if we shall deal falsely with our God in this work we have undertaken, and so cause Him to withdraw His present help from us, we shall be made a story and a by-word through the world.

The Puritans believed in the necessity for a trained and educated ministry. They founded Harvard College and Yale College to ensure an adequate supply of ministers. Boys, but not girls, were formally educated to prepare them for Harvard and Yale. As a result, male literacy was nearly universal by 1750 in New England, and, despite their lack of formal training, increasing numbers of women were literate as well.

Although the Puritans immigrated to America for religious freedom, they did not tolerate religious dissent or diversity. Both Roger Williams and Anne Hutchinson were expelled for challenging the Puritan authorities. Roger Williams founded Rhode Island. He advanced the cause of religious toleration and freedom of thought. Williams believed that the state was an improper and ineffectual agency in matters of spirit. Massachusetts Bay officials banished Anne Hutchinson to Rhode Island after she challenged clerical authority and claimed to have had revelations from God. Hutchinson is best known for her struggle with the Massachusetts Bay authorities over religious doctrine and gender roles.

Connecticut, New Hampshire, and Maine were settled by people from Massachusetts in search of land for the growing population. The Massachusetts Bay Colony purchased Maine outright and kept it until shortly before Maine became a state in 1820, which is why Maine is not counted among the original thirteen colonies.

The Middle Colonies: Pennsylvania, New Jersey, New York, Delaware

The Dutch first settled what became the colony of **New York**. **The British Navigation Act of 1660** restricted all transportation of goods to and from the colonies to British ships. The Dutch had a profitable business in marine transportation so the British declaration was provocative. Furthermore, King Charles II granted the area between

Connecticut and Maryland to his brother, the Duke of York, essentially declaring war against the Dutch. Finally, in 1664, the British captured the Dutch settlement of New Amsterdam and changed the name to New York. The Dutch adapted well to British rule and their settlements along the Hudson River continued to prosper as part of the British colony of New York.

In 1664, the Duke of York gave New Jersey to two proprietors who attracted many settlers by offering land on easy terms, freedom of religion, and democratic local government. By 1680, Quakers had purchased New Jersey from the original proprietors.

The colony most famously associated with the Quakers was, of course, Pennsylvania. Founded by William Penn, the colony was unusually liberal and included a representative assembly elected by the landowners. Pennsylvania granted freedom of religion and did not have a state-supported church. Other important Quaker beliefs and practices included pacifism, according women a larger role in church services than other religious sects in the colonies, and being among the first to oppose slavery.

A Snapshot of the Colonial Society on the Eve of the Revolution

Education

- The highest literacy rates were in New England, thanks to Puritan emphasis on an educated ministry and individual reading of the Bible.

- The lowest literacy rates were in the South because the population was so spread out geographically that the cost of building churches, let alone schools, was prohibitive.

- By the mid-eighteenth century, colonists read newspapers printed in the colonies— or listened to them read aloud in taverns—as well as almanacs, the Bible, and captivity narratives; the latter being accounts of colonists captured by Indians.

- Although literacy was higher in the colonies than in many European countries, colonial culture was still primarily an oral culture, with stories and traditions being handed down in the telling.

Society

- Northern merchants and Southern planters amassed great wealth and held public offices and high social status. Nonetheless, colonial society did not have a hereditary aristocracy. White men who achieved economic success despite humble beginnings were welcomed into the social hierarchy.

- The major industry in colonial North America was agriculture; however, as towns and cities arose, artisans became integral to the urban economy and social hierarchy. The most fortunate artisans were master craftsmen who owned their shops and employed journeymen and apprentices. Property-owning craftsmen and independent farmers made up the large middle class of the colonies.

- Property-less men held the lowest social status among white male colonists.

- The number of non-English settlers continued to increase. For example, Scotch-Irish and German immigrants moved into Appalachia as the Native Americans were defeated.

- During the colonial period, a woman usually lost control of her property when she married and she had no separate legal identity apart from her husband.

- Single women and widows had the right to own property.

Religion

- The 13 colonies were religiously diverse. As a result of this religious pluralism, there was no single dominant Protestant denomination.

- By the mid-eighteenth century, even New England, which had been so staunchly Congregationalist Puritan, saw increasing diversity among its Protestant denominations, including Anglicans, Presbyterians, Methodists, and Baptists. Maryland had its Catholics, but was predominantly Protestant. Small communities of Jews worshipped in several cities in the colonies, most notably in New York City and Newport, Rhode Island. Pennsylvania and New Jersey were home to many Quakers.

Economics

• Slavery was generally accepted as a labor system. The institution was legally established in all of the colonies.

• Colonial cities functioned primarily as mercantile centers for collecting agricultural goods and distributing imported manufactured goods. Most colonial cities were ports that maintained close economic and cultural ties with England.

• Mercantilism was England's dominant economic philosophy during the seventeenth and eighteenth centuries. The goal of mercantilism was for England to have a favorable balance of trade. To achieve this goal, the colonies were expected to export raw materials and import finished goods.

• Mercantilism was designed to protect English industry and promote England's prosperity. The Navigation Acts were part of the British policy of mercantilism. They listed colonial products that could be shipped only to England. The mercantilist system led to the subordination of the colonial economy to that of the mother country. Despite the Navigation Acts, however, the North American colonies were able to profit from Great Britain's policy of "salutary neglect," which means that until the end of the French and Indian War in 1763, the British government was preoccupied with European affairs and looked the other way when the colonies worked out trade agreements so they could acquire needed products from other countries.

Political Institutions

The British king chose the governors in the royal colonies, while the proprietors of Maryland, Delaware, and Pennsylvania appointed their governors.

Each colony had a legislature consisting of two houses, except for Pennsylvania which had only one house. In the royal colonies, the king appointed the members of the upper house, except in Massachusetts where the Massachusetts General Court elected them. The lower house members were elected by men who owned property. In the New England colonies, these property-owning voters also met in town meetings to decide on local issues.

The upper houses in the colonial legislatures served as councils that advised the governor, although the councils also had some judicial and legislative powers.

The lower houses had legislative powers and controlled the finances in the colony. They imposed taxes and decided on expenditures. There were no taxes imposed directly by the British government until the infamous Stamp Act of 1765.

The Enlightenment

As the 18th century progressed, Americans came to be more or less influenced by European ways of thought, culture, and society. Some Americans embraced the European intellectual movement known as the "Enlightenment." The key concept of the Enlightenment was rationalism—the belief that human reason was adequate to solve all of mankind's problems and, correspondingly, much less faith was needed in the central role of God as an active force in the universe.

A major English political philosopher of the Enlightenment was John Locke. Writing partially to justify England's 1688 Glorious Revolution, he strove to find in the social and political world the sort of natural laws Isaac Newton had recently discovered in the physical realm. He held that such natural laws included the rights of life, liberty, and property; that to secure these rights people submit to governments; and that governments which abuse these rights may justly be overthrown. His writings were enormously influential in America, though usually indirectly, by way of early 18th-century English political philosophers. Americans tended to equate Locke's law of nature with the universal law of God. The most notable Enlightenment man in America was Benjamin Franklin. While Franklin never denied the existence of God, he focused his attention on human reason and what it could accomplish.

The First Great Awakening took the form of a wave of religious revivals that began in New England in the 1730s. The wave soon swept across all the colonies during the1740s. In the southern colonies, many slaves were converted to Christianity.

Itinerant ministers advocated an emotional approach to religious practice, finding the established churches too rational in their practices. These "New Light" ministers promoted the growth of New Light institutions of higher learning, such as Princeton. The divisions between the "Old Light" and "New Light" practices affected both the Presbyterian and Congregational churches, resulting in growing religious diversity within the colonies. The most significant effect of the First Great Awakening is that it was the first national event that affected all of the colonies.

ESTABLISHING A NEW NATION (1763–1791)

Great Britain created two new policies in the wake of winning the French and Indian War: imposing revenue taxes on American colonists and prohibiting colonists from moving west of the crest of the Appalachian Mountains (the Proclamation of 1763). From the colonists' perspective, the British government was unfairly keeping them from moving onto new lands acquired from the French as a result of the war. The British government's goal was to prevent conflict between the trans-Appalachian Indians and the colonists looking to establish new settlements. Defending the colonists had become a drain on the British treasury.

In 1763 the strongly anti-American **George Grenville** became prime minister and set out to solve some of the empire's more pressing problems. Chief among these was the large national debt incurred in the recent war in defense of the American frontier, recently the scene of a bloody Indian uprising led by an Ottawa chief named **Pontiac**. Goaded by French traders, Pontiac had aimed to drive the entire white population into the sea. While failing in that endeavor, he had succeeded in killing a large number of settlers along the frontier. Grenville created a comprehensive program to deal with these problems and moved energetically to put it into effect. He sent the Royal Navy to suppress American smuggling and vigorously enforce the **Navigation Acts**.

It was the new tax policy, however, that ignited the fires of resentment among American colonists. The British Parliament decided it was time that the colonists contributed as well. In 1764, the **Sugar Act** placed import tariffs on sugar, coffee, and wine, among other things. In 1765, the **Stamp Act** placed a direct tax on printed matter sold in the colonies. Americans protested that Parliament had no right to tax them as they had no representation in Parliament. Parliament responded that the colonies' interests were represented by all of the members of Parliament. Americans, used to electing representatives to the lower houses of the colonial legislatures, became more steadfast in support of the principle of "no taxation without representation."

Meanwhile, Parliament passed the **Quartering Act**, which required local legislatures to feed and house British troops stationed in their locale. Americans resented not only the added drain on their finances, but also the idea that a standing army was necessary not only on the frontier, but in colonial cities such as Boston and New York.

In the end, Patriot leaders organized a boycott of British goods which hurt British merchants. Violent attacks on stamp agents also occurred. Under pressure at home as well as in the colonies, Parliament rescinded the Stamp Act. But the next year, 1767, the so-called **Townshend Acts**, import taxes on glass, lead, paint, paper, and tea, were levied on the colonists. This time, the boycott of British goods cut imports by half. When British troops killed five Bostonians in the so-called **Boston Massacre of 1770**, another crisis point erupted. Again, the Parliament blinked and rescinded all of the Townshend Duties except for the **threepenny tax** on tea. The boycott of British goods collapsed.

Three years later, however, the British government, in an effort to help the nearly bankrupt **British East India Company**, allowed the company to sell tea directly to the colonists at a considerably reduced price. The threepenny tea tax remained in place, however. Tempted by the inexpensive tea, colonists nevertheless organized against allowing the ships to dock and unload when they realized that if Britain was successful with establishing a tea monopoly, they might attempt to monopolize other aspects of colonial trade. In Boston, the colonial resistance turned into the famous **"Boston Tea Party."**

Infuriated by the Bostonians' willful destruction of British property, the British responded with four acts collectively titled the **Coercive Acts**. First, the **Boston Port Act** closed the Port of Boston to all trade until local citizens would agree to pay for the lost tea (they would not). Secondly, the **Massachusetts Government Act** greatly increased the power of Massachusetts' royal governor at the expense of the legislature. Thirdly, the **Administration of Justice Act** provided that royal officials accused of crimes in Massachusetts could be tried elsewhere, where chances of acquittal might be greater. Finally, a strengthened **Quartering Act** allowed the new governor, General Thomas Gage, to quarter his troops anywhere, including unoccupied private homes. A further act of Parliament also angered and alarmed Americans. This was the **Quebec Act**, which extended the province of Quebec to the Ohio River, established Roman Catholicism as Quebec's official religion, and set up a government, without a representative assembly, for Quebec.

For Americans this was a denial of the hopes and expectations of westward expansion for which they had fought the French and Indian War. In addition, New Englanders especially saw it as a threat that in their colonies too, Parliament could establish autocratic government and the hated Church of England. Americans lumped the Quebec

Act together with the Coercive Acts and referred to them all as the **Intolerable Acts**. In response to the Coercive Acts, the **First Continental Congress** was called and met in Philadelphia in September 1774. It once again petitioned Parliament for relief but also passed the Suffolk Resolves (so called because they were first passed in Suffolk County, Massachusetts), denouncing the Intolerable Acts and calling for strict non-importation and rigorous preparation of local militia companies in case the British should resort to military force.

The Congress then narrowly rejected a plan, submitted by Joseph Galloway of Pennsylvania, calling for a union of the colonies within the empire and a rearrangement of relations with Parliament. Most of the delegates felt matters had already gone too far for such a mild measure. Finally, before adjournment, it was agreed that there should be a **Second Continental Congress** to meet in May of the following year if the colonies' grievances had not been righted by then.

Finally, the Americans had coalesced around certain beliefs:

- The colonists believed that King George III was a tyrant.

- They believed that Parliament wanted to control the internal affairs of the colonies without the consent of the colonists.

- They wanted greater political participation in policies affecting the colonies.

- They resented the quartering of British troops in colonial homes.

- They wanted to preserve their local autonomy and way of life from British interference.

Key Individuals and their Roles in the Emergence of a New Nation

- **King George III** succeeded his grandfather as king of Great Britain in 1760. Determined to have more control of the government than George II had had, George III appointed ministers who were not the ablest. George III could be stubborn and he refused to listen to the American colonists' complaints. This was unfortunate because many colonists believed that their king was getting bad advice, not that he personally agreed with taxing Americans and punishing them when they did not comply. By 1776, the colonists had turned against King George III as can be seen in the list of grievances in the Declaration of Independence.

- **John Adams,** a well-known Harvard-educated lawyer from Massachusetts defended the British soldiers ("redcoats") accused of the Boston Massacre. Adams was a delegate to the First and Second Continental Congresses, and led in the movement for independence. During the Revolutionary War he served in France and Holland in diplomatic roles, and helped negotiate the treaty of peace. From 1785 to 1788 he was minister to the Court of St. James's, returning to be elected Vice President under George Washington. Adams served as the second President of the United States.

- **George Washington,** a Virginia man, made his military debut in the French and Indian War. In spite of his losses during the war the Virginia House of Burgess gave him commendations and the rank of Colonel. Washington wore his military uniform to the Second Continental Congress in Philadelphia in May 1775 where he was appointed commander-in-chief of the Continental Army. He became a prime mover in the steps leading to the Constitutional Convention at Philadelphia in 1787. When the new Constitution was ratified, the Electoral College unanimously elected Washington the first President of the United States.

- **Thomas Jefferson,** a delegate from Virginia, at age 33 was the youngest to attend the Continental Congress. Jefferson, while not much of an orator, was an eloquent writer and drafted the Declaration of Independence. In years following he labored to make its words a reality. Jefferson succeeded Benjamin Franklin as minister to France in 1785. As a reluctant candidate for President in 1796, he came within three votes of election. Through a flaw in the Constitution, he became Vice President, although he was an opponent of President Adams. In 1800 the defect caused a more serious problem. Republican electors, attempting to name both a President and a Vice President from their own party, cast a tie vote between Jefferson and Aaron Burr. The House of Representatives settled the tie. Alexander Hamilton, disliking both Jefferson and Burr, nevertheless urged Jefferson's election.

- **Thomas Paine** was born in England and, after meeting Benjamin Franklin in England, immigrated to the American colonies in October 1774. In his political pamphlet, "Common Sense," published in January 1776, Paine called for independence from Great Britain. Paine opposed monarchy and strongly favored republican government. Republicanism is the belief that government should be based on the consent of the governed. Paine's strong words helped overcome the loyalty many still felt for the monarchy and the mother country.

The War for Independence

The British government paid little attention to the First Continental Congress, having decided to teach the Americans a military lesson. More troops were sent to Massachusetts, which was officially declared to be in a state of rebellion. Orders were sent to General Gage to arrest the leaders of the resistance, or failing that, to provoke any sort of confrontation that would allow him to turn British military might loose on the Americans.

Gage decided on a reconnaissance-in-force to find and destroy a reported stockpile of colonial arms and ammunition at Concord. Seven hundred British troops set out on this mission on the night of April 18, 1775, which resulted in skirmishes with the colonists at **Lexington** and **Concord**.

Open warfare had begun, and the myth of British invincibility was destroyed. Militia came in large numbers from all the New England colonies to join the force besieging Gage and his army in Boston. The following month the Americans tightened the noose around Boston by fortifying Breed's Hill (a spur of Bunker Hill).

The British determined to remove them by a frontal attack. Twice the British were thrown back, but they finally succeeded when the Americans ran out of ammunition. Over a thousand British soldiers were killed or wounded in what turned out to be the bloodiest battle of the war (June 17, 1775). Yet the British had gained very little and remained bottled up in Boston. Meanwhile, in May 1775, American forces under Ethan Allen (1738–1789) and Benedict Arnold (1741–1801) took Fort Ticonderoga on Lake Champlain.

While these events were taking place in New England and Canada, the **Second Continental Congress** met in Philadelphia in May 1775. Congress was divided into two main factions. One was composed mostly of New Englanders and leaned toward declaring independence from Britain. The other drew its strength primarily from the Middle Colonies and was not yet ready to go that far.

The **Declaration of Independence** was primarily the work of **Thomas Jefferson** (1743–1826) of Virginia. The authors of the Declaration of Independence used the philosophy of natural rights, derived from the writings of John Locke. The idea of natural rights is most clearly expressed in the second paragraph of the Declaration of Independence:

> We hold these truths to be self-evident that all men are created equal; that they are endowed by their Creator with certain inalienable rights; that among these are life, liberty, and the pursuit of happiness.

It was a restatement of political ideas by then commonplace in America, and showed why the former colonists felt justified in separating from Great Britain. It was formally adopted by Congress on July 4, 1776.

The British landed that summer at New York City, where they hoped to find many loyalists. Washington narrowly avoided being trapped there (an escape partially due to General Howes' slowness). Defeated again at the Battle of Washington Heights (August 29–30, 1776) in Manhattan, Washington was forced to retreat across New Jersey with the aggressive British **General Lord Charles Cornwallis** (1738–1805) in pursuit.

With his victory almost complete, General Howe decided to wait until spring to finish annihilating Washington's army. Scattering his troops in small detachments so as to hold all of New Jersey, he went into winter quarters.

Washington, with his small army melting away as demoralized soldiers deserted, decided on a bold stroke. On Christmas night 1776, his army crossed the Delaware River and struck the Hessians at Trenton. The Hessians, still groggy from their hard-drinking Christmas party, were easily defeated. A few days later, Washington defeated a British force at Princeton (January 3, 1777). Much of New Jersey was regained, and Washington's army was saved from disintegration.

Hoping to weaken Britain, France began making covert shipments of arms to the Americans early in the war. Shipments from France were vital for the Americans. The

American victory at **Saratoga** convinced the French to join openly in the war against England. Eventually the Spanish (1779) and the Dutch (1780) joined as well.

American commander **Nathaniel Greene's** (1742–1786) brilliant southern strategy led to a crushing victory at Cowpens, South Carolina (January 17, 1781), by troops under Greene's subordinate, General Daniel Morgan (1736–1802) of Virginia. It also led to a near victory by Greene's own force at Guilford Court House, North Carolina (March 15, 1781).

The frustrated and impetuous Cornwallis now abandoned the southern strategy and moved north into Virginia, taking a defensive position at **Yorktown**. With the aid of a French fleet which took control of Chesapeake Bay and a French army which joined him in sealing off the land approaches to Yorktown, Washington succeeded in trapping Cornwallis. After three weeks of siege, Cornwallis surrendered on October 17, 1781.

News of the debacle at Yorktown brought the collapse of Lord North's ministry, and the new cabinet opened peace negotiations. The final agreement became known as the **Treaty of Paris of 1783**. Its terms stipulated the following:

1) The United States was recognized as an independent nation by the major European powers, including Britain;

2) Its western boundary was set at the Mississippi River.

3) Its southern boundary was set at 31° north latitude (the northern boundary of Florida). Britain retained Canada, but had to surrender Florida to Spain.

4) Private British creditors would be free to collect any debts owed by United States citizens; and Congress was to recommend that the states restore confiscated loyalist property.

The Creation of New Governments

After the collapse of British authority in 1775, it became necessary to form new state governments. By the end of 1777, ten new state constitutions had been formed. Most state constitutions included bills of rights—lists of things the government would guarantee its citizens.

In the summer of 1776, Congress appointed a committee to begin devising a framework for a national government. The end result preserved the sovereignty of the states and created a very weak national government.

The **Articles of Confederation** provided for a unicameral Congress in which each state would have one vote, as had been the case in the Continental Congress. Executive authority under the articles would be vested in a committee of 13, with one member from each state. In order to amend the articles, the unanimous consent of all the states was required.

The Articles of Confederation government was empowered to make war, make treaties, determine the amount of troops and money each state should contribute to the war effort, settle disputes between states, admit new states to the Union, and borrow money. But it was not empowered to levy taxes, raise troops, or regulate commerce.

Ratification of the Articles of Confederation was delayed by disagreements over the future status of the lands that lay to the west of the original 13 states. Maryland, which had no such claim, withheld ratification until 1781 when Virginia agreed to surrender its western claims to the new national government.

THE UNITED STATES CONSTITUTION (1787–1789)

Development and Ratification

In practice, the inadequacy of the Articles of Confederation became increasingly apparent. The most important accomplishment of the government under the Articles of Confederation was the **Northwest Ordinance of 1787**. That ordinance did the following:

- Provided for the orderly creation of territorial governments and new states (Ohio was the first state admitted to the Union from the Northwest Territory.)

- Excluded slavery north of the Ohio River

- Supported public education

Without the authority to raise revenue for national expenses, the government was dependent on the goodwill of the states in providing financial resources. In 1787 Congress called a convention of all the states to meet in Philadelphia for the purpose of revising the Articles of Confederation. The men who met in Philadelphia were supposed to revise the Articles, instead they scrapped them and wrote the United States Constitution.

The men who met in Philadelphia in 1787 were remarkably able, highly educated, and exceptionally accomplished. For the most part they were lawyers, merchants, and planters. Though representing individual states most thought in terms of national unity. George Washington was unanimously elected to preside, and the enormous respect that he commanded helped hold the convention together through difficult times.

As students of Enlightenment political philosophy, the delegates shared a basic belief in the innate selfishness of man, which must somehow be kept from abusing the power of government. For this purpose, the document that they finally produced contained many **checks and balances**, designed to prevent the government, or any one branch of the government, from gaining too much power.

Benjamin Franklin played an important role in reconciling the often heated debates among delegates and in making various suggestions that eventually helped the convention arrive at the **"Great Compromise,"** proposed by Roger Sherman (1721–1793) and Oliver Ellsworth (1745–1807). The Great (or Connecticut) Compromise provided for a presidency, a Senate with all states represented equally (by two senators each), and a House of Representatives with representation according to population.

Another crisis involved North-South disagreement over the issue of slavery. Here also a compromise was reached. Slavery was neither endorsed nor condemned by the Constitution. Each slave was to count as three-fifths of a person for purposes of apportioning representation and direct taxation on the states (the **Three-Fifths Compromise**). The federal government was prohibited from stopping the importation of slaves prior to 1808.

The third major area of compromise was the nature of the presidency. The result was a **strong presidency** with control of foreign policy and the power to veto Congress's legislation. Should the president commit an actual crime, Congress would have the power to impeach him. Otherwise, the president would serve for a term of four years and be re-electable without limit. As a check to the possible excesses of democracy, the president was to be elected by an electoral college, in which each state would have the same number of electors as it did senators and representatives combined. The person with the second highest total in the Electoral College would be vice president. If no one

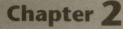

gained a majority in the Electoral College, the president would be chosen by the House of Representatives.

The following provisions were in the Constitution, as submitted to the states in 1787:

- The separation of powers, which organizes the national government into three branches

- The authority of Congress to declare war

- A guarantee of the legality of slavery

- The creation of an Electoral College to safeguard the presidency from direct popular election

- Provision for impeachment of the President

- Provision for the presidential State of the Union message

- Provision for ratifying the Constitution

- Federalism

- A bicameral legislature, as created by the Great Compromise

- Enumeration of the powers of Congress

- The Three-Fifths Compromise (Slaves counted as three-fifths of a person for purposes of representation and taxation)

The following provisions were not in the Constitution, as submitted to the states in 1787:

- A two-term limit for presidents

- Universal manhood suffrage

- A presidential cabinet

- The direct election of senators

- The idea of political parties (The framers opposed political parties. They believed that political parties promoted selfish interests, caused divisions, and thus threatened the existence of republican government.)

- The Bill of Rights

Table 2.2   Major Differences between Federalists and Anti–federalists.

ISSUE	FEDERALISTS	ANTI–FEDERALISTS	NOTES
A Constitution establishing a strong central government	Favored	Opposed	The main concern of the Anti-federalists was that the states would lose power and influence with the growth in the national government.
Power of thirteen states	Favored limiting state power. Argued that the Senate (with two representatives per state) adequately represented state interests.	Favored strong support and influence of states	Local control was key to Anti-federalist concept of Democracy. This issue would boil up in states' rights fights in the 1800's and beyond.
Bill of Rights	Not necessary	Essential to balance the powers given by the Constitution	The absence of a Bill of Rights in the original Constitution was seen as a real threat to individual citizens' liberties.
Articles of Confederation	Opposed as ineffectual as a governing document. Congress' power was limited to requesting cooperation from states.	Articles only needed amending	The decision at the Annapolis Convention (1786) to suggest a national convention to modify the Articles proved to be crucial.
Nation's Size	A large republic was seen as the best protection for individual freedoms	Only a small republic was capable of protecting the rights of individuals	No experiment in democracy on a scale as large as America had ever been attempted.
Supporters	Large farmers, merchants, artisans	Small farmers, often from rural areas	Only a few wealthy men (Mason and Randolph of Virginia, Gerry of Massachusetts) joined the Anti-federalists.

Source: Goldfield, Abbott, Anderson, Argersinger, Argersinger, Barney, Weir *The American Journey: A History of the United States,* Teaching and Learning Classroom Edition, Brief Third Edition

The new Constitution was to take effect when nine states, through special state conventions, had ratified it. As the struggle over ratification got under way, those favoring the Constitution astutely named themselves **Federalists** (i.e., advocates of centralized power) and labeled their opponents **Anti-federalists**.

By June 21, 1788, the required nine states had ratified, but the crucial states of New York and Virginia still held out. Ultimately, the promise of the addition of a bill of rights helped win the final states. March 1789, George Washington was inaugurated as the nation's first president on April 20, 1789, in New York City.

EARLY YEARS OF THE NEW NATION (1791–1829)

The Federalist Era

Few Anti-federalists were elected to Congress, and many of the new legislators had served as delegates to the Philadelphia Convention two years before. George Washington received virtually all the votes of the presidential electors, and John Adams received the next highest number, thus becoming the vice-president. After a triumphant journey from Mount Vernon, Washington was inaugurated in New York City, the temporary seat of government (April 30, 1789).

Ten amendments were ratified by the states by the end of 1791 and became the **Bill of Rights**. The first nine spelled out specific guarantees of personal freedoms, and the Tenth Amendment reserved to the states all those powers not specifically withheld or granted to the federal government.

The **Judiciary Act of 1789** provided for a Supreme Court with six justices, and invested it with the power to rule on the constitutional validity of state laws. It was to be the interpreter of the "supreme law of the land." A system of district courts was set up to serve as courts of original jurisdiction, and three courts of appeal were established.

Congress established three departments of the executive branch—state, treasury, and war—as well as the offices of attorney general and postmaster general.

Table 2.3   The Bill of Rights

1	protects the freedom of religion, speech, press, assembly, as well as the right to petition the government for the redress of grievances
2	protects the right to bear arms in a regulated militia (on a state basis; it was not intended to guarantee an individual's rights)
3	ensures that troops will not be housed in private citizen's homes
4	protects against unreasonable search and seizure (need for search warrant)
5	protects the rights for the accused, including required indictments, double jeopardy, self-incrimination, due process, and just compensation
6	guarantees a speedy and public trial, the confrontation by witnesses, and the right to call witnesses on one's own behalf
7	guarantees a jury trial
8	protects against excessive bail and cruel and unusual punishment
9	all rights not enumerated are nonetheless retained by the people
10	all powers not specifically delegated to the federal government are retained by the states

Washington's Administration (1789–1797)

Treasury Secretary Alexander Hamilton, in his "Report on the Public Credit," proposed the funding of the national debt at face value, federal assumption of state debts, and the establishment of a national bank. In his "Report on Manufactures," Hamilton proposed an extensive program for federal stimulation of industrial development through subsidies and tax incentives. The money needed to fund these programs would come from an excise tax on distillers and from tariffs on imports.

Thomas Jefferson, Secretary of State, and others objected to the funding proposal because they believed it would enrich a small elite group at the expense of the more worthy common citizen.

Hamilton interpreted the Constitution as having vested extensive powers in the federal government. This "implied powers" stance claimed that the government was given all powers that were not expressly denied to it. This is the "broad" interpretation.

Jefferson and Madison held the view that any action not specifically permitted in the Constitution was thereby prohibited. This is the "strict" interpretation, and the Republicans opposed the establishment of Hamilton's national bank based on this view of government. The Jeffersonian supporters, primarily under the guidance of James

Madison, began to organize political groups in opposition to the Federalist program. They called themselves Republicans.

The Federalists, as Hamilton's supporters were called, received their strongest support from the business and financial groups in the commercial centers of the Northeast and from the port cities of the South. The strength of the Republicans lay primarily in the rural and frontier areas of the South and West.

Foreign and Frontier Affairs

The U.S. proclaimed neutrality when France went to war with much of Europe, including England, in 1792, and American merchants traded with both sides. In retaliation, the British began to seize American merchant ships and force their crews into service with the British navy.

John Jay negotiated a treaty with the British that attempted to settle the conflict at sea, as well as to curtail English agitation of their Native American allies on the western borders in 1794. In the Pinckney Treaty, ratified by the Senate in 1796, the Spanish opened the Mississippi River to American traffic and recognized the 31st parallel as the northern boundary of Florida.

Internal Problems

In 1794, western farmers refused to pay the excise tax on whiskey which formed the backbone of Hamilton's revenue program. When a group of Pennsylvania farmers terrorized the tax collectors, President Washington sent out a federalized militia force of some 15,000 men and the rebellion evaporated, thus strengthening the credibility of the young government.

John Adams' Administration (1797–1801)

In the Election of 1796 John Adams was the Federalist candidate and Thomas Jefferson the Republican. Jefferson received the second highest number of electoral votes and became vice president.

Repression and Protest

The elections in 1798 increased the Federalists' majorities in both houses of Congress and they used their "mandate" to enact legislation to stifle foreign influences. The **Alien**

Act raised new hurdles in the path of immigrants trying to obtain citizenship, and the **Sedition Act** widened the powers of the Adams administration to muzzle its newspaper critics.

Republican leaders were convinced that the Alien and Sedition Acts were unconstitutional, but the process of deciding on the constitutionality of federal laws was as yet undefined. Jefferson and James Madison decided that state legislatures should have that power, and they drew up a series of resolutions which were presented to the Kentucky and Virginia legislatures. They proposed that state bodies could "nullify" federal laws within those states. These resolutions were adopted only in these two states, and so the issue died, but the principle of states' rights would have great force in later years.

The Revolution of 1800

Thomas Jefferson and Aaron Burr (1756–1836) ran on the Republican ticket against John Adams and Charles Pinckney (1746–1825) for the Federalists. The Republican candidates won handily, but both received the same number of electoral votes, thus throwing the selection of the president into the House of Representatives. After a lengthy deadlock, Alexander Hamilton threw his support to Jefferson and Burr had to accept the vice-presidency, the result obviously intended by the electorate. Jefferson appointed James Madison as secretary of state and Albert Gallatin (1761–1849) to the treasury.

The Federalist Congress passed a new **Judiciary Act** early in 1801, and President Adams filled the newly created vacancies with party supporters, many of them with last-minute commissions. **John Marshall** (1755–1835) was then appointed chief justice of the United States Supreme Court, thus guaranteeing continuation of Federalist policies from the bench of the high court.

The Jefferson Administration (1801–1809)

Thomas Jefferson and his Republican followers envisioned a nation of independent farmers living under a central government that exercised a minimum of control and served merely to protect the individual liberties guaranteed by the Constitution. This agrarian paradise would be free from the industrial smoke and urban blight of Europe, and would serve as a beacon light of Enlightenment rationalism to a world searching for direction. But Jefferson presided over a nation that was growing more industrialized and urban, and which seemed to need an ever-stronger president.

Domestic Affairs

The **Twelfth Amendment** was adopted and ratified in 1804, ensuring that a tie vote between candidates of the same party could not again cause the confusion of the Jefferson-Burr affair.

Following the Constitutional mandate, the importation of slaves was stopped by law in 1808.

The Louisiana Purchase: An American delegation purchased the trans-Mississippi territory from Napoleon for $15 million in April 1803, even though they had no authority to buy more than the city of New Orleans.

Exploring the West: Meriwether Lewis (1774–1809) and William Clark's (1770–1838) group left St. Louis in 1804 and returned two years later with a wealth of scientific and anthropological information. At the same time, Zebulon Pike and others had been traversing the middle parts of Louisiana and mapping the land.

Madison's Administration (1809–1817)

The Election of 1808: Republican James Madison won the election over Federalist Charles Pinckney, but the Federalists gained seats in both houses of the Congress.

The Native American tribes of the Northwest and the Mississippi Valley were resentful of the government's policy of pressured removal to the West, and the British authorities in Canada exploited their discontent by encouraging border raids against the American settlements.

At the same time, the British interfered with American transatlantic shipping, including impressing sailors and capturing ships.

The Congress in 1811 contained a strong pro-war group called the **War Hawks** led by Henry Clay (1777–1852) and John C. Calhoun (1782–1850). They gained control of both houses and began agitating for war with the British. On June 1, 1812, President Madison asked for a declaration of war and Congress complied.

The **War of 1812** is one of the forgotten wars of the United States. The war lasted for over two years, and while it ended much like it started— in stalemate—it was in fact a war that once and for all confirmed American Independence. The offensive actions of the United States failed in every attempt to capture Canada. On the other hand, the British army was successfully stopped when it attempted to capture Baltimore and New Orleans. There were a number of American naval victories in which American vessels proved themselves superior to similarly sized British vessels. These victories coming after victories in the Quasi War (an even more forgotten war) launched American naval traditions.

After three years of inconclusive war, in 1815 the **Treaty of Ghent** provided for the acceptance of the status quo that had existed at the beginning of hostilities and both sides restored their wartime conquests to the other.

The Federalists had increasingly become a minority party. They vehemently opposed the war, and Daniel Webster (1782–1852) and other New England congressmen consistently blocked the Administration's efforts to prosecute the war effort. On December 15, 1814, delegates from the New England states met in Hartford, Connecticut, and drafted a set of resolutions suggesting nullification—and even secession—if their interests were not protected against the growing influence of the South and the West.

Soon after the convention adjourned, the news of Andrew Jackson's victory over the British on January 8, 1815 at New Orleans was announced and their actions were discredited. The Federalist Party ceased to be a political force from this point on.

Postwar Developments

Protective Tariff (1816): The first protective tariff in the nation's history was passed in 1816 to slow the flood of cheap British manufactures into the country.

Rush-Bagot Treaty (1817): An agreement was reached in 1817 between Britain and the United States to stop maintaining armed fleets on the Great Lakes. This first "disarmament" agreement is still in effect.

The Adams-Onis Treaty (1819): Spain had decided to sell the remainder of the Florida territory to the Americans before they took it anyway. Under this agreement, the Spanish surrendered all their claims to Florida. The United States agreed to assume $5 million in debts owed to American merchants.

The Monroe Doctrine

As Latin American nations began declaring independence, British and American leaders feared that European governments would try to restore the former New World colonies to their erstwhile royal owners.

In December 1823, President James Monroe (1758–1831) included in his annual message to Congress a statement that the peoples of the American hemisphere were "henceforth not to be considered as subjects for future colonization by any European powers."

The years following the War of 1812 were years of rapid economic and social development, followed by a severe depression in 1819. But this slump was temporary, and it became obvious that the country was moving rapidly from its agrarian origins toward an industrial, urban future.

The Monroe Presidency (1817–1823): James Monroe, the last of the "Virginia dynasty," had been handpicked by the retiring Madison and he was elected with only one electoral vote opposed—a symbol of national unity.

The Marshall Court

John Marshall delivered the majority opinions in a number of critical decisions in these formative years, all of which served to strengthen the power of the federal government and restrict the powers of state governments.

Marbury vs. Madison (1803): This case established the precedent of the Supreme Court's power to rule on the constitutionality of federal laws.

Gibbons vs. Ogden (1824): In a case involving competing steamboat companies, Marshall ruled that commerce included navigation, and that only Congress has the right to regulate commerce among states. Thus, the state-granted monopoly was voided.

National Expansion

The Missouri Compromise (1820): The Missouri Territory, the first to be organized from the **Louisiana Purchase,** applied for statehood in 1819. Since the Senate membership was evenly divided between slaveholding and free states at that time, the admission of a new state would give the voting advantage either to the North or to the South.

As the debate dragged on, the northern territory of Massachusetts applied for admission as the state of Maine. The two admission bills were combined, with Maine coming in free and Missouri coming in as a slave state. To make the package palatable for the House, a provision was added that prohibited slavery in the remainder of the Louisiana Territory north of the southern boundary of Missouri (latitude 36° 30′).

CONTINUED NATIONAL DEVELOPMENT (1829–1850)

Manifest Destiny and Westward Expansion

Although the term "**Manifest Destiny**" was not actually coined until 1844, the belief that the American nation was destined to eventually expand all the way to the Pacific Ocean, and to possibly embrace Canada and Mexico, had been voiced for years by many who believed that American liberty and ideals should be shared with everyone possible, by force if necessary. The rising sense of **nationalism** which followed the War of 1812 was fed by the rapidly expanding population, the reform impulse of the 1830s, and the desire to acquire new markets and resources for the burgeoning economy of "Young America."

The Election of 1824

Although John Quincy Adams, through the controversial action of the House of Representatives, became president in the 1824 election, Andrew Jackson instigated a campaign for the presidency immediately. He won the election of 1828.

Jackson was popular with the common man. He seemed to be the prototype of the self-made westerner: rough-hewn, violent, vindictive, with few ideas but strong convictions. He ignored his appointed cabinet officers and relied instead on the counsel of his "Kitchen Cabinet," a group of partisan supporters.

Jackson expressed the conviction that government operations could be performed by untrained, common folk, and he threatened to dismiss large numbers of government employees and replace them with his supporters. He exercised his veto power more than any other president before him.

The War on the Bank of the United States

The **Bank of the United States** had operated under the direction of Nicholas Biddle (1786–1844) since 1823. He was a cautious man, and his conservative economic policy enforced conservatism among the state and private banks—which many bankers resented. In 1832 Jackson vetoed the Bank's renewal, and it ceased being a federal institution in 1836.

Jackson had handpicked his Democratic successor, Martin Van Buren (1782–1862) of New York. The opposition Whig party had emerged from the ruins of the National Republicans and other groups who opposed Jackson's policies.

Van Buren inherited all the problems and resentments generated by his mentor. He spent most of his term in office dealing with the financial chaos left by the death of the Second Bank. The best he could do was to eventually persuade Congress to establish an Independent Treasury to handle government funds. It began functioning in 1840.

The Election of 1840

The Whigs nominated William Henry Harrison, "Old Tippecanoe (1773–1841)," a western fighter against the Native Americans. Their choice for vice-president was John Tyler (1790–1862), a former Democrat from Virginia. The Democrats put up Van Buren again.

Harrison won but died only a month after the inauguration, having served the shortest term in presidential history.

The **Age of Jackson** was the beginning of the modern two-party system. Popular politics, based on emotional appeal, became the accepted style. The practice of meeting in mass conventions to nominate national candidates for office was established during these years.

The Democrats opposed big government and the requirements of modernization: urbanization and industrialization. Their support came from the working classes, small merchants, and small farmers.

The Whigs promoted government participation in commercial and industrial development, the encouragement of banking and corporations, and a cautious approach to westward expansion. Their support came largely from northern business and manufacturing interests and large southern planters. Calhoun, Clay, and Webster dominated the Whig party during the early decades of the nineteenth century.

Remaking Society: Organized Reform

The early antislavery movement advocated freed the colonization of slaves in Liberia, Africa. The American Colonization Society was organized in 1817, and established the colony of Liberia in 1830, but by that time the movement had reached a dead end.

In 1831, William Lloyd Garrison (1805–1879) started his paper, *The Liberator*, and began to advocate total and immediate emancipation. He founded the New England Anti-slavery Society in 1832 and the American Anti-slavery Society in 1833. Theodore Weld (1803–1895) pursued the same goals, but advocated more gradual means.

The movement split into two wings: Garrison's radical followers, and the moderates who favored "moral suasion" and petitions to Congress. In 1840, the Liberty party, the first national anti-slavery party, fielded a presidential candidate on the platform of "free soil" (non-expansion of slavery into the new western territories).

Diverging Societies—Life in the North

As the nineteenth century progressed, the states seemed to polarize more into the two sections we call the North and the South, with the expanding West becoming ever more identified with the North.

The Role of Minorities

The women's rights movement focused on social and legal discrimination, and women like Lucretia Mott (1793–1880) and Sojourner Truth (ca. 1797–1883) became well-known figures on the speakers' circuit.

CIVIL WAR ERA (1850–1870's)

Causes of the Civil War ("The War of Northern Aggression")

Growth of Sectionalism. The differences between the Southern plantation cotton economy and the Northern industrial economy resulted in not only differences in income levels but also differences in economic attitudes that manifested themselves in considerations of race. For instance, the South, based on the advantages of agrarian life, was not as tuned in as the North, where different cultures and classes rubbed shoulders all day. The differences in the way of life—agrarian communities versus factories—further polarized the North and the South as the South remained almost completely agricultural, with an economy and a social order largely founded on slavery and the plantation system where the South derived its wealth. The North was not as reliant upon the South for its agricultural products, but instead it was able to develop more commercially and industrially in ways the South was not. In many ways, the North was more self-sufficient than the South. Over time, tensions mounted. Let's review some reasons why:

Unfair taxation. The development of the North and South into different types of economies caused some polarization. The South had an agrarian economy that was dependent upon slave labor in order to realize profits. The Northern economy was based upon manufacturing. In the early days of the country the South preferred to trade with England rather than the North – it would send its cotton to English mills and would buy European goods in return. The North was irritated that its southern neighbors were eschewing their goods in favor of European ones. So, by the early 1800s, the Northern politicians made efforts to attack the foundations of the Southern economy (or so the South perceived it) through abolition movements, of course, but also through taxes. They pushed through heavy taxes on European goods so Southerners would be forced to buy goods from the North instead. The South perceived this as blatantly unfair and as a tax directed at them.

States versus federal rights. Unresolved issues of state versus federal authority festered as Southern states argued that they should have the right to decide if they wanted to accept certain federal legislation. Not only was slavery an issue that they wanted to be able to bypass federal rules about import taxes that they felt jeopardized their well being. These states asserted that they had the right of **nullification** where they could rule federal acts as nullified. The federal government refused to allow nullification, and proponents of federal rights, primarily Northerners, argued that nullification was a dangerous precedent that would just make the country weaker and more open to take-over or dissolution.

Growing controversy between proslavery versus no-slavery proponents. Each time the United States gained more territory, there were disagreements over whether or not the new state should allow slavery. The vociferousness of these disagreements was a little odd as the average U.S. citizen in *both* the North and the South did not own slaves, but the politicians became interested in slaves and the concept of slavery. The North viewed it as a moral issue, and the South viewed slavery as an economic issue. Efforts to reach compromises resulted in legislation like the Fugitive Slave Act, which allowed slaveholders to capture their slaves in free territory. The Kansas-Nebraska Act of 1854 created two new territories that allowed popular sovereignty to determine whether or not it would be a free state or a slave state. In Kansas, the violence of the proslavery forces from Missouri named "Border Ruffians" **exacerbated the conflict**, and the fighting caused it to be called **Bleeding Kansas**. The ruckus extended itself to the Senate floor where pro-slavery Senator Preston Brooks from South Carolina beat Senator Charles Sumner of the antislavery movement over the head.

Growth of the Abolitionist Movement. Feelings in the North intensified with the passage of the Fugitive Slave Act, the Dred Scott Case, the publication of Harriet Beecher Stowe's *Uncle Tom's Cabin*, and John Brown's Raid. Religious and reform groups sprang up that targeted the immorality of slavery, and media campaigns as well as groups dedicated to rescuing slaves sprang up, to the consternation of the South.

The 1860 election of Abraham Lincoln. The run-up to the election caused political rifts within the Whig party, which resulted in its dissolution and the Southern members joining the Democratic Party and the Northerners joining the Republic Party. In the razor-thin 1860 Presidential election. Abraham Lincoln defeated three candidates—Stephen A. Douglas (Northern Democrat), John C. Breckinridge (Southern Democrat), and John Bell of the Constitutional Union party. Before Lincoln was sworn in, South Carolina seceded from the Union and six other states joined it.

The Civil War and Reconstruction (1860–1877)

Hostilities Begin

On **December 20, 1860,** South Carolina passed a secession ordinance and shortly thereafter, Mississippi, Florida, Alabama, Georgia, Louisiana, and Texas joined it. By **February 1861,** the **Confederate States of America**, a government formed by 11 southern states, had been formed in Alabama. In his inaugural address, Lincoln urged Southerners to reconsider their actions, but warned that the Union was perpetual, that states could not secede, and that he would therefore hold the federal forts and installations in the South. Only two remained in federal hands: Fort Pickens, off Pensacola, Florida; and **Fort Sumter**, in the harbor of Charleston, South Carolina. Lincoln soon received word from Major Robert Anderson, commander of the small garrison at Fort Sumter, that supplies were running low. Desiring to send in the needed supplies,

Lincoln informed the governor of South Carolina of his intention, but promised that no attempt would be made to send arms, ammunition, or reinforcements unless Southerners initiated hostilities.

Confederate General P.G.T. Beauregard, acting on orders from Confederate President Jefferson Davis, demanded Anderson's surrender. Anderson said he would surrender if not resupplied. Knowing supplies were on the way, the Confederates opened fire at 4:30 a.m. on **April 12, 1861**. The next day, the fort surrendered. The day following Sumter's surrender, Lincoln declared an insurrection and called for the states to provide 75,000 volunteers to put it down. In response to this, Virginia, Tennessee, North Carolina, and Arkansas declared their secession. The remaining slave states, Delaware, Kentucky, Maryland, and Missouri, wavered but stayed with the Union.

Comparative Advantages of the Confederacy and the Union

The North enjoyed at least five major advantages over the South. It had overwhelming preponderance in wealth and was vastly superior in industry, giving them vast resources to draw upon. The North also had an advantage of almost three to one in manpower; and over one-third of the South's population was composed of slaves, whom Southerners would not use as soldiers. Unlike the South, the North received large numbers of immigrants during the war. The North retained control of the U.S. Navy, and thus, would command the sea and be able to blockade the South. Finally, the North enjoyed a far superior system of railroads.

The South did, however, have several advantages. It was vast in size, making it difficult to conquer. Its troops would be fighting on their own ground, a fact that would give them the advantage of familiarity with the terrain, as well as the added motivation of defending their homes and families. Its armies would often have the opportunity of fighting on the defensive, a major advantage in the warfare of that day.

Progress of the War

At a creek called **Bull Run** near the town of Manassas Junction, Virginia, just southwest of Washington, D.C., the Union Army under General Scott met a Confederate force under Generals P.G.T. Beauregard and Joseph E. Johnston on July 21, 1861. In the **First Battle of Bull Run** (called First Manassas in the South), the Union army was forced to retreat in confusion back to Washington, alarming Union picnickers who had come to watch what they had thought would be an entertaining rout. The reaction among the Union officials was to embark on a series of command changes throughout 1861–1862, hoping to turn back the Southern troops. Some victories, such as at the **Battle of Antietam**, the bloodiest battle in the Civil War, in which a total of 31,000 men perished from each side, gave the North a bit of confidence, but was not enough to make the North confident in its military leadership. Nevertheless, after claiming the Battle of Antietam a victory, Lincoln issued the **Emancipation Proclamation**, which took effect on **New Year's Day 1863**, freeing all of the slaves in the areas of rebellion.

As the war dragged on, the greater population and material advantages of the North became a significant factor. The blockade and Union victories that gave them control of the Mississippi allowed Union forces to divide the South in half and to interrupt its trade and supply lines. The Union had a better Navy and, in addition to blocking Southern ports, also shelled land forts and took part in joint Army and Navy actions. The one battle between the newly constructed Union ironclad, **The Monitor**, and the Confederate ironclad, **The Virginia**, demonstrated the superiority of the Union Navy even though neither side actually won the battle between the two ships.

Furthermore, several key Confederate officers, such as Stonewall Jackson and Johnston, were severely injured or killed. The replacement of the North's largely ineffective McClellan only made an impact when he was permanently removed from the command of the Army in favor of **Ulysses S. Grant**. After 1863, the Union was able to go on the offensive and invade the South. **Vicksburg** and **Gettysburg** were besieged and ultimately fell to the Union. Lincoln's **Gettysburg Address** stressed the honor of the dead on both sides and the need to bind up the wounds of a nation. This conciliatory attitude, as well as his determination to readmit the Southern states as quickly as possible, would be reflected in his **Ten Percent Plan**.

The final Union campaign consisted of a series of coordinated offensives in the South. Sherman's "March to the Sea" created a path of destruction and aroused bitter feelings in the South that would not end with the war. The final Confederate collapse was only a matter of time. Grant cut off all supplies to Lee and the Army of Northern Virginia, which had withdrawn to the area around Richmond, and on April 9, 1865, Lee surrendered at **Appomattox Court House**. Other Confederate armies still holding out in various parts of the South surrendered over the next few weeks. Lincoln did not live to receive news of the final surrenders. On April 14, 1865, he was shot in the back of the head while watching a play in Ford's Theater in Washington.

The Ordeal of Reconstruction

Reconstruction began well before the fighting of the Civil War came to an end. The North was faced with four basic concerns: (1) who would the local rulers be for the South and what role would they have; (2) whether governmental control of the South be in the hands of the President or Congress; (3) issues with the freedom of former slaves; and (4) whether they should reestablish the old system that had been in place, or build something anew so that these problems would not happen again. There were two main views to address these problems, one that rested with the executive branch, Lincoln, and another with the legislative branch, under sway of the Radical Republicans in Congress. Lincoln favored leniency and the Radical Republicans, a loose faction within Congress that had opposed slavery, favored revenge.

To restore legal governments in the seceded states, Lincoln developed a policy called the **Ten Percent Plan** that made it relatively easy for Southern states to enter the collateral process. Lincoln's plan stipulated that Southerners, except for high-ranking rebel officials, could take an oath promising future loyalty to the Union and acknowledge the end of slavery. When the number of people who had taken this oath within any one state reached 10% of the number who had been registered to vote in 1860, a loyal state government could be formed. Tennessee, Arkansas, and Louisiana formed loyal governments under Lincoln's plan but were refused recognition by a Congress dominated by Radical Republicans.

Radical Republicans such as **Thaddeus Stevens** of Pennsylvania believed that Lincoln's plan did not adequately punish the South, restructure Southern society, or boost the political prospects of the Republican Party. Instead, the radicals in Congress drew up the more stringent **Wade-Davis Bill,** which required a majority of individuals who had been alive and registered to vote in 1860 to swear an "iron-clad" oath stating that they were loyal and had never been disloyal. Under these terms, no confederate state could have been readmitted unless African-Americans were given the vote. Until a majority of individuals took the oath, the state could not send representatives to Congress. Lincoln killed the bill with a "pocket veto," and the radicals were furious. When Lincoln was assassinated, the radicals rejoiced, believing that Vice President Andrew Johnson would be less generous to the South, or at least easier to control. However, Johnson, although having pledged earlier to be harsh with the South, changed his mind and embraced Lincoln's Ten Percent Plan to be more lenient with the Southern states. His plan was not totally magnanimous, however.

Now president, Johnson's plans for reconstruction waffled a bit. First he stated that certain Southerners, like officers, officials, and members of the planter class whose prop-

United States History   **Chapter 2**

erty was worth more than $20,000, would not be allowed to take the oath of loyalty, and would have to apply personally to the president for a pardon. But this policy lacked teeth, as Johnson proceeded to grant thousands of pardons, which then allowed the previous social and governmental power brokers in the South to remain in place. After only eight months, Johnson declared that Reconstruction was over and former Confederates could return to Congress in December 1865. Congress, on the other hand, was agitated by Johnson's overtures to the South and decided to refuse to admit ex-Confederates to its ranks. Congress justified its position by arguing that the Constitution gave it, not the president, the power to admit new states.

Thirteenth and Fourteenth Amendments and Congressional Reconstruction

Tensions between Congress and President Johnson continued to build, and Congress decided that it would go ahead and embark on their own reconstruction plans. The **Thirteenth Amendment,** officially ending slavery, had already been passed. After Johnson's succession to the presidency, Congress passed a Civil Rights Act and extended the authority of the Freedman's Bureau. Johnson vetoed both bills, claiming they were unconstitutional, but Congress overrode the vetoes. Congress then approved the **Fourteenth Amendment** and sent it to the states for ratification in June 1866. The Fourteenth Amendment defined citizenship and forbade any states to deny various rights to citizens. Any state that denied the vote or other rights to eligible citizens, including African-Americans, would have their representation in Congress reduced. The Amendment also prohibited the paying of any Confederate debts and made former Confederates ineligible to hold public office. Johnson tried to block the Fourteenth Amendment throughout the country, urging Southern state legislatures to vote against it and organizing a National Union Convention in the North to do the same.

In response to Johnson's machinations, Congress embarked on some manipulating of its own with the passage of a series of Reconstruction Acts, which would give Union generals control of military districts in the South and supervision of elections. It also forced states to ratify the Fourteenth Amendment, to make changes to their state constitutions, and to submit them to Congress for approval. Johnson continued to work against Congressional policies so it fought back by passing the Tenure of Office Act, which was passed over Johnson's veto. This act forbade Johnson from dismissing his cabinet members without permission of Congress. In particular, Congress limited Johnson's power over the army by forcing him to issue orders through Grant, who in turn was not allowed to be dismissed without Congressional approval. Congress also passed this measure in order to protect the Secretary of War, Edwin M. Stanton, who was the last Radical Republican Cabinet member still in office.

69

In response, Johnson issued orders to commanders in the South that limited their powers, removed some of the best officers, and then, as a last straw, dismissed Stanton in order to test the constitutionality of the Tenure of Office Act. Before the matter could be taken up in court, Congress responded by impeaching Johnson but was one vote shy of removing him from office. Johnson remained in office but offered little resistance to the Radical Republicans during his last months in office.

The Election of 1868 and the Fifteenth Amendment

In 1868, the Republicans nominated Ulysses S. Grant for president. Grant had no political record and his views—if any—on national issues were unknown. The narrow victory of even such a strong candidate as Grant prompted Republican leaders to decide that it would be politically expedient to give the vote to all blacks, in the North as well as the South. For this purpose, the Fifteenth Amendment was drawn up and submitted to the states. Ironically, the idea was so unpopular in the North that it won the necessary three-fourths approval only with its ratification by southern states. Though personally of unquestioned integrity, Grant naively placed his faith in a number of thoroughly dishonest men. His administration was rocked by one scandalous revelation of government corruption after another.

Many of the economic difficulties that the country faced during Grant's administration were caused by the necessary readjustments from a wartime economy back to a peacetime economy. The central economic question was deflation versus inflation, or more specifically, whether to retire the un-backed paper money, greenbacks, printed to meet the wartime emergency, or to print more.

Early in Grant's second term, the country was hit by an economic depression known as the **Panic of 1873**. Brought on by the over-expansive tendencies of railroad builders and businessmen during the immediate postwar boom, the Panic was triggered by economic downturns in Europe and more immediately, by the failure of Jay Cooke and Company, a major American financial firm.

The Panic led to clamor for the printing of more greenbacks. In 1874, Congress authorized a small new issue of greenbacks, but it was vetoed by Grant. Pro-inflation forces were further enraged when Congress demonetized silver in 1873, going to a straight gold standard. Silver was becoming more plentiful due to Western mining and was seen by some as a potential source of inflation. Pro-inflation forces referred to the demonetization of silver as the "Crime of '73." In the election of 1876, the Democrats campaigned against corruption and nominated New York Governor Samuel J. Tilden

(1814–1886), who had broken the Tweed political machine of New York City. The Republicans passed over Grant and turned to Governor Rutherford B. Hayes of Ohio. Like Tilden, Hayes was decent, honest, in favor of hard money and civil service reform, and opposed to government regulation of the economy. Tilden won the popular vote and led in the electoral vote 184 to 165. However, 185 electoral votes were needed for election, and 20 votes, from the three Southern states still occupied by federal troops and run by Republican governments, were disputed. A deal was made whereby those 20 votes went to Hayes in return for removal of federal troops from the South. Reconstruction was over.

Consequences of Reconstruction

The power struggle between the President and the Congress and between the North and the South had finally ended, but the impact of both the war and the efforts to restore the Union would continue to exert an influence on the development of the United States. The Union had been preserved, but at what cost and to what extent was the nation that emerged after 1877 fundamentally different from the one that had gone to war in 1861?

The abolition of slavery led to real changes in the lives of former slaves, but it did not end their economic dependence on Southern whites nor did it end discrimination in the South. African-Americans after the Civil War were able to marry and divorce, and hundreds published letters and ads seeking loved ones from whom they had been separated as a result of the internal slave trade. African-Americans immediately began to form their own schools and churches. The restrictions that forbade slaves from learning to read and write in the old slave codes were now nullified, and former slaves emphasized the importance of education, especially for children. Former slaves also began to leave white churches and form their own church communities, which often had distinctive elements such as music or dance as part of the service. African-Americans also gained control over their time and their movements, but in terms of their economic status, little had changed. The failure of the government to provide former slaves with land or other economic opportunities meant that many blacks ended up renting land or sharecropping from their former masters. White southerners could no longer exercise complete control over former slaves—for instance, many African-American males refused to allow their wives to work for whites—but they could demand a large portion of their crop as rent payment. Whites could also charge African-Americans high prices for seed and other supplies that had to be purchased from stores owned by whites.

Despite these efforts by conservative southerners, the new Southern Republican Party came to power in the constitutional conventions of 1868–1870, and as a result, the new

Southern state constitutions were more democratic. Initially both blacks and Republicans were elected to serve in the new governments.

Reconstruction laws encouraged investment and industrialization; which helped in some areas, but also increased corruption. The question of land redistribution was very important to blacks but was not paid adequate attention by Republicans. The effects on the Southern economy were terrible. Government industrialization plans geared toward helping the South industrialize did not work well. High tax rates turned public opinion against reconstructionists whose governments had to raise taxes substantially to pay for the Civil War damage.

Reconstruction transformed Southern society and culture and increased divisions within the population. The first division was between those who supported and those who disagreed with Reconstruction. Opponents called Southerners who cooperated with reconstruction or who joined the Republican Party **scalawags,** and the Northerners who ran such programs were referred to as **carpetbaggers** and considered to be greedy, corrupt businessmen trying to take advantage of the South. The influx of these Northern "carpetbaggers" to the South resulted in the Republican Party gaining power in the South and passing some civil rights laws like ones that legalized interracial marriage and that allowed black students to attend schools. In many of the state legislatures, blacks gained positions of power.

The rapid cultural and economic changes that were occurring in the South resulted in racial tensions, as former slaves also faced campaigns of terror and intimidation by white Southerners who wanted to keep them in their place in society, sabotage black civil rights, and persuade them not to try to exercise their right to vote. The **Ku Klux Klan** targeted all of those who supported Reconstruction—black and white. Klansmen often attacked and murdered scalawags and leaders of all races, community activists, and teachers. In response to the violence in the South, Congress passed the **Enforcement Acts** and an **Anti-Klan Law** in 1870–1871; making actions against the civil rights of others to be criminal offenses. The laws did not have much impact, however, and Klan violence continued.

Eventually, the North lost interest in continuing its pursuit of enforcing the laws and measures designed to advance civil rights for blacks. Many of the civil rights laws were overturned, and conditions worsened for blacks in the South. Congress passed the **Posse Comitatus Act**, which prohibited federal authorities from exercising any power or control over local enforcement agencies, so that the interpretation of laws was left to individual Southern districts. In 1883, a rewrite of the Fourteenth Amendment declared that Congress only had the power to outlaw public rather than private discrimination. The **Plessy v. Ferguson** case ruled that state-mandated segregation was legal as long as there were "separate but equal" facilities. In response to this case, Southern states introduced **Jim Crow Laws** designed to segregate whites from African-Americans.

It was not just in the South that African-Americans encountered discrimination and hostility, although the worst abuses did take place in the South. All in all, reconstruction was a mixed bag, but in terms of achieving equality within the United States, it was clearly a failure.

EMERGENCE OF THE MODERN UNITED STATES (1877–1900)

The presidencies of Abraham Lincoln and Theodore Roosevelt (1858–1919) mark the boundaries of a half century of relatively weak executive leadership and legislative domination by Congress and the Republican party.

"Stalwarts," led by New York senator Roscoe Conkling (1829–1888) favored the old spoils system of political patronage. "Half-Breeds," headed by Maine senator James G. Blaine (1830–1893), pushed for civil service reform and merit appointments to government posts.

The Economy (1877–1882)

Between 1860 and 1894, the United States moved from the fourth-largest manufacturing nation to the world's leader through capital accumulation, natural resources, especially in iron, oil, and coal, an abundance of labor helped by massive immigration, railway transportation, and communications and major technical innovations such as the development of the modern steel industry and electrical energy.

By 1880, northern capital erected the modern textile industry in the New South by bringing factories to the cotton fields.

Social and Cultural Developments (1877–1882)

In time, advocates of the "social gospel" such as Jane Addams (1860–1939) and Washington Gladden (1836–1918) urged the creation of settlement houses and better health and education services to accommodate the new immigrants. In 1881, Booker T. Washington (1856–1915) became president of Tuskegee Institute in Alabama, a school devoted to teaching and vocational education for African Americans.

The Economy (1882–1887)

Captains of industry such as John D. Rockefeller in oil, J. P. Morgan (1837–1919) in banking, Gustavus Swift (1839–1903) in meat processing, Andrew Carnegie in steel, and E. H. Harriman (1848–1909) in railroads, put together major industrial empires.

The concentration of wealth and power in the hands of a relatively small number of giant firms led to a monopoly capitalism that minimized competition. This led to a demand by smaller businessmen, farmers, and laborers for government regulation of the economy in order to promote competition.

The Interstate Commerce Act (1887): Popular resentment of railroad abuses such as price-fixing, kickbacks, and discriminatory freight rates created demands for federal regulation of the railway industry. The Interstate Commerce Act was passed providing that a commission be established to oversee fair and just railway rates, prohibit rebates, end discriminatory practices, and require annual reports and financial statements.

American Federation of Labor (1886): Samuel Gompers (1850–1924) and Adolph Strasser put together a combination of national craft unions to represent labor's concerns with wages, hours, and safety conditions. Although militant in its use of the strike and in its demand for collective bargaining in labor contracts with large corporations, it did not promote violence or radicalism.

Frederick W. Taylor (1856–1915), an engineer credited as the father of scientific management, introduced modern concepts of industrial engineering, plant management, and time and motion studies. This gave rise to a separate class of managers in industrial manufacturing — efficiency experts.

The Economy (1887–1892)

Despite a protective tariff policy, the United States became increasingly international as it sought to export surplus manufactured and agricultural goods. Foreign markets were viewed as a safety valve for labor employment problems and agrarian unrest.

Corporate monopolies (trusts) which controlled whole industries were subject to federal prosecution if they were found to be combinations or conspiracies in restraint of trade. Although supported by smaller businesses, labor unions, and farm associations, the Sherman Antitrust Act of 1890 was in time interpreted by the Supreme Court to apply to labor unions and farmers' cooperatives as much as to large corporate combinations. Monopoly was still dominant over laissez-faire, free-enterprise economics during the 1890s.

Foreign Relations (1887–1892)

As secretary of state, James G. Blaine was concerned with international trade, political stability, and excessive militarism in Latin America. His international Bureau of American Republics was designed to promote a Pan-American customs union and peaceful conflict resolution. To achieve his aims, Blaine opposed U.S. military intervention in the hemisphere.

Displacement of Native Americans from Western Lands (1870–1900)

Federal Indian policy during this period departed from earlier policies dominated by removal, treaties, reservations, and even war. The new policy focused specifically on breaking up reservations by granting land allotments to individual Native Americans. Very sincere individuals reasoned that if a person adopted white clothing and ways, and was responsible for his own farm, he would gradually drop his Indian-ness and be assimilated into the population. Then there would be no more necessity for the government to oversee Indian welfare in the paternalistic way it had been obligated to do, or provide meager annuities that seemed to keep the Indian in a subservient and poverty stricken position.

On February 8, 1887, Congress passed the **Dawes Act**, also known as the **General Allotment Act**; the law allowed for the president to break up reservation land, which was held in common by the members of a tribe, into small allotments to be parceled out to individuals. Thus, Native Americans registering with the Bureau of Indian Affairs were granted allotments of reservation land.

> To each head of a family, one-quarter of a section; To each
> single person over eighteen years of age, one-eighth of a section;
> To each orphan child under eighteen years of age, one-eighth of

a section; and To each other single person under eighteen years now living, or who may be born prior to the date of the order of the President directing an allotment of the lands embraced in any reservation, one-sixteenth of a section…

The purpose of the Dawes Act and the subsequent acts that extended its initial provisions was originally to protect Indian property rights, particularly during the land rushes of the 1890s; however, the results were vastly different. The land allotted to the Indians included desert or near-desert lands unsuitable for farming. In addition, the techniques of self-sufficient farming were much different from their tribal way of life. Many Indians did not want to take up agriculture, and those who did want to farm could not afford the tools, animals, seed, and other supplies necessary to get started. There were also problems with inheritance. Often young children inherited allotments that they could not farm because they had been sent away to boarding schools. Multiple heirs also caused a problem; when several people inherited an allotment, the size of the holdings became too small for efficient farming.

Economic Depression and Social Crisis (1892–1897)

The economic depression that began in 1893 brought about a collective response from organized labor, militant agriculture, and the business community. Each group called for economic safeguards and a more humane free-enterprise system which would expand economic opportunities in an equitable manner.

Politics of the Period (1892–1897)

The most marked development in American politics was the emergence of a viable third-party movement in the form of the essentially agrarian Populist party.

Democrat Grover Cleveland (New York) regained the White House by defeating Republican president Benjamin Harrison (Indiana). Cleveland's conservative economic stand in favor of the gold standard brought him the support of various business interests. The Democrats won control of both houses of Congress.

The People's party (Populist) nominated James Weaver (Iowa) for president in 1892. The party platform called for the enactment of a program espoused by agrarians, but also for a coalition with urban workers and the middle class. Specific goals were the coinage of silver to gold at a ratio of 16 to 1; federal loans to farmers; a graduated income tax;

postal savings banks; public ownership of railroads and telephone and telegraph systems; prohibition of alien land ownership; immigration restriction; a ban on private armies used by corporations to break up strikes; an eight-hour working day; a single six-year term for president and direct election of senators; the right of initiative and referendum; and the use of the secret ballot.

In the election of 1896, the Republicans nominated William McKinley (Ohio) for president on a platform which promised to maintain the gold standard and protective tariffs. The Democratic party repudiated Cleveland's conservative economics and nominated William Jennings Bryan (1860–1925) (Nebraska) for president on a platform similar to the Populists. Bryan delivered one of the most famous speeches in American history when he declared that the people must not be "crucified upon a cross of gold."

The **Populist Party** also nominated Bryan. Having been outmaneuvered by the Silver Democrats, the Populists lost the opportunity to become a permanent political force.

McKinley won a hard-fought election by only about one-half million votes, as Republicans succeeded in creating the fear among business groups and middle-class voters that Bryan represented a revolutionary challenge to the American system. The Republicans retained control over Congress, which they had gained in 1894.

The Economy (1892–1897)

Homestead Strike (1892): Iron and steel workers went on strike in Pennsylvania against the Carnegie Steel Company to protest salary reductions.

Depression of 1893: The primary causes for the depression were dramatic growth of the federal deficit, withdrawal of British investments from the American market and the outward transfer of gold, and loss of business confidence. Twenty percent of the workforce was eventually unemployed. The depression would last four years.

March of Unemployed (1894): The Populist businessman Jacob Coxey (1854–1951) led a march of hundreds of unemployed workers on Washington asking for a government work-relief program.

Pullman Strike (1894): Eugene Debs's (1855–1926) American Railway Union struck the Pullman Palace Car Co. in Chicago over wage cuts and job losses. The strikes were all ended by force.

Social and Cultural Developments (1892–1897)

The **Anti-Saloon League** was formed in 1893. Women were especially concerned about the increase of drunkenness during the depression.

Immigration declined by almost 400,000 during the depression. Settlement houses helped poor immigrants. Such institutions also lobbied against sweatshop labor conditions, and for bans on child labor.

Foreign Relations (1892–1897)

The Cuban revolt against Spain in 1895 threatened American business interests in Cuba. Sensational "yellow" journalism, and nationalistic statements from officials such as Assistant Secretary of the Navy Theodore Roosevelt (1858–1919), encouraged popular support for direct American military intervention on behalf of Cuban independence. President McKinley, however, proceeded cautiously through 1897.

The Sino-Japanese War (1894–1895)

Japan's easy victory over China signaled to the United States and other nations trading in Asia that China's weakness might result in its colonization by industrial powers, and thus, in the closing of the China market. This concern led the United States to announce the Open Door policy with China, designed to protect equal opportunity of trade and China's political independence (1899 and 1900).

Foreign Policy (1897–1902)

On March 27, President McKinley asked Spain to call an armistice, accept American mediation to end the war, and end the use of concentration camps in Cuba. Spain refused to comply. On April 21, Congress declared war on Spain with the objective of establishing Cuban independence (Teller Amendment). The first U.S. forces landed in Cuba on June 22, 1898, and by July 17 had defeated the Spanish forces.

On May 1, 1898, the Spanish fleet in the Philippines was destroyed, and Manila surrendered on August 13. Spain agreed to a peace conference to be held in Paris in October 1898, where it ceded the Philippines, Puerto Rico, and Guam to the United States, in return for a payment of $20 million to Spain for the Philippines. The **Treaty of Paris** was ratified by the Senate on February 6, 1900.

Filipino nationalists under Emilio Aguinaldo (1869–1964) rebelled against the United States (February 1899) when they learned the Philippines would not be given independence. The United States used 70,000 men to suppress the revolutionaries by June 1902. A special U.S. commission recommended eventual self-government for the Philippines.

During the war with Spain, the United States annexed Hawaii on July 7, 1898. In 1900, the United States claimed Wake Island, 2,000 miles west of Hawaii.

Although Cuba was granted its independence, the **Platt Amendment** of 1901 guaranteed that it would become a virtual protectorate of the United States. Cuba could not:

1) make a treaty with a foreign state impairing its independence, or

2) contract an excessive public debt.

Cuba was required to allow the United States to preserve order on the island, and to lease a naval base for 99 years to the United States at Guantanamo Bay.

PROGRESSIVE ERA THROUGH THE NEW DEAL (1900–1939)

Politics of the Period (1900–1902)

The unexpected death of Vice President Garrett Hobart led the Republican party to choose the war hero and reform governor of New York, Theodore Roosevelt, as President William McKinley's vice-presidential running mate. Riding the crest of victory against Spain, the G.O.P platform called for upholding the gold standard for full economic recovery, promoting economic expansion and power in the Caribbean and the Pacific, and building a canal in Central America. The Democrats once again nominated William Jennings Bryan on a platform condemning imperialism and the gold standard. McKinley easily won reelection and the Republicans retained control of both houses of Congress.

While attending the Pan American Exposition in Buffalo, New York, the president was shot on September 6, 1901, by Leon Czolgosz, an anarchist. The president died on

September 14. Theodore Roosevelt became the nation's 25th president, and at age 42, its youngest to date.

Theodore Roosevelt and Progressive Reforms (1902–1907)

President Roosevelt did much to create a bipartisan coalition of liberal reformers whose objective was to restrain corporate monopoly and promote economic competition at home and abroad.

The president pledged strict enforcement of the Sherman Antitrust Act (1890), which was designed to break up illegal monopolies and regulate large corporations for the public good.

Hepburn Act (1906): Membership of the Interstate Commerce Commission was increased from five to seven. The I.C.C. could set its own fair freight rates, had its regulatory power extended over pipelines, bridges, and express companies, and was empowered to require a uniform system of accounting by regulated transportation companies.

Pure Food and Drug Act (1906): This prohibited the manufacture, sale, and transportation of adulterated or fraudulently labeled foods and drugs in accordance with consumer demands.

Meat Inspection Act (1906): This provided for federal and sanitary regulations and inspections in meat packing facilities. Wartime scandals in 1898 involving spoiled canned meats were a powerful force for reform.

The Economy (1902–1907)

Antitrust Policy (1902): Attorney General P. C. Knox (1853–1921) first brought suit against the Northern Securities Company, a railroad holding corporation put together by J. P. Morgan (1837–1913), and then moved against Rockefeller's Standard Oil Company. By the time he left office in 1909, Roosevelt had indictments against 25 monopolies.

Department of Commerce and Labor (1903): A new cabinet position was created to address the concerns of business and labor. Within the department, the Bureau of Corporations was empowered to investigate and report on the illegal activities of corporations.

Coal Strike (1902): Roosevelt interceded with government mediation to bring about negotiations between the United Mine Workers union and the anthracite mine owners after a bitter strike over wages, safety conditions, and union recognition. This was the first time that the government intervened in a labor dispute without automatically siding with management.

A brief economic recession and panic occurred in 1907 as a result, in part, of questionable bank speculations, a lack of flexible monetary and credit policies, and a conservative gold standard. This event called attention to the need for banking reform which would lead to the establishment of the Federal Reserve System in 1913.

Social and Cultural Developments (1902–1907)

There was not one unified progressive movement, but a series of reform causes designed to address specific social, economic, and political problems. Progressive reforms might best be described as evolutionary change from above rather than revolutionary upheaval from below.

Muckrakers (a term coined by Roosevelt) were investigative journalists and authors who were often the champions of reforms.

Foreign Relations (1902–1907)

Panama Canal: Roosevelt engineered the separation of Panama from Colombia and the recognition of Panama as an independent country. The Hay-Bunau-Varilla Treaty of 1903 granted the United States control of the canal zone in Panama for $10 million and an annual fee of $250,000, beginning nine years after ratification of the treaty by both parties. Construction of the canal began in 1904 and was completed in 1914.

Roosevelt Corollary to the Monroe Doctrine: The United States reserved the right to intervene in the internal affairs of Latin American nations to keep European powers from using military force to collect debts in the Western Hemisphere. The United States by 1905, had intervened in the affairs of Venezuela, Haiti, the Dominican Republic, Nicaragua, and Cuba.

Taft-Katsura Memo (1905): The United States and Japan pledged to maintain the Open Door principles in China. Japan recognized American control over the Philippines, and the United States granted a Japanese protectorate over Korea.

Gentleman's Agreement with Japan (1907): After numerous incidents of racial discrimination against Japanese in California, Japan agreed to restrict the emigration of unskilled Japanese workers to the United States.

The Regulatory State and the Ordered Society (1907–1912)

Deciding not to run for reelection, Theodore Roosevelt opened the way for William H. Taft (1857–1930) (Ohio) to run on a Republican platform calling for a continuation of antitrust enforcement, environmental conservation, and a lower tariff policy to promote international trade. The Democrats nominated William Jennings Bryan for a third time on an anti-monopoly and low-tariff platform. Taft easily won and the Republicans retained control of both houses of Congress. For the first time, the American Federation of Labor entered national politics officially with an endorsement of Bryan. This decision began a long alliance between organized labor and the Democratic party in the twentieth century.

Antitrust Policy: In pursuing anti-monopoly law enforcement, Taft chose as his attorney general George Wickersham (1858–1936), who brought 44 indictments in antitrust suits.

Taft was less successful in healing the Republican split between conservatives and progressives over such issues as tariff reform, conservation, and the almost dictatorial power held by the reactionary Republican Speaker of the House, Joseph Cannon (Illinois).

The 1912 election was one of the most dramatic in American history. President Taft's inability to maintain party harmony led Theodore Roosevelt to return to national politics. When denied the Republican nomination, Roosevelt and his supporters formed the **Progressive** (Bull Moose) party and nominated Roosevelt for president on a political platform nicknamed "The New Nationalism." It called for stricter regulation of large corporations, creation of a tariff commission, women's suffrage, minimum wages, and benefits, direct election of senators, initiative, referendum and recall, presidential primaries, and prohibition of child labor. Roosevelt also called for a Federal Trade Commission to regulate the economy, a stronger executive, and more government planning. Theodore Roosevelt did not see big business as evil, but as a permanent development that was necessary in a modern economy.

The Republicans: President Taft and Vice President Sherman were nominated on a platform of "Quiet Confidence," which called for a continuation of the progressive programs pursued by Taft.

The Democrats: A compromise gave the nomination to New Jersey Governor Woodrow Wilson. Wilson, who had also served as president of Princeton University, called his campaign the "New Freedom"; it borrowed pieces from the Progressive and Republican platforms. Wilson called for breaking up large corporations rather than just regulating them. He differed from the other two party candidates by favoring independence for the Philippines, and by advocating the exemption from prosecution of labor unions under the Sherman Antitrust Act. Wilson also supported such measures as lower tariffs, a graduated income tax, banking reform, and direct election of senators.

The Republican split paved the way for Wilson's victory. Although a minority president, Wilson garnered the largest electoral majority in American history up to that time. Democrats won control of both houses of Congress.

The Wilson Presidency (1913–1921)

Before the outbreak of **World War I** in 1914, President Wilson, working with cooperative majorities in both houses of Congress, achieved much of the remaining progressive agenda, including lower tariff reform (**Underwood-Simmons Act,** 1913), the **Sixteenth Amendment** (graduated income tax, 1913), the **Seventeenth Amendment** (direct election of senators, 1913), the **Federal Reserve** banking system (which provided regulation and flexibility to monetary policy, 1913), the **Federal Trade Commission** (to investigate unfair business practices, 1914), and the **Clayton Antitrust Act** (improving the old Sherman act and protecting labor unions and farm cooperatives from prosecution, 1914).

Other goals such as the protection of children in the work force (**Keating-Owen Act,** 1916), credit reform for agriculture (**Federal Farm Loan Act**, 1916), and an independent tariff commission (1916) came later. By the end of Wilson's presidency, the New Freedom and the New Nationalism had merged into one government philosophy of regulation, order, and standardization in the interest of an increasingly diverse nation.

Social and Cultural Developments (1907–1912)

In 1905, the African-American intellectual militant **W.E.B. DuBois** (1868–1963) founded the **Niagara Movement,** which called for federal legislation to protect racial equality and for full rights of citizenship. The **National Association for the Advancement of Colored People (NAACP)** was organized in 1909.

A radical labor organization called the **Industrial Workers of the World** (I.W.W., or Wobblies, 1905–1924) was active in promoting violence and revolution. The I.W.W. organized effective strikes in the textile industry in 1912, and among a few western miners groups, but had little appeal to the average American worker. After the **Red Scare** of 1919, the government worked to smash the I.W.W. and deported many of its immigrant leaders and members.

Foreign Relations (1907–1915)

President Taft sought to avoid military intervention, especially in Latin America, by replacing "big stick" policies with "dollar diplomacy" in the expectation that American financial investments would encourage economic, social, and political stability. This idea proved an illusion.

Wilson urged Mexican President Huerta to hold democratic elections and adopt a constitutional government. Huerta refused, and Wilson invaded Mexico with troops at Veracruz in 1914. A second U.S. invasion came in northern Mexico in 1916.

The United States kept a military presence in the Dominican Republic and Haiti, and intervened militarily in Nicaragua (1911) to quiet fears of revolution and help manage foreign financial problems.

Wilson and World War I (1912–1920)

The Early Years of the Wilson Administration

Wilson was only the second Democrat (Cleveland was the first) elected president since the Civil War. Key appointments to the cabinet were William Jennings Bryan as secretary of state and William Gibbs McAdoo (1863–1941) as secretary of the treasury.

The Federal Reserve Act of 1913: The law divided the nation into 12 regions, with a Federal Reserve bank in each region. Federal Reserve banks loaned money to member banks at interest less than the public paid to the member banks, and the notes of indebtedness of businesses and farmers to the member banks were held as collateral. This allowed the Federal Reserve to control interest rates by raising or lowering the discount rate.

The money loaned to the member banks was in the form of a new currency, Federal Reserve notes, which was backed 60 percent by commercial paper and 40 percent by gold. This currency was designed to expand and contract with the volume of business activity and borrowing.

The Federal Reserve system serviced the financial needs of the federal government. The system was supervised and policy was set by a national Federal Reserve Board composed of the secretary of the treasury, the comptroller of the currency, and five other members appointed by the president of the United States.

The **Clayton Antitrust Act** of 1914: This law supplemented and interpreted the Sherman Antitrust Act of 1890. Under its provisions, stock ownership by a corporation in a competing corporation was prohibited, and the same persons were prohibited from managing competing corporations. Price discrimination (charging less in some regions than in others to undercut the competition) and exclusive contracts which reduced competition were prohibited.

The Election of 1916

The Democrats, the minority party nationally in terms of voter registration, nominated Wilson and adopted his platform calling for continued progressive reforms and neutrality in the European war.

The Republican convention bypassed Theodore Roosevelt and chose Charles Evans Hughes (1862–1948), an associate justice of the Supreme Court and formerly a progressive Republican governor of New York.

Wilson won the election.

Social Issues in the First Wilson Administration

In 1913, Treasury Secretary William G. McAdoo and Postmaster General Albert S. Burleson segregated workers in some parts of their departments with no objection from Wilson. Many northern blacks and whites protested, especially black leader W.E.B. DuBois (1868–1963), who had supported Wilson in 1912.

Wilson opposed immigration restrictions and vetoed a literacy test for immigrants in 1915, but in 1917, Congress overrode a similar veto.

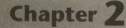

Wilson's Foreign Policy and the Road to War

Wilson's Basic Premise: Wilson promised a more moral foreign policy than that of his predecessors, denouncing imperialism and dollar diplomacy, and advocating the advancement of democratic capitalist governments throughout the world.

Wilson signaled his repudiation of Taft's dollar diplomacy by withdrawing American involvement from the six-power loan consortium of China.

In 1912, American marines had landed in Nicaragua to maintain order, and an American financial expert had taken control of the customs station. The Wilson administration kept the marines in Nicaragua and negotiated the Bryan-Chamorro Treaty of 1914, which gave the United States an option to build a canal through the country.

Claiming that political anarchy existed in Haiti, Wilson sent marines in 1915 and imposed a treaty making the country a protectorate, with American control of its finances and constabulary. The marines remained until 1934.

In 1916, Wilson sent marines to the Dominican Republic to stop a civil war and established a military government under an American naval commander.

Wilson feared in 1915 that Germany might annex Denmark and its Caribbean possession, the Danish West Indies or Virgin Islands. After extended negotiations, the United States purchased the islands from Denmark by treaty on August 4, 1916, for $25 million and took possession of them on March 31, 1917.

The Road to War in Europe

When World War I broke out in Europe, Wilson issued a proclamation of American neutrality on August 4, 1914. The value of American trade with the Central Powers fell from $169 million in 1914 to almost nothing in 1916, but trade with the Allies rose from $825 million to $3.2 billion during the same period. In addition, the British and French had borrowed about $3.25 billion from American sources by 1917. The United States had become a major supplier of Allied munitions, food, and raw materials.

The sinking of the British liner *Lusitania* off the coast of Ireland on May 7, 1915, with the loss of 1,198 lives, including 128 Americans, brought strong protests from Wilson. Secretary of State Bryan, who believed Americans should stay off belligerent ships, resigned rather than insist on questionable neutral rights and was replaced by Robert Lansing.

The House-Grey Memorandum: Early in 1915, Wilson sent his friend and adviser Colonel Edward M. House on an unsuccessful visit to Europe to offer American mediation in the war. Late in the year, House returned to London to propose that Wilson call a peace conference; if Germany refused to attend or was uncooperative at the conference, the United States could enter the war on the Allied side. An agreement to that effect, called the House-Grey memorandum, was signed by the British foreign secretary, Sir Edward Grey, on February 22, 1916.

In an address to Congress on January 22, 1917, Wilson made his last offer to serve as a neutral mediator. He proposed a "peace without victory," based not on a "balance of power" but on a "community of power."

Germany announced on January 31, 1917, that it would sink all ships, belligerent or neutral, without warning in a large war zone off the coasts of the Allied nations in the eastern Atlantic and the Mediterranean. Wilson broke diplomatic relations with Germany on February 3. During February and March several American merchant ships were sunk by submarines.

The British intercepted a secret message from the German foreign secretary, Arthur Zimmerman, to the German minister in Mexico, and turned it over to the United States on February 24, 1917. The Germans proposed that, in the event of a war between the United States and Germany, Mexico attack the United States. After the war, the "lost territories" of Texas, New Mexico, and Arizona would be returned to Mexico. When the telegram was released to the press on March 1, many Americans became convinced that war with Germany was necessary. A declaration of war against Germany was signed by Wilson on April 6.

World War I: The Military Campaign

The American force of about 14,500, which had arrived in France by September 1917, was assigned a quiet section of the line near Verdun. When the Germans mounted a major drive toward Paris in the spring of 1918, the Americans experienced their first important engagements. In June, they prevented the Germans from crossing the Marne at Chateau-Thierry, and cleared the area of Belleau Woods. In July, eight American divisions aided French troops in attacking the German line between Reims and Soissons. The American First Army, with over half a million men under Pershing's immediate command, was assembled in August 1918, and began a major offensive at St. Mihiel on the southern part of the front on September 12. Following the successful operation, Pershing began a drive against the German defenses between Verdun and Sedan, an action called the Meuse-Argonne offensive. He reached Sedan on November 7. During the same period the English in the north and the French along the central front also broke through the German lines. The fighting ended with the armistice on November 11, 1918.

Mobilizing the Home Front

A number of volunteer organizations sprang up around the country to search for draft dodgers, enforce the sale of bonds, and report any opinion or conversation considered suspicious. Such groups publicly humiliated people accused of not buying war bonds, and persecuted, beat, and sometimes killed people of German descent. The anti-German and anti-subversive war hysteria in the United States far exceeded similar public moods in Britain and France during the war.

The **Espionage Act of 1917** provided for fines and imprisonment for persons who made false statements that aided the enemy, incited rebellion in the military or obstructed recruitment or the draft. Printed matter advocating treason or insurrection could be excluded from the mails. **The Sedition Act** of May 1918 forbade any criticism of the government, flag, or uniform, even if there were not detrimental consequences, and expanded the mail exclusion. The laws were applied in ways that trampled on civil liberties. The Espionage Act was upheld by the Supreme Court in the case of **Schenck v. United States** in 1919. The opinion, written by Justice Oliver Wendell Holmes, Jr. (1841–1935), stated that Congress could limit free speech when the words represented a "clear and present danger," and that a person cannot cry "fire" in a crowded theater. The Sedition Act was similarly upheld in **Abrams v. United States** a few months later. Ultimately 2,168 persons were prosecuted under the laws, and 1,055 were convicted, of whom only 10 were charged with actual sabotage.

Wartime Social Trends

Large numbers of women, mostly white, were hired by factories and other enterprises in jobs never before open to them. When the war ended, almost all returned to traditional "women's jobs" or to homemaking. Returning veterans replaced them in the labor market.

The labor shortage opened industrial jobs to Mexican-Americans and to African-Americans. W.E.B. DuBois, the most prominent African-American leader of the time, supported the war effort in the hope that the war would make the world safe for democracy and bring a better life for African-Americans in the United States. About half a million rural southern African-Americans migrated to cities, mainly in the North and Midwest, to obtain employment in war and other industries, especially in steel and meatpacking. In 1917, there were race riots in 26 cities in the North and South, with the worst in East St. Louis, Illinois.

In December 1917, a constitutional amendment to prohibit the manufacture and sale of alcoholic beverages in the United States was passed by Congress and submitted to the states for ratification.

Peacemaking and Domestic Problems (1918–1920)

From the time of the American entry into the war, Wilson had maintained that the war would make the world safe for democracy. He insisted that there should be **peace without victory**, meaning that the victors would not be vindictive toward the losers, so that a fair and stable international situation in the postwar world would ensure lasting peace. In an address to Congress on January 8, 1918, he presented his specific peace plan in the form of the Fourteen Points. The first five points called for open rather than secret peace treaties, freedom of the seas, free trade, arms reduction, and a fair adjustment of colonial claims. The next eight points were concerned with the national aspirations of various European peoples and the adjustment of boundaries. The fourteenth point, which he considered the most important and had espoused as early as 1916, called for a "general association of nations" to preserve the peace.

Wilson decided that he would lead the American delegation to the peace conference, which opened in Paris on January 12, 1919. In doing so he became the first president to leave the country during his term of office. In the negotiations, which continued until May 1919, Wilson found it necessary to make many compromises in forging the text of the treaty.

Following a protest by 39 senators in February 1919, Wilson obtained some changes in the **League of Nations** structure to exempt the Monroe Doctrine and domestic matters from League jurisdiction. Then, on July 26, 1919, he presented the treaty with the League within it to the Senate for ratification. Almost all of the 47 Democrats supported Wilson and the treaty, but the 49 Republicans were divided. About a dozen were "irreconcilables" who thought that the United States should not be a member of the League under any circumstances. The remainder included 25 "strong" and 12 "mild" reservationists who would accept the treaty with some changes. The main objection centered on Article X of the League Covenant, where the reservationists wanted it understood that the United States would not go to war to defend a League member without the approval of Congress.

On September 3, 1919, Wilson set out on a national speaking tour to appeal to the people to support the treaty and the League and to influence their senators. He collapsed after a speech in Pueblo, Colorado, on September 25, and returned to Washington, where he suffered a severe stroke on October 2 which paralyzed his left side. He was seriously ill for several months, and never fully recovered. The treaty failed to get a two-thirds majority either with or without the reservationists.

Many people, including British and French leaders, urged Wilson to compromise on reservationists, including the issue of Article X. Many historians think that Wilson's ill health impaired his judgment, and that he would have worked out a compromise had he not had the stroke. The Senate took up the treaty again in February 1920, and on March 19 it was again defeated both with and without the reservationists. The United States officially ended the war with Germany by a resolution of Congress signed on July 2, 1921, and a separate peace treaty was ratified on July 25. The United States did not join the League.

Domestic Problems and the End of the Wilson Administration

In January 1919, the Eighteenth Amendment to the Constitution prohibiting the manufacture, sale, transportation, or importation of intoxicating liquors was ratified by the states, and it became effective in January 1920. The **Nineteenth Amendment** providing for **women's suffrage**, which had been defeated in the Senate in 1918, was approved by Congress in 1919. It was ratified by the states in time for the election of 1920.

Americans feared the spread of the Russian communist revolution to the United States, and many interpreted the widespread strikes of 1919 spurred by inflation, as Communist-inspired and the beginning of the revolution. Bombs sent through the mail to prominent government and business leaders in April 1919 seemed to confirm their fears, although the origin of the bombs has never been determined. The anti-German hysteria of the war years was transformed into the anti-Communist and anti-foreign hysteria of 1919 and 1920, and continued in various forms through the 1920s.

Attorney General A. Mitchell Palmer, who aspired to the 1920 presidential nomination, was one of the targets of the anonymous bombers in the spring of 1919. In

August 1919, he named J. Edgar Hoover (1895–1972) to head a new Intelligence Division in the Justice Department to collect information about radicals. After arresting nearly 5,000 people in late 1919 and early 1920, Palmer announced that huge Communist riots were planned for major cities on May Day (May 1, 1920). Police and troops were alerted, but the day passed with no radical activity. Palmer was discredited and the Red Scare subsided.

White hostility based on competition for lower-paying jobs and black encroachment into neighborhoods led to race riots in 25 cities, with hundreds killed or wounded and millions of dollars in property damage. The Chicago riot in July was the worst. Fear of returning African-American veterans in the South led to an increase of lynchings from 34 in 1917 to 60 in 1918 and 70 in 1919. Some of the victims were veterans still in uniform.

The Roaring Twenties and Economic Collapse (1920–1929)

The Election of 1920

The Republican Convention: Senator Warren G. Harding (1865–1923) of Ohio was nominated as a dark-horse candidate, and Governor Calvin Coolidge (1872–1933) of Massachusetts was chosen as the vice presidential nominee. The platform opposed the League and promised low taxes, high tariffs, immigration restriction, and aid to farmers.

The Democratic Convention: Governor James Cox was nominated on the 44th ballot, and Franklin D. Roosevelt (1882–1945), an assistant secretary of the Navy and distant cousin of Theodore, was selected as his running mate. The platform endorsed the League, but left the door open for reservations.

The Twenties: Economic Advances and Social Tensions

The principal driving force of the economy of the 1920s was the automobile. Automobile manufacturing stimulated supporting industries such as steel, rubber, and glass, as well as gasoline refining and highway construction. During the 1920s, the United States became a nation of paved roads. The Federal Highway Act of 1916 started the federal highway system and gave matching funds to the states for construction.

Unlike earlier boom periods, which had involved large expenditures for capital investments such as railroads and factories, the prosperity of the 1920s depended heavily on the sale of consumer products. Purchases of "big ticket" items such as automobiles, refrigerators, and furniture were made possible by installment or time payment credit. The idea was not new, but the availability of consumer credit expanded tremendously during the 1920s. Consumer interest and demand was spurred by the great increase in professional advertising, which used newspapers, magazines, radio, billboards, and other media.

There was a trend toward corporate consolidation during the 1920s. In most fields, an oligopoly of two to four firms dominated. This is exemplified by the automobile industry, where Ford, General Motors, and Chrysler produced 83 percent of the vehicles in 1929. Government regulatory agencies such as the Federal Trade Commission and the Interstate Commerce Commission were passive and generally controlled by persons from the business world.

There was also a trend toward bank consolidation. Because corporations were raising much of their money through the sale of stocks and bonds, the demand for business loans declined. Commercial banks then put more of their funds into real estate loans, loans to brokers against stocks and bonds, and the purchase of stocks and bonds themselves.

American Society in the 1920s

By 1920, for the first time, a majority of Americans (51 percent) lived in an urban area with a population of 2,500 or more. A new phenomenon of the 1920s was the tremendous growth of suburbs and satellite cities, which grew more rapidly than the central cities. Streetcars, commuter railroads, and automobiles contributed to the process, as well as the easy availability of financing for home construction. The suburbs had once been the domain of the wealthy, but the technology of the 1920s opened them to working-class families.

Traditional American moral standards regarding premarital sex and marital fidelity were widely questioned for the first time during the 1920s. The automobile, by giving people mobility and privacy, was generally considered to have contributed to sexual license. Birth control, though illegal, was promoted by Margaret Sanger (1883–1966) and others and was widely accepted.

When it became apparent that women did not vote as a block, political leaders gave little additional attention to the special concerns of women. Divorce laws were liberalized in many states at the insistence of women. Domestic service was the largest job category.

Most other women workers were in traditional female occupations such as secretarial and clerical work, retail sales, teaching, and nursing. Rates of pay were below those for men. Most women still pursued the traditional role of housewife and mother, and society accepted that as the norm.

The migration of southern rural African-Americans to the cities continued, with about 1.5 million moving during the 1920s. By 1930, about 20 percent of American blacks lived in the North, with the largest concentrations in New York, Chicago, and Philadelphia. While they were generally better off economically in the cities than they had been as tenant farmers, they generally held low-paying jobs and were confined to segregated areas of the cities.

A native of Jamaica, Marcus Garvey (1887–1940) founded the Universal Negro Improvement Association, advocating African-American racial pride and separatism rather than integration, and called for a return of African-Americans to Africa. In 1921, he proclaimed himself the provisional president of an African empire, and sold stock in the Black Star Steamship Line which would take migrants to Africa. The line went bankrupt in 1923, and Garvey was convicted and imprisoned for mail fraud in the sale of the line's stock and then deported. His legacy was an emphasis on African-American pride and self-respect.

Many writers of the 1920s were disgusted with the hypocrisy and materialism of contemporary American society. Often called the "Lost Generation," many of them, such as novelists Ernest Hemingway (1899–1961), Gertrude Stein (1874–1946), F. Scott Fitzgerald (1896–1940) and poets Ezra Pound (1885–1972) and T. S. Eliot (1888–1965) moved to Europe.

Social Conflicts

Many white Protestant families saw their traditional values gravely threatened. The traditionalists were largely residents of rural areas and small towns, and the clash of farm values with the values of an industrial society of urban workers was evident. The traditionalist backlash against modern urban industrial society expressed itself primarily through intolerance.

On Thanksgiving Day in 1915, the Knights of the Ku Klux Klan, modeled on the organization of the same name in the 1860s and 1870s, was founded near Atlanta by William J. Simmons. Its purpose was to intimidate African-Americans, who were experiencing an apparent rise in status during World War I. By 1923, the Klan had about five million members throughout the nation. The largest concentrations of members were in the South, the Southwest, the Midwest, California, and Oregon.

There had been calls for immigration restriction since the late nineteenth century. Labor leaders believed that immigrants depressed wages and impeded unionization. Some progressives believed that they created social problems. In June 1917, Congress, over Wilson's veto, had imposed a literacy test for immigrants, and excluded many Asian nationalists. In 1921, Congress passed the **Emergency Quota Act**. In practice, the law admitted about as many as wanted to come from such nations as Britain, Ireland, and Germany, while severely restricting Italians, Greeks, Poles, and east European Jews. It became effective in 1922 and reduced the number of immigrants annually to about 40 percent of the 1921 total. Congress then passed the **National Origins Act** of 1924, which further reduced the number of southern and eastern Europeans, and cut the annual immigration to 20 percent of the 1921 figure. In 1927, the annual maximum was reduced to 150,000.

The Eighteenth Amendment, which prohibited the manufacture, sale, or transportation of intoxicating liquors, took effect in January 1920.

Fundamentalist Protestants, under the leadership of William Jennings Bryan, began a campaign in 1921 to prohibit the teaching of evolution in the schools, and thus protect belief in the literal biblical account of creation. The idea was especially well received in the South.

Sacco and Vanzetti: On April 15, 1920, two unidentified gunmen robbed a shoe factory and killed two men in South Braintree, Massachusetts. Nicola Sacco and Bartolomeo Vanzetti, Italian immigrants and admitted anarchists, were tried for the murders. After they were convicted and sentenced to death in July 1921, there was much protest in the United States and in Europe that they had not received a fair trial. After six years of delays, they were executed on August 23, 1927. Fifty years later, on July 19, 1977, the pair were vindicated by Governor Michael Dukakis.

Government and Politics in the 1920s: The Harding Administration

Harding was a handsome and amiable man of limited intellectual and organizational abilities. He had spent much of his life as the publisher of a newspaper in the small city of Marion, Ohio. He recognized his limitations, but hoped to be a much-loved president.

Harding appointed some outstanding persons to his cabinet, including Secretary of State Charles Evans Hughes, a former Supreme Court justice and presidential candidate; Secretary of the Treasury Andrew Mellon (1855–1937), a Pittsburgh aluminum and banking magnate and reportedly the richest man in America; and Secretary of Commerce Herbert Hoover, a dynamic multimillionaire mine owner famous for his wartime relief efforts. Less impressive was his appointment of his cronies Albert B. Fall as secretary of the interior and Harry M. Daugherty as attorney general.

The **Teapot Dome Scandal** began when Secretary of the Interior Albert B. Fall, in 1921, secured the transfer of several naval oil reserves to his jurisdiction. In 1922, he secretly leased reserves at Teapot Dome in Wyoming to Harry F. Sinclair of Monmouth Oil and at Elk Hills in California to Edward Doheny of Pan-American Petroleum. Sinclair and Doheny were acquitted in 1927 of charges of defrauding the government, but in 1929, Fall was convicted, fined, and imprisoned for bribery.

Vice President Calvin Coolidge became president upon Harding's death in 1923.

The Election of 1924

The Republicans: Calvin Coolidge was nominated. The platform endorsed business development, low taxes, and rigid economy in government. The party stood on its record of economic growth and prosperity since 1922.

The Progressives: Robert M. LaFollette, after failing in a bid for the Republican nomination, formed a new Progressive party, with support from Midwest farm groups, socialists, and the American Federation of Labor. The platform attacked monopolies, and called for the nationalization of railroads, the direct election of the president, and other reforms.

The Democrats: John W. Davis was nominated and presented little contrast with the Republicans.

The Election of 1928

The Republicans: Coolidge did not seek another term, and the convention quickly nominated Herbert Hoover, the secretary of commerce, for president. The platform endorsed the policies of the Harding and Coolidge administrations.

The Democrats: Governor Alfred E. Smith (1873–1944) of New York, a Catholic and an anti-prohibitionist, controlled most of the nonsouthern delegations. Southerners supported his nomination with the understanding that the platform would not advocate repeal of prohibition. The platform differed little from that of the Republicans, except in advocating lower tariffs.

The Great Depression: The Crash

Herbert Hoover, an Iowa farm boy and an orphan, graduated from Stanford University with a degree in mining engineering. He became a multimillionaire from mining and other investments around the world. After serving as the director of the Food Administration under Wilson, he became Secretary of Commerce under Harding and Coolidge. He believed that cooperation between business and government would enable the United States to abolish poverty through continued economic growth.

Stock prices increased throughout the decade. The boom in prices and volume of sales was especially active after 1925, and was intensive during 1928–29.

Careful investors, realizing that stocks were overpriced, began to sell to take their profits. During October 1929, prices declined as more stock was sold. On "Black Thursday," October 24, 1929, almost 13 million shares were traded, a large number for that time, and prices fell precipitously. Investment banks tried to boost the market by buying, but on October 29, **"Black Tuesday,"** the market fell about 40 points, with 16.5 million shares traded.

The Great Depression and The New Deal (1929–1941)

Reasons for the Depression

A stock-market crash does not mean that a depression must follow. In 1929, a complex interaction of many factors caused the decline of the economy.

Many people had bought stock on a margin of 10 percent, meaning that they had borrowed 90 percent of the purchase through a broker's loan and put up the stock as collateral. When the price of a stock fell more than 10 percent, the lender sold the stock for whatever it would bring and thus further depressed prices. The forced sales brought great losses to the banks and businesses that had financed the broker's loans, as well as to the investors.

There were already signs of recession before the market crash in 1929. The farm economy, which involved almost 25 percent of the population, had been depressed throughout the decade. Coal, railroads, and New England textiles had not been prosperous. After 1927, new construction declined and auto sales began to sag. Many workers had been laid off before the crash of 1929.

During the early months of the depression, most people thought it was just an adjustment in the business cycle which would soon be over. As time went on, the worst depression in American history set in, reaching its bottom point in early 1932.

Hoover's Depression Policies

The Agricultural Marketing Act: Passed in June 1929, before the market crash, this law, proposed by the president, created the Federal Farm Board. It had a revolving fund of $500 million to lend agricultural cooperatives to buy commodities, such as wheat and cotton, and hold them for higher prices.

The Hawley-Smoot Tariff: This law, passed in June 1930, raised duties on both agricultural and manufactured imports.

The Reconstruction Finance Corporation: Chartered by Congress in 1932, the RFC loaned money to railroads, banks, and other financial institutions. It prevented the failure of basic firms, on which many other elements of the economy depended, but was criticized by some as relief for the rich.

The Federal Home Loan Bank Act: This law, passed in July 1932, created home-loan banks, to make loans to building and loan associations, savings banks, and insurance companies to help them avoid foreclosures on homes.

Election of 1932

The Republicans renominated Hoover while the Democrats nominated Franklin D. Roosevelt, governor of New York. Although calling for a cut in spending, Roosevelt communicated optimism and easily defeated Hoover.

The First New Deal

In February 1933, before Roosevelt took office, Congress passed the **Twenty-First Amendment** to repeal prohibition, and sent it to the states. In March, the new

Congress legalized light beer. The amendment was ratified by the states and took effect in December 1933.

When Roosevelt was inaugurated on March 4, 1933, the American economic system seemed to be on the verge of collapse. Roosevelt assured the nation that "the only thing we have to fear is fear itself," called for a special session of Congress to convene on March 9, and asked for "broad executive powers to wage war against the emergency." Two days later, he closed all banks and forbade the export of gold or the redemption of currency in gold.

Legislation of the First New Deal

The special session of Congress, from March 9 to June 16, 1933, passed a great body of legislation which has left a lasting mark on the nation. The period has been referred to ever since as the "**Hundred Days.**" Historians have divided Roosevelt's legislation into the **First New Deal** (1933–1935) and a new wave of programs beginning in 1935 called the **Second New Deal**.

The **Emergency Banking Relief Act** was passed on March 9, the first day of the special session. The law provided additional funds for banks from the RFC and the Federal Reserve, allowed the Treasury to open sound banks after 10 days and to merge or liquidate unsound ones, and forbade the hoarding or export of gold. Roosevelt, on March 12, assured the public of the soundness of the banks in the first of many "fireside chats," or radio addresses. People believed him, and most banks were soon open with more deposits than withdrawals.

The **Banking Act of 1933**, or the **Glass-Steagall Act,** established the **Federal Deposit Insurance Corporation (FDIC)** to insure individual deposits in commercial banks, and separated commercial banking from the more speculative activity of investment banking.

The **Truth-in-Securities Act required** that full information about stocks and bonds be provided by brokers and others to potential purchasers.

The **Home Owners Loan Corporation (HOLC)** had authority to borrow money to refinance home mortgages and thus prevent foreclosures. Eventually, it lent more than three billion dollars to more than one million homeowners.

Gold was taken out of circulation following the president's order of March 6, and the nation went off the gold standard. Eventually, on January 31, 1934, the value of the dollar was set at $35 per ounce of gold, 59 percent of its former value. The object of the devaluation was to raise prices and help American exports.

The **Securities and Exchange Commission** was created in 1934 to supervise stock exchanges and to punish fraud in securities trading.

The **Federal Housing Administration (FHA)** was created by Congress in 1934 to insure long-term, low-interest mortgages for home construction and repair.

These programs, intended to provide temporary relief for people in need, were to be disbanded when the economy improved.

The **Federal Emergency Relief Act** appropriated $500 million for aid to the poor to be distributed by state and local governments. It also established the Federal Emergency Relief Administration under Harry Hopkins (1890–1946).

The **Civilian Conservation Corps** enrolled 250,000 young men aged 18 to 24 from families on relief to go to camps where they worked on flood control, soil conservation, and forest projects under the direction of the War Department.

The **Public Works Administration**, under Secretary of the Interior Harold Ickes, had $3.3 billion to distribute to state and local governments for building projects such as schools, highways, and hospitals.

In November 1933, Roosevelt established the **Civil Works Administration** to hire four million unemployed workers. The temporary and makeshift nature of the jobs, such as sweeping streets, brought much criticism, and the experiment was terminated in April 1934.

The **Agricultural Adjustment Act** of 1933 created the **Agricultural Adjustment Administration (AAA)**. Farmers agreed to reduce production of principal farm commodities and were paid a subsidy in return. The money came from a tax on the processing of the commodities. Farm prices increased, but tenants and sharecroppers were hurt when owners took land out of cultivation. The law was repealed in January 1936 on the grounds that the processing tax was not constitutional.

The **Federal Farm Loan Act** consolidated all farm credit programs into the Farm Credit Administration to make low-interest loans for farm mortgages and other agricultural purposes.

The **Commodity Credit Corporation** was established in October 1933 by the AAA to make loans to corn and cotton farmers against their crops so that they could hold them for higher prices.

The **Frazier-Lemke Farm Bankruptcy Act** of 1934 allowed farmers to defer foreclosure on their land while they obtained new financing, and helped them to recover property already lost through easy financing.

National Industrial Recovery Act: This law was viewed as the cornerstone of the recovery program. It sought to stabilize the economy by preventing extreme competition, labor-management conflicts, and overproduction. A board composed of industrial and labor leaders in each industry or business drew up a code for that industry which set minimum prices, minimum wages, maximum work hours, production limits, and quotas. The antitrust laws were temporarily suspended.

The **Tennessee Valley Authority (TVA),** a public corporation under a three-member board, was proposed by Roosevelt as the first major experiment in regional public planning. Starting from the nucleus of the government's Muscle Shoals property on the Tennessee River, the TVA built 20 dams in an area of 40,000 square miles to stop flooding and soil erosion, improve navigation, and generate hydroelectric power. It also manufactured nitrates for fertilizer, conducted demonstration projects for farmers, engaged in reforestation, and attempted to rehabilitate the whole area.

The economy improved but did not recover. The GNP, money supply, salaries, wages, and farm income rose. Unemployment dropped from about 25 percent of nonfarm workers in 1933 to about 20.1 percent, or 10.6 million, in 1935.

The Second New Deal: Opposition

The **Share Our Wealth Society** was founded in 1934 by **Senator Huey "The Kingfish" Long** (1893–1935) of Louisiana. Long was a populist demagogue who was elected governor of Louisiana in 1928, established a practical dictatorship over the state, and moved to the United States Senate in 1930. He supported Roosevelt in 1932, but then broke with him, calling him a tool of Wall Street for not doing more to combat the depression. Long called for the confiscation of all fortunes over five million dollars and a tax of one hundred percent on annual incomes over one million. His society had more than five million members when he was assassinated on the steps of the Louisiana Capitol on September 8, 1935.

The Second New Deal Begins

The **Works Progress Administration (WPA)** was started in May 1935, following the passage of the **Emergency Relief Appropriations Act** of April 1935. The WPA employed people from the relief rolls for 30 hours of work a week at pay double the relief payment but less than private employment.

The **National Youth Administration (NYA)** was established as part of the WPA in June 1935, to provide part-time jobs for high school and college students to enable them to stay in school, and to help young adults not in school to find jobs.

The **Rural Electrification Administration (REA)** was created in May 1935, to provide loans and WPA labor to electric cooperatives so they could build lines into rural areas not served by private companies.

The **Social Security Act** was passed in August 1935. It established a retirement plan for persons over age 65, which was to be funded by a tax on wages paid equally by employee and employer. The first benefits, ranging from $10 to $85 per month, were paid in 1942. Another provision of the act had the effect of forcing the states to initiate unemployment insurance programs.

The **Banking Act of 1935** created a strong central Board of Governors of the Federal Reserve system with broad powers over the operations of the regional banks.

The Election of 1936

Roosevelt had put together a coalition of followers who made the Democratic party the majority party in the nation for the first time since the Civil War. While retaining the Democratic base in the South and among white ethnics in the big cities, Roosevelt also received strong support from midwestern farmers. Two groups that made a dramatic shift into the Democratic ranks were union workers and African-Americans.

The Last Years of the New Deal

Frustrated by a conservative Supreme Court which had overturned much of his New Deal legislation, Roosevelt, in February 1937, proposed to Congress the Judicial Reorganization Bill, which would allow the president to name a new federal judge for each judge who did not retire by the age of $70^1/_2$. The appointments would be limited to a maximum of 50, with no more than six added to the Supreme Court. The president was astonished by the wave of opposition from Democrats and Republicans alike, but he uncharacteristically refused to compromise. In doing so, he not only lost the bill but control of the Democratic Congress, which he had dominated since 1933. Nonetheless, the Court changed its position, as Chief Justice Charles Evans Hughes and Justice Owen Roberts began to vote with the more liberal members.

Most economic indicators rose sharply between 1935 and 1937. Roosevelt decided that the recovery was sufficient to warrant a reduction in relief programs and a move toward a balanced budget. The budget for fiscal year 1938 was reduced from $8.5 billion to $6.8 billion, with the WPA experiencing the largest cut. During the winter of 1937–1938, the economy slipped rapidly and unemployment rose to 12.5 percent. In April 1938, Roosevelt requested and received from Congress an emergency appropriation of about $3 billion for the WPA, as well as increases for public works and other programs. In July 1938, the economy began to recover, and it regained the 1937 levels in 1939.

Social Dimensions of the New Deal Era

Unemployment for African-Americans was much higher than for the general population, and before 1933 they were often excluded from state and local relief efforts. Roosevelt seems to have given little thought to the special problems of African-Americans, and he was afraid to endorse legislation such as an anti-lynching bill for fear of alienating the southern wing of the Democratic party. More African-Americans were appointed to government positions by Roosevelt than ever before, but the number was still small. Roosevelt issued an executive order on June 25, 1941, establishing the **Fair Employment Practices Committee** to ensure consideration for minorities in defense employment.

John Collier, the commissioner of the **Bureau of Indian Affairs**, persuaded Congress to repeal the **Dawes Act of 1887** by passing the **Indian Reorganization Act of 1934**. The law restored tribal ownership of lands, recognized tribal constitutions and government, and provided loans to tribes for economic development.

Labor Unions

Labor unions lost members and influence during the 1920s and early 1930s. The **National Industrial Recovery Act** gave them new hope when it guaranteed the right to unionize, and during 1933 about 1.5 million new members joined unions.

The passage of the **National Labor Relations** or **Wagner Act** in 1935 resulted in a massive growth of union membership, but at the expense of bitter conflict within the labor movement. The **American Federation of Labor** was made up primarily of craft unions. Some leaders wanted to unionize the mass-production industries, such as automobiles and rubber, with industrial unions. In November 1935, John L. Lewis and others established the **Committee for Industrial Organization** to unionize basic industries, presumably within the AFL. President William Green of the AFL ordered the CIO to disband in January 1936. When the rebels refused, they were expelled by the AFL in March 1937. The insurgents then reorganized the CIO as the independent Congress of Industrial Organizations.

During its organizational period, the CIO sought to initiate several industrial unions, particularly in the steel, auto, rubber, and radio industries. In late 1936 and early 1937, it used a tactic called the sit-down strike, with the strikers occupying the workplace to prevent any production. By the end of 1941, the CIO was larger than the AFL. Union members comprised about 11.5 percent of the work force in 1933 and 28.2 percent in 1941.

New Deal Diplomacy and the Road to War

Roosevelt and Secretary of State Cordell Hull continued the policies of their predecessors by endeavoring to improve relations with Latin American nations, and formalized their position by calling it the **Good Neighbor Policy**.

At the **Montevideo Conference of American Nations** in December of 1933, the United States renounced the right of intervention in the internal affairs of Latin American countries. In 1936, in the **Buenos Aires Convention**, the United States agreed to submit all American disputes to arbitration.

United States Neutrality Legislation

Belief that the United States should stay out of foreign wars and problems began in the 1920s and grew in the 1930s. Examinations of World War I profiteering and revisionist history that asserted Germany had not been responsible for World War I and that the United States had been misled were also influential during the 1930s. A Gallup poll in April 1937 showed that almost two-thirds of those responding thought that American entry into World War I had been a mistake.

The Johnson Act of 1934: This law prohibited any nation in default on World War I payments from selling securities to any American citizen or corporation.

The Neutrality Acts of 1935: On outbreak of war between foreign nations, all exports of American arms and munitions to them would be embargoed for six months. In addition, American ships were prohibited from carrying arms to any belligerent, and the president was to warn American citizens not to travel on belligerent ships.

The Neutrality Acts of 1936: The laws gave the president authority to determine when a state of war existed, and prohibited any loans or credits to belligerents.

The Neutrality Acts of 1937: The laws gave the president authority to determine if a civil war was a threat to world peace and if it was covered by the Neutrality Acts. It also prohibited all arms sales to belligerents, and allowed the cash-and-carry sale of nonmilitary goods to belligerents.

The American Response to the War in Europe

In August 1939, Roosevelt created the **War Resources Board** to develop a plan for industrial mobilization in the event of war. The next month, he established the **Office of Emergency Management** in the White House to centralize mobilization activities.

The Neutrality Act of 1939: Roosevelt officially proclaimed the neutrality of the United States on September 5, 1939. The Democratic Congress, in a vote that followed party lines, passed a new Neutrality Act in November. It allowed the cash-and-carry sale of arms and short-term loans to belligerents, but forbade American ships to trade with belligerents or Americans to travel on belligerent ships.

Almost all Americans recognized Germany as a threat. They were divided on whether to aid Britain or to concentrate on the defense of America. **The Committee to Defend America by Aiding the Allies** was formed in May 1940, and the **America First Committee**, which opposed involvement, was incorporated in September 1940.

In April 1940, Roosevelt declared that Greenland, a possession of conquered Denmark, was covered by the Monroe Doctrine, and he supplied military assistance to set up a coastal patrol there.

In May 1940, Roosevelt appointed a **Council of National Defense**, chaired by William S. Knudson (1879–1948), the president of General Motors, to direct defense production and to build 50,000 planes. The **Office of Production Management** was created to allocate scarce materials, and the **Office of Price Administration** was established to prevent inflation and protect consumers.

Congress approved the nation's first peacetime draft, the **Selective Service and Training Act**, in September 1940.

Roosevelt determined that to aid Britain in every way possible was the best way to avoid war with Germany. In September 1940, he signed an agreement to give Britain 50 American destroyers in return for a 99-year lease on air and naval bases in British territories in Newfoundland, Bermuda, and the Caribbean.

The Election of 1940

The Republicans: The Republicans nominated Wendell L. Willkie (1892–1944) of Indiana, a dark-horse candidate. The platform supported a strong defense program, but severely criticized New Deal domestic policies.

The Democrats: Roosevelt was nominated for a third term, breaking a tradition which had existed since George Washington. The platform endorsed the foreign and domestic policies of the administration.

The Election: Roosevelt won by a much narrower margin than in 1936.

American Involvement with the European War

The Lend-Lease Act: This let the United States provide supplies to Britain in exchange for goods and services after the war. It was signed on March 11, 1941.

In April 1941, Roosevelt started the American Neutrality Patrol. The American navy would search out but not attack German submarines in the western half of the Atlantic and warn British vessels of their location. Also in April, U.S. forces occupied Greenland, and in May, the president declared a state of unlimited national emergency.

American marines occupied Iceland, a Danish possession, in July 1941 to protect it from seizure by Germany. The American navy began to convoy American and Icelandic ships between the United States and Iceland.

On August 9, 1941, Roosevelt and Winston Churchill issued the **Atlantic Charter**.

Germany invaded Russia in June 1941, and in November the United States extended lend-lease assistance to the Russians.

The American destroyer *Greer* was attacked by a German submarine near Iceland on September 4, 1941. Roosevelt ordered the American military forces to shoot on sight any German or Italian vessel in the patrol zone. An undeclared naval war had begun. The American destroyer *Kearny* was attacked by a submarine on October 16, and the destroyer *Reuben James* was sunk on October 30, with 115 lives lost. In November, Congress authorized the arming of merchant ships.

The Road to Pearl Harbor

In late July 1941, the United States placed an embargo on the export of aviation gasoline, lubricants, and scrap iron and steel to Japan, and granted an additional loan to China. In December, the embargo was extended to include iron ore and pig iron, some chemicals, machine tools, and other products.

In October 1941, a new military cabinet headed by General Hideki Tojo took control of Japan. The Japanese secretly decided to make a final effort to negotiate, and to go to war if no solution was found by November 25. A new round of talks followed in Washington, but neither side would make a substantive change in its position, and on November 26, Hull repeated the American demand that the Japanese remove all their forces from China and Indochina immediately. The Japanese gave final approval on December 1 for an attack on the United States.

The Japanese planned a major offensive to take the Dutch East Indies, Malaya, and the Philippines in order to obtain the oil, metals, and other raw materials they needed. At the same time, they would attack Pearl Harbor in Hawaii to destroy the American Pacific fleet to keep it from interfering with their plans.

The United States had broken the Japanese diplomatic codes and knew that trouble was imminent. Between December 1 and December 6, 1941, it became clear to administration leaders that Japanese task forces were being ordered into battle. American commanders in the Pacific were warned of possible aggressive action there, but not forcefully.

At 7:55 a.m. on Sunday, December 7, 1941, the first wave of Japanese carrier-based planes attacked the American fleet in Pearl Harbor. A second wave followed at 8:50 a.m. The United States suffered the loss of two battleships sunk, six damaged and out of action, three cruisers and three destroyers sunk or damaged, and a number of lesser vessels destroyed or damaged. All of the 150 aircraft at Pearl Harbor were destroyed on the ground. Worst of all, 2,323 American servicemen were killed and about 1,100 wounded. The Japanese lost 29 planes, five midget submarines, and one fleet submarine.

THE SECOND WORLD WAR AND THE POSTWAR PERIOD (1939–1963)

Declared War Begins

On December 8, 1941, Congress declared war on Japan, with one dissenting vote. On December 11, Germany and Italy declared war on the United States. Great Britain and the United States then established the **Combined Chiefs of Staff**, headquartered in Washington, to direct Anglo-American military operations.

On January 1, 1942, representatives of 26 nations met in Washington, D.C., and signed the Declaration of the United Nations, pledging themselves to the principles of the Atlantic Charter and promising not to make a separate peace with their common enemies.

The Home Front

War Production Board: The WPB was established in 1942 by President Franklin D. Roosevelt for the purpose of regulating the use of raw materials.

Wage and Price Controls: In April 1942, the General Maximum Price Regulation Act froze prices and extended rationing. In April 1943, prices, wages, and salaries were frozen.

Revenue Act of 1942: The Revenue Act of 1942 extended the income tax to the majority of the population. Payroll deduction for the income tax began in 1944.

Social Changes: Rural areas lost population, while population in coastal areas increased rapidly. Women entered the work force in increasing numbers. African-Americans moved from the rural South to northern and western cities, with racial tensions often resulting, most notably in the June 1943 racial riot in Detroit.

Smith-Connolly Act: Passed in 1943, the Smith-Connolly Antistrike Act authorized government seizure of a plant or mine idled by a strike if the war effort was impeded. It expired in 1947.

Korematsu v. United States: In 1944, the Supreme Court upheld President Roosevelt's 1942 order that Issei (Japanese-Americans who had emigrated from Japan) and Nisei (native born Japanese-Americans) be relocated to concentration camps. The camps were closed in March 1946.

Presidential Election of 1944: President Franklin D. Roosevelt, together with new vice-presidential candidate Harry S. Truman (1884–1972) of Missouri, defeated his Republican opponent, Governor Thomas E. Dewey of New York.

Roosevelt died on April 12, 1945, at Warm Springs, Georgia. Harry S. Truman became president.

The North African and European Theaters

The United States joined in the bombing of the European continent in July 1942. Bombing increased during 1943 and 1944 and lasted to the end of the war.

The Allied army under Dwight D. Eisenhower attacked French North Africa in November 1942. The Vichy French forces surrendered.

In the Battle of Kassarine Pass, North Africa, February 1943, the Allied army met General Erwin Rommel's Africa Korps. Although the battle is variously interpreted as a standoff or a defeat for the United States, Rommel's forces were soon trapped by the British moving in from Egypt. In May 1943, Rommel's Africa Korps surrendered.

Allied armies under George S. Patton (1885–1945) invaded Sicily from Africa in July 1943, and gained control by mid-August. Moving from Sicily, the Allied armies invaded the Italian mainland in September. The Germans, however, put up a stiff resistance, with the result that Rome did not fall until June 1944.

In March 1944, the Soviet Union began pushing into Eastern Europe.

On "D-Day," June 6, 1944, Allied armies under Dwight D. Eisenhower, now commander-in-chief of the Allied Expeditionary Forces, began an invasion of Normandy, France.

Allied armies liberated Paris in August. By mid-September, they had arrived at the Rhine, on the edge of Germany.

Beginning December 16, 1944, at the Battle of the Bulge, the Germans counterattacked, driving the Allies back about 50 miles into Belgium. By January, the Allies were once more advancing toward Germany. The Allies crossed the Rhine in March 1945. In the last week of April, Eisenhower's forces met the Soviet army at the Elbe. On May 7, 1945, Germany surrendered.

The Yalta Conference

The Yalta Conference was held in the resort town Yalta, on the Crimea, on February 4th–11th in 1945. The "Big Three" met there to decide the fate of post-war Europe. The United States was represented by Franklin D. Roosevelt, Great Britain was represented by Winston Churchill, and Josef Stalin was there on the Soviet Union's behalf. The goal of this conference was to discuss many aspects of the time. Among them were:

- The dividing up of Germany

- The formation of the United Nations

- German war reparations

- The entry of Soviet forces into the Far-Eastern front (Japan)

- The final, and most difficult issue, the future of Poland

The discussion and subsequent agreement of the entry of Soviet forces into the war against Japan was almost exclusively between Roosevelt and Stalin. President Roosevelt was strongly opposed to increased British involvement in the war, because he knew Churchill would demand more colonies. At the same time however, he knew that he needed help on the Pacific Front because the atomic bomb had not yet been tested. Therefore, the Soviet Union seemed to be the only logical alternative. Stalin agreed to enter the war on the side of the Allies within three months after the fall of Germany. In return, Roosevelt promised Stalin that he would have certain strategic lands.

The Pacific Theater

By the end of December 1941, Guam, Wake Island, the Gilbert Islands, and Hong Kong had fallen to the Japanese. In January 1942, Raboul, New Britain, fell, followed in February by Singapore and Java, and in March by Rangoon, Burma. U.S. forces surrendered at Corregidor, Philippines, on May 6, 1942.

The Battle of the Coral Sea, May 7–8, 1942, stopped the Japanese advance on Australia.

The **Battle of Midway**, June 4–7, 1942, proved to be the turning point in the Pacific.

A series of land, sea, and air battles took place around Guadalcanal in the Solomon Islands from August 1942 to February 1943, stopping the Japanese.

The Allied strategy of island hopping, begun in 1943, sought to neutralize Japanese strongholds with air and sea power and then move on.

U.S. forces advanced into the Gilberts (November 1943), the Marshalls (January 1944), and the Marianas (June 1944). After the American capture of the Marianas, General Tojo resigned as premier of Japan.

The Battle of Leyte Gulf, October 25, 1944, resulted in Japan's loss of most of its remaining naval power. Forces under General Douglas MacArthur (1880–1964) liberated Manila in March 1945.

Between April and June 1945, in the battle for Okinawa, nearly 50,000 American casualties resulted from the fierce fighting, but the battle virtually destroyed Japan's remaining defenses.

The Atomic Bomb

The Manhattan Engineering District was established by the army engineers in August 1942 for the purpose of developing an atomic bomb (it eventually became known as the Manhattan Project). J. Robert Oppenheimer directed the design and construction of a transportable atomic bomb at Los Alamos, New Mexico.

On December 2, 1942, Enrico Fermi (1901–1954) and his colleagues at the University of Chicago produced the first atomic chain reaction.

On July 16, 1945, the first atomic bomb was exploded at Alamogordo, New Mexico.

The *Enola Gay* dropped an atomic bomb on Hiroshima, Japan, on August 6, 1945, killing about 78,000 persons and injuring 100,000 more. On August 9, a second bomb was dropped on Nagasaki, Japan.

On August 8, 1945, ninety days after Germany was defeated, the Soviet Union entered the war against Japan. Japan surrendered on August 14, 1945. The formal surrender was signed on September 2.

Diplomacy

Casablanca Conference: On January 14–25, 1943, Franklin D. Roosevelt and Winston Churchill, prime minister of Great Britain, declared a policy of unconditional surrender for "all enemies."

Moscow Conference: In October 1943, Secretary of State Cordell Hull obtained Soviet agreement to enter the war against Japan after Germany was defeated, and to participate in a world organization after the war was over.

Declaration of Cairo: Issued on December 1, 1943, after Roosevelt met with General Chiang Kai-shek in Cairo from November 22 to 26, the Declaration of Cairo called for Japan's unconditional surrender and stated that all Chinese territories occupied by Japan would be returned to China and that Korea would be free and independent.

The Emergence of the Cold War and Containment

In 1947, career diplomat and Soviet expert George F. Kennan wrote an anonymous article for *Foreign Affairs* in which he called for a counterforce to Soviet pressures, for the purpose of "containing" communism.

Truman Doctrine: In February 1947, Great Britain notified the United States that it could no longer aid the Greek government in its war against Communist insurgents. The next month President Harry S. Truman asked Congress for $400 million in military and economic aid for Greece and Turkey. In what became known as the "Truman Doctrine," he argued that the United States must support free peoples who were resisting Communist domination.

Marshall Plan: Secretary of State George C. Marshall (1880–1959) proposed in June 1947 that the United States provide economic aid to help rebuild Europe. The following March, Congress passed the European Recovery Program, popularly known as the Marshall Plan, which provided more than $12 billion in aid.

After the United States, France, and Great Britain announced plans to create a West German Republic out of their German zones, the Soviet Union in June 1948 blocked surface access to Berlin. The United States then instituted an airlift to transport supplies to the city until the Soviets lifted their blockade in May 1949.

NATO

In April 1949, the North Atlantic Treaty Organization was signed by the United States, Canada, Great Britain, and nine European nations. The signatories pledged that an attack against one would be considered an attack against all. The Soviets formed the Warsaw Treaty Organization in 1955 to counteract NATO.

International Cooperation

Representatives from Europe and the United States, at a conference held July 1–22, 1944, signed agreements for an international bank and a world monetary fund to stabilize international currencies and rebuild the economies of war-torn nations.

From April to June 1945, representatives from 50 countries met in San Francisco to establish the United Nations. The U.N. charter created a General Assembly composed of all member nations which would act as the ultimate policy-making body. A Security

Council, made up of 11 members, including the United States, Great Britain, France, the Soviet Union, and China as permanent members and six additional nations elected by the General Assembly for two-year terms, would be responsible for settling disputes among U.N. member nations.

Containment in Asia

General Douglas MacArthur headed a four-power Allied Control Council which governed Japan, allowing it to develop economically and politically.

Between 1945 and 1948, the United States gave more than $2 billion in aid to the Nationalist Chinese under Chiang Kai-shek, and sent George C. Marshall to settle the conflict between Chiang's Nationalists and Mao Tse-tung's Communists. In 1949, however, Mao defeated Chiang and forced the Nationalists to flee to Formosa (Taiwan). Mao established the People's Republic of China on the mainland.

Korean War

On June 25, 1950, North Korea invaded South Korea. President Truman committed U.S. forces commanded by General MacArthur, but under United Nations auspices. By October, the U.N. forces (mostly American) had driven north of the 38th parallel, which divided North and South Korea. Chinese troops attacked MacArthur's forces on November 26, pushing them south of the 38th parallel, but by spring 1951, the U.N. forces had recovered their offensive.

In June 1953, an armistice was signed, leaving Korea divided along virtually the same boundary that had existed prior to the war.

Eisenhower-Dulles Foreign Policy

Dwight D. Eisenhower, elected president in 1952, chose John Foster Dulles (1888–1959) as secretary of state. Dulles talked of a more aggressive foreign policy, calling for "massive retaliation" and "liberation" rather than containment. He wished to emphasize nuclear deterrents rather than conventional armed forces.

After several years of nationalist war against French occupation, France, Great Britain, the Soviet Union, and China signed the Geneva Accords in July 1954, dividing Vietnam along the 17th parallel. The North would be under Ho Chi Minh and the South under Emperor Bao Dai. Elections were scheduled for 1956 to unify the country, but Ngo Dinh Diem overthrew Bao Dai and prevented the elections from taking place. The United States supplied economic aid to South Vietnam.

Dulles attempted to establish a Southeast Asia Treaty Organization parallel to NATO, but was able to obtain only the Philippine Republic, Thailand, and Pakistan as signatories in September 1954.

President Eisenhower announced in January 1957 that the United States was prepared to use armed force in the Middle East against Communist aggression. Under this doctrine, U.S. marines entered Beirut, Lebanon, in July 1958 to promote political stability during a change of governments. The marines left in October.

The United States supported the overthrow of President Jacobo Arbenz Guzman of Guatemala in 1954 because he began accepting arms from the Soviet Union.

In January 1959, Fidel Castro overthrew Fulgencio Batista, dictator of Cuba. Castro soon began criticizing the United States and moved closer to the Soviet Union, signing a trade agreement with the Soviets in February 1960. The United States prohibited the importation of Cuban sugar in October 1960, and broke off diplomatic relations in January 1961.

The Politics of Affluence: Demobilization and Domestic Policy

Harry S. Truman, formerly a senator from Missouri and vice president of the United States, became president on April 12, 1945. Congress created the **Atomic Energy Commission** in 1946, establishing civilian control over nuclear development and giving the president sole authority over the use of atomic weapons in warfare.

Taft-Hartley Act (1947): The Republicans, who had gained control of Congress in 1946, sought to control the power of the unions through the Taft-Hartley Act. This act made the "closed-shop" illegal; labor unions could no longer force employers to hire only union members. The act slowed down efforts to unionize the South, and by 1954, 15 states had passed "right to work" laws, forbidding the "union-shop."

In 1948, the president banned racial discrimination in federal government hiring practices and ordered desegregation of the armed forces.

The **Presidential Succession Act of 1947** placed the Speaker of the House and the president pro tempore of the Senate ahead of the secretary of state and after the vice president in the line of succession. The **Twenty-Second Amendment** to the Constitution, ratified in 1951, limited the president to election to two terms.

Election of 1948

Truman was the Democratic nominee, but the Democrats were split by the States' Rights Democratic party (Dixiecrats), which nominated Governor Strom Thurmond of South Carolina, and the Progressive party, which nominated former Vice President Henry Wallace. The Republicans nominated Governor Thomas E. Dewey of New York. After traveling widely, and attacking the "do-nothing Congress," Truman won a surprise victory.

Anticommunism

In 1950, Julius and Ethel Rosenberg and Harry Gold were charged with giving atomic secrets to the Soviet Union. The Rosenbergs were convicted and executed in 1953.

On February 9, 1950, Senator Joseph R. McCarthy (1908–1957) of Wisconsin alleged that he had a list of known Communists who were working in the State Department. He later expanded his attacks. After making unproved charges against the army, he was censured by the Senate in 1954.

Eisenhower's Dynamic Conservatism

The Republicans nominated Dwight D. Eisenhower, most recently NATO commander, for the presidency. The Democrats nominated Governor Adlai E. Stevenson (1900–1965) of Illinois for president. Eisenhower won by a landslide; for the first time since Reconstruction, the Republicans won some southern states.

Eisenhower sought to balance the budget and lower taxes but did not attempt to roll back existing social and economic legislation. Eisenhower first described his policy as "dynamic conservatism," and then as "progressive moderation." The administration abolished the Reconstruction Finance Corporation, ended wage and price controls, and reduced farm price supports. It cut the budget and in 1954 lowered tax rates for corporations and individuals with high incomes; an economic slump, however, made balancing the budget difficult.

Social Security was extended in 1954 and 1956 to an additional 10 million people, including professionals, domestic and clerical workers, farm workers, and members of the armed services.

The Rural Electrification Administration announced in 1960 that 97 percent of American farms had electricity.

In 1954, Eisenhower obtained congressional approval for joint Canadian–U.S. construction of the St. Lawrence Seaway, which was to give oceangoing vessels access to the Great Lakes. In 1956, Congress authorized construction of the Interstate Highway System, with the federal government supplying 90 percent of the cost and the states 10 percent.

The launching of the Soviet space satellite *Sputnik* on October 4, 1957, created fear that America was falling behind technologically. Although the United States launched *Explorer I* on January 31, 1958, the concern continued. In 1958, Congress established the National Aeronautics and Space Administration (NASA) to coordinate research and development, and passed the National Defense Education Act to provide grants and loans for education.

On January 3, 1959, Alaska became the 49th state, and on August 21, 1959, Hawaii became the 50th.

Civil Rights

Eisenhower completed the formal integration of the armed forces, desegregated public services in Washington, D.C., naval yards, and veteran's hospitals, and appointed a Civil Rights Commission.

Brown v. Board of Education of Topeka: In this 1954 case, NAACP lawyer Thurgood Marshall challenged the doctrine of "separate but equal" (*Plessy v. Ferguson*, 1896). The Court declared that separate educational facilities were inherently unequal. In 1955, the Court ordered states to integrate "with all deliberate speed."

Although he did not personally support the Supreme Court decision, Eisenhower sent 10,000 National Guardsmen and 1,000 paratroopers to Little Rock, Arkansas, to control mobs and enable African-Americans to enroll at Central High in September 1957.

On December 11, 1955, in Montgomery, Alabama, Rosa Parks, a black woman, refused to give up her seat on a city bus to a white and was arrested. Under the leadership of Martin Luther King (1929–1968), an African-American pastor, African-Americans of Montgomery organized a bus boycott that lasted for a year, until in December 1956, the Supreme Court refused to review a lower court ruling that stated that separate but equal was no longer legal.

In 1959, state and federal courts nullified Virginia laws that prevented state funds from going to integrated schools. This proved to be the beginning of the end for "massive resistance."

On February 1, 1960, upon being denied service, four African-American students staged a sit-in at a Woolworth lunch counter in Greensboro, North Carolina. This inspired sit-ins by thousands elsewhere in the South and led to the formation of the Student Nonviolent Coordinating Committee.

The Election of 1960

Vice President Richard M. Nixon won the Republican presidential nomination, and the Democrats nominated Senator John F. Kennedy (1917–1963) for the presidency, with Lyndon B. Johnson (1908–1973), majority leader of the Senate, as his running mate.

Kennedy won the election by slightly more than 100,000 popular votes and 94 electoral votes, based on majorities in New England, the Middle Atlantic, and the South.

RECENT DEVELOPMENTS (1960's–PRESENT)

- Vietnam War-major causes, events, and outcomes; student protests in the United States

- African American Civil Rights movement; the leadership and assassination of Martin Luther King Jr.

- The women's movement, peace movement, migrant farm workers movement, and environmentalism movement

- Social policy initiatives: the "Great Society" and the "War on Poverty"

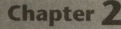

- Watergate scandal

- Increase in the number of working women and changes in family structure

- Changing demographics—subcultures and ethnic and cultural identities

- Conservative movements-religious conservatives, tax revolts, the drive to reduce the size of government

- Industrial trends—decline of unions; the growth of the service sector; the growth of the budget deficit; the impact of deregulation; energy and environmental issues

- International relations, including United States relations with the Soviet Union and its successor stares and the changing role of the United States in world political and economic affairs

- Development of computers and information systems and their impact on the economy and jobs

Kennedy's "New Frontier" and the Liberal Revival

Kennedy was unable to get much of his program through Congress because of the opposition of an alliance of Republicans and southern Democrats.

Kennedy did gain congressional approval for raising the minimum wage from $1.00 to $1.25 an hour and extending it to 3 million more workers.

The 1961 Housing Act provided nearly $5 billion over four years for the preservation of open urban spaces, development of mass transit, and the construction of middle-class housing.

Civil Rights

In May 1961, blacks and whites boarded buses in Washington, D.C., and traveled across the South to New Orleans to test federal enforcement of regulations prohibiting discrimination. They met violence in Alabama but continued to New Orleans.

The Justice Department, under Attorney General Robert F. Kennedy (1925–1968), began to push for civil rights, including desegregation of interstate transportation in the South, integration of schools, and supervision of elections.

In the fall of 1962, President Kennedy called the Mississippi National Guard to federal duty to enable an African-American, James Meredith, to enroll at the University of Mississippi.

Kennedy presented a comprehensive civil rights bill to Congress in 1963. With the bill held up in Congress, 200,000 people marched, demonstrating on its behalf on August 28, 1963, in Washington, D.C. Martin Luther King gave his "I Have a Dream" speech.

The Cold War Continues

Under Eisenhower, the Central Intelligence Agency had begun training some 2,000 men for an invasion of Cuba to overthrow Fidel Castro, the left-leaning revolutionary who had taken power in 1959. On April 19, 1961, this force invaded at the Bay of Pigs, but was pinned down and forced to surrender. Some 1,200 men were captured.

In August 1961, Khrushchev closed the border between East and West Berlin and ordered the erection of the Berlin Wall.

The Soviet Union began the testing of nuclear weapons in September 1961. Kennedy then authorized resumption of underground testing by the United States.

On October 14, 1962, a U-2 reconnaissance plane brought photographic evidence that missile sites were being built in Cuba. Kennedy, on October 22, announced a blockade of Cuba and called on Khrushchev to dismantle the missile bases and remove all weapons capable of attacking the United States from Cuba. Six days later, Khrushchev backed down, withdrew the missiles, and Kennedy lifted the blockade.

In July 1963, a treaty banning the atmospheric testing of nuclear weapons was signed by all the major powers except France and China.

In 1961, Kennedy announced the Alliance for Progress, which would provide $20 million in aid to Latin America.

Johnson and the Great Society

On November 22, 1963, Kennedy was assassinated by Lee Harvey Oswald in Dallas, Texas. Jack Ruby, a nightclub owner, killed Oswald two days later.

Succeeding Kennedy, Lyndon B. Johnson had extensive experience in both the House and Senate, and as a Texan, was the first southerner to serve as president since Woodrow Wilson.

A tax cut of more than $10 billion passed Congress in 1964, and an economic boom resulted.

The 1964 **Civil Rights Act** outlawed racial discrimination by employers and unions, created the Equal Employment Opportunity Commission to enforce the law, and eliminated the remaining restrictions on black voting.

Michael Harrington's *The Other America* (1962) showed that 20 to 25 percent of American families were living below the governmentally defined poverty line. The Economic Opportunity Act of 1964 sought to address the problem by establishing a Job Corps, community action programs, educational programs, work-study programs, job training, loans for small businesses and farmers, and Volunteers in Service to America (VISTA), a "domestic peace corps." The Office of Economic Opportunity administered many of these programs.

Election of 1964

Lyndon Johnson was nominated for president by the Democrats. The Republicans nominated Senator Barry Goldwater, a conservative from Arizona. Johnson won more than 61 percent of the popular vote and could now launch his own "Great Society" program.

The Medicare Act of 1965 combined hospital insurance for retired people with a voluntary plan to cover physician's bills. Medicaid provided grants to states to help the poor below retirement age.

Emergence of Black Power

In 1965, Rev. Martin Luther King Jr. announced a voter registration drive. With help from the federal courts, he dramatized his effort by leading a march from Selma to Montgomery, Alabama, between March 21 and 25. **The Voting Rights Act of 1965** authorized the attorney general to appoint officials to register voters.

Seventy percent of African-Americans lived in city ghettos. In 1966, New York and Chicago experienced riots, and the following year there were riots in Newark and Detroit. The Kerner Commission, appointed to investigate the riots, concluded that they were directed at a social system that prevented African-Americans from getting good jobs and crowded them into ghettos.

Stokely Carmichael, in 1966, called for the civil rights movements to be "black-staffed, black-controlled, and black-financed." Later, he moved on to the **Black Panthers**, self-styled urban revolutionaries based in Oakland, California. Other leaders such as H. Rap Brown also called for Black Power.

On April 4, 1968, Martin Luther King was assassinated in Memphis by James Earl Ray. Riots in more than 100 cities followed.

The New Left

Students at the University of California at Berkeley staged sit-ins in 1964 to protest the prohibition of political canvassing on campus. In December, police broke up a sit-in; protests spread to other campuses across the country.

Student protests began focusing on the Vietnam War. In the spring of 1967, 500,000 gathered in Central Park in New York City to protest the war, many burning their draft cards. **Students for a Democratic Society (SDS)** became more militant and willing to use violence.

More than 200 large campus demonstrations took place in the spring, culminating in the occupation of buildings at Columbia University to protest the university's involvement in military research and its poor relations with minority groups. Police wielding billy clubs eventually broke up the demonstration. In August, thousands gathered in Chicago to protest the war during the Democratic convention. Beginning in 1968, SDS began breaking up into rival factions. By the early 1970s, the New Left had lost political influence, having abandoned its original commitment to democracy and nonviolence.

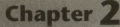

Other Liberation Movements

The Civil Rights movement and changing views among the young regarding sexual behavior provided an environment in which homosexuals could also claim rights, beginning with a riot against police harassment in 1969 in Greenwich Village in New York. The feminist movement, however, was more immediately visible, marked by the publication of Betty Friedan's *The Feminine Mystique* (1963) and the formation of the National Organization for Women (NOW) in 1966. Focusing on such issues as equality in employment opportunities and pay, the feminist movement also won a major victory with the Supreme Court's ruling in *Roe v. Wade* (1973) legalizing abortion.

Vietnam

After the French defeat in 1954, the United States sent military advisors to South Vietnam to aid the government of Ngo Dinh Diem. The pro-Communist Vietcong forces gradually grew in strength, partly because Diem failed to follow through on promised reforms. They received support from North Vietnam, the Soviet Union, and China.

In August 1964—after claiming that North Vietnamese gunboats had fired on American destroyers in the Gulf of Tonkin—Lyndon Johnson pushed the Gulf of Tonkin resolution through Congress, authorizing him to use military force in Vietnam. After a February 1965 attack by the Vietcong on Pleiku, Johnson ordered operation "Rolling Thunder," the first sustained bombing of North Vietnam. Johnson then sent combat troops to South Vietnam; under the leadership of General William C. Westmoreland, they conducted search and destroy operations. The number of troops increased to 184,000 in 1965, 385,000 in 1966, 485,000 in 1967, and 538,000 in 1968.

"Hawks" defended the president's policy drawing on "containment theory" which said that the nation had the responsibility to resist aggression. This Cold War "containment" notion was born of the Domino Theory, which held that if one country fell under communist influence or control, its neighboring countries would soon follow. Containment was the cornerstone of the Truman Doctrine as defined by a Truman speech on March 12, 1947. If Vietnam should fall, it was said, all Southeast Asia would eventually go. The administration stressed its willingness to negotiate the withdrawal of all "foreign" forces from the war. Johnson, in a television interview in 1964, affirmed his support for the theory this way:

> "I think it would be a very dangerous thing, and I share President Kennedy's view, and I think the whole of Southeast Asia would be involved and that would involve hundreds of millions of people, and I think it's—it cannot be ignored, we must do everything that we can, we must be responsible, we must stay there and help them, and that is what we are going to do." (www.mtholyoke.edu/acad/intrel/pentagon3/ps2.htm, accessed November 11, 2009)

Opposition began quickly, with "teach-ins" at the University of Michigan in 1965 and a 1966 congressional investigation led by Senator J. William Fulbright. Antiwar demonstrations were gaining large crowds by 1967. "Doves" argued that the war was a civil war in which the United States should not meddle.

On January 31, 1968, the first day of the Vietnamese New Year (Tet), the Vietcong attacked numerous cities and towns, American bases, and even Saigon. Although they suffered large losses, the Vietcong won a psychological victory, as American opinion began turning against the war.

The Election of 1968

In November 1967, Senator Eugene McCarthy of Minnesota announced his candidacy for the 1968 Democratic presidential nomination, running on the issue of opposition to the war.

In February, McCarthy won 42 percent of the Democratic vote in the New Hampshire primary, compared with Johnson's 48 percent. Robert F. Kennedy then announced his candidacy for the Democratic presidential nomination.

Lyndon Johnson withdrew his candidacy on March 31, 1968, and Vice President Hubert H. Humphrey took his place as a candidate for the Democratic nomination.

After winning the California primary over McCarthy, Robert Kennedy was assassinated by Sirhan Sirhan, a young Palestinian. This event assured Humphrey's nomination.

The Republicans nominated Richard M. Nixon. Governor George C. Wallace of Alabama ran for the presidency under the banner of the American Independent party, appealing to fears generated by protestors and big government.

Johnson suspended air attacks on North Vietnam shortly before the election. Nonetheless Nixon, who emphasized stability and order, defeated Humphrey by a margin of 1 percent. Wallace's 13.5 percent was the best showing by a third-party candidate since 1924.

The Nixon Conservative Reaction

The Nixon administration sought to block renewal of the Voting Rights Act and delay implementation of court-ordered school desegregation in Mississippi.

In 1969, Nixon appointed Warren E. Burger, a conservative, as chief justice. Although more conservative than the Warren court, the Burger court did declare the death penalty, as used at the time, unconstitutional in 1972 and struck down state antiabortion legislation in 1973.

The president turned to **"Vietnamization,"** the effort to build up South Vietnamese forces while withdrawing American troops. In 1969, Nixon reduced American troop strength by 60,000, but at the same time ordered the bombing of Cambodia, a neutral country.

In April 1970, Nixon announced that Vietnamization was succeeding but a few days later, he sent troops into Cambodia to clear out Vietcong sanctuaries and resumed bombing of North Vietnam.

Protests against escalation of the war were especially strong on college campuses. After several students were killed during protests, several hundred colleges were closed down by student strikes, as moderates joined the radicals. Congress repealed the Gulf of Tonkin Resolution.

The publication in 1971 of classified Defense Department documents, called "The Pentagon Papers," revealed that the government had misled the Congress and the American people regarding its intentions in Vietnam during the mid-1960s.

Nixon drew American forces back from Cambodia but increased bombing. In March 1972, after stepped-up aggression from the North, Nixon ordered the mining of Haiphong and other northern ports.

In the summer of 1972, negotiations between the United States and North Vietnam began in Paris. A few days before the 1972 presidential election, Henry Kissinger, the president's national security advisor, announced that "peace was at hand."

Nixon resumed bombing of North Vietnam in December 1972, claiming that the North Vietnamese were not bargaining in good faith. In January 1973, the opponents reached a settlement in which the North Vietnamese retained control over large areas of the South and agreed to release American prisoners of war within 60 days. Nearly 60,000 Americans had been killed and 300,000 more wounded and the war had cost Americans $109 billion. On March 29, 1973, the last American combat troops left South Vietnam.

Foreign Policy

With his national security advisor, Henry Kissinger, Nixon took some bold diplomatic initiatives. In February 1972, Nixon and Kissinger went to China to meet with Mao Tse-tung and his associates. The United States agreed to support China's admission to the United Nations and to pursue economic and cultural exchanges.

Nixon and Kissinger called their policy *détente*, a French term meaning a relaxation in the tensions between two governments.

The Election of 1972

Richard M. Nixon, who had been renominated by the Republicans, won a landslide victory over the Democratic nominee, Senator George McGovern.

Watergate

What became known as the **Watergate** crisis began during the 1972 presidential campaign. Early on the morning of June 17, James McCord, a security officer for the Committee to Re-Elect the President, and four other men broke into Democratic headquarters at the Watergate apartment and office complex in Washington, D.C., and were caught while going through files and installing electronic eavesdropping devices.

In March 1974, a grand jury indicted Haldeman, Ehrlichman, former Attorney General John Mitchell, and four other White House aides and named Nixon an unindicted coconspirator.

Meanwhile, the House Judiciary Committee televised its debate over impeachment, adopting three articles of impeachment. It charged the president with obstructing justice, misusing presidential power, and failing to obey the committee's subpoenas.

Before the House began to debate impeachment, Nixon announced his resignation on August 8, 1974, to take effect at noon the following day. Gerald Ford then became president.

The Ford Presidency

Gerald Ford was in many respects the opposite of Nixon. Although a partisan Republican, he was well liked and free from any hint of scandal. Ford almost immediately encountered controversy when in September 1974 he offered to pardon Nixon. Nixon accepted the offer, although he admitted no wrongdoing and had not yet been charged with a crime.

Vietnam Falls

As North Vietnamese forces pushed back the South Vietnamese, Ford asked Congress to provide more arms for the South. Congress rejected the request, and in April 1975 Saigon fell to the North Vietnamese.

Carter's Moderate Liberalism

Ronald Reagan, a former movie actor and governor of California, opposed Ford for the Republican presidential nomination, but Ford won by a slim margin. The Democrats nominated James Earl Carter, formerly governor of Georgia, who ran on the basis of his integrity and lack of Washington connections. Carter narrowly defeated Ford in the election.

Carter offered amnesty to Americans who had fled the draft and gone to other countries during the Vietnam War. He established the Departments of Energy and

Education and placed the civil service on a merit basis. He created a "superfund" for cleanup of chemical waste dumps, established controls over strip mining, and protected 100 million acres of Alaskan wilderness from development.

Carter's Foreign Policy

Carter negotiated a controversial treaty with Panama, affirmed by the Senate in 1978, that provided for the transfer of ownership of the canal to Panama in 1999 and guaranteed its neutrality.

Carter ended official recognition of Taiwan and in 1979 recognized the People's Republic of China. Conservatives called the decision a "sell-out."

In 1978, Carter negotiated the **Camp David Agreement** between Israel and Egypt. Israel promised to return occupied land in the Sinai to Egypt in exchange for Egyptian recognition, a process completed in 1982. An agreement to negotiate the Palestinian refugee problem proved ineffective.

The Iranian Crisis

In 1978, a revolution forced the shah of Iran to flee the country, replacing him with a religious leader, Ayatollah Ruhollah Khomeini. Because the United States had supported the shah with arms and money, the revolutionaries were strongly anti-American, calling the United States the "Great Satan."

After Carter allowed the exiled shah to come to the United States for medical treatment in October 1979, some 400 Iranians broke into the American embassy in Teheran on November 4, taking the occupants captive. They demanded that the shah be returned to Iran for trial and that his wealth be confiscated and given to Iran. Carter rejected these demands; instead, he froze Iranian assets in the United States and established a trade embargo against Iran.

The Election of 1980

Republican Ronald Reagan defeated Carter by a large electoral majority, and the Republicans gained control of the Senate and increased their representation in the House.

After extensive negotiations with Iran, in which Algeria acted as an intermediary, American hostages were freed on January 20, 1981, the day of Reagan's inauguration.

The Reagan Presidency: Attacking Big Government

An ideological though pragmatic conservative, Ronald Reagan acted quickly and forcefully to change the direction of government policy. He placed priority on cutting taxes. His approach was based on "supply-side" economics, the idea that if government left more money in the hands of the people, they would invest rather than spend the excess on consumer goods. The results would be greater production, more jobs, and greater prosperity, and thus more income for the government despite lower tax rates.

Reagan asked for a 30 percent tax cut, and despite fears of inflation on the part of Congress, in August 1983 obtained a 25 percent cut, spread over three years.

Congress passed the **Budget Reconciliation Act** in 1981, cutting $39 billion from domestic programs, including education, food stamps, public housing, and the National Endowments for the Arts and Humanities. While cutting domestic programs, Reagan increased the defense budget by $12 billion.

From a deficit of $59 billion in 1980, the federal budget was running $195 billion in the red by 1983.

Because of rising deficits, Reagan and Congress increased taxes in various ways. The 1982 Tax Equity and Fiscal Responsibility Act reversed some concessions made to business in 1981. Social Security benefits became taxable income in 1983. In 1984, the Deficit Reduction Act increased taxes by another $50 billion. But the deficit continued to increase.

Reagan ended ongoing antitrust suits against International Business Machines and American Telephone and Telegraph, thereby fulfilling his promise to reduce government interference with business.

Asserting American Power

Reagan took a hard line against the Soviet Union, calling it an "evil empire." He placed new cruise missiles in Europe, despite considerable opposition from Europeans.

Reagan also concentrated on obtaining funding for the development of a computer-controlled strategic defense initiative system (SDI), popularly called "Star Wars" after the widely seen movie, that would destroy enemy missiles from outerspace.

In Nicaragua, Reagan encouraged the opposition (*contras*) to the leftist Sandinista government with arms, tactical support, and intelligence, and supplied aid to the government of El Salvador in its struggles against left-wing rebels. In October 1983, the president also sent American troops into the Caribbean island of Grenada to overthrow a newly established Cuban-backed regime.

The Election of 1984

Walter Mondale, a former senator from Minnesota and vice president under Carter, won the Democratic nomination. Mondale criticized Reagan for his budget deficits, high unemployment and interest rates, and reduction of spending on social services. However, Reagan was elected to a second term in a landslide.

Second-Term Foreign Concerns

After Mikhail S. Gorbachev became the premier of the Soviet Union in March 1985 and took a more flexible approach toward both domestic and foreign affairs, Reagan softened his anti-Soviet stance.

Reagan and Gorbachev had difficulty in reaching an agreement on arms limitations at summit talks in 1985 and 1986. Finally, in December 1987, they signed an agreement eliminating medium-range missiles throughout Europe.

Iran-Contra

In 1985 and 1986, several Reagan officials sold arms to the Iranians in hopes of encouraging them to use their influence in getting American hostages in Lebanon released. The profits from these sales were then diverted to the Nicaraguan *contras* in an attempt to get around congressional restrictions on funding the *contras*. The president was forced to appoint a special prosecutor, and Congress held hearings on the affair in May 1987.

Second-Term Domestic Affairs: The Economy

The Tax Reform Act of 1986 lowered tax rates. At the same time, it removed many tax shelters and tax credits. The law did away with the concept of progressive taxation, the requirement that the percentage of income taxed increased as income increased.

The federal deficit reached $179 billion in 1985. At about the same time, the United States experienced trade deficits of more than $100 billion annually.

Black Monday: On October 19, 1987, the Dow Jones Industrial Average dropped more than 500 points. Between August 25 and October 20, the market lost over a trillion dollars in paper value.

NASA: The explosion of the shuttle *Challenger* soon after take-off on January 28, 1986, damaged NASA's credibility and reinforced doubts about the complex technology required for the SDI program.

Supreme Court: Reagan reshaped the Court in 1986, replacing Chief Justice Warren C. Burger with Associate Justice William H. Rehnquist, probably the most conservative member of the Court. Although failing in his nomination of Robert Bork for associate justice, Reagan did appoint other conservatives to the Court: Sandra Day O'Connor, Antonin Scalia, and Anthony Kennedy.

The Election of 1988

Vice President George H. W. Bush won the Republican nomination. Bush easily defeated Michael Dukakis, the Democratic nominee, but the Republicans were unable to make any inroads in Congress.

The First Bush Administration

Soon after George H.W Bush took office, the budget deficit for 1990 was estimated at $143 billion. In September, the administration and Congress agreed to increase taxes on gasoline, tobacco, and alcohol, establish an excise tax on luxury items, and raise Medicare taxes. Cuts were also to be made in medicare and other domestic programs. In a straight party vote, Republicans voting against and Democrats voting in favor, Congress in December transferred the power to decide whether new tax and spending proposals violated the deficit cutting agreement from the White House Office of Management and Budget to the Congressional Budget Office.

The Commission on Base Realignment and Closure proposed in December 1989 that 54 military bases be closed. In June 1990, Secretary of Defense Richard Cheney sent to Congress a plan to cut military spending by 10 percent and the armed forces by 25 percent over the next five years. The following April, Cheney recommended the closing of 43 domestic military bases, plus many more abroad.

With the savings and loan industry in financial trouble in 1989, largely because of bad real-estate loans, Bush signed a bill which created the Resolution Trust Corporation to oversee the closure and merging of savings and loans, and which provided $166 billion over 10 years to cover the bad debts. Estimates of the total costs of the debacle were over $300 billion.

Bush's Activist Foreign Policy

Panama: Since coming to office, the Bush administration had been concerned with Panamanian dictator Manuel Noriega because he allegedly served as an important link in the drug traffic between South America and the United States. After economic sanctions, diplomatic efforts, and an October 1989 coup failed to oust Noriega, Bush ordered 12,000 troops into Panama on December 20. The Americans installed a new government headed by Guillermo Endara, who had earlier won a presidential election that was promptly nullified by Noriega. On January 3, 1990, Noriega surrendered to the Americans and was taken to the United States to stand trial on drug trafficking charges; he was convicted and jailed for assisting the Medellín drug cartel. Twenty-three United States soldiers and three American civilians were killed in the operation. The Panamanians lost nearly 300 soldiers and more than 500 civilians.

Nicaragua: After years of civil war, Nicaragua held a presidential election in February 1990. Because of an economy largely destroyed by civil war and large financial debt to the United States, Violeta Barrios de Chamorro of the National Opposition Union defeated Daniel Ortega Saavedra of the Sandinistas, thereby fulfilling a long-standing American objective. The United States lifted its economic sanctions in March and put together an economic aid package for Nicaragua. In September 1991, the Bush administration forgave Nicaragua most of its debt to the United States.

China: After the death in April 1989 of reformer Hu Yaobang, formerly general secretary and chairman of the Chinese Communist party, students began pro-democracy marches in Beijing. By the middle of May, more than one million people were gathering on Beijing's Tiananmen Square, and other protestors elsewhere in China, calling for political reform. Martial law was imposed and in early June the army fired on the demonstrators. Estimates of the death toll in the wake of the nationwide crackdown on demonstrators ranged between 500 and 7,000. In July 1989, United States National Security Advisor Brent Scowcroft and Deputy Secretary of State Lawrence Eagleburger secretly met with Chinese leaders. When they again met the Chinese in December and revealed their earlier meeting, the Bush administration faced a storm of criticism for its policy of "constructive engagement" from opponents arguing that sanctions should be imposed. While establishing sanctions in 1991 on Chinese high-technology satellite-part exports, Bush continued to support renewal of Most Favored Nation trading status.

Africa: To rescue American citizens threatened by civil war, Bush sent 230 marines into Liberia in August 1990, evacuating 125 people. South Africa in 1990 freed Nelson Mandela, the most famous leader of the African National Congress, after 28 years of imprisonment. South Africa then began moving away from apartheid, and in 1991 Bush lifted economic sanctions imposed five years earlier. Mandela and his wife, Winnie, toured the U.S. in June 1990 to a tumultuous welcome, particularly from African-Americans. During their visit, they also addressed Congress.

Collapse of East European Communism

In August 1989 Hungary opened its borders with Austria. The following October, the Communists reorganized their party, calling it the Socialist party. Hungary then proclaimed itself a "Free Republic."

With thousands of East Germans passing through Hungary to Austria, after the opening of the borders in August 1989, Erich Honecker stepped down as head of state in October. On November 1, the government opened the border with Czechoslovakia and eight days later the Berlin Wall fell. On December 6, a non-Communist became head of state, followed on December 11 by large demonstrations demanding German reunification. Reunification took place in October 1990.

After anti-government demonstrations were forcibly broken up in Czechoslovakia in October 1989, changes took place in the Communist leadership the following month.

Then, on December 8, the Communists agreed to relinquish power and Parliament elected Václav Havel, a playwright and anti-Communist leader, to the presidency on December 29.

When anti-government demonstrations in Romania were met by force in early December, portions of the military began joining the opposition which captured dictator Nicolae Ceausescu and his wife, Elena, killing them on December 25, 1989. In May 1990 the National Salvation Front, made up of many former Communists, won the parliamentary elections.

In January 1990 the Bulgarian national assembly repealed the dominant role of the Communist party. A multi-party coalition government was formed the following December.

Albania opened its border with Greece and legalized religious worship in January 1990, and in July ousted hardliners from the government.

Amid the collapse of Communism in Eastern Europe, Bush met with Mikhail Gorbachev in Malta from December 1 through December 3, 1989; the two leaders appeared to agree that the Cold War was over. On May 30 and 31, 1990, Bush and Gorbachev met in Washington to discuss the possible reunification of Germany, and signed a trade treaty between the United States and the Soviet Union. The meeting of the two leaders in Helsinki on September 9 addressed strategies for the developing Persian Gulf crisis. At the meeting of the "Group of 7" nations (Canada, France, Germany, Italy, Japan, United Kingdom, and the United States) in July 1991, Gorbachev requested economic aid from the West. A short time later, on July 30 and 31, Bush met Gorbachev in Moscow where they signed the START treaty, which cut U.S. and Soviet nuclear arsenals by 30 percent, and pushed for Middle Eastern talks. With the collapse of the Soviet Union, the United States remained the lone world super-power.

Persian Gulf Crisis

Saddam Hussein of Iraq charged that Kuwait had conspired with the United States to keep oil prices low and began massing troops at the Iraq-Kuwait border.

On August 2, 1990 Iraq invaded Kuwait, an act that Bush denounced as "naked aggression." One day later 100,000 Iraqi soldiers were poised south of Kuwait City near the Saudi Arabian border. The United States quickly banned most trade with Iraq, froze Iraq's and Kuwait's assets in the United States, and sent aircraft carriers to the Persian Gulf. After the United Nations Security Council condemned the invasion, on August 6, Bush ordered the deployment of air, sea, and land forces to Saudi Arabia, dubbing the operation "Desert Shield." At the end of August there were 100,000 American soldiers in Saudi Arabia.

Bush encouraged Egypt to support American policy by forgiving Egypt its debt to the United States and obtaining pledges of financial support from Saudi Arabia, Kuwait, and Japan, among other nations, to help pay for the operation. On October 29, the Security Council warned Saddam Hussein that further actions might be taken if he did not withdraw from Kuwait. In November, Bush ordered that U.S. forces be increased to more than 400,000. On November 29, the United Nations set January 15, 1991, as the deadline for Iraqi withdrawal from Kuwait.

On January 9, Iraq's foreign-minister, Tariq Aziz, rejected a letter written by Bush to Hussein. Three days later, after an extensive debate, Congress authorized the use of force in the Gulf. On January 17, an international force including the United States, Great Britain, France, Italy, Saudi Arabia, and Kuwait launched an air and missile attack on Iraq and occupied Kuwait. The U.S. called the effort "Operation Desert Storm." Under the overall command of Army General H. Norman Schwarzkopf, the military effort emphasized high-technology weapons, including F-15 E fighter-bombers, F-117 A stealth fighters, Tomahawk cruise missiles, and Patriot anti-missile missiles. Beginning on January 17, Iraq fired SCUD missiles into Israel in an effort to draw that country into the war and splinter the U.S.-Arabian coalition. On January 22 and 23, Hussein's forces set Kuwaiti oil fields on fire and spilled oil into the Gulf.

On February 23, the allied ground assault began. Four days later Bush announced that Kuwait was liberated and ordered offensive operations to cease. The United Nations established the terms for the cease-fire: Iraqi annexation of Kuwait to be rescinded, Iraq to accept liability for damages and return Kuwaiti property, Iraq to end all military actions and identify mines and booby traps, and Iraq to release captives.

On April 3, the Security Council approved a resolution to establish a permanent cease-fire; Iraq accepted U.N. terms on April 6. The next day the United States began airlifting food to Kurdish refugees on the Iraq-Turkey border who were fleeing the Kurdish rebellion against Hussein, a rebellion that was seemingly encouraged by Bush, who nonetheless refused to become militarily involved. The United States estimated that 100,000 Iraqis had been killed during the war while the Americans had lost about 115 lives.

On February 6, 1991, the United States had set out its postwar goals for the Middle East. These included regional arms control and security arrangements, international aid for reconstruction of Iraq and Kuwait, and resolution of the Israeli-Palestinian conflict. Immediately after cessation of the conflict, Secretary of State James Baker toured the Middle East attempting to promote a conference to address the problems of the region. After several more negotiating sessions, Saudi Arabia, Syria, Jordan, and Lebanon had accepted the U.S. proposal for an Arab-Israeli peace conference by the middle of July; Israel conditionally accepted in early August. Despite continuing conflict with Iraq, including United Nations inspections of its nuclear capabilities, and new Israeli settlements in disputed territory—which kept the conference agreement tenuous—the nations met in Madrid, Spain, at the end of October. Bilateral talks in early November between Israel and the Arabs concentrated on procedural issues.

Breakup of the Soviet Union

Following the collapse of Communism in Eastern Europe, the Baltic republic of Lithuania, which had been taken over by the Soviet Union in 1939 through an agreement with Adolf Hitler, declared its independence from the Soviet Union on March 11, 1990.

Two days later, on March 13, the Soviet Union removed the Communist monopoly of political power, allowing non-Communists to run for office. The process of liberalization went haltingly forward in the Soviet Union. Perhaps the most significant event was the election of Boris Yeltsin, who had left the Communist party, as president of the Russian republic on June 12, 1991.

On August 19, Soviet hard-liners attempted a coup to oust Gorbachev, but a combination of their inability to control communication with the outside world, a failure to quickly establish military control, and the resistance of Yeltsin, members of the military, and people in the streets of cities such as Moscow and Leningrad, ended the coup on August 21, returning Gorbachev to power.

In the aftermath of the coup, much of the Communist structure came crashing down, setting the stage for opposition parties to emerge. The remaining Baltic republics of Latvia and Estonia declared their independence, which was recognized by the United States several days after other nations had done so. Most of the other Soviet republics then followed suit in declaring their independence. The Bush administration wanted some form of central authority to remain in the Soviet Union; hence, it did not seriously consider recognizing the independence of any republics except the Baltics. Bush also resisted offering economic aid to the Soviet Union until it presented a radical economic reform plan to move toward a free market. However, humanitarian aid such as food was pledged in order to preserve stability during the winter.

In September 1991, George Bush announced unilateral removal and destruction of ground-based tactical nuclear weapons in Europe and Asia, removal of nuclear-armed Tomahawk cruise missiles from surface ships and submarines, immediate destruction of intercontinental ballistic missiles covered by START, and an end to the 24-hour alert for strategic bombers that the U.S. had maintained for decades. Gorbachev responded the next month by announcing the immediate deactivation of intercontinental ballistic missiles covered by START, removal of all short-range missiles from Soviet ships, submarines, and aircraft, and destruction of all ground-based tactical nuclear weapons. He also said that the Soviet Union would reduce its forces by 700,000 troops, and he placed all long-range nuclear missiles under a single command. Gorbachev's hold on the presidency progressively weakened in the final months of 1991, with the reforms he had put in place taking on a life of their own. The dissolution of the U.S.S.R. led to his resignation in December, making way for Boris Yeltsin, who had headed popular resistance. The United States was now the world's only superpower.

The Democrats Reclaim the White House

William Jefferson Clinton, governor of Arkansas, overcame several rivals to win the Democratic presidential nomination in 1992 and with his running mate, Senator Albert Gore of Tennessee, went on to win the White House. During the campaign, Clinton and independent candidate H. Ross Perot, a wealthy Texas businessman, emphasized jobs and the economy while attacking the mounting federal debt. The incumbent, Bush, stressed traditional values and his foreign policy accomplishments. In the 1992 election, Clinton won 43 percent of the popular vote and 370 electoral votes, defeating Bush and Perot. Perot took 19 percent of the popular vote, but was unable to garner any electoral votes.

Clinton came to be dogged by a number of controversies, ranging from alleged ill-gotten gains in a complex Arkansas land deal that came to be known as the Whitewater Affair to charges of sexual misconduct, brought by a former Arkansas state employee (with whom he would ultimately reach an out-of-court settlement), that dated to an incident she said had occurred when Clinton was governor. In December 1998 Clinton was impeached by the House on charges that stemmed from an adulterous affair with a White House intern, Monica Lewinsky. The affair had been uncovered by Independent Counsel Kenneth Starr in the course of a long-running investigation into alleged malfeasance by the president and his wife, Hillary, in the Whitewater land deal and other matters. Extraordinary detail about Clinton's encounters with Lewinsky was revealed in a voluminous report from Starr's office. Its release triggered the impeachment proceedings, which ended with Clinton's acquittal by the Senate in February 1999.

On the legislative front, Clinton was strongly rebuffed in an attempt during his first term to reform the nation's healthcare system. In the 1994 mid-term elections, in what Clinton himself considered a repudiation of his administration, the Republicans took both houses of Congress from the Democrats and voted in Newt Gingrich of Georgia as Speaker of the House. Gingrich had helped craft the Republican congressional campaign strategy to dramatically shrink the federal government and give more power to the states.

Clinton, however, was not without his successes, both on the legislative and diplomatic fronts. He signed legislation establishing a five-day waiting period for handgun purchases as well as a crime bill emphasizing community policing. He signed the Family and Medical Leave Act, which requires large companies to provide up to 12 weeks' unpaid leave to workers for family and medical emergencies. He also championed welfare reform (a central theme of his campaign), but made it clear that the legislation he signed into law in August 1996 radically overhauling FDR's welfare system disturbed him on two counts—its exclusion of legal immigrants from getting most federal benefits and its deep cut in federal outlays for food stamps; Clinton said these flaws could be repaired with further legislation. In foreign affairs, Clinton signed the North American Free Trade Agreement (NAFTA), which lifted most trade barriers with Mexico and Canada as of 1994. Clinton sought to ease tensions between Israelis and Palestinians, and he helped bring together Itzhak Rabin, prime minister of Israel, and Yasir Arafat, chairman of the Palestine Liberation Organization, for a summit at the White House. Ultimately, the two Middle East leaders signed an accord in 1994 establishing Palestinian self-rule in the Gaza Strip and Jericho. In October 1994 Israel and Jordan signed a treaty to begin the process of establishing full diplomatic relations. Rabin was assassinated a year later by a radical, right-wing Israeli. The Clinton administration also played a central role in hammering out peace agreements in 1995 in war-torn former Yugoslavia—where armed conflict had broken out four years earlier among Serbs, Croats, Bosnian Muslims, and other factions and groups—and in 1998 in Northern Ireland.

Clinton recaptured the Democratic nomination without a serious challenge, while longtime GOP Senator Robert Dole of Kansas, the Senate majority leader, overcame several opponents but orchestrated a harmonious nominating convention with running mate Jack Kemp, a former New York congressman and Cabinet member. In November 1996, with most voters citing a healthy economy and the lack of an enticing alternative in Dole or the Reform Party's Perot, Clinton received 49 percent of the vote, becoming the first Democrat to be re-elected since FDR, in 1936. The GOP retained control of both houses of Congress.

Clinton, intent on mirroring the diversity of America in his Cabinet appointments, chose Hispanics Henry Cisneros (Housing and Urban Development) and Federico Peña (Transportation and, later, Energy), African Americans Ron Brown (Commerce) and Mike Espy (Agriculture), and women, including the nation's first woman attorney general, Janet Reno, and Madeleine Albright, the first woman secretary of state in U.S. history (Albright succeeded Warren Christopher, who served through Clinton's first term). Brown and 34 others on a trade mission died when his Air Force plane crashed in Croatia in April 1996. Cisneros and Espy both resigned under ethics clouds.

The Election of 2000—Republicans Retake the Whitehouse

In 2000, Republican George W. Bush, the son of former President George H.W. Bush, defeated Democrat Al Gore in a close and controversial election with Bush receiving a majority of the electoral votes (after a decision by the Supreme Court to stop a third recount—essentially awarding Florida's electoral votes to him), but Gore receiving a majority of the popular vote. Eight months after Bush was sworn in, the September 11th attacks occurred. In response to the attacks, President Bush declared a War on Terror, which led to the creation of a new cabinet-level agency, the Department of Homeland Security, an invasion of Afghanistan, and an invasion of Iraq. On the domestic front, President Bush signed into law tax cuts, the No Child Left Behind Act, and Medicare prescription drug benefits for seniors.

After defeating Democrat John Kerry in the 2004 election, President Bush's second term was beset by scandals and criticism related to the War on Terror, the perceived failure of the government's response to Hurricane Katrina, and an economy that went into recession. While extremely popular for much of his first term, his public approval ratings went from 90% approval to a low of 25% while finally rising to 34% as he left office. Only Harry Truman and Richard Nixon had lower ratings at the end of their presidencies.

The 2008 Presidential Election

The 2008 election cycle was one of firsts. It was the first time since 1952 that neither party had an incumbent in the race. It was the first time that two sitting Senators, Democrat Barack Obama from Illinois and Republican John McCain from Arizona, had vied for the White House. And the Republican Party nominated Alaska Governor Sarah Palin, its first woman on a presidential ticket. In another significant first, the 2008 election was the first in which an African-American man, Senator Obama, and a white woman, Hillary R. Clinton, ran viable races in a major party primary.

Senator Obama won and became the 44th president of the United States and its first African-American president. Obama inherited a national economic crisis, and two major wars. While he entered the presidency with large public support, his job approval rating has fallen, affected by economic and political issues, some inherited as noted, and some due to Obama's own policy initiatives.

New Technologies

Personal Computing Comes of Age

As of the early twenty-first century, the world is in the fourth generation of computer technology, which began in 1970 with an idea for personal computing. At the dawn of the early computer technology, Ted Hoff, an employee of Intel, believed that all the processing units of a computer would one day be placed on a single chip; at the time many people were skeptical. Today, every electronic component has a microprocessor built into it, just as Hoff had predicted.

The microcomputer was born in 1976 when Steve Jobs and Steve Wozniak sold a Volkswagen and a calculator for $1300 to build the first Apple in Wozniak's garage, just two years before IBM announced the release of the IBM PC. Over the next 18 months the IBM would become an industry standard. Beginning in 1980, the demand for a personal computer in industry and in the home grew. Brands, unknown today, were cutting edge—the Commodore, Tandy, and the Atari. As demand grew, so grew competition to make a faster, better chip, and therefore, a better computer. The names associated with the personal computer today, Microsoft and Bill Gates, were certainly part of the movement to bring computers into the home, but they were not the only, nor the first to have envisioned the "connected home" of the twenty-first century.

Late 20th Century Social and Cultural Developments

The United States, as it entered the second decade of the twenty-first century, faced the paradox of power: the enormous economic, military, and technological capacity that allowed it to impose its will on other nations did not extend to an ability to prevent anti-American actions by deeply enraged individuals. Acts of terror became a constant threat—with September 11, 2001 delivering the appalling blow of a foreign-orchestrated terror attack on our soil. In response, Congress gave the president sweeping powers; the Patriot Act and new Department of Homeland Security, the military response in Afghanistan, and continued hunt for the Al-Qaeda network, and the war with Iraq have all come in the aftermath of the events of September 2001.

Domestic Issues

In 2012, the chief domestic issues that the United States faces are the economy, financial reform, housing reform, environmental disasters such as the oil spill in the Gulf of Mexico, and health care reform.

Current issues:

Abortion: Debate centers on the immorality of abortion versus the immorality of not providing for unwanted children. The idea of a "woman's right to choose" has sparked controversy and discussion. Currently some religious groups and the Republican Party have adopted a virulent anti-abortion/"pro-life" stance; however, there are Republicans who favor "pro-choice" just as there are Democrats who support the "pro-life" position.

College Costs: Rising college costs and the inability of middle-class Americans to pay for them has ignited discussion about where this will eventually lead. With the current state of the economy and the inability of new graduates to find jobs that pay enough for them to pay off college loans, the nation is facing the prospect of a declining percentage of college graduates among its adult population.

Credit Crisis: Tied to the economic downturn in 2009, the idea of how credit is granted, how much, and what goes into making those decisions remains a chief concern among government, financial, and consumer advocate institutions. **President George W. Bush's** administration pushed through the Temporary Aid to Reform Program (TARP) just before leaving office in 2009. TARP saved many large banks, but, midway through his presidency, **President Barack Obama** was facing an increasingly angry public as unemployment continued and Americans were unable to solve their personal credit crises because the banks have tightened credit. As of 2011 the housing market flucuated, although there was a decrease in the number of home foreclosures.

Energy: Since the 1973–1974 Arab oil embargo, production of alternative sources of energy has increased, albeit slowly. With conflict continuing to broil between the United States and oil producing countries, the United States has become more concerned about finding alternative sources of oil and energy. Before the Gulf of Mexico oil spill in 2010, many were pushing for an extension of off-shore drilling rights. It remains to be seen what long-term effect the spill will have on energy policy.

Same-Sex Marriage: States have begun to pass legislation allowing for marriage or civil unions between two people of the same sex. Debate continues to rage that crosses traditional Republican/Democrat lines about the legality and morality of it.

Gun Control: Concerns about the proliferation of guns, easy access to buying them at gun shows, permits to conceal these weapons, who should not be permitted to buy them, and training associated with gun ownership continue to be questions that are debated, particularly in the West.

Health Care: Escalating health-care costs, reluctance of insurance companies to cover procedures, and the lack of health care for everyone was a primary focus for President Obama. Debate raged over whether or not his plan would worsen the system, make things better, or did not go far enough, consuming American society during the first year and a half of his administration.

Immigration: Arizona passed controversial anti-immigration laws, in the spring of 2010. The laws made many, including federal officials, uncomfortable. Immigration remains a prime issue in the United States. The same sort of fears expressed during the height of the immigration boom in the late-nineteenth/early twentieth-centuries continue to reveal themselves. Claims of racism, fairly or not, follow anti-immigration supporters.

Poverty in the United States: As the economy struggled to recover from the Great Recession, the gap between rich and poor, which had been increasing in the first decade of the new century, continued to widen. All of the issues attendant to the poor—housing, health care, and schooling, for example—will receive new focus. Faith-based initiatives as a way to cope with the increase in poverty will surely provide one avenue of help.

Public Education: Debate continues over the old, unfunded mandates prescribed in the *No Child Left Behind Act*. Opponents of the measure claim that testing destroys good schools, means little to students, and punishes schools that tend to be over-crowded and poorly-funded and who thus have no avenue for relief available to them. Proponents argue that holding teachers and administrators more accountable, via test results, is necessary in order to improve public education.

Social Security: The availability of social security for this and future generations remains in doubt, particularly with the escalating financial crises, increasing numbers of retirees who are also living longer, and mixed public support for privatizing the nearly 80-year-old public safety net for the elderly.

Stem Cell Research: Conservatives and Liberals continue to debate the viability, morality, and the ethical questions associated with using stem cells for research and/or medical treatment.

Tax Cuts: Concerns about whether or not to eliminate President George W. Bush's tax breaks for the wealthy and the impracticality and fairness of the Alternative Minimum Tax have also taken center stage in the midst of the current economic crisis.

Foreign Issues

Afghanistan: President Obama is trying to refocus American efforts in Afghanistan to eliminate the sources of terror that facilitated the 9/11 attacks.

China: Issues of developing a balance of trade with China continue to dominate economic issues. Moreover, the Chinese stake in the U.S. financial system seems to remain a concern to many in the U.S. financial industry.

Climate Change: Coming up with a worldwide agreement on whether or not climate change is occurring and what we should do about it remains a topic of debate. The United States, in particular, is seen by the world community as being unwilling to help out. The new administration has opened the doors to discussions about global warming and climate change.

Cuba: With the rise of Fidel Castro's brother, Raul, debate about whether or not to resume trade and diplomatic relations between the United States and Cuba continues. The Cuban-American lobby is particularly interested in this issue.

Darfur: The role of the United States toward helping victims of genocide in areas not apparently of high economic or military interest to the United States has been a concern among activists who have claimed U.S. racism and self-interest as the reasons the United States has not become more involved.

Economic Development: Policy about when and how to help out which foreign countries, particularly in this climate of economic difficulty in the United States, which has its own infrastructure issues, remains a concern among foreign aid workers.

European Union: Maintaining good relations with Europeans who are already questioning the wisdom of U.S. foreign policy since 9/11 remains a bit of a thorny issue.

Guantanamo: Early in 2011, President Obama, withdrew an Election promise to close Guantanamo Bay detention camp due to lack of congressional support for federal trials for certain prisioners. U.S. treatment of prisoners continues to ignite debate as U.S. policies there and abroad have fueled criticism.

Iran: Iran continues to be ruled by fundamentalist Islamists more than 30 years after the revolution that ousted the U.S.-backed Shah Reza Pahlavi. Although President Reagan allowed the secret sale of arms to Iran during its war with Iraq in the 1980s, tensions between the Americans and the Iranians have remained high for decades. Currently, Iran's refusal to eliminate their nuclear program has resulted in American-led efforts at the United Nations and elsewhere to force Iran to stop.

Iraq: Nearly a decade after invading Iraq believing that its dictator, Saddam Hussein, was hiding weapons of mass destruction, the United States continues to try to figure out how, when, where, and under what conditions it could pull all of its troops out of Iraq. A drawdown of combat troops has begun, but about 50,000 troops are scheduled to remain in Iraq for the time being. The issues there are complicated, and it makes movement in any direction quite difficult.

Israel: Criticism of Israeli treatment of Palestinians has slowly become more of an issue in the United States, with the advent of citizen journalists who can more easily record atrocities there. On the other hand, the U.S. government continues to stress that it is a friend of Israel. The Israeli lobby in the United States is particularly effective in keeping a strong presence and strong media influence. The American Israel Public Affairs Committee (AIPAC) the largest of the lobbying organizations was founded in 1963.

Japan: On March 10, 2011, a deadly 8.9 earthquake spawned a ferocious tsunami that ravaged Japan leaving thousands dead, millions more homeless, and cities and towns flattened. The subsequent nuclear crisis continued to plague Japan as two of its nuclear reactor cores were breached due to the earthquake and tsunami.

North Korea: North Korea has nuclear capabilities; therefore the United States has approached it differently from its approach to other nations in the Middle East which are seeking nuclear capabilities. North Korea has also isolated itself, diplomatically and economically, from most of the world, with the exception of China.

Osama bin Laden: In the ten years since the 9/11 attacks efforts to capture Osama bin Laden had been unsucessful—until May 1, 2011. In an early-morning raid by Navy SEAL and CIA operatives, bin Laden was captured and killed at his compound in Abbottabad, Pakistan. In an effort to stem any protests in the Middle East, bin Laden was buried at sea following a shipboard Muslim service.

Pakistan: Growing anti-Americanism and political instability there has made Pakistan a growing area of concern for the U.S. military. The American raid on a compound 31 miles north of the Pakistani capital of Islamabad which resulted in the death of the Osama bin Laden resulted in even more strained relations between the U.S. and Pakistan. Some American leaders believe some in the Pakistani military establishment must have had knowledge of bin Laden's five-year residency just down the street from the Military Academy in Abbottabad.

Russia: Relations with Russia have waxed and waned over the years. The recent exchange of spies between the two countries may have an effect on relations in the future.

War on Drugs: The U.S. position on the War on Drugs seems to have taken a bit of a backseat to focus on the War on Terrorism.

War on Terror: This continues to dominate U.S. foreign, and even domestic, policy, as not only is the United States embarking on military intervention abroad, but also it has employed reactive policies whenever there is a terrorist attack or foiled attack. For instance, in reaction to the "shoe bomber," Americans now have to take their shoes off and run them through the detectors at airports.

SUGGESTIONS TO HELP YOU STUDY

Make your own timeline of United States history, starting with space for each century: 1400's, 1500's, 1600's, etc. (recognizing, of course, that Native Americans were here for thousands of years before that). Put the events listed in the study topics on your timeline in the correct century; then trace and describe in your own words important trends in cultural, intellectual, social, economic, political, and diplomatic history.

Other trends to identify and describe in your timeline:

- Migration—patterns and effects

- Technology—important developments and their effects

- Urbanization—patterns and effects

- Religions—dominant religions, conflicts with each other and government, influence on society and politics

- The emergence of the United States as a world leader in the areas of military power, industry, finance, and politics

World History

HUMAN SOCIETY TO APPROXIMATELY 3500 BCE

The Appearance of Civilization

Between 6000 and 3000 BCE, humans invented the plow, utilized the wheel, harnessed the wind, discovered how to smelt copper ores, and began to develop accurate solar calendars. Small villages gradually grew into populous cities. The invention of writing in Mesopotamia around 3500 BCE, in combination with heightened refinement in sculpture, architecture, and metal working from about 3000 BCE, marks the beginning of civilization and divides prehistoric from historic times.

DEVELOPMENT OF CITY CIVILIZATIONS AND ANCIENT EMPIRES (CA. 3500 BCE–500 CE)

Mesopotamia

Sumer (4000 to 2000 BCE) included the city of Ur. The *Gilgamesh* is an epic Sumerian poem. The **Sumerians** constructed dikes and reservoirs and established a loose confederation of city-states. They probably invented writing (called "cuneiform" because of its wedge-shaped letters). The Amorites, or Old Babylonians (2000 to 1550

BCE), established a new capital at Babylon, known for its famous Hanging Gardens. **King Hammurabi** (reigned 1792–1750 BCE) promulgated a legal code that called for retributive punishment ("an eye for an eye") and provided that one's social class determined punishment for a crime.

The **Assyrians** (1100–612 BCE) conquered Syria, Palestine, and much of Mesopotamia. They controlled a brutal, militaristic empire. The Chaldeans, or New Babylonians (612–538 BCE), conquered the Assyrian territory, including Jerusalem. In 538 BCE, Cyrus, king of the southern Persians, defeated the Chaldeans. The Persians created a huge empire and constructed a road network. Their religion, Zoroastrianism, promoted worship of a supreme being in the context of a cosmic battle with the forces of evil. After 538 BCE, the peoples of Mesopotamia came under the rule of a series of different empires and dynasties.

Egypt

During the end of the Archaic Period (5000–2685 BCE), Menes, or Narmer, unified Upper and Lower Egypt around 3200 BCE. During the Old Kingdom (2685–2180 BCE), the pharaohs came to be considered living gods. The capital moved to Memphis during the Third Dynasty (ca. 2650 BCE). The pyramids at Giza were built during the Fourth Dynasty (ca. 2613–2494 BCE).

After the Hyksos invasion (1785–1560 BCE), the New Kingdom (1560–1085 BCE) expanded into Nubia and invaded Palestine and Syria, enslaving the Jews. King Amenhotep IV or Akhenaton (reigned c. 1372–1362 BCE) promulgated the idea of a single god, Aton, and closed the temples of all other Gods and Goddesses. His successor, Tutankhamen, reestablished pantheism in Egypt.

In the **Post-Empire Period** (1085–1030 BCE), Egypt came under the successive control of the Assyrians, the Persians, Alexander the Great, and finally, in 30 BCE, the Roman Empire. The Egyptians developed papyrus and made many medical advances. Other peoples would elaborate their ideas of monotheism and the notion of an afterlife.

Palestine and the Hebrews

Phoenicians settled along the present-day coast of Lebanon (Sidon, Tyre, Beirut, Byblos) and established colonies at Carthage and in Spain. They spread Mesopotamian culture through their trade networks.

The **Hebrews** probably moved to Egypt around 1700 BCE and were enslaved about 1500 BCE. The Hebrews fled Egypt under Moses and around 1200 BCE returned to Palestine. Under **King David** (reigned ca. 1012–972 BCE), the Philistines were defeated and a capital established at Jerusalem. Ultimately, Palestine divided into Israel (10 tribes) and Judah (two tribes). The 10 tribes of Israel—also known as the Lost Tribes—disappeared after Assyria conquered Israel in 722 BCE.

The poor and less attractive state of Judah continued until 586 BCE, when the Chaldeans transported the Jews to Chaldea as advisors and slaves (Babylonian captivity). When the Persians conquered Babylon in 539 BCE, the Jews were allowed to return to Palestine. Alexander the Great conquered Palestine in 325 BCE. During the Hellenistic period (323–63 BCE) the Jews were allowed to govern themselves. Under Roman rule, Jewish autonomy was restricted. The Jews revolted in 70 BCE. The Jews also revolted in 132–135 CE. These uprisings led to the Jews' loss of their Holy Land. The Romans quashed the revolt and ordered the dispersion of the Jews. The Jews contributed the ideas of monotheism and humankind's convenant and responsibility to God to lead ethical lives.

Greece

Homer's **Iliad and Odyssey** were poems that dramatized for Ancient Greek civilization ideas like excellence (*arete*), courage, honor, and heroism. Hesiod's *Works and Days* summarized everyday life. His *Theogony* recounted Greek myths. Greek religion was based on their writings.

In the **Archaic Period** (800–500 BCE), Greek life was organized around the polis (city-state). Oligarchs controlled most of the polis until the end of the sixth century, when individuals holding absolute power (tyrants) replaced them. By the end of the sixth century, democratic governments replaced many tyrants.

Sparta, however, developed into an armed camp. Sparta seized control of neighboring Messenia around 750 BCE. To prevent rebellions, every Spartan entered lifetime military service (as hoplites) beginning at age 7. Around 640 BCE, Lycurgus promulgated a constitution. Around 540 BCE, Sparta organized the Peloponnesian League.

Athens was the principal city of Attica. Draco (ca. 621 BCE) first codified Athenian law. His Draconian Code was known for its harshness. Solon (ca. 630–560 BCE) reformed the laws in 594 BCE. He enfranchised the lower classes and gave the state responsibility for administering justice. Growing indebtedness of small farmers and insufficient land strengthened the nobles. Peisistratus (ca. 605–527 BCE) seized control and governed as a tyrant. In 527 BCE, Cleisthenes led a reform movement that established the basis of Athens's democratic government, including an annual assembly to identify and exile those considered dangerous to the state.

The Fifth Century (Classical Age)

The fifth century marked the high point of Greek civilization. It opened with the Persian Wars (480–479 BCE) after which Athens organized the Delian League. Pericles (ca. 495–429 BCE) used League money to rebuild Athens, including construction of the Parthenon and other Acropolis buildings. Athens's dominance spurred war with Sparta.

The Peloponnesian War between Athens and Sparta (431–404 BCE) ended with Athens's defeat, but weakened Sparta as well. Sparta fell victim to Thebes, and the other city-states warred amongst themselves until Alexander the Great's conquest. It was his conquest that unified the Greek city-states in the fourth century BCE, the beginning of the Hellenistic Age.

A revolution in philosophy occurred in classical Athens. The Sophists emphasized the individual and his/her attainment of excellence through rhetoric, grammar, music, and mathematics. Socrates (ca. 470–399 BCE) criticized the Sophists' emphasis on rhetoric and emphasized a process of questioning, or dialogues, with his students. Like Socrates, Plato (ca. 428–348 BCE) emphasized ethics. His *Theory of Ideas or Forms* said that what we see is but a dim shadow of the eternal Forms or Ideas. Philosophy should seek to penetrate to the real nature of things. Plato's *Republic* described an ideal state ruled by a philosopher king.

Aristotle (ca. 384–322 BCE) was Plato's pupil. He criticized Plato, arguing that ideas or forms did not exist outside of things. He contended that it was necessary to examine four factors in treating any object: its matter, its form, its cause of origin, and its end or purpose.

Greek art emphasized the individual. In architecture, the Greeks developed the Doric and Ionian forms. Euripides (484–406 BCE) is often considered the most modern tragedian because he was so psychologically minded. In comedy, Aristophanes (ca. 450–

388 BCE) was a pioneer who used political themes. The New Comedy, exemplified by Menander (ca. 342–292 BCE), concentrated on domestic and individual themes.

The Greeks were the first to develop the study of history. They were skeptical and critical and banished myth from their works. Herodotus (ca. 484–424 BCE), called the "father of history," wrote *History of the Persian War*. Thucydides (ca. 460–400 BCE) wrote *History of the Peloponnesian War*.

The Hellenistic Age and Macedonia

The Macedonians were a Greek people who were considered semibarbaric by their southern Greek relatives. They never developed a city-state system and had more territory and people than any of the polis.

In 359 BCE Philip II (382–336 BCE) became king. To finance his state and secure a seaport, he conquered several city-states. In 338 BCE, Athens fell. In 336 BCE, Philip was assassinated.

Philip's son, Alexander the Great (356–323 BCE), killed or exiled rival claimants to his father's throne. He established an empire that included Syria and Persia and extended to the Indus River Valley. At the time of his death, Alexander had established 70 cities and created a vast trading network. With no succession plan, Alexander's realm was divided among three of his generals. By 30 BCE, all of the successor states had fallen to Rome.

Rome

The traditional founding date for Rome is 753 BCE. Between 800 and 500 BCE, Greek tribes colonized southern Italy, bringing their alphabet and religious practices to Roman tribes. In the sixth and seventh centuries, the Etruscans expanded southward and conquered Rome.

Late in the sixth century (the traditional date is 509 BCE), the Romans expelled the Etruscans and established an aristocratically based republic in place of the monarchy. In the early Republic, power was in the hands of the patricians (wealthy landowners). A Senate composed of patricians governed. The Senate elected two consuls to serve one-year terms. Roman executives had great power (the imperium). They were assisted by two quaestors, who managed economic affairs.

Rome's expansion and contact with Greek culture disrupted the traditional agrarian basis of life. Tiberius Gracchus (163–133 BCE) and Gaius Gracchus (153–121 BCE) led the People's party (or *Populares*). They called for land reform and lower grain prices to help small farmers. They were opposed by the *Optimates* (best men). Tiberius was assassinated. Gaius continued his work, assisted by the *Equestrians*. After several years of struggle, Gaius committed suicide.

Power passed into the hands of military leaders for the next 80 years. During the 70s and 60s, Pompey (106–48 BCE) and Julius Caesar (100–44 BCE) emerged as the most powerful men. In 73 BCE, Spartacus led a slave rebellion, which General Crassus suppressed.

In 60 BCE, Caesar convinced Pompey and Crassus (ca. 115–53 BCE) to form the First Triumvirate. When Crassus died, Caesar and Pompey fought for leadership. In 49 BCE, Caesar crossed the Rubicon, the stream separating his province from Italy, and a civil war followed. In 47 BCE, the Senate proclaimed Caesar as dictator, and later named him consul for life. Brutus and Cassius believed that Caesar had destroyed the Republic. They formed a conspiracy, and on March 15, 44 BCE (the Ides of March), Caesar was assassinated in the Roman Forum. His 18-year-old nephew and adopted son, Octavian, succeeded him. Caesar reformed the tax code and eased burdens on debtors. He instituted the Julian calendar, in use until 1582. The Assembly under Caesar had little power.

In literature and philosophy, Plautus (254–184 BCE) wrote Greek-style comedy. Terence, a slave (ca. 186–159 BCE), wrote comedies in the tradition of Menander. Catullus (87–54 BCE) was the most famous lyric poet. Lucretius's (ca. 94–54 BCE) *Order of Things* described Epicurean atomic metaphysics, while arguing against the immortality of the soul. Cicero (106–43 BCE), the great orator and stylist, defended the Stoic concept of natural law. He was an important advocate of the Roman Republic and an opponent of Caesar. His *Orations* described Roman life. Roman religion was family centered and more civic-minded than Greek religion.

DISRUPTION AND REVERSAL (CA. 500–1400 CE)

The Roman Empire

After a period of struggle, Octavian (63 BCE–14 CE), named as Caesar's heir, gained absolute control while maintaining the appearance of a republic. When he offered to relinquish his power in 27 BCE, the Senate gave him a vote of confidence and a new title, "Augustus." Augustus ruled for 44 years (31 BCE–14 CE). He introduced many reforms, including new coinage, new tax collection, fire and police protection, and land for settlers in the provinces.

Between 27 BCE and 180 CE, Rome's greatest cultural achievements occurred under the Pax Romana. The period between 27 BCE and 14 CE is called the **Augustan Age**. Vergil (70–19 BCE) wrote the *Aeneid,* an account of Rome's rise. Horace (65–8 BCE) wrote the lyric *Odes*. Ovid (43 BCE–18 CE) published the *Ars Amatoria,* a guide to seduction, and the *Metamorphoses,* about Greek mythology. Livy (57 BCE–17 CE) wrote a narrative history of Rome based on earlier accounts.

The **Silver Age** lasted from 14–180 CE Writings in this period were less optimistic. Seneca (5 BCE to 65 CE) espoused Stoicism in his tragedies and satires. Juvenal (50–127 CE) wrote satire, Plutarch's (46–120 CE) *Parallel Lives* portrayed Greek and Roman leaders, and Tacitus (55–120 CE) criticized the follies of his era in his histories.

Stoicism was the dominant philosophy of the era. Epictetus (ca. 60–120 CE), a slave, and Emperor Marcus Aurelius were its chief exponents. In law, Rome made a lasting contribution. It distinguished three orders of law: civil law (*jus civile*), which applied to Rome's citizens, law of the people (*jus gentium*), which merged Roman law with the laws of other peoples of the Empire, and natural law (*jus naturale*), governed by reason.

After the **Pax Romana**, the third century was a period of great tumult for Rome. Civil war was nearly endemic in the third century. Between 235 and 284 CE, 26 "barracks emperors" governed, taxing the population heavily to pay for the Empire's defense.

Rome's frontiers were attacked constantly by barbarians. Emperors Diocletian (reigned 285–305 CE) and Constantine (reigned 306–337 CE) tried to stem Rome's decline. Diocletian divided the Empire into four parts and moved the capital to Nicomedia in Asia Minor. Constantine moved the capital to Constantinople.

Some historians argue that the rise of Christianity was an important factor in Rome's decline. Jesus was born around 4 BCE, and began preaching and ministering to the poor and sick at the age of 30. The Gospels provide the fullest account of his life and teachings. Saul of Tarsus, or Paul (10–67 CE), transformed Christianity from a small sect of Jews who believed Jesus was the Messiah into a world religion. Paul won followers through his missionary work. He also shifted the focus from the early followers' belief in Jesus' imminent return to concentrate on personal salvation. His *Epistles* (letters to Christian communities) laid the basis for the religion's organization and sacraments.

The **Pax Romana** allowed Christians to move freely through the Empire. In the Age of Anxiety, many Romans felt confused and alienated, and thus drawn to the new religion. And unlike other mystery religions, Christianity included women. By the first century, the new religion had spread throughout the Empire.

Around 312 CE, Emperor Constantine converted to Christianity and ordered toleration in the Edict of Milan (ca. 313 CE). In 391 CE, Emperor Theodosius I (reigned 371–395 CE) proclaimed Christianity as the Empire's official religion. By the second century, the church hierarchy had developed. Eventually, the Bishop of Rome came to have preeminence, based on the interpretation that Jesus had chosen Peter as his successor.

The Byzantine Empire

Emperor Theodosius II (reigned 408–450 CE) divided his empire between his sons, one ruling the East, the other the West. After the Vandals sacked Rome in 455 CE, Constantinople was the undisputed leading city of the Empire.

In 527 CE, Justinian I (483–565 CE) became emperor in the East and reigned with his controversial wife Theodora until 565 CE. The Nika revolt broke out in 532 CE and demolished the city. It was crushed by General Belisarius in 537 CE, after 30,000 had died in the uprising.

The Crusaders further weakened the state. In 1204 CE, Venice contracted to transport the Crusaders to the Near East in return for the Crusaders capturing and looting Constantinople. The Byzantines were defeated in 1204 CE. Though they drove out the Crusaders in 1261 CE, the empire never regained its former power. In 1453 CE, Constantinople fell to the Ottoman Turks.

Islamic Civilization in the Middle Ages

Mohammed was born about 570 CE and received a revelation from the Angel Gabriel around 610 CE. In 630 CE, Mohammed marched into Mecca. The **Sharia** (code of law and theology) outlines five pillars of faith for Muslims to observe. First is the belief that there is one God and that Mohammed is his prophet. The faithful must pray five times a day, perform charitable acts, fast from sunrise to sunset during the holy month of Ramadan, and make a *haj*, or pilgrimage, to Mecca. The **Koran**, which consists of 114 *suras* (verses), contains Mohammed's teachings. *Mullahs* (teachers) occupy positions of authority, but Islam did not develop a hierarchical system comparable to that of Christianity.

A leadership struggle developed after Mohammed's death. His father-in-law, Abu Bakr (573–634 CE), succeeded as caliph (successor to the prophet) and governed for two years, until his death in 634 CE. Omar succeeded him. Between 634 and 642 CE, Omar established the Islamic Empire.

The Omayyad caliphs, based in Damascus, governed from 661–750 CE. They called themselves Shiites and believed they were Mohammed's true successors. (Most Muslims were Sunnites, from *sunna*, oral traditions about the prophet.) They conquered Spain by 730 CE and advanced into France until they were stopped by Charles Martel (ca. 688–741 CE) in 732 CE at Poitiers and Tours. Muslim armies penetrated India and China. They transformed Damascus into a cultural center and were exposed to Hellenistic culture from the nearby Byzantine Empire.

The Abbasid caliphs ruled from 750–1258 CE. They moved the capital to Baghdad and treated Arab and non-Arab Muslims as equals. Islam assumed a more Persian character under their reign. In the late tenth century, the empire began to disintegrate. In 1055 CE, the Seljuk Turks captured Baghdad, allowing the Abbasids to rule as figureheads. Genghis Khan (ca. 1162–1227 CE) and his army invaded the Abbasids. In 1258 CE, they seized Baghdad and murdered the last caliph.

Feudalism in Japan

Feudalism in Japan began with the arrival of mounted nomadic warriors from throughout Asia during the **Kofun Era** (300–710). Some members of these nomadic groups formed an elite class and became part of the court aristocracy in the capital city of Kyoto, in western Japan. During the **Heian Era** (794–1185), a hereditary military aristocracy arose in the Japanese provinces, and by the late Heian Era, many of these formerly nomadic warriors had established themselves as independent land owners, or as managers of landed estates *(shoen)* owned by Kyoto aristocrats. These aristocrats depended on these warriors to defend their *shoen,* and in response to this need, the warriors organized into small groups called *bushidan.*

As the years passed, these warrior clans grew larger, and alliances formed among them, led by imperial descendants who moved from the capital to the provinces. After victory in the Taira-**Minamoto War** (1180–1105), Minamoto no Yoritomo forced the emperor to award him the title of *shogun,* which is short for "barbarian subduing generalissimo." He used this power to found the **Kamakura Shogunate** which survived for 148 years. Under the Kamakura Shogunate, many vassals were appointed to the position of *jitro* or land steward, or the position of provincial governors *(shugo)* to act as liaisons between the Kamakura government and local vassals.

By the fourteenth century, the *shugo* had augmented their power enough to become a threat to the Kamakura, and in 1333 lead a rebellion that overthrew the shogunate. Under the Ashikaga Shogunate, the office of *shogu* was made hereditary, and its powers were greatly extended. These new *shogu* turned their vassals into aggressive local warriors called *kokujin,* or *jizamurai.* Following this move, the Ashikaga shoguns lost a great deal of their power to political fragmentation, which eventually lead to the Warring States Era (1467–1568).

By the middle of the sixteenth century, the feudal system had evolved considerably. At the center of this highly evolved system was the *daimyo,* a local feudal lord who ruled over one of the many autonomous domains.

Far reaching alliances of *daimyo* were forged under the Tokugawa Shogunate, the final and most unified of the three shogunates. Under the Tokugawa, the *daimyo* were considered direct vassals of the shoguns, and were kept under strict control. The warriors were gradually transformed into scholars and bureaucrats under the *bushido,* or code of chivalry, and the principles of Neo-Confucianism. A merchant class, or *chonin,* gained wealth as the samurai class began to lose power, and the feudal system effectively ended when power was returned to the emperor under the Meji Restoration of 1868, when all special privileges of the samurai class were abolished.

Chinese and Indian Empires

The Harappan or Indus civilization was confined to the Indus basin. Around 1500 BCE, during the so-called Vedic age, India came to be ruled by the Indo-Aryans, a mainly pastoral people with a speech closely related to the major languages of Europe.

The religion of the Harappan peoples revolved around the god Siva, the belief in reincarnation, in a condition of "liberation" beyond the cycle of birth and death, and in the technique of mental concentration which later came to be called *yoga*. The religion of the Indo-Aryans was based on a pantheon of gods of a rather worldly type, and sacrifices were offered to them. The traditional hymns that accompanied them were the Vedas, which form the basic scriptures for the religion of Hinduism. Indian society also came to be based on a *caste* system.

In the third century BCE, the Indian kingdoms fell under the Mauryan Empire. The grandson of the founder of this empire, named Asoka, opened a new era in the cultural history of India by introducing the Buddhist religion. Buddha had disregarded the Vedic gods and the institutions of caste and had preached a relatively simple ethical religion that had two levels of aspiration—a monastic life of renunciation of the world and a high, but not too difficult morality for the layman. The two religions of Hinduism and Buddhism flourished together for centuries in a tolerant rivalry, and in the end Buddhism virtually disappeared from India by the thirteenth century CE.

Chinese civilization originated in the Yellow River Valley and gradually extended to the southern regions. Three dynasties ruled early China: the Xia or Hsia, the Shang (c. 1500 to 1122 BCE), and the Zhou (c. 1122 to 211 BCE). After the Zhous fell, China welcomed the teachings of Confucius, as warfare between states and philosophical speculation created circumstances ripe for such teachings. Confucius made the good order of society depend on an ethical ruler, who should be advised by scholar-moralists like Confucius himself.

In contrast to the Confucians, the Taoists professed a kind of anarchism; the best kind of government was none at all. The wise man did not concern himself with political affairs, but by means of mystical contemplation identified himself with the forces of nature.

Sub-Saharan Kingdoms and Cultures

The Nok were a people that lived in the area now known as Nigeria. Artifacts indicate that they were peaceful farmers who built small communities consisting of houses of wattle and daub.

The people referred to as the Ghana lived about 500 miles from what we now call Ghana. The Ghana peoples traded with Berber merchants. The Ghana offered these traders gold from deposits found in the south of their territory. In the 1200s the Mali kingdom conquered Ghana and the civilization mysteriously disappeared.

The people known as the Mali lived in a huge kingdom that lay mostly on the savanna bordering the Sahara Desert. The city of Timbuktu, built in the thirteenth century, was a thriving city of culture where traders visited stone houses, shops, libraries, and mosques.

The Songhai lived near the Niger River and gained their independence from the Mali in the early 1400s. The major growth of the empire came after 1464 CE under the leadership of Sunni Ali, who devoted his reign to warfare and expansion of the empire.

The Bantu peoples, numbering about 100,000,000 lived across large sections of Africa. Bantu societies lived in tiny chiefdoms, starting in the third millennium BCE, and each group developed its own version of the original Bantu language.

Civilizations of the Americas

The great civilizations of early America were agricultural, and foremost of these was the Mayan, in Yucatan, Guatemala, and eastern Honduras.

Mayan history is divided into three parts, the Old Empire, Middle Period, and the New Empire. By the time the Spanish conquerors arrived, most of the Mayan religious centers had been abandoned and their civilization had deteriorated seriously, perhaps due to the wide gulf between the majority of the people, who were peasants, and the priests and nobles.

Farther north, in Mexico, there arose a series of advanced cultures that derived much of their substance from the Maya. Such peoples as the Zapotecs, Totonacs, Olmecs, and Toltecs evolved a high level of civilization. By 500 BCE agricultural peoples had begun to use a ceremonial calendar and had built stone pyramids on which they performed religious observances.

The Aztecs then took over Mexican culture. A major feature of their culture was human sacrifice in repeated propitiation of their chief god. Aztec government was centralized, with an elective king and a large army. Like their predecessors, the Aztecs were skilled builders and engineers, accomplished astronomers and mathematicians.

Andean civilization was characterized by the evolution of beautifully made pottery, intricate fabrics, and flat-topped mounds called *huacas*.

The Incas, a tribe from the interior of South America who termed themselves "Children of the Sun," controlled an area stretching from Ecuador to central Chile. They were Sun worshippers, and believed themselves to be the vice regent on earth of the sun god; the Inca were all powerful; every person's place in society was fixed and immutable; the state and the army were supreme. They were at the apex of their power just before the Spanish conquest.

In the southwestern U.S. and northern Mexico, meanwhile, two ancient cultures are noteworthy. The Anasazi, who lived in the plateau region extending through today's northern Arizona and New Mexico, southern Utah and Colorado, developed adobe architecture, worked the land extensively, had a highly developed system of irrigation, and made cloth and baskets. Their time ran approximately from 100 to 1300 CE. The Hohokam, roughly contemporaneous to the Anasazi, built separate stone and timber houses around central plazas in the desert Southwest.

Europe in Antiquity

Between 486 and 1050 CE, Europe acquired a distinctive identity. In antiquity, much of Europe was occupied by Germanic tribes.

Nomadic tribes from the central Asian steppes invaded Europe and pushed Germanic tribes into conflict with the Roman Empire. Ultimately, in 410 CE, the Visigoths sacked Rome, followed by the Vandals in 455 CE. In 476 CE, the Ostrogoth king forced the boy emperor Romulus Augustulus to abdicate, ending the empire in the West.

The Frankish Kingdom was the most important medieval Germanic state. Under Clovis I (reigned 481–511 CE), the Franks conquered France and the Gauls in 486 CE. Clovis converted to Christianity and founded the Merovingian dynasty.

Pepin's son, known as Charles the Great or Charlemagne (reigned 768–814 CE), founded the Carolingian dynasty. In 800 CE, Pope Leo III named Charlemagne Emperor of the Holy Roman Empire. In the Treaty of Aix-la-Chapelle (812 CE), the Byzantine emperor recognized Charles's authority in the West.

The Holy Roman Empire was intended to reestablish the Roman Empire in the West. Charles vested authority in 200 counts, who were each in charge of a county. Charles's son, Louis the Pious (reigned 814–840 CE), succeeded him. On Louis's death, his three sons vied for control of the Empire. The three eventually signed the Treaty of Verdun in 843 CE This gave Charles the Western Kingdom (France), Louis the Eastern Kingdom (Germany), and Lothair the Middle Kingdom, a narrow strip of land running from the North Sea to the Mediterranean.

In the ninth and tenth centuries, Europe was threatened by attacks from the Vikings in the north, the Muslims in the south, and the Magyars in the east. Under the leadership of William the Conqueror (reigned 1066–1087), the Normans conquered England in 1066 CE (Battle of Hastings).

Rome's collapse had ushered in the decline of cities, a reversion to a barter economy from a money economy, and a fall in agricultural productivity with a shift to subsistence agriculture.

Manorialism and feudalism developed in this period. Manorialism refers to the economic system in which large estates, granted by the king to nobles, strove for self-sufficiency. Large manors might incorporate several villages. The lands surrounding the villages were usually divided into long strips, with common land in-between. Ownership was divided among the lord and his serfs (also called villeins).

Feudalism describes the decentralized political system of personal ties and obligations that bound vassals to their lords. The nature of feudalism varied in different areas and changed over time. But at its base were serfs—peasants who were bound to the land. They worked on the demesne, or lord's property, three or four days a week in return for the right to work their own land. In difficult times, the nobles were supposed to provide for the serfs.

The church was the only institution to survive the Germanic invasions intact. The power of the popes grew in this period. Gregory I (reigned 590–604 CE) was the first member of a monastic order to rise to the papacy. He advanced the ideas of penance and purgatory. He centralized church administration and was the first pope to rule as the secular head of Rome. Monasteries preserved the few remnants of antiquity that survived the decline.

The High Middle Ages (1050–1300)

The year 1050 CE marked the beginning of the High Middle Ages. Europe was poised to emerge from five centuries of decline. Between 1000 and 1350 CE, the population grew from 38 million to 75 million. Agricultural productivity grew, aided by new technologies, such as heavy plows, and a slight temperature rise, which produced a longer growing season. Horses were introduced into agriculture in this period, and the three-field system replaced the two-field system.

Enfranchisement, or freeing of serfs, grew in this period, and many other serfs simply fled their manors for the new lands.

The Holy Roman Empire

Charlemagne's grandson, Louis the German, became Holy Roman Emperor under the Treaty of Verdun. Under the weak leadership of his descendants, the dukes in Saxony, Franconia, Swabia, Bavaria, and the Lorraine eroded Carolingian power. The last Carolingian died in 911 CE. The German dukes elected the leader of Franconia to lead the German lands. He was replaced in 919 CE by the Saxon dynasty, which ruled until 1024 CE. Otto became Holy Roman Emperor in 962 CE. His descendants governed the Empire until 1024 CE, when the Franconian dynasty assumed power, reigning until 1125 CE. When the Franconian line died out in 1125 CE, the Hohenstaufen family (Conrad III, reigned 1138–1152 CE) won power over a contending family. The Hapsburg line gained control of the Empire in 1273 CE.

The Romans abandoned their last outpost in England in the fourth century. Alfred the Great (ca. 849–899 CE) defeated the Danes who had begun invading during the previous century in 878 CE. In 959 CE, Edgar the Peaceable (reigned 959–975 CE) became the first king of all England.

William (reigned 1066–1087 CE) stripped the Anglo-Saxon nobility of its privileges and instituted feudalism. He ordered a survey of all property of the realm, which was recorded in the *Domesday Book* (1086 CE).

In 1215 CE, the English barons forced John I to sign the Magna Carta Libertatum, acknowledging their "ancient" privileges. The Magna Carta established the principle of a limited English monarchy. Henry III reigned from 1216–1272 CE. In 1272 CE, Edward I became king. His need for revenue led him to convene a parliament of English nobles, which would act as a check upon royal power.

In 710 CE, the Muslims conquered Spain from the Visigoths. Under the Muslims, Spain enjoyed a stable, prosperous government. The caliphate of Córdoba became a center of scientific and intellectual activity. Internal dissent caused the collapse of Córdoba and the division of Spain into more than 20 Muslim states in 1031 CE.

The Reconquista (1085–1340 CE) wrested control from the Muslims. Rodrigo Diaz de Bivar, known as El Cid (ca. 1043–1099 CE), was the most famous of its knights. The fall of Córdoba in 1234 CE completed the Reconquista, except for the small state of Granada.

Most of Russia and Eastern Europe was never under Rome's control, and it was cut off from Western influence by the Germanic invasions. Poland converted to Christianity in the tenth century, and after 1025 CE was dependent on the Holy Roman Empire. In the twelfth and thirteenth centuries, powerful nobles divided control of the country.

In Russia, Vladimir I converted to Orthodox Christianity in 988 CE. He established the basis of Kievian Russia. After 1054 CE, Russia broke into competing principalities. The Mongols (Tatars) invaded in 1221 CE, completing their conquest in 1245 CE, and cutting Russia's contact with the West for almost a century.

The Crusades were an attempt to liberate the Holy Land from infidels. There were seven major crusades between 1096 and 1300 CE. Urban II called Christians to the First Crusade (1096–1099 CE) with the promise of a plenary indulgence (exemption from punishment in purgatory). Younger sons who would not inherit their fathers' lands were also attracted. The Crusades helped to renew interest in the ancient world. But thousands of Jews and Muslims were massacred as a result of the Crusades, and relations between Europe and the Byzantine Empire collapsed.

Charlemagne mandated that bishops open schools at each cathedral, and founded a school in his palace for his court. The expansion of trade and the need for clerks and officials who could read and write spurred an 1179 CE requirement that each cathedral set aside enough money to support one teacher.

Scholasticism was an effort to reconcile reason and faith and to instruct Christians on how to make sense of the pagan tradition.

Peter Abelard (ca. 1079–1144 CE) was a controversial proponent of Scholasticism. In *Sic et Non* (Yes and No), Abelard collected statements in the Bible and by church leaders that contradicted each other. Abelard believed that reason could resolve the apparent contradictions between the two authorities, but the church judged his views as heretical.

Thomas Aquinas (ca. 1225–1274 CE) believed that there were two orders of truth. The lower, reason, could demonstrate propositions such as the existence of God, but on a higher level, some of God's mysteries such as the nature of the Trinity must be accepted on faith. Aquinas viewed the universe as a great chain of being, with humans midway on the chain, between the material and the spiritual.

Latin was the language used in universities. But the most vibrant works were in the vernacular. The *chansons de geste* were long epic poems composed between 1050 and 1150 CE Among the most famous are the *Song of Roland,* the *Song of the Nibelungs,* the Icelandic *Eddas,* and *El Cid.*

The fabliaux were short stories, many of which ridiculed the clergy. Boccaccio (1313–1375 CE) and Chaucer (ca. 1342–1400 CE) belonged to this tradition. The work of Dante (1265–1321 CE), the greatest medieval poet, synthesized the pagan and Christian traditions.

In this period, polyphonic (more than one melody at a time) music was introduced. In architecture, Romanesque architecture (rounded arches, thick stone walls, tiny windows) flourished between 1000 and 1150 CE. After 1150 CE, Gothic architecture, which emphasized the use of light, came into vogue.

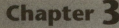

EMERGING GLOBAL INTERACTIONS (CA. 1400–1750)

The Renaissance, Reformation, and the Wars of Religion (1300–1648)

The Late Middle Ages

The Middle Ages fell chronologically between the classical world of Greece and Rome and the modern world. The papacy and monarchs, after exercising much power and influence in the high Middle Ages, were in eclipse after 1300. During the late Middle Ages (1300–1500), all of Europe suffered from the Black Death. While England and France engaged in destructive warfare in northern Europe, in Italy the Renaissance had begun.

Toward the end of the period, monarchs began to assert their power and control. The major struggle, between England and France, was the Hundred Years' War (1337–1453).

The war was fought in France, though the Scots (with French encouragement) invaded northern England. A few major battles occurred—Crécy (1346), Poitiers (1356), Agincourt (1415)—although the fighting consisted largely of sieges and raids. Eventually, the war became one of attrition; the French slowly wore down the English. Technological changes during the war included the use of English longbows and the increasingly expensive plate armor for knights.

Joan of Arc (1412–1431), an illiterate peasant girl who said she heard voices of saints, rallied the French army for several victories. But she was captured by the Burgundians, allies of England, and sold to the English who tried her for heresy (witchcraft). She was burned at the stake at Rouen.

England lost all of its Continental possessions, except Calais. French farmland was devastated, with England and France both expending great sums of money. Population, especially in France, declined. In addition, both countries suffered internal disruption as soldiers plundered and local officials left to fight the war. Trade everywhere was disrupted and England's wool trade with the Low Countries slumped badly. To cover these financial burdens, heavy taxation was inflicted on the peasants.

Because of the war, nationalism grew. Literature also came to express nationalism, as it was written in the language of the people instead of in Latin. Geoffrey Chaucer portrayed a wide spectrum of English life in the *Canterbury Tales*, while François Villon (1431–1463), in his *Grand Testament*, emphasized the ordinary life of the French with humor and emotion.

The New Monarchs

The defeat of the English in the Hundred Years' War and of the duchy of Burgundy in 1477 removed major military threats. Trade was expanded, fostered by the merchant Jacques Coeur (1395–1456). Louis XI (1461–1483) demonstrated ruthlessness in dealing with his nobility as individuals and collectively in the Estates General.

The marriage of Isabella of Castile (reigned 1474–1504) and Ferdinand of Aragon (reigned 1474–1516) created a united Spain. The Muslims were defeated at Granada in 1492. Navarre was conquered in 1512.

The Black Death and Social Problems

The bubonic plague ("Black Death") is a disease affecting the lymph glands. It causes death quickly. Conditions in Europe encouraged the quick spread of disease. There was no urban sanitation, and streets were filled with refuse, excrement, and dead animals. Living conditions were overcrowded, with families often sleeping in one room or one bed. Poor nutrition was rampant. There was little personal cleanliness.

Carried by fleas on rats, the plague was brought from Asia by merchants, and arrived in Europe in 1347. The plague affected all of Europe by 1350 and killed perhaps 25 to 40 percent of the population, with cities suffering more than the countryside.

The Renaissance (1300–1600)

The Renaissance emphasized new learning, including the rediscovery of much classical material, and new art styles. Italian city-states, such as Venice, Milan, Padua, Pisa, and especially Florence, were the home to many Renaissance developments, which were limited to the rich elite.

Literature, Art, and Scholarship

Humanists, as both orators and poets, were inspired by and imitated works of the classical past. The literature was more secular and wide-ranging than that of the Middle Ages.

Dante (1265–1321) was a Florentine writer whose *Divine Comedy*, describing a journey through hell, purgatory, and heaven, shows that reason can only take people so far and that God's grace and revelation must be used.

Petrarch (1304–1374) encouraged the study of ancient Rome, collected and preserved work of ancient writers, and produced much work in the classical literary style.

Boccaccio (1313–1375) wrote *The Decameron*, a collection of short stories in Italian, which were meant to amuse, not edify, the reader.

Artists also broke with the medieval past, in both technique and content. Renaissance art sometimes used religious topics, but often dealt with secular themes or portraits of individuals. Oil paints, chiaroscuro, and linear perspectives produced works of energy in three dimensions.

Leonardo da Vinci (1452–1519) produced numerous works, including *The Last Supper* and *Mona Lisa*. Raphael (1483–1520), a master of Renaissance grace and style, theory and technique, represented these skills in *The School of Athens*. Michelangelo (1475–1564) produced masterpieces in architecture, sculpture (*David*), and painting (the Sistine Chapel ceiling). His work was a bridge to a new, non-Renaissance style called Mannerism.

Renaissance scholars were more practical and secular than medieval ones. Manuscript collections enabled scholars to study the primary sources and to reject all traditions which had been built up since classical times. Also, scholars participated in the lives of their cities as active politicians.

Leonardo Bruni (1370–1444), a civic humanist, served as chancellor of Florence, where he used his rhetorical skills to rouse the citizens against external enemies.

Machiavelli (1469–1527) wrote *The Prince*, which analyzed politics from the standpoint of expedience. His work, amoral in tone, describes how a political leader could obtain and hold power by acting only in his own self-interest.

The Reformation

The Reformation destroyed Western Europe's religious unity and introduced new ideas about the relationships between God, the individual, and society. Its course was greatly influenced by politics and led, in most areas, to the subjection of the church to the political rulers.

Martin Luther (1483–1546)

Martin Luther, to his personal distress, could not reconcile the problem of the sinfulness of the individual with the justice of God. How could a sinful person attain the righteousness necessary to obtain salvation? he wondered. During his studies of the Bible, especially of Romans 1:17, Luther came to believe that personal efforts—good works such as a Christian life and attention to the sacraments of the church—could not "earn" the sinner salvation, but that belief and faith were the only way to obtain grace. By 1515 Luther came to believe that "justification by faith alone" was the road to salvation.

On October 31, 1517, Luther nailed 95 theses, or statements, about indulgences, the cancellation of a sin in return for money, to the door of the Wittenberg church and challenged the practice of selling them. At this time he was seeking to reform the church, not divide it.

In 1519 Luther presented various criticisms of the church and was driven to say that only the Bible, not religious traditions or papal statements, could determine correct religious practices and beliefs. In 1521 Pope Leo X excommunicated Luther for his beliefs.

In 1521 Luther appeared in the city of Worms before a meeting (Diet) of the important figures of the Holy Roman Empire, including the Emperor, Charles V. He was again condemned. At the Diet of Worms Luther made his famous statement about his writings and the basis for them: "Here I stand. I can do no other." After this, Luther could not go back; the break with the pope was permanent.

Frederick III of Saxony, the ruler of the territory in which Luther resided, protected Luther in Wartburg Castle for a year. Frederick never accepted Luther's beliefs but protected him because Luther was his subject. The weak political control of the Holy Roman Emperor contributed to Luther's success in avoiding the pope's and the Emperor's penalties.

Other Reformers

Anabaptist (derived from a Greek word meaning to baptize again) is a name applied to people who rejected the validity of child baptism and believed that such children had to be rebaptized when they became adults. A prominent leader was Menno Simons (1496-1561).

Anabaptists sought to return to the practices of the early Christian church, which was a voluntary association of believers with no connection to the state. Anabaptists adopted pacifism and avoided involvement with the state whenever possible.

In 1536 John Calvin (1509–1564), a Frenchman, arrived in Geneva, a Swiss city-state which had adopted an anti-Catholic position. He left after his first efforts at reform failed. Upon his return in 1540, Geneva became the center of the Reformation. Calvin's *Institutes of the Christian Religion* (1536), a strictly logical analysis of Christianity, had a universal appeal.

Calvin emphasized the doctrine of predestination (God knew who would obtain salvation before those people were born) and believed that church and state should be united. Calvinism triumphed as the majority religion in Scotland, under the leadership of John Knox (ca. 1514–1572), and in the United Provinces of the Netherlands. Puritans in England and New England also accepted Calvinism.

Reform in England

England underwent reforms in a pattern different from the rest of Europe. Personal and political decisions by the rulers determined much of the course of the Reformation there, when in 1533 Henry VIII defied the pope and turned to Archbishop Thomas Cranmer to dissolve his marriage to Catherine of Aragon.

Protestant beliefs and practices made little headway during Henry's reign, as he accepted transubstantiation, enforced celibacy among the clergy, and otherwise made the English church conform to most medieval practices.

Under Henry VIII's son, Edward VI (1547–1553), who succeeded to the throne at age 10, the English church adopted Calvinism. Clergy were allowed to marry, communion by the laity expanded, and images were removed from churches. Doctrine included justification by faith, the denial of transubstantiation, and only two sacraments.

Some reformers wanted to purify (hence "Puritans") the church of its remaining Catholic aspects. The resulting church, Protestant in doctrine and practice but retaining most of the physical possessions, such as buildings, and many of the powers, such as church courts, of the medieval church, was called Anglican.

The Counter Reformation

The Counter Reformation brought changes to the portion of the Western church which retained its allegiance to the pope.

Ignatius of Loyola (1491–1556), a former soldier, founded the Society of Jesus in 1540 to lead the attack on Protestantism. Jesuits became the leaders of the Counter Reformation.

The Sack of Rome in 1527, when soldiers of the Holy Roman Emperor captured and looted Rome, was seen by many as a judgment of God against the lives of the Renaissance popes. In 1534 Paul III became pope and attacked abuses while reasserting papal leadership.

The Wars of Religion (1560–1648)

The period from approximately 1560 to 1648 witnessed continuing warfare, primarily between Protestants and Catholics. In the latter half of the sixteenth century, the fighting was along the Atlantic seaboard between Calvinists and Catholics; after 1600 the warfare spread to Germany, where Calvinists, Lutherans, and Catholics fought.

The Catholic Crusade: The territories of Charles V, the Holy Roman Emperor, were divided in 1556 between Ferdinand, Charles's brother, and Philip II (1556–1598),

Charles's son. Ferdinand received Austria, Hungary, Bohemia, and the title of Holy Roman Emperor. Philip received Spain, Milan, Naples, the Netherlands, and the New World. It was Philip, not the pope, who led the Catholic attack on Protestants.

Spain dominated the Mediterranean following a series of wars led by Philip's half-brother, Don John, against Moslem (largely Turkish) forces. Don John secured the Mediterranean for Christian merchants with a naval victory over the Turks at Lepanto off the coast of Greece in 1571.

Portugal was annexed by Spain in 1580 following the death of the king without a clear successor. This gave Philip the only other large navy of the day as well as Portuguese territories around the globe.

England and Spain

England was ruled by two queens, Mary I (reigned 1553–1558), who married Philip II, and then Elizabeth I (reigned 1558–1603), while three successive kings of France from 1559 to 1589 were influenced by their mother, Catherine de' Medici (1519–1589).

Mary I sought to make England Catholic. She executed many Protestants, earning the name "Bloody Mary" from opponents. Mary married Philip II, king of Spain, and organized her foreign policy around Spanish interests. They had no children.

Elizabeth I, a Protestant, achieved a religious settlement between 1559 and 1563 which left England with a church governed by bishops and practicing Catholic rituals, but maintaining a Calvinist doctrine.

Catholics participated in several rebellions and plots. Mary, Queen of Scots, had fled to England from Scotland in 1568, after alienating the nobles there. In Catholic eyes, she was the legitimate queen of England. Several plots and rebellions to put Mary on the throne led to her execution in 1587. Elizabeth was formally excommunicated by the pope in 1570.

In 1588, as part of his crusade and to stop England from supporting the rebels in the Netherlands, Philip II sent the Armada, a fleet of more than 125 ships, to convey troops from the Netherlands to England as part of a plan to make England Catholic. The Armada was defeated by a combination of superior English naval tactics and a wind which made it impossible for the Spanish to accomplish their goal. A peace treaty between Spain and England was signed in 1604, but England remained an opponent of Spain.

The Thirty Years' War

Calvinism was spreading throughout Germany. The Peace of Augsburg (1555), which settled the disputes between Lutherans and Catholics, had no provision for Calvinists. Lutherans gained more territories through conversions and often took control of previous church-states—a violation of the Peace of Augsburg. A Protestant alliance under the leadership of the Calvinist ruler of the Palatinate opposed a Catholic League led by the ruler of Bavaria. Religious wars were common.

The war brought great destruction to Germany, leading to a decline in population of perhaps one-third, or more, in some areas. Germany remained divided and without a strong government until the nineteenth century.

After 1648, warfare, though often containing religious elements, would not be executed primarily for religious goals.

The Catholic crusade to reunite Europe failed, largely due to the efforts of the Calvinists. The religious distribution of Europe has not changed significantly since 1648.

Nobles, resisting the increasing power of the state, usually dominated the struggle. France, then Germany, fell apart due to the wars. France was reunited in the seventeenth century. Spain began a decline which ended its role as a great power of Europe.

The Growth of the State and the Age of Exploration

In the seventeenth century the political systems of the countries of Europe began dividing into two types, absolutist, and constitutionalist. England, the United Provinces, and Sweden moved towards constitutionalism, while France was adopting absolutist ideas.

Overseas exploration, begun in the fifteenth century, expanded. Governments supported such activity in order to gain wealth and to preempt other countries.

England

The English church was a compromise of Catholic practices and Protestant beliefs and was criticized by both groups. The monarchs, after 1620, gave leadership of the church to men with Arminian beliefs, a modified Calvinist creed that de-emphasized predestination. Opponents to this shift in belief were called Puritans, a term that covered a wide range of beliefs and people. To escape the church in England, many Puritans began moving to the New World, especially Massachusetts.

In financial matters, inflation and Elizabeth's wars left the government short of money. Contemporaries blamed the shortage on the extravagance of the courts of James I and Charles I. The monarchs lacked any substantial source of income and had to obtain the consent of a Parliament to levy a tax.

Parliament met only when the monarch summoned it. Though Parliaments had existed since the Middle Ages, there were long periods of time between parliamentary meetings. Parliaments consisted of nobles and gentry, and a few merchants and lawyers. The men in a Parliament usually wanted the government to remedy grievances as part of the agreement to a tax.

Charles I inherited both the English and Scottish thrones at the death of his father, James I. He claimed a "divine right" theory of absolute authority for himself as king and sought to rule without Parliament. That rule also meant control of the Church of England.

Charles stumbled into wars with both Spain and France during the late 1620s. A series of efforts to raise money for the wars led to confrontations with his opponents in Parliament. A "forced loan" was collected from taxpayers with the promise it would be repaid when a tax was voted by a Parliament. Soldiers were billeted in subjects' houses during the wars. In 1628 Parliament passed the Petition of Right, which declared royal actions involving loans and billeting illegal. Charles ruled without calling a Parliament during the 1630s.

In August 1642 Charles abandoned all hope of negotiating with his opponents and instead declared war against them. Charles's supporters were called Royalists or Cavaliers. His opponents were called Parliamentarians or Roundheads, due to many who wore their hair cut short. This struggle is called the Puritan Revolution, the English Civil War, or the Great Rebellion. Charles was defeated. His opponents had allied with the Scots who still had an army in England. Additionally, the New Model Army, with its general, Oliver Cromwell (1599–1658), was superior to Charles's army, and became a cauldron of radical ideas.

France

The regions of France had long had a large measure of independence, and local parliaments could refuse to enforce royal laws. The centralization of all government proceeded by replacing local authorities with intendants, civil servants who reported to the king.

Henry IV relied on the Duke of Sully (1560–1641), the first of a series of strong ministers in the seventeenth century. Sully and Henry increased the involvement of the state in the economy, acting on a theory known as mercantilism.

Louis XIII reigned from 1610 to 1643, but Cardinal Richelieu became the real power in France. The unique status of the Huguenots was reduced through warfare and the Peace of Alais (1629), when their separate armed cities were eliminated. The nobility was reduced in power through constant attention to the laws and the imprisonment of offenders.

Cardinal Mazarin governed while Louis XIV (reigned 1643–1715) was a minor. During the Fronde, from 1649 to 1652, the nobility controlled Paris, drove Louis XIV and Mazarin from the city, and attempted to run the government. Noble ineffectiveness, the memories of the chaos of the wars of religion, and the overall anarchy convinced most people that a strong king was preferable to a warring nobility.

Louis XIV saw the need to increase royal power and his own glory and dedicated his life to these goals. He steadily pursued a policy of "one king, one law, one faith."

Explorations and Conquests

Portugal. Prince Henry the Navigator (1394–1460) supported exploration of the African coastline, largely in order to seek gold. Bartholomew Dias (1450–1500) rounded the southern tip of Africa in 1487. Vasco de Gama (1460–1524) reached India in 1498 and, after some fighting, soon established trading ports at Goa and Calicut. Albuquerque (1453–1515) helped establish an empire in the Spice Islands after 1510.

Spain. Christopher Columbus (1451–1506), seeking a new route to the (East) Indies, "discovered" the Americas in 1492. Ferdinand Magellan (1480–1521) circumnavigated the globe in 1521–1522. Conquests of the Aztecs by Hernando Cortes (1485–1547), and the Incas by Francisco Pizarro (ca. 1476–1541), enabled the Spanish to send much gold and silver back to Spain.

Other Countries. In the 1490s the Cabots, John (1450–1498) and Sebastian (ca. 1483–1557), explored North America, and after 1570, various Englishmen, including Francis Drake (ca. 1540–1596), fought the Spanish around the world. Jacques Cartier (1491–1557) explored parts of North America for France in 1534.

Samuel de Champlain (1567–1635) and the French explored the St. Lawrence River, seeking furs to trade. The Dutch established settlements at New Amsterdam and in the Hudson River Valley. The Dutch founded trading centers in the East Indies, the West Indies, and southern Africa. Swedes settled on the Delaware River in 1638.

POLITICAL AND INDUSTRIAL REVOLUTIONS, NATIONALISM (1750–1914)

Through the Treaty of Paris (1763), France lost all possessions in North America to Britain. (In 1762 France had ceded to Spain all French claims west of the Mississippi River and New Orleans.)

France entered the French-American Alliance of 1778 in an effort to regain lost prestige in Europe and to weaken her British adversary. In 1779 Spain joined France in the war, hoping to recover Gibraltar and the Floridas.

With the Treaty of Paris (1783) Britain recognized the independence of the United States of America and retroceded the Floridas to Spain. Britain left France no territorial gains by signing a separate and territorially generous treaty with the United States.

Economic Developments

There were several basic assumptions of mercantilism: 1) Wealth is measured in terms of commodities, especially gold and silver, rather than in terms of productivity and income-producing investments; 2) Economic activities should increase the power of the national government in the direction of state controls; 3) Since a favorable balance of trade was important, a nation should purchase as little as possible from nations regarded as enemies. The concept of the mutual advantage of trade was not widely accepted; 4) Colonies existed for the benefit of the mother country, not for any mutual benefit that would be gained by economic development.

Absentee landlords and commercial farms replaced feudal manors, especially in England. Urbanization, increased population, and improvements in trade stimulated the demand for agricultural products.

The steam engine, developed by James Watt between 1765 and 1769, became one of the most significant inventions in human history. It was no longer necessary to locate factories on mountain streams where water wheels were used to supply power. Its portability meant that both steamboats and railroad engines could be built to transport goods across continents. Ocean-going vessels were no longer dependent on winds to power them. At the same time, textile machines revolutionized that industry.

Bourbon France

Louis XIV (reigned 1643–1715) believed in absolute, unquestioned authority. Louis XIV deliberately chose his chief ministers from the middle class in order to keep the aristocracy out of government.

Council orders were transmitted to the provinces by intendants, who supervised all phases of local administration (especially courts, police, and the collection of taxes).

Louis XIV never called the Estates General. His intendants arrested the members of the three provincial estates who criticized royal policy, and the *parlements* were too intimidated by the lack of success of the *Frondes* to offer further resistance.

Control of the peasants, who comprised 95 percent of the French population, was accomplished by numerous means. Some peasants kept as little as 20 percent of their cash crops after paying the landlord, the government, and the Church. Peasants also were subject to the *corvée*, a month's forced labor on the roads. People not at work on the farm were conscripted into the French army or put into workhouses. Finally, rebels were hanged or forced to work as galley slaves.

Under Louis XV (reigned 1715–1774) French people of all classes desired greater popular participation in government and resented the special privileges of the aristocracy.

All nobles were exempt from certain taxes. Many were subsidized with regular pensions from the government. The highest offices of government were reserved for aristocrats. Promotions were based on political connections rather than merit.

There was no uniform code of laws and little justice. The king had arbitrary powers of imprisonment. Government bureaucrats were often petty tyrants, many of them merely serving their own interests. The bureaucracy became virtually a closed class. Vestiges of the feudal and manorial systems taxed peasants excessively compared to other segments of society. The *philosophes* gave expression to these grievances and discontent grew.

Louis XVI (reigned 1774–1792) married Marie Antoinette (1770), daughter of the Austrian Empress Maria Theresa. Louis XVI was honest, conscientious, and sought genuine reforms, but he was indecisive and lacking in determination. One of his first acts was to restore judicial powers to the French parlements. When he sought to impose new taxes on the undertaxed aristocracy, the parlements refused to register the royal decrees. In 1787 he granted toleration and civil rights to French Huguenots (Protestants).

In 1787 the king summoned the Assembly of the Notables, a group of 144 representatives of the nobility and higher clergy. Louis XVI asked them to tax all lands, without regard to privilege of family; to establish provincial assemblies; to allow free trade in grain; and to abolish forced labor on the roads. The Notables refused to accept these reforms and demanded the replacement of certain of the king's ministers.

The climax of the crisis came in 1788 when the king was no longer able to achieve either fiscal reform or new loans. He could not even pay the salaries of government officials. By this time one-half of government revenues went to pay interest on the national debt.

For the first time in 175 years, the king called for a meeting of the Estates General (1789). The Estates General formed itself into the National Assembly, and the French Revolution was under way.

England, Scotland, and Ireland

One of the underlying issues in this conflict was the constitutional issue of the relationship between the King and Parliament. In short, the question was whether England was to have a limited constitutional monarchy, or an absolute monarchy as in France and Prussia.

The theological issue focused on the form of church government England was to have. The episcopal form meant that the King, the **Archbishop of Canterbury**, and the bishops of the church would determine policy, theology, and the form of worship and service in the presbyterian form. Each congregation would have a voice in the life of the church, and a regional group of ministers, or "presbytery," would attempt to ensure "doctrinal purity."

The political implications for representative democracy were present in both issues. That is why most Presbyterians, Puritans, and Congregationalists sided with Parliament and most Anglicans and Catholics sided with the King.

The Parliament in effect bribed the king by granting him a tax grant in exchange for his agreement to the Petition of Right in 1628. It stipulated that no one should pay any tax, gift, loan, or contribution except as provided by an act of Parliament; no one should be imprisoned or detained without due process of law; all were to have the right to the writ of *habeas corpus;* there should be no forced billeting of soldiers in the homes of private citizens; and martial law was not to be declared in England.

In 1629 Charles I dissolved Parliament—for 11 years. Puritan leaders and leaders of the opposition in the House of Commons were imprisoned by the king, some for several years.

The established **Church of England** was the only legal church under Charles I, a Catholic. Archbishop of Canterbury William Laud (1573–1645) sought to enforce the king's policies vigorously. Arminian clergymen were to be tolerated, but Puritan clergymen silenced. Criticism was brutally suppressed. Several dissenters were executed.

The king, however, had no money, no army, and no popular support. He summoned the Parliament to meet in November 1640. With mobs in the street and rumors of an army enroute to London to dissolve Parliament, a bare majority of an under attended House of Commons passed a bill of attainder to execute the Earl of Strafford, one of the king's principal ministers. Fearing mob violence as well as Parliament itself, the king signed the bill and Strafford was executed in 1641. Archbishop William Laud was also arrested and eventually tried and executed in 1645.

The House of Commons passed a series of laws to strengthen its position and protect civil and religious rights. The **Triennial Act** (1641) provided that no more than three years should pass between Parliaments. Another act provided that the current Parliament should not be dissolved without its own consent. Various hated laws, taxes, and institutions were abolished: the Star Chamber, the High Commission, and power of the Privy Council to deal with property rights.

Men began identifying themselves as Cavaliers if they supported the king, or Roundheads if they supported Parliament.

The king withdrew to Hampton Court and sent the queen to France for safety. In March 1642 Charles II went to York, and the English Civil War began. Charles put together a sizeable force with a strong cavalry and moved on London, winning several skirmishes.

Oliver Cromwell (1599–1658) led the parliamentary troops to victory, first with his cavalry, which eventually numbered 1,100, and then as lieutenant general in command of the well-disciplined and well-trained New Model Army. He eventually forced the king to flee.

During the Civil War, under the authority of Parliament, the Westminster Assembly convened to write a statement of faith for the Church of England that was Reformed or Presbyterian in content. Ministers and laymen from both England and Scotland participated for six years and wrote the *Westminster Confession of Faith*, still a vital part of Presbyterian theology.

The army tried Charles Stuart, formerly king of England, and sentenced him to death for treason. After the execution of the king, Parliament abolished the office of king and the House of Lords. The new form of government was to be a Commonwealth, or Free State, governed by the representatives of the people in Parliament. This commonwealth lasted four years, between 1649 and 1653.

Royalists and Presbyterians both opposed Parliament for its lack of broad representation and for regicide. The army was greatly dissatisfied that elections were not held, as one of the promises of the Civil War was popular representation. Surrounded by foreign enemies, the Commonwealth became a military state with a standing army of 44,000. The North American and West Indian colonies were forced to accept the government of the Commonwealth.

When it became clear that Parliament intended to stay in office permanently, Cromwell agreed to serve as Lord Protector from 1653–1659, with a Council of State and a Parliament. The new government permitted religious liberty, except for Catholics and Anglicans.

The new Parliament restored the monarchy from 1660–1688, but the Puritan Revolution clearly showed that the English constitutional system required a limited monarchy. Parliament in 1660 was in a far stronger position in its relationship to the king than it ever had been before.

Two events in 1688 goaded Parliament to action. In May, James reissued the Declaration of Indulgence with the command that it be read on two successive Sundays in every parish church. On June 10, 1688, a son was born to the king and his queen, Mary of Modena. As long as James was childless by his second wife, the throne would go to one of his Protestant daughters, Mary or Anne. The birth of a son, who would be raised Roman Catholic, changed the picture completely.

A group of Whig and Tory leaders, speaking for both houses of Parliament, invited William and Mary to assume the throne of England.

On November 5, 1688, William and his army landed at Torbay in Devon. King James offered many concessions, but it was too late. He finally fled to France. William assumed temporary control of the government and summoned a free Parliament. In February 1689 William and Mary were declared joint sovereigns, with the administration given to William.

The **English Declaration of Rights (1689)** declared the following:

1) The king could not be a Roman Catholic.

2) A standing army in time of peace was illegal without Parliamentary approval.

3) Taxation was illegal without Parliamentary consent.

4) Excessive bail and cruel and unusual punishments were prohibited.

5) Right to trial by jury was guaranteed.

6) Free elections to Parliament would be held.

The Toleration Act (1689) granted the right of public worship to Protestant Nonconformists, but did not permit them to hold office. The Act did not extend liberty to Catholics or Unitarians, but normally they were left alone. The Trials for Treason Act (1696) stated that a person accused of treason should be shown the accusations against him and should have the advice of counsel. They also could not be convicted except upon the testimony of two independent witnesses. Freedom of the press was permitted, but with very strict libel laws.

Control of finances was to be in the hands of the Commons, including military appropriations. There would no longer be uncontrolled grants to the king. Judges were made independent of the Crown. Thus, England declared itself a limited monarchy and a Protestant nation.

Russia Under the Muscovites and the Romanovs

In 1480, Ivan III (1440–1505), "Ivan the Great," put an end to Mongol domination over Russia. Ivan took the title of Caesar (Tsar) as heir of the Eastern Roman Empire (Byzantine Empire). He encouraged the Eastern Orthodox Church and called Moscow the "Third Rome."

Ivan IV (1530–1584), "Ivan the Terrible," grandson of Ivan III, began westernizing Russia. A contemporary of Queen Elizabeth, he welcomed both the English and Dutch and opened new trade routes to Moscow and the Caspian Sea. English merchant adventurers opened Archangel on the White Sea and provided a link with the outer world free from Polish domination.

After a "Time of Troubles" following Ivan's death in 1584, stability returned to Russia in 1613 when the Zemsky Sobor (Estates General representing the Russian Orthodox church, landed gentry, townspeople, and a few peasants) elected Michael Romanov, who ruled as tsar from 1613 to 1645.

Under Michael Romanov, Russia extended its empire to the Pacific. Romanov continued westernization. By the end of the seventeenth century, 20,000 Europeans lived in Russia, developing trade and manufacturing, practicing medicine, and smoking tobacco, while Russians began trimming their beards and wearing Western clothing.

In 1649 three monks were appointed to translate the Bible for the first time into Russian. The Raskolniki (Old Believers) refused to accept any Western innovations or liturgy in the Russian Orthodox church and were severely persecuted as a result.

Peter I (reigned 1682–1725) was one of the most extraordinary people in Russian history. The driving ambitions of Peter the Great's life were to modernize Russia and to compete with the great powers of Europe on equal terms. By the end of Peter's reign, Russia produced more iron than England.

Peter built up the army through conscription and a 25-year term of enlistment. He gave flintlocks and bayonets to his troops instead of the old muskets and pikes. Artillery was improved and discipline enforced. By the end of his reign, Russia had a standing army of 210,000, despite a population of only 13 million. The tsar ruled by decree (*ukase*). Government officials and nobles acted under government authority, but there was no representative body.

All landowners owed lifetime service to the state, either in the army, the civil service, or at court. In return for government service, they received land and serfs to work their fields. Conscription required each village to send recruits for the Russian army. By 1709 Russia manufactured most of its own weapons and had an effective artillery.

After a series of largely ineffective rulers, Catherine II "the Great," (reigned 1762–1796) continued the westernization process begun by Peter the Great. The three partitions of Poland, in 1772, 1793, and 1795 respectively, occurred under Catherine II's rule. Russia also annexed the Crimea and warred with Turkey during her reign.

Italy and the Papacy

Italy in the seventeenth and eighteenth centuries remained merely a geographic expression divided into small kingdoms, most of which were under foreign domination. Unification of Italy into a national state did not occur until the mid-nineteenth century.

The Scientific Revolution and Scientific Societies

Science and religion were not in conflict in the seventeenth and eighteenth centuries. Scientists universally believed they were studying and analyzing God's creation, not an autonomous phenomenon known as "Nature." There was no attempt, as in the nineteenth and twentieth centuries, to secularize science.

For the first time in human history, the eighteenth century saw the appearance of a secular worldview. This became known as **the Age of the Enlightenment**. In the past, some kind of a religious perspective had always been central to Western civilization. The philosophical starting point for the Enlightenment was the belief in the autonomy of man's intellect apart from God. The most basic assumption was faith in reason rather than faith in revelation.

The Enlightenment believed in the existence of God as a rational explanation of the universe and its form; "God" was a deistic Creator who made the universe and then was no longer involved in its mechanistic operation. That mechanistic operation was governed by "natural law."

Rationalists stressed deductive reasoning or mathematical logic as the basis for their epistemology (source of knowledge). They started with "self-evident truths," or postulates, from which they constructed a coherent and logical system of thought.

René Descartes (1596–1650) sought a basis for logic and thought he found it in man's ability to think. "I think; therefore, I am" was his most famous statement.

Benedict de Spinoza (1632–1677) developed a rational pantheism in which he equated God and nature. He denied all free will and ended up with an impersonal, mechanical universe.

Gottfried Wilhelm Leibniz (1646–1716) worked on symbolic logic and calculus, and invented a calculating machine. He, too, had a mechanistic world- and life- view and thought of God as a hypothetical abstraction rather than a persona.

Empiricists stressed inductive observation—the "scientific method"—as the basis for their epistemology.

John Locke (1632–1704) pioneered in the empiricist approach to knowledge and stressed the importance of environment in human development. He classified knowledge as 1) according to reason, 2) contrary to reason or, 3) above reason. Locke thought reason and revelation were both complementary and derived from God.

David Hume (1711–1776) was a Scottish historian and philosopher who began by emphasizing the limitations of human reasoning and later became a dogmatic skeptic.

The Enlightenment believed in a closed system of the universe in which the supernatural was not involved in human life, in contrast to the traditional view of an open system in which God, angels, and devils were very much a part of human life on earth.

The "Counter-Enlightenment" is a comprehensive term encompassing diverse and disparate groups who disagreed with the fundamental assumptions of the Enlightenment and pointed out its weaknesses.

Roman Catholic Jansenism in France argued against the idea of an uninvolved or impersonal God. Hasidism in Eastern European Jewish communities, especially in the 1730s, stressed a joyous religious fervor in direct communion with God.

The French Revolution I (1789–1799)

Radical ideas about society and government were developed during the eighteenth century in response to the success of the "scientific" and "intellectual" revolutions of the preceding two centuries. Armed with new scientific knowledge of the physical universe, as well as new views of the human capacity to detect "truth," social critics assailed existing modes of thought governing political, social, religious, and economic life. Ten years of upheaval in France (1789–1799) further shaped modern ideas and practices.

Napoleon Bonaparte spread some of the revolutionary ideas about the administration of government as he conquered much of Europe. The modern world that came of age in the eighteenth century was characterized by rapid, revolutionary changes which paved the way for economic modernization and political centralization throughout Europe.

Influence of the Enlightenment (c. 1700–1800)

While they came from virtually every country in Europe, most of the famous social activists were French, and France was the center of this intellectual revolution. Voltaire,

Denis Diderot, Baron de Montesquieu, and Jean-Jacques Rousseau were among the more famous philosophers.

The major assumptions of the Enlightenment were as follows:

- Human progress was possible through changes in one's environment; in other words: better people, better societies, better standard of living.

- Humans were free to use reason to reform the evils of society.

- Material improvement would lead to moral improvement.

- Natural science and human reason would discover the meaning of life.

- Laws governing human society would be discovered through application of the scientific method of inquiry.

- Inhuman practices and institutions would be removed from society in a spirit of humanitarianism.

- Human liberty would ensue if individuals became free to choose what reason dictated was good.

The Enlightenment's Effect on Society:

- **Religion.** Deism or "natural religion" rejected traditional Christianity by promoting an impersonal God who did not interfere in the daily lives of the people. The continued discussion of the role of God led to a general skepticism associated with Pierre Bayle (1647–1706), a type of religious skepticism pronounced by David Hume (1711–1776), and a theory of atheism or materialism advocated by Baron d'Holbach (1723–1789).

- **Political Theory.** John Locke (1632–1704) and Jean-Jacques Rousseau (1712–1778) believed that people were capable of governing themselves, either through a political (Locke) or social (Rousseau) contract forming the basis of society. However, most philosophes opposed democracy, preferring a limited monarchy that shared power with the nobility.

- **Economic Theory**. The assault on mercantilist economic theory was begun by the physiocrats in France, who proposed a "laissez-faire" (nongovernmental interference) attitude toward land usage, and culminated in the theory of economic capitalism associated with Adam Smith (1723–1790) and his slogans of free trade, free enterprise, and the law of supply and demand.

- **Education.** Attempting to break away from the strict control of education by the church and state, Jean-Jacques Rousseau advanced the idea of progressive education, where children learn by doing and where self-expression is encouraged. This idea was carried forward by Johann Pestalozzi, Johann Basedow, and Friedrich Fröbel, and influenced a new view of childhood.

- **Psychological Theory**. In the *Essay Concerning Human Understanding* (1690), John Locke offered the theory that all human knowledge was the result of sensory experience, without any preconceived notions.

Causes of the French Revolution

The rising expectations of "enlightened" society were demonstrated by the increased criticism directed toward government inefficiency and corruption, and toward the privileged classes. The clergy (First Estate) and nobility (Second Estate), representing only two percent of the total population of 24 million, were the privileged classes and were essentially tax exempt. The remainder of the population (Third Estate) consisted of the middle class, urban workers, and the mass of peasants, who bore the entire burden of taxation and the imposition of feudal obligations. As economic conditions worsened in the eighteenth century, the French state became poorer, and totally dependent on the poorest and most depressed sections of the economy for support at the very time this tax base had become saturated.

Designed to represent the three estates of France, the Estates General had only met twice, once at its creation in 1302 and again in 1614. When the French parlements insisted that any new taxes must be approved by this body, King Louis XVI reluctantly ordered it to assemble at Versailles by May 1789.

Election fever swept over France for the very first time. The election campaign took place in the midst of the worst subsistence crisis in eighteenth-century France, with widespread grain shortages, poor harvests, and inflated bread prices. Finally, on May 5, 1789, the Estates General met and argued over whether to vote by estate or individual. Each estate was ordered to meet separately and vote as a unit. The Third Estate refused and insisted that the entire assembly stay together.

Phases of Revolution

The National Assembly (1789–1791): After a six-week deadlock over voting methods, representatives of the Third Estate declared themselves the true National Assembly of France (June 17). Defections from the First and Second Estates then caused the king to recognize the National Assembly (June 27) after dissolving the Estates General. At the same time, Louis XVI ordered troops to surround Versailles.

The "Parisian" revolution began at this point. Angry because of food shortages, unemployment, high prices, and fear of military repression, the workers and tradespeople began to arm themselves.

The Legislative Assembly (1791–1792): While the National Assembly had been rather homogeneous in its composition, the new government began to fragment into competing political factions. The most important political clubs were republican groups such as the Jacobins (radical urban) and Girondins (moderate rural), while the *Sans-culottes* (working-class, extremely radical) were a separate faction with an economic agenda.

The National Convention (1792–1795): Meeting for the first time in September 1792, the Convention abolished monarchy and installed republicanism. Louis XVI was charged with treason, found guilty, and executed on January 21, 1793. Later the same year, the queen, Marie Antoinette, met the same fate.

The most notorious event of the French Revolution was the famous "Reign of Terror" (1793–1794), the government's campaign against its internal enemies and counterrevolutionaries.

The Directory (1795–1799): The Constitution of 1795 restricted voting and office holding to property owners. The middle class was in control. It wanted peace in order to gain more wealth and to establish a society in which money and property would become the only requirements for prestige and power. Despite rising inflation and mass public dissatisfaction, the Directory government ignored a growing shift in public opinion. When elections in April 1797 produced a triumph for the royalist right, the results were annulled, and the Directory shed its last pretense of legitimacy.

But the weak and corrupt Directory government managed to hang on for two more years because of great military success. French armies annexed the Austrian Netherlands, the left bank of the Rhine, Nice, and Savoy. The Dutch republic was made a satellite state of France. The greatest military victories were won by Napoleon Bonaparte, who drove the Austrians out of northern Italy and forced them to sign the Treaty of Campo Formio (October 1797), in return for which the Directory government agreed to Bonaparte's scheme to conquer Egypt and threaten English interests in the East.

The French Revolution II: The Era of Napoleon (1799–1815)

Consulate Period, 1799–1804 (Enlightened Reform): The new government was installed on December 25, 1799, with a constitution which concentrated supreme power in the hands of Napoleon. His aim was to govern France by demanding obedience, rewarding ability, and organizing everything in orderly hierarchical fashion. Napoleon's domestic reforms and policies affected every aspect of society.

Empire Period, 1804–1814 (War and Defeat): After being made Consul for Life (1801), Napoleon felt that only through an empire could France retain its strong position in Europe. On December 2, 1804, Napoleon crowned himself emperor of France in Notre Dame Cathedral.

Militarism and Empire Building: Beginning in 1805 Napoleon engaged in constant warfare that placed French troops in enemy capitals from Lisbon and Madrid to Berlin and Moscow, and temporarily gave Napoleon the largest empire since Roman times. Napoleon's Grand Empire consisted of an enlarged France, satellite kingdoms, and coerced allies.

French-ruled peoples viewed Napoleon as a tyrant who repressed and exploited them for France's glory and advantage. Enlightened reformers believed Napoleon had betrayed the ideals of the Revolution. The downfall of Napoleon resulted from his inability to conquer England, economic distress caused by the Continental System (boycott of British goods), the Peninsular War with Spain, the German War of Liberation, and the invasion of Russia. The actual defeat of Napoleon was the result of the Fourth Coalition and the

Battle of Leipzig ("Battle of Nations"). Napoleon was exiled to the island of Elba as a sovereign with an income from France.

After learning of allied disharmony at the Vienna peace talks, Napoleon left Elba and began the Hundred Days by seizing power from the restored French king, Louis XVIII. Napoleon's gamble ended at Waterloo in June 1815. He was exiled as a prisoner of war to the South Atlantic island of St. Helena, where he died in 1821.

The Post-War Settlement: The Congress of Vienna (1814–1815)

The Congress of Vienna met in 1814 and 1815 to redraw the map of Europe after the Napoleonic era, and to provide some way of preserving the future peace of Europe. Europe was spared a general war throughout the remainder of the nineteenth century. But the failure of the statesmen who shaped the future in 1814–1815 to recognize the forces, such as nationalism and liberalism, unleashed by the French Revolution, only postponed the ultimate confrontation between two views of the world—change and accommodation, or maintaining the status quo.

The Vienna settlement was the work of the representatives of the four nations that had done the most to defeat Napoleon: England (Lord Castlereagh), Austria (Prince Klemens Von Metternich), Russia (Tsar Alexander I), and Prussia (Karl Von Hardenberg).

Arrangements to guarantee the enforcement of the status quo as defined by the Vienna settlement included two provisions: The "Holy Alliance" of Tsar Alexander I of Russia, an idealistic and unpractical plan, existed only on paper. No one except Alexander took it seriously. But the "Quadruple Alliance" of Russia, Prussia, Austria, and England provided for concerted action to arrest any threat to the peace or balance of power.

From 1815 to 1822, European international relations were controlled by the series of meetings held by the great powers to monitor and defend the status quo: the Congress of Aix-la-Chapelle (1818), the Congress of Troppau (1820), the Congress of Laibach (1821), and the Congress of Verona (1822).

The Industrial Revolution

Twentieth-century English historian Arnold Toynbee came to refer to the period since 1750 as "the Industrial Revolution." The term was intended to describe a time of transition when machines began to significantly displace human and animal power in methods of producing and distributing goods, and an agricultural and commercial society converted into an industrial one.

These changes began slowly, almost imperceptibly, gaining momentum with each decade, so that by the middle of the ninteenth century, industrialism had swept across Europe west to east, from England to Eastern Europe. Few countries purposely avoided industrialization, because of its promised material improvement and national wealth. The economic changes that constitute the Industrial Revolution have done more than any other movement in Western civilization to revolutionize Western life.

Roots of the Industrial Revolution could be found in the following: 1) the Commercial Revolution (1500–1700), which spurred the great economic growth of Europe and brought about the Age of Discovery and Exploration, which in turn helped to solidify the economic doctrines of mercantilism; 2) the effect of the Scientific Revolution, which produced the first wave of mechanical inventions and technological advances; 3) the increase in population in Europe from 140 million people in 1750, to 266 million people by the mid-part of the nineteenth century (more producers, more consumers); and 4) the political and social revolutions of the nineteenth century, which began the rise to power of the "middle class," and provided leadership for the economic revolution.

The revolution occurred first in the cotton and metallurgical industries, because those industries lent themselves to mechanization. A series of mechanical inventions (1733–1793) would enable the cotton industry to mass-produce quality goods. The need to replace wood as an energy source led to the use of coal, which increased coal mining, and resulted ultimately in the invention of the steam engine and the locomotive. The development of steam power allowed the cotton industry to expand and transformed the iron industry. The factory system, which had been created in response to the new energy sources and machinery, was perfected to increase manufactured goods.

A transportation revolution ensued in order to distribute the productivity of machinery and deliver raw materials to the eager factories. This led to the growth of canal systems, the construction of hard-surfaced "macadam" roads, the commercial use of the steamboat (demonstrated by Robert Fulton, 1765–1815), and the railway locomotive (made commercially successful by George Stephenson, 1781–1848).

A subsequent revolution in agriculture made it possible for fewer people to feed the population, thus freeing people to work in factories, or in the new fields of communications, distribution of goods, or services like teaching, medicine, and entertainment.

The Industrial Revolution created a unique new category of people who were dependent on their job alone for income, a job from which they might be dismissed without cause. Until 1850 workers as a whole did not share in the general wealth produced by the Industrial Revolution. Conditions would improve as the century wore on, as union action combined with general prosperity and a developing social conscience to improve the working conditions, wages, and hours first of skilled labor, and later of unskilled labor.

The most important sociological result of industrialism was urbanization. The new factories acted as magnets, pulling people away from their rural roots and beginning the most massive population transfer in history. Cities made the working class a powerful force by raising consciousness and enabling people to unite for political action and to remedy economic dissatisfaction.

Impact of Thought Systems ("Isms") on the European World

Romanticism was a reaction against the rigid classicism, rationalism, and deism of the eighteenth century. Strongest between 1800 and 1850, the romantic movement differed from country to country and from romanticist to romanticist. Because it emphasized change, it was considered revolutionary in all aspects of life.

English literary Romantics like Wordsworth and Coleridge epitomized the romantic movement. Other romantics included Goethe of Germany, Hugo of France, and Pushkin of Russia. Romanticism also affected music and the visual arts.

Romantic philosophy stimulated an interest in Idealism, the belief that reality consists of ideas, as opposed to materialism. This school of thought (Philosophical Idealism), founded by Plato, was developed through the writings of Immanuel Kant, Johann Gottlieb Fichte, and Georg Wilhelm Hegel, the greatest exponent of this school of thought. Hegel believed that an impersonal God rules the universe and guides humans along a progressive evolutionary course by means of a process called dialecticism; this is a historical process by which one thing is constantly reacting with its opposite (the thesis and antithesis), producing a result (synthesis) that automatically meets another opposite and continues the series of reactions.

Conservatism arose in reaction to liberalism and became a popular alternative for those who were frightened by the violence, terror, and social disorder unleashed by the French Revolution. Early conservatism was allied to the restored monarchical governments of Austria, Russia, France, and England. Support for conservatism came from the traditional ruling classes as well as the peasants who still formed the majority of the population. In essence, conservatives believed in order, society, and the state; faith and tradition.

The theory of **liberalism** was the first major theory in the history of Western thought to teach that the individual is a self-sufficient being whose freedom and well-being are the sole reasons for the existence of society. Liberalism was more closely connected to the spirit and outlook of the Enlightenment than to any of the other "isms" of the early nineteenth century. Liberalism was reformist and political rather than revolutionary in character.

Liberals also advocated economic individualism (i.e., laissez-faire capitalism), heralded by Adam Smith (1723–1790) in his 1776 economic masterpiece, *Wealth of Nations*.

The regenerative force of liberal thought in early nineteenth-century Europe was dramatically revealed in the explosive force of the power of nationalism. Raising the level of consciousness of people having a common language, soil, traditions, history, culture, and experience to seek political unity around an identity of what or who constitutes the nation, nationalism was aroused and made militant during the turbulent French Revolutionary era.

Nationalistic thinkers and writers examined the language, literature, and folkways of their people, thereby stimulating nationalist feelings. Emphasizing the history and culture of the various European peoples reinforced and glorified national sentiment.

Socialism

The Utopian Socialists (from *Utopia*, Saint Thomas More's (1478–1535) book on a fictional ideal society) were the earliest writers to propose an equitable solution to improve the distribution of society's wealth. While they endorsed the productive capacity of industrialism, they denounced its mismanagement. Human society was to be organized as a community rather than a mixture of competing, selfish individuals. All the goods a person needed could be produced in one community.

The Anarchists rejected industrialism and the dominance of government.

"Scientific" Socialism, or Marxism, was the creation of Karl Marx (1818–1883), a German scholar who, with the help of Friedrich Engels (1820–1895), intended to replace utopian hopes and dreams with a militant blueprint for socialist working-class success. The principal works of this revolutionary school of socialism were *The Communist Manifesto* and *Das Kapital*.

The theory of dialectical materialism enabled Marx to explain the history of the world. By borrowing Hegel's dialectic, substituting materialism and realism in place of Hegel's idealism and inverting the methodological process, Marx was able to justify his theoretical conclusions. Marxism consisted of a number of key propositions: 1) An economic interpretation of history, i.e., all human history has been determined by economic factors (mainly who controls the means of production and distribution); 2) Class struggle, i.e., since the beginning of time there has been a class struggle between the rich and the poor or the exploiters and the exploited; 3) Theory of surplus value, i.e., the true value of a product was labor, and since the worker received a small portion of his just labor price, the difference was surplus value, "stolen" from him by the capitalist; and 4) Socialism was inevitable, i.e., capitalism contained the seeds of its own destruction (overproduction, unemployment, etc.); the rich would grow richer and the poor would grow poorer until the gap between each class (proletariat and bourgeoisie) is so great that the working classes would rise up in revolution and overthrow the elite bourgeoisie to install a "dictatorship of the proletariat." As modern capitalism was dismantled, the creation of a classless society guided by the principle "from each according to his abilities, to each according to his needs" would take place.

The Revolutionary Tradition

The year 1848 is considered the watershed of the nineteenth century. The revolutionary disturbances of the first half of the nineteenth century reached a climax in a new wave of revolutions that extended from Scandinavia to southern Italy, and from France to central Europe. Only England and Russia avoided violent upheaval.

The issues were substantially the same as they had been in 1789. What was new in 1848 was that these demands were far more widespread and irrepressible than ever. Whole classes and nations demanded to be fully included in society. Aggravated by rapid population growth and the social disruption caused by industrialism and urbanization, a massive tide of discontent swept across the Western world.

Generally speaking, the 1848 upheavals shared the strong influences of romanticism, nationalism, and liberalism, as well as a new factor of economic dislocation and instability.

Specifically, a number of similar conditions existed in several countries: 1) Severe food shortages caused by poor harvests of grain and potatoes (e.g., Irish potato famine); 2) Financial crises caused by a downturn in the commercial and industrial economy; 3) Business failures; 4) Widespread unemployment; 5) A sense of frustration and discontent among urban artisan and working classes as wages diminished; 6) A system of poor relief which became overburdened; 7) Living conditions, which deteriorated in the cities; 8) The power of nationalism in the Germanies, Italies and in Eastern Europe to inspire the overthrow of existing governments. Middle-class predominance within the unregulated economy continued to drive liberals to push for more government reform and civil liberty. They enlisted the help of the working classes to put more pressure on the government to change.

In France, working-class discontent and liberals' unhappiness with the corrupt regime of King Louis Philippe (reigned 1830–1848)—especially his minister Guizot (1787–1874)—erupted in street riots in Paris on February 22–23, 1848. With the workers in control of Paris, King Louis Philippe abdicated on February 24, and a provisional government proclaimed the Second French Republic.

The "June Days" revolt was provoked when the government closed the national workshop. This new revolution (June 23–26) was unlike previous uprisings in France. It marked the inauguration of genuine class warfare; it was a revolt against poverty and a cry for the redistribution of property. It foreshadowed the great social revolutions of the twentieth century. The revolt was extinguished after General Cavaignac was given dictatorial powers by the government. The June Days confirmed the political predominance of conservative property holders in French life.

The new Constitution of the Second French Republic provided for a unicameral legislature and executive power vested in a popularly elected president of the Republic. When the election returns were counted, the government's candidate was defeated by a "dark horse" candidate, Prince Louis Napoleon Bonaparte (1808–1873), a nephew of the great emperor. On December 20, 1848, Louis Napoleon was installed as president of the Republic. In December 1852 Louis Napoleon became Emperor Napoleon III (reigned 1852–1870), and France retreated from republicanism again.

Italian nationalists and liberals wanted to end Hapsburg (Austrian), Bourbon (Naples and Sicily), and papal domination and unite these disparate Italian regions into a unified liberal nation. A revolt by liberals in Sicily in January 1848 was followed by the granting of liberal constitutions in Naples, Tuscany, Piedmont, and the Papal States. Milan and Venice expelled their Austrian rulers. In March 1848 upon hearing the news of the revolution in Vienna, a fresh outburst of revolution against Austrian rule occurred in Lombardy and Venetia, with Sardinia-Piedmont declaring war on Austria. Simultaneously, Italian patriots attacked the Papal States, forcing the pope, Pius IX (1792–1878), to flee to Naples for refuge.

The temporary nature of these initial successes was illustrated by the speed with which the conservative forces regained control. In the north Austrian Field Marshal Radetzky (1766–1858) swept aside all opposition, regaining Lombardy and Venetia and crushing Sardinia-Piedmont. In the Papal States the establishment of the Roman Republic (February 1849) under the leadership of Giuseppe Mazzini and the protection of Giuseppe Garibaldi (1807–1882), would fail when French troops took Rome in July 1849 after a heroic defense by Garibaldi. Pope Pius IX returned to Rome cured of his liberal leanings. In the south and in Sicily the revolts were suppressed by the former rulers.

The immediate effect of the 1848 Revolution in France was a series of liberal and nationalistic demonstrations in the German states (March 1848), with the rulers promising liberal concessions. The liberals' demand for constitutional government was coupled with another demand—some kind of union or federation of the German states.

Great Britain and the Victorian Compromise

The Victorian Age (1837–1901) is associated with the long reign of Queen Victoria, who succeeded her uncle King William IV at the age of 18, and married her cousin, Prince Albert. The early years of her reign coincided with the continuation of liberal reform of the British government, accomplished through an arrangement known as the "Victorian Compromise." The Compromise was a political alliance of the middle class and aristocracy to exclude the working class from political power. The middle class gained control of the House of Commons, the aristocracy controlled the government, the army, and the Church of England. This process of accommodation worked successfully.

Parliamentary reforms continued after passage of the 1832 Reform Bill. Laws were enacted abolishing slavery throughout the Empire (1833). The Factory Act (1831) forbade the employment of children under the age of nine. The New Poor Law (1834) required the needy who were able and unemployed to live in workhouses. The Municipal Reform Law (1835) gave control of the cities to the middle class. The last remnants of the mercantilistic age fell with the abolition of the Corn Laws (1846) and repeal of the old navigation acts (1849).

The revolutions of 1848 began with much promise, but all ended in defeat for a number of reasons. They were spontaneous movements which lost their popular support as people lost their enthusiasm. Initial successes by the revolutionaries were due less to their strength than to the hesitancy of governments to use their superior force. Once this hesitancy was overcome, the revolutions were smashed. They were essentially urban movements, and the conservative landowners and peasants tended, in time, to nullify the spontaneous actions of the urban classes. The middle class, who led the revolutions, came to fear the radicalism of their working-class allies. Divisions among national groups, and the willingness of one nationality to deny rights to other nationalities, helped to destroy the revolutionary movements in Central Europe.

However, the results of 1848–1849 were not entirely negative. Universal male suffrage was introduced in France; serfdom remained abolished in Austria and the German states; parliaments were established in Prussia and other German states, though dominated by princes and aristocrats; and Prussia and Sardinia-Piedmont emerged with new determination to succeed in their respective unification schemes.

A new age followed the revolutions of 1848–1849, as Otto von Bismarck (1815–1898), one of the dominant political figures of the second half of the nineteenth century, was quick to realize. If the mistake of these years was to believe that great decisions could be brought about by speeches and parliamentary majorities, the sequel showed that in an industrial era new techniques involving ruthless force were all too readily available. The period of *Realpolitik*—of realistic, iron-fisted politics and diplomacy—followed.

Realpolitik and the Triumph of Nationalism

After the collapse of the revolutionary movements of 1848, the leadership of Italian nationalism was transferred to Sardinian leaders Victor Emmanuel II (1820–1878), Camillo de Cavour (1810–1861), and Giuseppe Garibaldi (1807–1882). The new leaders did not entertain romantic illusions about the process of transforming Sardinia into a new Italian kingdom; they were practitioners of the politics of realism, *Realpolitik*.

In 1855, under Cavour's direction, Sardinia joined Britain and France in the Crimean War against Russia. At the Paris Peace Conference (1856), Cavour addressed the delegates on the need to eliminate the foreign (Austrian) presence in the Italian peninsula and attracted the attention and sympathy of the French Emperor, Napoleon III.

After being provoked, the Austrians declared war on Sardinia in 1859. French forces intervened and the Austrians were defeated in the battles of Magenta (June 4) and Solferino (June 24).

Napoleon III, without consulting Cavour, signed a secret peace (The Truce of Villafranca) on July 11, 1859. Sardinia received Lombardy but not Venetia; the other terms indicated that Sardinian influence would be restricted and that Austria would remain a power in Italian politics. The terms of Villafranca were clarified and finalized with the Treaty of Zurich (1859).

In 1860, Cavour arranged the annexation of Parma, Modena, Romagna, and Tuscany into Sardinia. These actions were recognized by the Treaty of Turin between Napoleon III and Victor Emmanuel II; Nice and Savoy were transferred to France.

Giuseppe Garibaldi and his Red Shirts landed in Sicily in May 1860 and extended the nationalist activity to the south. Within three months, Sicily was taken and by September 7, Garibaldi was in Naples and the Kingdom of the Two Sicilies had fallen under Sardinian influence. Cavour distrusted Garibaldi, but Victor Emmanuel II encouraged him.

In February 1861, in Turin, Victor Emmanuel was declared King of Italy and presided over an Italian Parliament which represented the entire Italian peninsula with the exception of Venetia and the Patrimony of St. Peter (Rome). Cavour died in June 1861.

Venetia was incorporated into the Italian Kingdom in 1866 as a result of an alliance between Bismarck's Prussia and the Kingdom of Italy which preceded the Austro-Prussian War between Austria and Prussia. In return for opening a southern front against Austria, Prussia, upon its victory, arranged for Venetia to be transferred to Italy.

Bismarck was again instrumental in the acquisition of Rome into the Italian Kingdom in 1870. In 1870, the Franco-Prussian War broke out and the French garrison, which had been in Rome providing protection for the Pope, was withdrawn to serve on the front against Prussia. Italian troops seized Rome, and in 1871, as a result of a plebiscite, Rome became the capital of the Kingdom of Italy.

Bismarck and the Unification of Germany

In the period after 1815, Prussia emerged as an alternative to a Hapsburg-based Germany.

Otto von Bismarck (1810–1898) entered the diplomatic service of Wilhelm I as the Revolutions of 1848 were being suppressed. By the early 1860s, Bismarck had emerged as the principal adviser and minister to the king. Bismarck was an advocate of a Prussian-based (Hohenzollern) Germany.

In 1863, the Schleswig-Holstein crisis broke. These provinces, which were occupied by Germans, were under the personal rule of Christian IX (1818–1906) of Denmark. The Danish government advanced a new constitution which specified that Schleswig and Holstein would be annexed into Denmark. German reaction was predictable and Bismarck arranged for joint Austro-Prussian military action. Denmark was defeated and agreed (Treaty of Vienna, 1864) to give up the provinces, and Schleswig and Holstein were to be jointly administered by Austria and Prussia.

In 1870, deteriorating relations between France and Germany collapsed over the Ems Dispatch. Wilhelm I was approached by representatives of the French government who requested a Prussian pledge not to interfere on the issue of the vacant Spanish throne. Wilhelm I refused to give such a pledge and informed Bismarck of these developments through a telegram from Ems.

Bismarck exploited the situation by initiating a propaganda campaign against the French. Subsequently, France declared war and the Franco-Prussian War (1870–1871) commenced. Prussian victories at Sedan and Metz proved decisive; Napoleon III and his leading general, Marshal MacMahon, were captured. Paris continued to resist but fell to the Prussians in January 1871. The Treaty of Frankfurt (May 1871) concluded the war and resulted in France ceding Alsace-Lorraine to Germany and a German occupation until an indemnity was paid.

The German Empire was proclaimed on January 18, 1871, with Wilhelm I becoming the Emperor of Germany. Bismarck became the Imperial Chancellor. Bavaria, Baden, Württemberg, and Saxony were incorporated into the new Germany.

The Crimean War

The Crimean War originated in the dispute between two differing groups of Christians and their protectors over privileges in the Holy Land. During the nineteenth century, Palestine was part of the Ottoman Turkish Empire. In 1852, the Turks negotiated an agreement with the French to provide enclaves in the Holy Land to Roman Catholic religious orders; this arrangement appeared to jeopardize already existing agreements which provided access to Greek Orthodox religious orders. Czar Nicholas I (reigned 1825–1855), unaware of the impact of his action, ordered Russian troops to occupy several Danubian principalities; his strategy was to withdraw from these areas once the Turks agreed to clarify and guarantee the rights of the Greek Orthodox orders. In October 1853, the Turks demanded that the Russians withdraw from the occupied principalities. The Russians failed to respond, and the Turks declared war. In February 1854, Nicholas advanced a draft for a settlement of the Russo-Turkish War; it was rejected and Great Britain and France joined the Ottoman Turks and declared war on Russia.

With the exception of some naval encounters in the Gulf of Finland off the Aaland Islands, the war was conducted on the Crimean Peninsula in the Black Sea. In September 1854, more than 50,000 British and French troops landed in the Crimea, determined to take the Russian port city of Sebastopol. In December 1854, Austria reluctantly became a co-signatory of the Four Points of Vienna, a statement of British and French war aims. In 1855, Piedmont joined Britain and France in the war. In March 1855, Czar Nicholas I died and was succeeded by Alexander II (reigned 1855–1881), who was opposed to continuing the war. In December 1855, the Austrians, under excessive pressure from the British, French, and Piedmontese, sent an ultimatum to Russia in which they threatened to renounce their neutrality. In response, Alexander II indicated that he would accept the Four Points.

The resulting Peace of Paris had the following major provisions: Russia had to acknowledge international commissions to regulate maritime traffic on the Danube, recognize Turkish control of the mouth of the Danube, renounce all claims to the Danubian Principalities of Moldavia and Wallachia (which later led to the establishment of Romania), agree not to fortify the Aaland Islands, renounce its previously espoused position of protector of the Greek Orthodox residents of the Ottoman Empire, and return all occupied territories to the Ottoman Empire. The Straits Convention of 1841 was revised by neutralizing the Black Sea. The Declaration of Paris specified rules to regulate commerce during periods of war. Lastly, the independence and integrity of the Ottoman Empire were recognized and guaranteed by the signatories.

The Eastern Question and the Congress of Berlin

In 1876, Turkish forces under the leadership of Osman Pasha soundly defeated Serbian armies. In March 1878, the Russians and the Turks signed the Peace of San Stephano; implementation of its provisions would have resulted in Russian hegemony in the Balkans and dramatically altered the balance of power in the eastern Mediterranean.

Britain, under the leadership of Prime Minister Benjamin Disraeli (1804–1881), denounced the San Stephano Accord, dispatched a naval squadron to Turkish waters, and demanded that the San Stephano agreement be scrapped. The German Chancellor, Otto von Bismarck, intervened and offered his services as mediator.

The delegates of the major powers convened in Berlin in June and July 1878 to negotiate a settlement. Prior to the meeting, Disraeli had concluded a series of secret arrangements with Austria, Russia, and Turkey. The combined impact of these accommodations was to restrict Russian expansion in the region, reaffirm the independence of Turkey, and maintain British control of the Mediterranean.

The Russians, who had won the war against Turkey and had imposed the harsh terms of the San Stephano Treaty, found that they left the conference with very little (Kars, Batum, etc.) for their effort. Although Disraeli was the primary agent of this anti-Russian settlement, the Russians blamed Bismarck for their dismal results. Their hostility toward Germany led Bismarck (1879) to embark upon a new system of alliances which transformed European diplomacy and rendered any additional efforts of the Concert of Europe futile.

Capitalism and the Emergence of the New Left (1848–1914)

During the nineteenth century, Europe experienced the full impact of the Industrial Revolution. The Industrial Revolution resulted in improving aspects of the physical lives of a greater number of Europeans; at the same time, it led to a factory system with undesirable working and living conditions and the abuses of child labor.

As the century progressed, the inequities of the system became increasingly evident. Trade-unionism and socialist political parties emerged which attempted to address these problems and improve the lives of the working class.

During the period from 1815 to 1848, Utopian Socialists such as Robert Owen (1771–1858), Saint Simon, and Charles Fourier advocated the establishment of a political-economic system which was based on romantic concepts of the ideal society. The failure of the Revolutions of 1848 and 1849 discredited the Utopian Socialists, and the new "Scientific Socialism" advanced by Karl Marx (1818–1883) became the primary ideology of protest and revolution. Marx stated that the history of humanity was the history of class struggle and that the process of the struggle (the dialectic) would continue until a classless society was realized. The Marxian dialectic was driven by the dynamics of materialism. The proletariat, or the industrial working class, needed to be educated and led towards a violent revolution which would destroy the institutions which perpetuated the struggle and the suppression of the majority. After the revolution, the people would experience the dictatorship of the proletariat, during which the Communist party would provide leadership. Marx advanced these concepts in a series of tracts and books including *The Communist Manifesto* (1848), *Critique of Political Economy* (1859), and *Capital* (1863–1864).

Britain

In 1865, Palmerston died, and during the next two decades significant domestic developments occurred which expanded democracy in Great Britain. The dominant leaders of this period were William Gladstone (1809–1898) and Benjamin Disraeli (1804–1881). As the leader of the Liberal party (until 1895), Gladstone supported Irish Home Rule, fiscal responsibility, free trade, and the extension of democratic principles. He was opposed to imperialism, the involvement of Britain in European affairs, and the further centralization of the British government. Disraeli argued for an aggressive foreign policy, the expansion of the British Empire, and, after opposing democratic reforms, the extension of the franchise.

The Second French Republic and the Second Empire

Louis Napoleon became the president of the Second French Republic in December 1848. During the three-year life of the Second Republic, Louis Napoleon demonstrated his skills as a gifted politician through the manipulation of the various factions in French politics. His deployment of troops in Italy to rescue and restore Pope Pius IX was condemned by the republicans, but strongly supported by the monarchists and moderates.

Louis Napoleon minimized the importance of the Legislative Assembly, capitalized on the developing Napoleonic Legend, and courted the support of the army, the Catholic church, and a range of conservative political groups. The Falloux Law returned control of education to the church. Further, Louis Napoleon was confronted with Article 45 of the constitution, which stipulated that the president was limited to one four-year term; he had no intention of relinquishing power. With the assistance of a core of dedicated supporters, Louis Napoleon arranged for a coup d'état on the night of December 1–2, 1851. The Second Republic fell and was soon replaced by the Second French Empire.

Louis Napoleon drafted a new constitution which resulted in a highly centralized government. On December 2, 1852, he announced that he was Napoleon III, Emperor of the French.

The Second Empire collapsed after the capture of Napoleon III during the Franco-Prussian War (1870–1871). After a regrettable Parisian experience with a communist type of government, the Third French Republic was established; it would survive until 1940.

Imperial Russia

The autocracy of Nicholas I's (reigned 1825–1855) regime was not threatened by the revolutionary movements of 1848. In 1848 and 1849, Russian troops suppressed disorganized Polish attempts to reassert Polish nationalism.

Russian involvement in the Crimean War met with defeat. Russian ambitions in the eastern Mediterranean had been thwarted by a coalition of Western European states. In 1855 Nicholas I died and was succeeded by Alexander II (reigned 1855–1881).

Fearing the transformation of Russian society from below, Alexander II instituted a series of reforms which altered the nature of the social contract in Russia. In 1861, Alexander II declared that serfdom was abolished. Further, he issued the following reforms: 1) The serf (peasant) would no longer be dependent upon the lord; 2) all people were to have freedom of movement and were free to change their means of livelihood; and 3) the serf could enter into contracts and could own property.

The last years of the reign of Alexander II witnessed increased political opposition, manifested in demands for reforms from an ever more hostile group of intellectuals, the emergence of a Russian populist movement, and attempts to assassinate the czar. As the regime matured, greater importance was placed on traditional values. This attitude developed at the same time that nihilism, which rejected romantic illusions of the past in favor of a rugged realism, was being advanced by such writers as Ivan Turgenev in his *Fathers and Sons*.

The notion of the inevitability and desirability of a social and economic revolution was promoted through the Russian populist movement. Originally, the populists were interested in an agrarian utopian order. The populists had no national support. Government persecution of the populists resulted in the radicalization of the movement. In the late 1870s and early 1880s, leaders such as Andrei Zheleabov and Sophie Perovsky became obsessed with the need to assassinate Alexander II. In March 1881, the czar was killed in St. Petersburg when his carriage was bombed. He was succeeded by Alexander III (reigned 1881–1894), who advocated a national policy based on "Orthodoxy, Autocracy, and Nationalism." Alexander III died in 1894 and was succeeded by the last of the Romanovs to hold power, Nicholas II (reigned 1894–1917). Nicholas II displayed lack of intelligence, wit, political acumen, and the absence of a firm will throughout his reign. From his ministers to his wife, Alexandra, to Rasputin (1872–1916), Nicholas was influenced by stronger personalities.

The opposition to the Czarist government became more focused and thus, more threatening, with the emergence of the Russian Social Democrats and the Russian Social Revolutionaries. Both groups were Marxist. Vladimir Ilyich Ulyanov, also known as Lenin, became the leader of the Bolsheviks, a splinter group of the Social Democrats. By winter (1904–1905), the accumulated consequences of inept management of the economy and the prosecution of the Russo-Japanese War reached a critical stage. A group under the leadership of the radical priest Gapon marched on the Winter Palace in St. Petersburg (January 9, 1905) to submit a list of grievances to the czar. Troops fired on the demonstrators and many casualties resulted on this "Bloody Sunday." In June 1905, naval personnel on the battleship *Potemkin* mutinied while the ship was in Odessa. In October 1905, Nicholas II issued the October Manifesto calling for the convocation of a Duma, or assembly of state, which would serve as an advisory body to the czar, extending civil liberties to include freedom of speech, assembly, and press, and announcing that Nicholas II would reorganize his government.

The leading revolutionary forces differed in their responses to the manifesto. The Octobrists indicated that they were satisfied with the arrangements; the Constitutional Democrats, also known as the Kadets, demanded a more liberal representative system.

The Duma convened in 1906 and, from its outset to the outbreak of the First World War, was paralyzed by factionalism which was exploited by the czar's ministers. By 1907, Nicholas II's ministers had recovered the real power of government. Russia experienced a general though fragile economic recovery by 1909, which lasted until the war.

Origins, Motives, and Implications of the New Imperialism (1870–1914)

By the 1870s, the European industrial economies required external markets to distribute products which could not be absorbed within their domestic economies. Further, excess capital was available and foreign investment, while risky, appeared to offer high returns. Finally, the need for additional sources of raw materials served as a rationale and stimulant for imperialism. Politicians were also influenced by the numerous missionary societies which sought government protection, in extending Christianity throughout the world. European statesmen, were also interested in asserting their national power overseas through the acquisition of strategic (and many not so strategic) colonies.

The focus of most of the European imperial activities during the late nineteenth century was Africa. Initially, European interest in these activities was romantic. With John Hanning Speke's discovery of Lake Victoria (1858), Livingstone's surveying of the Zambezi, and Stanley's work on the Congo River, Europeans became enraptured with the greatness and novelty of Africa south of the Sahara.

Disraeli was involved in the intrigue which would result in the British acquisition of the Suez Canal (1875), and during the 1870s and 1880s Britain was involved in a Zulu War and announced the annexation of the Transvaal, which the Boers regained after their great victory of Majuba Hill (1881). At about the same time, Belgium established its interest in the Congo; France, in addition to seizing Tunisia, extended its influence into French Equitorial Africa, and Italy established small colonies in East Africa. During the 1880s Germany acquired several African colonies including German East Africa, the Cameroons, Togoland, and German South West Africa. The Berlin Conference (1884–1885) resulted in an agreement which specified the following: 1) The Congo would be under the control of Belgium through an International Association; 2) More liberal use of the Niger and Congo rivers; and 3) European powers could acquire African territory through first occupation and second notifying the other European states of their occupation and claim.

British movement north of the Cape of Good Hope involved Europeans fighting one another rather than a native African force. The Boers had lived in South Africa since the beginning of the nineteenth century. With the discovery of gold (1882) in the Transvaal, many English Cape settlers moved into the region. The Boers, under the leadership of Paul Kruger, restricted the political and economic rights of the British settlers and developed alternative railroads through Mozambique which would lessen the Boer dependency on the Cape colony. The crisis mounted and, in 1899, the Boer War began. Until 1902, the British and Boers fought a war which was costly to both sides. Britain prevailed and by 1909, the Transvaal, Orange Free State, Natal, and the Cape of Good Hope were united into the Union of South Africa.

Another area of increased imperialist activity was the Pacific. In 1890, the American naval officer Captain Alfred Mahan published *The Influence of Sea Power Upon History*; in this book he argued that history demonstrated that nations which controlled the seas prevailed. During the 1880s and 1890s naval ships required coaling stations. While Britain, the Netherlands, and France demonstrated that they were interested in Pacific islands, the most active states in this region during the last 20 years of the nineteenth century were Germany and the United States. The United States acquired the Philippines in 1898. Germany gained part of New Guinea, and the Marshall, Caroline, and Mariana island chains. The European powers were also interested in the Asian mainland. Most powers agreed with the American Open Door Policy which recognized the independence and integrity of China and provided economic access for all the powers. Rivalry over China (Manchuria) was a principal cause of the outbreak of the Russo-Japanese War in 1904.

The Age of Bismarck (1871–1890)

During the period from the establishment of the German Empire in January 1871 to his dismissal as chancellor of Germany in March 1890, Otto von Bismarck dominated European diplomacy and established an integrated political and economic structure for the new German state. Bismarck established a statist system which was reactionary in political philosophy and based upon industrialism, militarism, and innovative social legislation.

During the 1870s and 1880s, Bismarck's domestic policies were directed at the establishment of a strong united German state which would be capable of defending itself from a French war of revenge designed to restore Alsace-Lorraine to France. Laws were enacted which unified the monetary system, established an Imperial Bank and strengthened existing banks, developed universal German civil and criminal codes, and required compulsory military service. All of these measures contributed to the integration of the German state.

In order to develop public support for the government and to minimize the threat from the left, Bismarck instituted a protective tariff, to maintain domestic production, and introduced many social and economic laws to provide social security, regulate child labor, and improve working conditions for all Germans.

Bismarck's foreign policy was centered on maintaining the diplomatic isolation of France. In the crisis stemming from the Russo-Turkish War (1877–1878), Bismarck tried to serve as the "Honest Broker" at the Congress of Berlin. Russia did not succeed at the conference and incorrectly blamed Bismarck for its failure. Early in the next year, a cholera epidemic affected Russian cattle herds, and Germany placed an embargo on the importation of Russian beef. The Russians were outraged by the German action and launched an anti-German propaganda campaign in the Russian press. Bismarck, desiring to maintain the peace and a predictable diplomatic environment, concluded a secret defensive treaty with Austria-Hungary in 1879. The Dual Alliance was very significant because it was the first "hard" diplomatic alliance of the era. A "hard" alliance involved the specific commitment of military support; traditional or "soft" alliances involved pledges of neutrality or to hold military conversations in the event of a war. The Dual Alliance, which had a five-year term and was renewable, directed that one signatory would assist the other in the event that one power was attacked by two or more states.

In 1882, another agreement, the Triple Alliance, was signed between Germany, Austria-Hungary, and Italy. In the 1880s, relations between Austria-Hungary and Russia became estranged over Balkan issues. Bismarck, fearing a war, intervened and by 1887, had negotiated the secret Reinsurance Treaty with Russia. This was a "hard" defensive alliance with a three-year term, which was renewable.

In 1888, Wilhelm I died and was succeeded by his son Friedrich III, who also died within a few months. Friedrich's son, Wilhelm II (reigned 1888–1918), came to power and soon found himself in conflict with Bismarck. Early in 1890, two issues developed which led ultimately to Bismarck's dismissal. First, Bismarck had evolved a scheme for a fabricated attempted coup by the Social Democratic Party (SDP); his intent was to use this situation to create a national hysteria through which he could restrict the SDP through legal action. Second, Bismarck intended to renew the Reinsurance Treaty with

Russia to maintain his policy of French diplomatic isolation. Wilhelm II opposed both of these plans; in March 1890, Bismarck, who had used the threat of resignation so skillfully in the past, suggested that he would resign if Wilhelm II would not approve of these actions. Wilhelm II accepted his resignation; in fact, Bismarck was dismissed.

The Movement toward Democracy in Western Europe

Even after the reform measures of 1867 and 1884 to 1885, the movement toward democratic reforms in Great Britain continued unabated.

The most significant political reform of this long-lived Liberal government was the Parliament Act of 1911, which eliminated the powers of the House of Lords and resulted in the House of Commons becoming the unquestioned center of national power.

The most recurring and serious problem which Great Britain experienced during the period from 1890 to 1914 was the "Irish Question." The Irish situation became more complicated when the Protestant counties of the north started to enjoy remarkable economic growth from the mid-1890s; they were adamant in their rejection of all measures of Irish Home Rule. In 1914, an Irish Home Rule Act was passed by both the Commons and the Lords, but the Protestants refused to accept it. Implementation was deferred until after the war.

The Third French Republic

In the fall of 1870, Napoleon III's Second Empire collapsed when it was defeated by the Prussian armies. Napoleon III and his principal aides were captured; later, he abdicated and fled to England. A National Assembly (1871–1875) was created and Adolphe Thiers was recognized as its chief executive. At the same time, a more radical political entity, the Paris Commune (1870–1871), came into existence and exercised extraordinary power during the siege of Paris. After the siege and the peace agreement with Prussia, the Commune refused to recognize the authority of the National Assembly. Led by radical Marxists, anarchists, and republicans, the Paris Commune repudiated the conservative and monarchist leadership of the National Assembly. From March to May 1871, the Commune fought a bloody struggle with the troops of the National Assembly. France began a program of recovery which led to the formulation of the Third French Republic in 1875. The National Assembly sought to 1) put the French political house in order; 2) establish a new constitutional government; 3) pay off an imposed indemnity and, in doing so, remove German troops from French territory; and 4) restore the honor and glory of France. In 1875 a constitution was adopted which provided for a republican government consisting of a president (with little power), a Senate, and a Chamber of Deputies, which was the center of political power. During the early years of the Republic, Leon Gambetta (1838–1882) led the republicans.

The most serious threat to the Republic came through the Dreyfus Affair. In 1894, Captain Alfred Dreyfus (1859–1935) was assigned to the French General Staff. A scandal broke when it was revealed that classified information had been provided to German spies. Dreyfus, a Jew, was charged, tried, and convicted. Later, it was determined that the actual spy was Commandant Marie Charles Esterhazy (1847–1923), who was acquitted in order to save the pride and reputation of the army. In 1906, the case was closed when Dreyfus was declared innocent and returned to the ranks. Rather than lead to the collapse of the Republic, the Dreyfus Affair demonstrated the intensity of anti-Semitism in French society, the level of corruption in the French army, and the willingness of the Catholic church and the monarchists to join in a conspiracy against an innocent man.

From 1905 to 1914 the socialists under Jean Jaurès gained seats in the Chamber of Deputies. The Third French Republic endured the crises which confronted it and, in 1914, enjoyed the support of the vast majority of French citizens.

CONFLICTS, IDEOLOGIES, AND EVOLUTIONS IN THE TWENTIETH CENTURY

During the late nineteenth century, the economically motivated "New Imperialism" resulted in further aggravating the relations among the European powers. The Fashoda Crisis (1898–1899), the Moroccan Crisis (1905–1906), the Balkan Crisis (1908), and the Agadir Crisis (1911) demonstrated the impact of imperialism in heightening tensions among European states and in creating an environment in which conflict became more acceptable.

In 1908, the decadent Ottoman Empire was experiencing domestic discord which attracted the attention of both the Austrians and the Russians. These two powers agreed that Austria would annex Bosnia and Herzegovina and Russia would be granted access to the Straits and thus the Mediterranean. Great Britain intervened and demanded that there be no change in the status quo in the Straits. Russia backed down from a confrontation, but Austria proceeded to annex Bosnia and Herzegovina.

World War I And Europe In Crisis (1914–1935)

The Origins of World War I

The long-range roots of the origins of World War I can be traced to numerous factors, beginning with the creation of modern Germany in 1871. Achieved through a series of wars, the emergence of this new German state completely destroyed Europe's traditional balance of power, and forced its diplomatic and military planners back to their drawing boards to rethink their collective strategies.

From 1871 to 1890, balance of power was maintained through the network of alliances created by the German Chancellor, Otto von Bismarck, and centered around his *Dreikaiserbund* (League of the Three Emperors) that isolated France, and the Dual (Germany, Austria) and Triple (Germany, Austria, Italy) Alliances. Bismarck's fall in 1890 resulted in new policies that saw Germany move closer to Austria, while England and France (Entente Cordiale, 1904), and later Russia (Triple Entente, 1907), drew closer.

Germany's dramatic defeat of France in 1870–1871 coupled with Kaiser William II's decision in 1890 to build up a navy comparable to that of Great Britain created a reactive arms race. This, blended with European efforts to carve out colonial empires in Africa and Asia—plus a new spirit of nationalism and the growing romanticization of war—helped create an unstable international environment in the years before the outbreak of World War I.

Immediate Cause of World War I

The Balkans, the area which today comprises the former Yugoslavia, Albania, Greece, Bulgaria, Macedonia, and Romania, were notably unstable. Part of the rapidly decaying Ottoman (Turkish) Empire, it saw two main forces at work: (1) ethnic nationalism among the various small groups who lived there, and (2) an intense rivalry between Austria-Hungary and Russia over spheres of influence. Existing friction between Austria and Serbia heated up all the more. In 1912, with Russia's blessing, the Balkan League (Serbia, Montenegro, Greece, and Bulgaria) went to war with Turkey. Serbia, which sought a port on the Adriatic, was rebuffed when Austria and Italy backed the creation of an independent Albania. Russia, meanwhile, grew increasingly protective of its southern Slavic cousins, supporting Serbia's and Montenegro's claims to Albanian lands.

The Outbreak of the World War

On June 28, 1914, Archduke Franz Ferdinand (1863–1914), heir to the Austrian throne, was assassinated by Gavrilo Princip, a young Serbian nationalist. Austria consulted with the German government on July 6 and received a "blank check" to take any steps necessary to punish Serbia. On July 23, 1914, the Austrian government presented Serbia with a 10-point ultimatum that required Serbia to suppress and punish all forms of anti-Austrian sentiment there with the help of Austrian officials. On July 25, 1914, three hours after mobilizing its army, the Serbians acceded to most of Austria's terms. In fact, they requested only that Austria's demand to participate in Serbian judicial proceedings be adjudicated by the International Tribunal at The Hague.

Austria immediately broke off official relations with Serbia and mobilized its army. On July 28, 1914, Austria went to war against Serbia, and began to bombard Belgrade the following day. At the same time, Russia gradually prepared for war against Austria and Germany, declaring full mobilization on July 30.

German military strategy, based in part on the plan of the Chief of the General Staff Count Alfred von Schlieffen, viewed Russian mobilization as an act of war. The Schlieffen Plan was based on a two-front war with Russia and France. It was predicated on a swift, decisive blow against France while maintaining a defensive position against slowly mobilizing Russia, which would be dealt with after France.

Germany demanded that Russia demobilize in 12 hours and appealed to the Russian ambassador in Berlin. Russia's offer to negotiate the matter was rejected, and Germany declared war on Russia on August 1, 1914. On August 3, Germany declared war on France. Berlin asked Belgium for permission to send its troops through its territory to attack France, which Belgium refused. On August 4, England, which agreed in 1839 to protect Belgian neutrality, declared war on Germany; Belgium followed suit. Between 1914 and 1915, the alliance of the Central Powers (Germany, Austria-Hungary, Bulgaria, and Turkey) faced the Allied Powers of England, France, Russia, Japan, and in 1917, the United States. A number of smaller countries were also part of the Allied coalition.

By the end of 1914, Allied fleets had gained control of the high seas, which caused Germany to lose control of its colonial empire. Germany's failure in 1914 to weaken British naval strength prompted German naval leaders to begin using the submarine as an offensive weapon to weaken the British. On February 4, Germany announced a war zone around the British Isles, and advised neutral powers to sail there at their own risk. On May 7, 1915, a German submarine sank the *Lusitania*, a British passenger vessel, because it was secretly carrying arms.

New Military Technology

Germany, Russia, and Great Britain all had submarines, but the German U-boats were the most effective. Designed principally for coastal protection, they increasingly used them to reduce British naval superiority through tactical and psychological means.

By the spring of 1915, British war planners finally awoke to the fact that the machine gun had become the mistress of defensive trench warfare. In a search for a weapon to counter trench defenses, the British developed tanks as an armored "land ship," and first used them on September 15, 1916, in the battle of the Somme.

Airplanes were initially used for observation purposes in the early months of the war. As their numbers grew, mid-air struggles using pistols and rifles took place, until the Germans devised a synchronized propeller and machine gun on its Fokker aircraft in May 1915. The Allies responded with similar equipment and new squadron tactics during the early days of the Verdun campaign in February 1916, and briefly gained control of the skies. They also began to use their aircraft for bombing raids against Zeppelin bases in Germany. Air supremacy shifted to the Germans in 1917.

During the first year of the war, the Germans began to use Zeppelin airships to bomb civilian targets in England. Though their significance was neutralized with the development of the explosive shell in 1916, Zeppelins played an important role as a psychological weapon in the first two years of the war.

In the constant search for methods to counter trench warfare, the Germans and the Allied forces experimented with various forms of internationally outlawed gas. On October 27, 1914, the Germans tried a nose/eye irritant gas at Neuve-Chapelle, and by the spring of 1915 had developed a poison chlorine gas at the Battle of Ypres. That fall, the British countered with a similar chemical at the battles of Champagne and Loos.

The Russian Revolutions of 1917

The February Revolution

The government's handling of the war prompted a new wave of civilian unrest. Estimates are that 1,140 riots and strikes swept Russia in January and February 1917. Military and police units ordered to move against the mobs either remained at their posts or joined them.

Though ordered by the czar not to meet until April, Duma leaders demanded dramatic solutions to the country's problems. Though dissolved on March 11, the Duma met in special session on March 13 and created a Provisional Committee of Elders to deal with the civil war. After two days of discussions, it decided that the czar must give up his throne, and on March 15, 1917, President Michael Rodzianko and Aleksandr Ivanovich Guchkov, leader of the Octobrist Party, convinced the czar to abdicate. He agreed, turning over the throne to his brother, the Grand Duke Michael, who himself abdicated the next day.

The Bolshevik October Revolution

On October 23–24, Lenin returned from Finland to meet with the party's Central Committee to plan the coup. Though he met with strong resistance, the Committee agreed to create a Political Bureau (Politburo) to oversee the revolution.

Leon Trotsky, head of the Petrograd Soviet and its Military Revolutionary Committee, convinced troops in Petrograd to support Bolshevik moves. While Trotsky gained control of important strategic points around the city, Alexander Kerensky, Prime Minister of the Russian Provisional Government at the time, and well-informed of Lenin's plans, finally decided on November 6 to move against the plotters. In response, Lenin and Trotsky ordered their supporters to seize the city's transportation and communication centers. The Winter Palace was captured later that evening, along with most of Kerensky's government.

The Second Congress opened at 11 p.m. on November 7, with Lev Kamenev (1883–1936), a member of Lenin's Politburo, as its head. Soon after it opened, many of the moderate socialists walked out in opposition to Lenin's coup, leaving the Bolsheviks and the Left Socialist Revolutionaries in control of the gathering.

At the Congress, it was announced that the government's new Cabinet, officially called the Council of People's Commissars (Sovnarkom), and responsible to a Central Executive Committee, would include Lenin as Chairman or head of government, Trotsky as Foreign Commissar, and Josef Stalin as Commissar of Nationalities. The Second Congress issued two decrees on peace and land. The first called for immediate peace without any consideration of indemnities or annexations, while the second adopted the Socialist Revolutionary land program that abolished private ownership of land and decreed that a peasant could only have as much land as he could farm. Village councils would oversee distribution.

The Constituent Assembly

The Constituent Assembly, long promised by the Provisional Government as the country's first legally elected legislature, presented serious problems for Lenin, since he knew the Bolsheviks could not win a majority of seats in it. Regardless, Lenin allowed elections for it to be held on November 25 under universal suffrage. When the assembly convened on January 18 in the Tauride Palace, it voted down Bolshevik proposals and elected Victor Chernov, a Socialist Revolutionary, as president, and declared the country a democratic federal republic. The Bolsheviks walked out. The next day, troops dissolved the Assembly.

World War I: The Final Phase (1917–1918)

Russia Leaves the War

As order collapsed among Russian units along the Eastern Front, the Soviet government began to explore cease fire talks with the Central Powers. Leon Trotsky, the Commissar of Foreign Affairs, offered general negotiations to all sides, and signed an initial armistice as a prelude to peace discussions with Germany at Brest-Litovsk on December 5, 1917.

The Soviets accepted terms that were integrated into the Treaty of Brest-Litovsk of March 3, 1918. According to its terms, in return for peace, Soviet Russia lost its Baltic provinces, the Ukraine, Finland, Byelorussia, and part of Transcaucasia. The area lost totaled 1,300,000 square miles and included 62 million people.

The American Presence: Naval and Economic Support

The United States, which had originally hoped that it could simply supply the Allies with naval and economic support, made its naval presence known immediately and helped Great Britain mount an extremely effective blockade of Germany and, through a convoy system, strengthened the shipment of goods across the Atlantic.

An initial token group, the American Expeditionary Force under General John J. Pershing (1860–1948), arrived in France on June 25, 1917, while by the end of April 1918, 300,000 Americans a month were placed as complete divisions alongside British and French units.

Stirred by the successes on the Marne, the Allies began their offensive against the Germans at Amiens on August 8, 1918. By September 3, the Germans retreated to the Hindenburg Line. On September 26, Foch began his final offensive, and took the Hindenburg Line the following day. Two days later, Ludendorff advised his government to seek a peace settlement. Over the next month, the French took St. Quetin (October 1), while the British occupied Cambrai, Le Cateau, and Ostend.

On September 14, Allied forces attacked in the Salonika area of Macedonia and forced Bulgaria to sue for peace on September 29. On September 19, General Allenby began an attack on Turkish forces at Megiddo in Palestine and quickly defeated them. In a rapid collapse of Turkish resistance, the British took Damascus, Aleppo, and finally forced Turkey from the war at the end of October. On October 24, the Italians began an assault against Austria-Hungary at Vitto Veneto and forced Vienna to sign armistice terms on November 3. Kaiser Wilhelm II, pressured to abdicate, fled the country on November 9, and a republic was declared. On November 11, at 11 a.m., the war ended, with Germany accepting a harsh armistice.

The Paris Peace Conference of 1919–1920

Preliminary Discussions

To a very great extent, the direction and thrust of the discussions at the Paris Peace Conference were determined by the destructive nature of the war itself and the political responsibilities, ideals, and personalities of the principle architects of the settlements at Paris. The sudden, unexpected end of the war, combined with the growing threat of communist revolution throughout Europe created an unsettling atmosphere at the conference. The "Big Four" of Wilson (U.S.), Clemenceau (France), Lloyd-George (England), and Orlando (Italy) took over the peace discussions. The delays caused by uncertainty over direction at the beginning of the conference, Wilson's insistence that the League of Nations be included in the settlement, and fear of European-wide revolution resulted in a hastily prepared, dictated peace settlement.

The Treaty of Versailles

The treaty's war guilt statements were the justification for its harsh penalties. The former German king, Wilhelm II, was accused of crimes against "international morality and the sanctity of treaties," while Germany took responsibility for itself and for its allies for all losses suffered by the Allied Powers and their supporters as a result of German and Central Power aggression.

Germany had to return Alsace and Lorraine to France and Eupen-Malmedy to Belgium. France got Germany's Saar coal mines as reparations, while the Saar Basin was to be occupied by the major powers for 15 years, after which a plebiscite would decide its ultimate fate. Poland got a number of German provinces and Danzig, now a free city, as its outlet to the sea. Additionally, Germany lost all of its colonies in Asia and Africa.

The German Army was limited to 100,000 men and officers with 12 year enlistments for the former and 25 for the latter. The General Staff was also abolished. The Navy lost its submarines and most offensive naval forces, and was limited to 15,000 men and officers with the same enlistment periods as the army. Aircraft and blimps were outlawed. A Reparations Commission was created to determine Germany's war debt to the Allies, which it figured in 1921 to be $32.4 billion, to be paid over an extended period of time. In the meantime, Germany was to begin immediate payments in goods and raw materials.

The Allies presented the treaty to the Germans on May 7, 1919, but the Germans stated that its terms were too much for the German people, and that it violated the spirit of Wilson's Fourteen Points. After some minor changes were made, the Germans were told to sign the document or face an Allied advance into Germany. The treaty was signed on June 28, 1919, at Versailles.

Treaties with Germany's Allies

The Allied treaty with Austria legitimized the breakup of the Austrian Empire in the latter days of the war and saw Austrian territory ceded to Italy and the new states of Czechoslovakia, Poland, and Yugoslavia. The agreement included military restrictions and debt payments.

Weimar Germany (1918–1929)

The dramatic collapse of the German war effort in the second half of 1918 ultimately created a political crisis that forced the abdication of the kaiser and the creation of a German Republic on November 9.

From the outset, the Provisional Government, formed by a coalition of Majority and Independent Social Democratic Socialists, was beset by divisions from within and threats of revolution throughout Germany.

Elections for the new National Constituent Assembly, which was to be based on proportional representation, gave no party a clear majority. A coalition of the Majority Socialists, the Catholic Center party, and the German Democratic party (DDP) dominated the new assembly. On February 11, 1919, the assembly met in the historic town of Weimar and selected Friedrich Ebert President of Germany. Two days later, Phillip Scheidemann (1865–1939) formed the first Weimar Cabinet and became its first Chancellor.

On August 11, 1919, a new constitution was promulgated, which provided for a bicameral legislature.

Politics and Problems of the Weimar Republic (1919–1923)

The territorial, manpower, and economic losses suffered during and after the war, coupled with a $32.4 billion reparations debt, had a severe impact on the German economy and society, and severely handicapped the new government's efforts to establish a stable governing environment.

In an effort of good faith based on hopes of future reparation payment reductions, Germany borrowed heavily and made payments in kind to fulfill its early debt obligations. The result was a spiral of inflation. After the Allied Reparations Commission declared

Germany in default on its debt, the French and the Belgians occupied the Ruhr on January 11, 1923.

Chancellor Wilhelm Cuno (1876–1933) encouraged the Ruhr's Germans passively to resist the occupation, and printed worthless marks. The occupation ended on September 26, and helped prompt stronger Allied sympathy to Germany's payment difficulties, though the inflationary spiral had severe economic, social, and political consequences.

Weimar Politics (1919–1923): Germany's economic and social difficulties deeply affected its infant democracy. From February 1919 to August 1923, the country had six chancellors.

Growing right-wing discontent with the Weimar Government resulted in the assassination of the gifted head of the Catholic Center Party, Matthias Erzberger (1875–1921), on August 29, 1921, and the murder of Foreign Minister Walter Rathenau (1867–1922) on June 24, 1922. These were two of the most serious of over 350 political murders in Germany since the end of the war.

Following the death of President Ebert on February 28, 1925, two ballots were held for a new president, since none of the candidates won a majority on the first vote. On the second ballot on April 26, the Reichsblock, a coalition of Conservative parties, was able to get its candidate elected. War hero Paul von Hindenburg was narrowly elected.

The elections of May 20, 1928, saw the Social Democrats get almost one-third of the popular vote which, blended with other moderate groups, created a stable, moderate majority in the Reichstag, which chose Hermann Müller (1876–1931) as chancellor.

Italy (1919–1925)

Benito Mussolini, capitalizing on the sympathy of unfulfilled war veterans, disaffected nationalists, and those fearful of communism, formed the Fascio Italiano di Combattimento (Union of Combat) in Milan on March 23, 1919. Initially, Mussolini's movement had few followers, and it did badly in the November 1919 elections. However, Socialist strikes and unrest enabled him to convince Italians that he alone could bring stability and prosperity to their troubled country.

The resignation of the Bonomi Cabinet on February 9, 1922, underlined the government's inability to maintain stability. In the meantime, the Fascists seized control of Bologna in May, and Milan in August. In response, Socialist leaders called for a nationwide strike on August 1, 1922; it was stopped by Fascist street violence within 24 hours. On October 24, 1922, Mussolini told followers that if he was not given power, he would "March on Rome." Three days later, Fascists began to seize control of other cities, while 26,000 began to move towards the capital. On October 29, the king, Victor Emmanuel III (1869–1947), asked Mussolini to form a new government as Premier of Italy.

Beginning in 1925, Mussolini arrested opponents, closed newspapers, and eliminated civil liberties in a new reign of terror. On December 24, 1925, the legislature's powers were greatly limited, while those of Mussolini were increased as the new Head of State. Throughout 1926, Mussolini intensified his control over the country with legislation that outlawed strikes and created the syndicalist corporate system. A failed assassination attempt prompted the "Law for the Defense of the State" of November 25, 1926, that created a Special Court to deal with political crimes and introduced the death penalty for threats against the king, his family, or the Head of State.

Italian Foreign Policy

The nation's wish for post-war peace and stability saw Italy participate in all of the international developments in the 1920s aimed at securing normalcy in relations with its neighbors. Because Italy did not receive its desired portions of Dalmatia at the Paris Peace Conference, Italian nationalist Gabriele D'Annunzio seized Fiume on the Adriatic in the fall of 1919. D'Annunzio's daring gesture as well as his deep sense of Italian national pride deeply affected Mussolini. However, in the atmosphere of detente prevalent in Europe at the time, he agreed to settle the dispute with Yugoslavia in a treaty on January 27, 1924, which ceded most of the port to Italy, and the surrounding area to Yugoslavia.

In the fall of 1923, Mussolini used the assassination of Italian officials, who were working to resolve a Greek-Albanian border dispute, to seize the island of Corfu. Within a month, however, the British and the French convinced him to return the island for an indemnity.

Soviet Russia (1922–1932)

The Civil War and "War Communism" had brought economic disaster and social upheaval throughout the country. On March 1, 1921, as the Soviet leadership met to decide on policies to guide the country in peace, a naval rebellion broke out at the Kronstadt naval base. The Soviet leadership sent Trotsky to put down the rebellion, which he did brutally by March 18.

Vladimir Ilyich Lenin, the founder of the Soviet State, suffered a serious stroke on May 26, 1922 and a second in December of that year. Lenin died on January 21, 1924.

Iosef Vissarionovich Dzugashvili (**Josef Stalin**, 1879–1953) took over numerous, and in some cases, seemingly unimportant party organizations after the Revolution and transformed them into important bases of power. Among them were Politburo (Political Bureau), which ran the country; the Orgburo (Organizational Bureau), which Stalin headed, and which appointed people to positions in groups that implemented Politiburo decisions; the Inspectorate (Rabkrin, Commissariat of the Workers' and Peasants' Inspectorate) which tried to eliminate party corruption, and the Secretariat, which worked with all party organs and set the Politburo's agenda. Stalin served as the party's General Secretary after 1921.

Lev Davidovich Bronstein (**Trotsky**, 1879–1940) was Chairman of the Petrograd Soviet, headed the early Brest-Litovsk negotiating team, served as Foreign Commissar, and was father of the Red Army. A brilliant organizer and theorist, Trotsky was also brusque and, some felt, overbearing.

In China the Soviets helped found a young Chinese Communist party (CCP) in 1921. When it became apparent that Sun Yat-sen's (1866–1925) revolutionary Kuomintang (KMT) was more mature than the infant CCP, the Soviets encouraged an alliance between its party and this movement. Sun's successor, Chiang Kai-shek (1887–1975), was deeply suspicious of the Communists and made their destruction part of his effort to militarily unite China.

Founded in 1919, the Soviet-controlled **Comintern** (Third International or Communist International) sought to coordinate the revolutionary activities of Communist parties abroad, though it often conflicted with Soviet diplomatic interests. It became an effectively organized body by 1924, and was completely Stalinized by 1928.

Europe in Crisis: Depression and Dictatorship (1929–1935)

In Great Britain in 1929, Ramsay MacDonald formed a minority Labour government that would last until 1931. The most serious problem facing the country was the

Depression, which caused unemployment to reach 1,700,000 by 1930 and over 3 million, or 25 percent of the labor force, by 1932. To meet growing budget deficits caused by heavy subsidies to the unemployed, a special government commission recommended budget cuts and tax increases. Cabinet and labor union opposition helped reduce the total for the cuts but this could not help restore confidence in the government, which fell on August 24, 1931.

The "National Government" (1931–1935)

The following day, King George VI (1895–1952) helped convince MacDonald to return to office as head of a National Coalition cabinet made up of four Conservatives, four Labourites, and two Liberals. MacDonald's coalition swept the November 1931 general elections winning 554 of 615 seats.

The British government abandoned the gold standard on September 21, 1931, and adopted a series of high tariffs on imports. Unemployment peaked at 3 million in 1932 and dropped to 2 million two years later.

MacDonald resigned his position in June 1935 because of ill health and was succeeded by Stanley Baldwin, whose conservative coalition won 428 seats in new elections in November.

France: Return of the Cartel des Gauches (1932–1934)

France remained plagued by differences over economic reform between the Radicals and the Socialists. The latter advocated nationalization of major factories, expanded social reforms, and public works programs for the unemployed, while the Radicals sought a reduction in government spending. This instability was also reflected in the fact that there were six Cabinets between June 1932 and February 1934. The government's inability to deal with the country's economic and political problems saw the emergence of a number of radical groups from across the political spectrum.

Germany: The Depression

The Depression had a dramatic effect on the German economy and politics. The country's national income dropped 20 percent between 1928 and 1932, while unemployment rose from 1,320,000 in 1929 to 6 million by January 1932. This meant that 43 percent of the German work force were without jobs (compared to one-quarter of the work force in the U.S.).

In 1919, Adolf Hitler joined the German Workers party (DAP), which he soon took over and renamed the National Socialist German Workers party (NAZI). In 1920, the party adopted a 25–point program that included treaty revision, anti-Semitism, economic, and other social changes. They also created a defense cadre of the *Sturm-abteilung* (SA)—"Storm Troopers" or "brown shirts"—which was to help the party seize power.

The Beer Hall Putsch (1923): In the midst of the country's severe economic crisis in 1923, the party, which now had 55,000 members, tried to seize power, first by a march on Berlin, and then, when this seemed impossible, on Munich. The march was stopped by police, and Hitler and his supporters were arrested. Though sentenced to five years imprisonment, he was released after eight months. While incarcerated, he dictated *Mein Kampf* to Rudolf Hess.

Hitler's failed coup and imprisonment convinced him to seek power through legitimate political channels, which would require transforming the Nazi party. To do this, he reasserted singular control over the movement from 1924 to 1926. Party districts were set up throughout Germany, overseen by *gauleiters* personally appointed by Hitler.

Hindenburg's seven-year presidential term expired in 1932, and he was convinced to run for reelection to stop Hitler from becoming president in the first ballot of March 13. Hitler got only 30 percent of the vote (11.3 million) to Hindenburg's 49.45 percent (18.6 million).

On June 1, Chancellor Bruenig was replaced by Franz von Papen (1879–1969), who formed a government made up of aristocratic conservatives and others that he and Hindenburg hoped would keep Hitler from power.

Later in the year, Von Papen convinced Hindenburg to appoint Hitler as chancellor and head of a new coalition cabinet with three seats for the Nazis. Hitler dissolved the Reichstag and called for new elections on March 5. Using presidential decree powers, he initiated a violent anti-Communist campaign that included the lifting of certain press and civil freedoms. On February 27, the Reichstag burned, which enabled Hitler to get Hindenburg to issue the "Ordinances for the Protection of the German State and Nation," that removed all civil and press liberties as part of a "revolution" against communism. In the Reichstag elections of March 5, the Nazis only got 43.9 percent of the vote and 288 Reichstag seats but, through an alliance with the Nationalists, got majority control of the legislature.

Once Hitler had full legislative power, he began a policy of *Gleichschaltung* (coordination) to bring all independent organizations and agencies throughout Germany under his control. All political parties were outlawed or forced to dissolve, and on July 14, 1933, the Nazi party became the only legal party in Germany. In addition, non-Aryans and Nazi opponents were removed from the civil service, the court system, and higher education. On May 2, 1933, the government declared strikes illegal, abolished labor unions, and later forced all workers to join the German Labor Front (DAF) under Robert Ley. In 1934 the Reichsrat was abolished and a special People's Court was created to handle cases of treason. Finally, the secret police or Gestapo (*Geheime Staatspolizei*) was created on April 24, 1933, under Hermann Göring to deal with opponents and operate concentration camps. The party had its own security branch, the SD (*Sicherheitsdienst*) under Reinhard Heydrich.

From the inception of the Nazi state in 1933, anti-Semitism was a constant theme and practice in all *Gleichschaltung* and nazification efforts. Illegal intimidation and harassment of Jews was coupled with rigid enforcement of civil service regulations that forbade employment of non-Aryans. This first wave of anti-Semitic activity culminated with the passage of the Nuremburg Laws on September 15, 1935, that deprived Jews of German citizenship and outlawed sexual or marital relations between Jews and other Germans, thus effectively isolating them from the mainstream of German society. The stage was being set for the systematic mass murder of 6 million Jews in concentration camps.

Hitler's international policies were closely linked to his rebuilding efforts to give him a strong economic and military base for an active, aggressive, independent foreign policy. The Reich simultaneously quit the League of Nations. On January 26, 1934, Germany signed a non-aggression pact with Poland, which ended Germany's traditional anti-Polish foreign policy and broke France's encirclement of Germany via the Little Entente. This was followed by the Saarland's overwhelming decision to return to Germany. The culmination of Hitler's foreign policy moves, though, came with his March 15, 1935, announcement that Germany would no longer be bound by the military restrictions of the Treaty of Versailles, that it had already created an air force (Luftwaffe), and that the Reich would institute a draft to create an army of 500,000 men.

Italy (1926–1936)

Until Mussolini's accession to power, the pope had considered himself a prisoner in the Vatican. In 1926, Mussolini's government began talks to resolve this issue, which resulted in the Lateran Accords of February 11, 1929. Italy recognized the Vatican as an independent state, with the pope as its head, while the papacy recognized Italian independence. Catholicism was made the official state religion of Italy, and religious teaching was required in all secondary schools.

In an effort to counter the significance of France's Little Entente with Czechoslovakia, Yugoslavia, and Romania, Mussolini concluded the Rome Protocols with Austria and Hungary which created a protective bond of friendship between the three countries.

In response to Hitler's announcement of German rearmament in violation of the Treaty of Versailles on March 16, 1935, France, England, and Italy met at Stresa in northern Italy on April 11–14, and concluded agreements that pledged joint military collaboration if Germany moved against Austria or along the Rhine.

Ethiopia (Abyssinia) became an area of strong Italian interest in the 1880s. The coastal region was slowly brought under Italian control until the Italian defeat at Ethiopian hands at Adowa in 1894. In 1906, the country's autonomy was recognized and in 1923 it joined the League of Nations. Mussolini, who had been preparing for war with Ethiopia since 1932, established a military base at Wal Wal in Ethiopian territory. Beginning in December 1934, a series of minor conflicts took place between the two countries, which gave Mussolini an excuse to plan for the full takeover of the country in the near future.

On October 2, 1935, Italy invaded Ethiopia, while the League of Nations, which had received four appeals from Ethiopia since January about Italian territorial transgressions, finally voted to adopt economic sanctions against Mussolini. Unfortunately, the League failed to stop shipments of oil to Italy and continued to allow it to use the Suez Canal. On May 9, 1936, Italy formally annexed the country and joined it to Somalia and Eritrea, which now became known as Italian East Africa.

International Developments (1918–1935)

Efforts to create an international body to arbitrate international conflicts gained credence with the creation of a **Permanent Court of International Justice** to handle such matters at the **First Hague Conference** (1899). But no major efforts towards this goal were initiated until 1915, when pro-League of Nations organizations arose in the United States and Great Britain. Support for such a body grew as the war lengthened, and creation of such an organization became the cornerstone of President Woodrow Wilson's post-war policy, enunciated in his "Fourteen Points" speech before Congress on January 8, 1918.

The Preamble of the League's Covenant defined the League's purposes, which were to work for international friendship, peace, and security. To attain this, its members agreed to avoid war, maintain peaceful relations with other countries, and honor international law and accords.

Headquartered in Geneva, the League came into existence as the result of an Allied resolution on January 25, 1919, and the signing of the Treaty of Versailles on June 28, 1919. The League had the right, according to Article 8 of the League Covenant, to seek ways to reduce arms strength, while Articles 10 through 17 gave it the authority to search for means to stop war. It could recommend ways to stop aggression, and could suggest economic sanctions and other tactics to enforce its decisions, though its military ability to enforce its decisions was vague.

The Locarno Pact (1925)

Signed on October 16, 1925, by England, France, Italy, Germany, and Belgium, the Locarno Pact guaranteed Germany's western boundaries and accepted the Versailles settlement's demilitarized zones. Italy and Great Britain agreed militarily to defend these lines if flagrantly violated.

In the same spirit, Germany signed arbitration dispute accords that mirrored the Geneva Protocol with France, Belgium, Poland, and Czechoslovakia, and required acceptance of League-determined settlements. Since Germany would only agree to arbitration and not finalize its eastern border, France separately signed guarantees with Poland and Czechoslovakia to defend their frontiers.

The Locarno Pact went into force when Germany joined the League on September 10, 1926, acquiring, after some dispute, the U.S.'s permanent seat on the Council. France and Belgium began to withdraw from the Rhineland, though they left a token force there until 1930.

The Pact of Paris (Kellogg-Briand Pact)

The Locarno Pact heralded a new period in European relations known as the "Era of Locarno" that marked the end of post-war conflict and the beginning of a more normal period of diplomatic friendship and cooperation. It reached its peak, with the Franco-American effort in 1928 to seek an international statement to outlaw war. On August 27, 1928, 15 countries, including the U.S., Germany, France, Italy, and Japan, signed this accord with some minor limitations, which renounced war as a means of solving differences and as a tool of national policy. Within five years, 50 other countries signed the agreement.

League and Allied Response to Aggression

On September 19, 1931, the Japanese Kwantung Army, acting independently of the government in Tokyo, began the gradual conquest of Manchuria after fabricating an incident at Mukden to justify their actions. Ultimately, they created a puppet state, Manchukuo, under the last Chinese emperor, Henry P'u-i. China's League protest resulted in the creation of an investigatory commission under the Earl of Lytton that criticized Japan's actions and recommended a negotiated settlement that would have allowed Japan to retain most of its conquest. Japan responded by resigning from the League on January 24, 1933.

Hitler's announcement on March 15, 1935, of Germany's decisions to rearm and to introduce conscription in violation of the Treaty of Versailles prompted the leaders of England, France, and Italy to meet in Stresa, Italy (April 11–14). They condemned Germany's actions, underlined their commitment to the Locarno Pact, and re-affirmed the support they collectively gave for Austria's independence in early 1934. Great Britain's decision, however, to separately protect its naval strength vis-à-vis a German buildup in the Anglo-German Naval Treaty of June 18, 1935, effectively compromised the significance of the Stresa Front.

From World War II to The Post-Communist Era (1935–1996)

Using a Franco-Soviet agreement of the preceding year as an excuse, Hitler, on March 7, 1936, repudiated the Locarno agreements and reoccupied the Rhineland (an area demilitarized by the Versailles Treaty). Neither France (which possessed military superiority at the time) nor Britain was willing to oppose these moves.

The Spanish Civil War (1936–1939) is usually seen as a rehearsal for World War II because of outside intervention. The government of the Spanish Republic (established in 1931) caused resentment among conservatives by its programs, including land reform and anti-clerical legislation aimed at the Catholic church. Following an election victory by a popular front of republican and radical parties, right-wing generals in July began a military insurrection. Francisco Franco, stationed at the time in Spanish Morocco, emerged as the leader of this revolt, which became a devastating civil war lasting nearly three years.

The democracies, including the United States, followed a course of neutrality. Nazi Germany, Italy, and the U.S.S.R. did intervene despite non-intervention agreements negotiated by Britain and France. Spain became a battlefield for fascist and anti-fascist forces with Franco winning by 1939 in what was seen as a serious defeat for anti-fascist forces everywhere.

The Spanish Civil War was a factor in bringing together Mussolini and Hitler in a Rome-Berlin Axis. Already Germany and Japan had signed the Anti-Comintern Pact in 1936. Ostensibly directed against international communism, this was the basis for a diplomatic alliance between those countries, and Italy soon adhered to this agreement, becoming Germany's ally in World War II.

In 1938 Hitler pressured the Austrian chancellor to make concessions and when this did not work, German troops annexed Austria (the *Anschluss*). Again Britain and France took no effective action, and about six million Austrians were added to Germany.

Hitler turned next to Czechoslovakia. Three million persons of German origin lived in the Sudetenland, a borderland between Germany and Czechoslovakia given to Czechoslovakia in order to provide it with a more defensible boundary. In 1938, after a series of demands from Hitler, a four-power conference was held in Munich with Hitler, Mussolini, Chamberlain, and Daladier in attendance, at which Hitler's terms were accepted. Britain and France, despite the French alliance with Czechoslovakia, put pressure on the Czech government to force it to comply with German demands. Hitler signed a treaty agreeing to this settlement as the limit of his ambitions. At the same time the Poles seized control of Teschen, and Hungary (with the support of Italy and Germany and over the protests of the British and French) seized 7,500 square miles of Slovakia. By the concessions forced on her at Munich, Czechoslovakia lost its frontier defenses and was totally unprotected against any further German encroachments.

In March 1939, Hitler annexed most of the Czech state while Hungary conquered Ruthenia. At almost the same time Germany annexed Memel from Lithuania. In April, Mussolini, taking advantage of distractions created by Germany, landed an army in Albania and seized that Balkan state in a campaign lasting about one week.

Disillusioned by these continued aggressions, Britain and France made military preparations. Guarantees were given to Poland, Romania, and Greece. The two democracies also opened negotiations with the U.S.S.R. for an arrangement to obtain that country's aid against further German aggression. Hitler, with Poland next on his timetable, also began a cautious rapprochement with the U.S.S.R. On August 23, 1939, the world was stunned by the announcement of a Nazi-Soviet Treaty of friendship. A secret protocol provided that in the event of a "territorial rearrangement" in Eastern Europe the two powers would divide Poland. In addition, Russia would have the Baltic states (Latvia, Lithuania, and Estonia) and Bessarabia (lost to Romania in 1918) as part of her sphere. Stalin agreed to remain neutral in any German war with Britain or France. World War II began with the German invasion of Poland on September 1, 1939, followed by British and French declarations of war against Germany on September 3.

World War II

The German attack (known as the "blitzkrieg" or "lightning war") overwhelmed the poorly equipped Polish army, which could not resist German tanks and airplanes.

On September 17 the Russian armies attacked the Poles from the east. They met the Germans two days later. Stalin's share of Poland extended approximately to the Curzon Line. Russia also made demands on Finland. Later, in June 1940, while Germany was attacking France, Stalin occupied the Baltic states of Latvia, Lithuania, and Estonia.

The only military action of any consequence during the winter of 1939–1940 resulted from Russian demands made on Finland, especially for territory adjacent to Leningrad (then only 20 miles from the border). Finnish refusal led to a Russian attack in November 1939. The Finns resisted with considerable vigor, receiving some supplies from Sweden, Britain, and France, but eventually by March they had to give in to the superior Russian forces. Finland was forced to cede the Karelian Isthmus, Viipuri, and a naval base at Hangoe.

On May 10, the main German offensive was launched against France. Belgium and the Netherlands were simultaneously attacked. According to plan, British and French forces advanced to aid the Belgians. At this point the Germans departed from the World War I strategy by launching a surprise armored attack through Luxembourg and the Ardennes Forest (considered by the British and French to be impassable for tanks). The Dutch could offer no real resistance and collapsed in four days after the May 13 German bombing of Rotterdam.

Paris fell to the Germans in mid-June. The Pétain government quickly made peace with Hitler, who added to French humiliation by dictating the terms of the armistice to the French at Compiégne in the same railroad car used by Marshal Foch when he gave terms to the Germans at the end of the First World War. The complete collapse of France quickly came as a tremendous shock to the British and Americans.

Mussolini declared war on both France and Britain on June 10. Hitler's forces remained in occupation of the northern part of France, including Paris. He allowed the French to keep their fleet and overseas territories probably in the hope of making them reliable allies. Pétain and his chief minister Pierre Laval established their capital at Vichy and followed a policy of collaboration with their former enemies. A few Frenchmen, however, joined the Free French movement started in London by the then relatively unknown General Charles de Gaulle (1890–1970).

From the French Defeat to the Invasion of Russia

By mid-summer 1940, Germany, together with its Italian ally, dominated most of Western and Central Europe. Germany began with no real plans for a long war, but continued resistance by the British made necessary the belated mobilization of German resources. Hitler's policy included exploiting areas Germany conquered. Collaborators were used to establish governments subservient to German policy. Germany began the policy of forcibly transporting large numbers of conquered Europeans to work in German war industries. Jews especially were forced into slave labor for the German war effort, and increasingly large numbers were rounded up and sent to concentration camps, where they were systematically murdered as the Nazis carried out Hitler's "final solution" of genocide against European Jewry. Although much was known about this during the war, the full horror of these atrocities was not revealed until Allied troops entered Germany in 1945.

With the fall of France, Britain remained the only power of consequence at war with the Axis. Hitler began preparations for invading Britain (Operation "Sea Lion"). Air control over the Channel was vital if an invasion force was to be transported safely to the

English Coast. The German Air Force (Luftwaffe) under Herman Göring began its air offensive against the British in the summer of 1940. The Germans concentrated first on British air defenses, then on ports and shipping, and finally in early September they began the attack on London. The Battle of Britain was eventually a defeat for the Germans, who were unable to gain decisive superiority over the British, although they inflicted great damage on both British air defenses and major cities such as London. Despite the damage and loss of life, British morale remained high and necessary war production continued. German losses determined that bombing alone could not defeat Britain. "Operation Sea Lion" was postponed October 12 and never seriously taken up again, although the British did not know this and had to continue for some time to give priority to their coastal and air defenses.

During the winter of 1940–1941, having given up "Operation Sea Lion," Hitler began to shift his forces to the east for an invasion of Russia ("Operation Barbarossa"). Russian expansion towards the Balkans dismayed the Germans, who hoped for more influence there themselves.

The German invasion of Russia began June 22, 1941. The invasion force of three million included Finnish, Romanian, Hungarian, and Italian contingents along with the Germans and advanced on a broad front of about 2,000 miles. They surrounded the city of Leningrad (although they never managed to actually capture it) and came within about 25 miles of Moscow. In November the enemy actually entered the suburbs, but then the long supply lines, early winter, and Russian resistance (strong despite heavy losses) brought the invasion to a halt. During the winter a Russian counterattack pushed the Germans back from Moscow and saved the capital.

With the coming of the Great Depression and severe economic difficulties, Japanese militarists gained more and more influence over the civilian government. On September 18, 1931, the Japanese occupied all of Manchuria. On July 7, 1937, a full-scale Sino-Japanese war began with a clash between Japanese and Chinese at the Marco Polo Bridge in Peking (now Beijing). An indication of ultimate Japanese aims came on November 3, 1938, when Prince Fumimaro Konoye's (1891–1946) government issued a statement on "A New Order in East Asia." This statement envisaged the integration of Japan, Manchuria (now the puppet state of Manchukuo), and China into one "Greater East Asia Co-Prosperity Sphere" under Japanese leadership. In July 1940, the Konoye government was re-formed with General Hideki Tojo (1884–1948), Japan's principal leader in World War I, as minister of war.

All of these events led to worsening relations between Japan and the two states in a position to oppose her expansion—the Soviet Union and the United States. Despite border clashes with the Russians, Japan avoided any conflict with that state, and Stalin wanted no war with Japan after he became fully occupied with the German invasion. In the few weeks after attacking the U.S. at Pearl Harbor, Japanese forces were able to occupy strategically important islands (including the Philippines and Dutch East Indies) and territory on the Asian mainland (Malaya, with the British naval base at Singapore, and all of Burma to the border of India).

The Japanese attack brought the United States not only into war in the Pacific, but resulted in German and Italian declarations of war which meant the total involvement of the United States in World War II.

American involvement in the war was ultimately decisive, for it meant that the greatest industrial power of that time was now arrayed against the Axis powers. The United States became, as President Roosevelt put it, "the arsenal of democracy." American aid was crucial to the immense effort of the Soviet Union. Lend-Lease aid was extended to Russia. By 1943 supplies and equipment were reaching Russia in considerable quantities.

The German forces launched a second offensive in the summer of 1942. This attack concentrated on the southern part of the front, aiming at the Caucasus and vital oil fields around the Caspian Sea. At Stalingrad on the Volga River the Germans were stopped. With the onset of winter, Hitler refused to allow the strategic retreat urged by his generals. As a result, the Russian forces crossed the river north and south of the city and surrounded 22 German divisions. On January 31, 1943, following the failure of relief efforts, the German commander Friedrich Paulus (1890–1957) surrendered the remnants of his army. From then on the Russians were almost always on the offensive.

After entering the war in 1940, the Italians invaded British-held Egypt. In December 1940, the British General Archibald Wavell (1883–1950) launched a surprise attack. The Italian forces were driven back about 500 miles and 130,000 were captured. Then Hitler intervened, sending General Erwin Rommel with a small German force (the Afrika Korps) to reinforce the Italians. Rommel took command and launched a counter-offensive which put his forces on the border of Egypt. By mid-1942 Rommel had driven to El Alamein, only 70 miles from Alexandria.

A change in the British high command now placed General Harold Alexander (1891–1969) in charge of Middle Eastern forces, with General Bernard Montgomery (1887–1976) in immediate command of the British Eighth Army. Montgomery attacked at El Alamein, breaking Rommel's lines and starting a British advance which was not stopped until the armies reached the border of Tunisia.

Meanwhile, the British and American leaders decided that they could launch a second offensive in North Africa ("Operation Torch") which would clear the enemy from the entire coast and make the Mediterranean once again safe for Allied shipping.

The landings resulted in little conflict with the French, and the French forces soon joined the war against the Axis. It was only a matter of time before German troops were forced into northern Tunisia and surrendered. American forces, unused to combat, suffered some reverses at the Battle of the Kasserine Pass, but gained valuable experience. The final victory came in May 1943, about the same time as the Russian victory at Stalingrad.

Relatively safe shipping routes across the North Atlantic to Britain were essential to the survival of Britain and absolutely necessary if a force was to be assembled to invade France and strike at Germany proper. New types of aircraft, small aircraft carriers, more numerous and better-equipped escort vessels, new radar and sonar (for underwater detection), extremely efficient radio direction finding, decipherment of German signals plus the building of more ships turned the balance against the Germans despite their development of improved submarines by early 1943, and the Atlantic became increasingly dangerous for German submarines.

Success in these three campaigns—Stalingrad, North Africa, and the Battle of the Atlantic—gave new hope to the Allied cause and made certain that victory was attainable. With the beginning of an Allied offensive in late 1942 in the Solomon Islands against the Japanese, 1943 became the turning point of the war.

At their conference at Casablanca in January 1943, Roosevelt and Churchill developed a detailed strategy for the further conduct of the war. Sicily was to be invaded, then Italy proper. Rome was not captured by the Allied forces until June 4, 1944. With a new Italian government now supporting the Allied cause, Italian resistance movements in northern Italy became a major force in helping to liberate that area from the Germans.

At the Teheran Conference, held in November 1943 and attended by all three major Allied leaders, the final decision reached by Roosevelt and Churchill some six months earlier to invade France in May 1944 was communicated to the Russians. Stalin promised to open a simultaneous Russian offensive.

The Normandy invasion (Operation "Overlord") was the largest amphibious operation in history. The landings actually took place beginning June 6, 1944. The first day, 130,000 men were successfully landed. Strong German resistance hemmed in the Allied forces for about a month. Then the Allies, now numbering about 1,000,000, managed a spectacular breakthrough. By the end of 1944, all of France had been seized. A second invasion force landed on the Mediterranean coast in August, freed southern France, and linked up with Eisenhower's forces. By the end of 1944, the Allied armies stood on the borders of Germany ready to invade from both east and west.

Stalin's armies crossed into Poland July 23, 1944, and three days later the Russian dictator officially recognized a group of Polish Communists (the so-called Lublin Committee) as the government of Poland. As the Russian armies drew near the eastern suburbs of Warsaw, the London Poles, a resistance group, launched an attack. Stalin's forces waited outside the city while the Germans brought in reinforcements and slowly wiped out the Polish underground army in several weeks of heavy street fighting. The offensive then resumed and the city was liberated by the Red Army, but the influence of the London Poles was now virtually nil. Needless to say, this incident aroused considerable suspicion concerning Stalin's motives and led both Churchill and Roosevelt to begin to think through the political implications of their alliance with Stalin.

By late summer of 1944, the German position in the Balkans began to collapse. The Red Army crossed the border into Romania, leading King Michael (1921–) to seize the opportunity to take his country out of its alliance with Germany and to open the way to the advancing Russians. German troops were forced to make a hasty retreat. At this point Bulgaria changed sides. The German forces in Greece withdrew in October.

From October 9–18, Winston Churchill visited Moscow to try to work out a political arrangement regarding the Balkans and Eastern Europe. Dealing from a position of weakness, he simply wrote out some figures on a sheet of paper: Russia to have the preponderance of influence in countries like Bulgaria and Romania, Britain to have the major say in Greece, and a fifty-fifty division in Yugoslavia and Hungary. Stalin agreed. The Americans refused to have anything to do with this "spheres of influence" arrangement.

In Greece, Stalin maintained a hands-off policy when the British used military force to suppress the Communist resistance movement and install a regent for the exiled government.

In early spring of 1945 the Allied armies crossed the Rhine. As the Americans and British and other Allied forces advanced into Germany, the Russians attacked from the east. While the Russian armies were fighting their way into Berlin, Hitler committed suicide in the ruins of the bunker where he had spent the last days of the war. Power was handed over to a government headed by Admiral Karl Dönitz (1891–1980). On May 7, General Alfred Jodl (1890–1946), acting for the German government, made the final unconditional surrender at General Eisenhower's headquarters near Reims.

The future treatment of Germany, and Europe in general, was determined by decisions of the "Big Three" (Churchill, Stalin, and Roosevelt).

The first major conference convened at Teheran on November 28, 1943, and lasted until December 1st. Here the two Western allies told Stalin of the May 1944 date for the planned invasion of Normandy. In turn, Stalin confirmed a pledge made earlier that Russia would enter the war against Japan after the war with Germany was concluded. The Yalta Conference was the second attended personally by Stalin, Churchill, and Roosevelt. It lasted from the 4th to the 11th of February 1945. A plan to divide Germany into zones of occupation, which had been devised in 1943 by a committee under British Deputy Prime Minister Clement Attlee, was formally accepted with the addition of a fourth zone taken from the British and American zones for the French to occupy. Berlin, which lay within the Russian Zone, was divided into four zones of occupation also.

The third summit meeting of the Big Three took place at Potsdam outside Berlin after the end of the European war but while the Pacific war was still going on. The conference began July 17, 1945, with Stalin, Churchill, and the new American President Harry Truman attending. A Potsdam Declaration, aimed at Japan, called for immediate Japanese surrender and hinted at the consequences that would ensue if it were not forthcoming. While at the conference, American leaders received the news of the successful testing of the first atomic bomb in the New Mexico desert, but the Japanese were given no clear warning that such a destructive weapon might be used against them.

On August 6, 1945, the bomb was dropped by a single plane on Hiroshima and an entire city disappeared, with the instantaneous loss of 70,000 lives. In time many other persons died from radiation poisoning and other effects. Since no surrender was received, a second bomb was dropped on Nagasaki, obliterating that city. Even the most fanatical of the Japanese leaders saw what was happening and surrender came quickly. The only departure from unconditional surrender was to allow the Japanese to retain their emperor (Hirohito, 1901–1989), but only with the proviso that he would be subject in every respect to the orders of the occupation commander. The formal surrender took place September 2, 1945, in Tokyo Bay on the deck of the battleship *Missouri*, and the occupation of Japan began under the immediate control of the American commander General Douglas MacArthur (1880–1964).

Europe after World War II: 1945 to 1953

Anglo-American ideas about what the postwar world should be like were expressed by Roosevelt and Churchill at their meeting off the coast of Newfoundland in August 1941. The Atlantic Charter was a general statement of goals: restoration of the sovereignty and self-government of nations conquered by Hitler, free access to world trade and resources, cooperation to improve living standards and economic security, and a peace that would ensure freedom from fear and want and stop the use of force and aggression as instruments of national policy.

At the Casablanca Conference, the policy of requiring unconditional surrender by the Axis powers was announced. This ensured that at the end of the war, all responsibility for government of the defeated nations would fall on the victors, and they would have a free hand in rebuilding government in those countries. No real planning was done in detail before the time arrived to meet this responsibility. It was done for the most part as the need arose.

At Teheran, the Big Three did discuss in a general way the occupation and demilitarization of Germany. They also laid the foundation for a post-war organization—the United Nations Organization—which like the earlier League of Nations was supposed to help regulate international relations and keep the peace and ensure friendly cooperation between the nations of the world.

At Potsdam, agreement was reached to sign peace treaties as soon as possible with former German allies. A Council of Foreign Ministers was established to draft the treaties. Several meetings were held in 1946 and 1947 and treaties were signed with Italy, Romania,

Hungary, Bulgaria, and Finland. These states paid reparations and agreed to some territorial readjustments as a price for peace. No agreement could be reached on Japan or Germany. In 1951, the Western powers led by the U.S. concluded a treaty with Japan without Russian participation. The latter made their own treaty in 1956. A final meeting of the Council of Foreign Ministers broke up in 1947 over Germany, and no peace treaty was ever signed with that country. The division of Germany for purposes of occupation and military government became permanent, with the three Western zones joining and eventually becoming the Federal Republic of Germany and the Russian zone becoming the German Democratic Republic.

Arrangements for the United Nations were confirmed at the Yalta Conference: the large powers would predominate in a Security Council, where they would have permanent seats together with several other powers elected from time to time from among the other members of the U.N. Consent of all the permanent members was necessary for any action to be taken by the Security Council (thus, giving the large powers a veto). The General Assembly was to include all members.

Much of European Russia had been devastated, and about 25 million people made homeless. In March 1946 a fourth five-year plan was adopted by the Supreme Soviet intended to increase industrial output to a level 50 percent higher than before the war. A bad harvest and food shortage in 1946 had been relieved by a good harvest in 1947, and in December 1947, the government announced the end of food rationing. At the same time a drastic currency devaluation was put through, which brought immediate hardship to many people but strengthened the Soviet economy in the long run. As a result of these and other forceful and energetic measures, the Soviet Union was able within a few years to make good most of the wartime damage and to surpass pre-war levels of production.

The fate of Eastern Europe (including Poland, Hungary, Romania, Bulgaria, Czechoslovakia, and the Russian zone of Germany) from 1945 on was determined by the presence of Russian armies in that area.

Communization of Eastern Europe and the establishment of regimes in the satellite areas of the Soviet Union occurred in stages over a three-year period following the end of the war. The timetable of events varied in each country.

As relations broke down between the four occupying powers, the Soviet authorities gradually created a Communist state in their zone. On October 7, 1948, a German

Democratic Republic was established. In June 1950, an agreement with Poland granted formal recognition of the Oder-Neisse Line as the boundary between the two states. Economic progress was unsatisfactory for most of the population, and on June 16–17, 1953, riots occurred in East Berlin which were suppressed by Soviet forces using tanks. In East Germany, a program of economic reform was announced which eventually brought some improvement.

In Yugoslavia, Marshal Tito (1892–1980) and his Communist partisan movement emerged from the war in a strong position because of their effective campaign against the German occupation. Tito was able to establish a Communist government in 1945 despite considerable pressure from Stalin, and pursue a course independent of the Soviet Union unique among the countries of Eastern Europe.

Western Europe: 1945–1953

The monarchy which had governed Italy since the time of unification in the mid-nineteenth century was now discarded in favor of a republic. King Victor Emmanuel III (1869–1947), compromised by his association with Mussolini, resigned in favor of his son, but a referendum in June 1946 established a republic. In simultaneous elections for a constituent assembly, three parties predominated: the Social Democrats, the Communists, and the Christian Democrats.

In the last two years of the war, France recovered sufficiently under the leadership of General Charles de Gaulle to begin playing a significant military and political role once again. In July 1944, the United States recognized de Gaulle's Committee of National Liberation as the de facto government of areas liberated from the German occupation.

In foreign affairs, France occupied Germany. In addition, the Fourth Republic was faced with two major problems abroad when it attempted to assert its authority over Indochina and Algeria. The Indochina situation resulted in a long and costly war against nationalists and Communists under Ho Chi Minh (1890–1969). French involvement ended with the Geneva Accords of 1954 and French withdrawal. The Algerian struggle reached a crisis in 1958 resulting in General de Gaulle's return to power and the creation of a new Fifth Republic.

In May 1945, when Germany surrendered unconditionally, the country lay in ruins. About three-quarters of city houses had been gutted by air raids, industry was in a shambles, and the country was divided into zones of occupation ruled by foreign military governors. Economic chaos was the rule, currency was virtually worthless, food was in short supply, and the black market flourished for those who could afford to buy in it. By the Potsdam agreements, Germany lost about one-quarter of its pre-war territory. In addition, some 12 million people of German origin driven from their homes in countries like Poland and Czechoslovakia had to be fed, housed, and clothed along with the indigenous population.

Demilitarization, denazification, and democratization were the initial goals of the occupation forces in Germany. All four wartime allies agreed on the trial of leading Nazis for a variety of war crimes and "crimes against humanity." An International Military Tribunal was established at Nuremburg to try 22 major war criminals, and lesser courts tried many others. Most of the defendants were executed, although a few like Rudolf Hess were given life imprisonment.

As relations between the three Western powers and the Soviets gradually broke down in Germany, East and West became separate states. In the West, the British and American zones were fused into one in 1946, with the French joining in 1948. Political parties were gradually re-established.

In February 1948, a charter granted further powers of government to the Germans in the American and British zones. Later that year, the Russians and East Germans, in an effort to force the Western powers out of their zones in Berlin, began a blockade of the city which was located within the Russian zone. The response was an allied airlift to supply the city, and eventually, after some months, the blockade was called off.

In 1951 a Conservative majority was returned in Great Britain, and Winston Churchill, who had been defeated in 1945, became prime minister again. The new regime immediately reversed the nationalization of iron and steel. Other measures survived, however, especially the universal health care program which proved to be one of the most popular parts of the Labour achievement. In April 1955, Churchill resigned for reasons of age and health and turned over the prime minister's office to Anthony Eden (1897–1977).

The Marshall Plan

European recovery from the effects of the war was slow for the first two or three years after 1945. The European Recovery Program (Marshall Plan, named after the American secretary of state and World War II army chief of staff) began in 1948 and showed substantial results in all the Western European countries that took part. The most remarkable gains were in West Germany. The Plan aimed to strengthen Western Europe's resistance to communism.

NATO

The United States joined eleven other states in the Atlantic region in a mutual defense pact called the North Atlantic Treaty Organization (NATO) in 1949. NATO was created to counterbalance the Soviet presence in Central and Eastern Europe.

British Overseas Withdrawal

Following World War II, there was a considerable migration of Jews who had survived the Nazi Holocaust to Palestine to join Jews who had settled there earlier. Conflicts broke out with the Arabs. The British occupying forces tried to suppress the violence and to negotiate a settlement between the factions. In 1948, after negotiations failed, the British, feeling they could no longer support the cost of occupation, announced their withdrawal. Zionist leaders then proclaimed the independent state of Israel and took up arms to fight the armies of Egypt, Syria, and other Arab states which invaded the Jewish-held area. The new Israeli state quickly proved its technological and military superiority by defeating the invaders.

The Jews of Israel created a modern parliamentary state on the European model with an economy and technology superior to their Arab neighbors. The new state was thought by many Arabs to be simply another manifestation of European imperialism made worse by religious antagonisms.

In 1967, Israel defeated Egypt, Syria, and Jordan in a six-day war, and the Israelis occupied additional territory including the Jordanian sector of the city of Jerusalem. An additional million Arabs came under Israeli rule as a result of this campaign.

Although defeated, the Arabs refused to sign any treaty or to come to terms with Israel. Palestinian refugees living in camps in states bordering Israel created grave problems. A Palestine Liberation Organization (PLO) was formed to fight for the establishment of an Arab Palestinian state on territory taken from Israel on the west bank of the Jordan River. The PLO resorted to terrorist tactics against both Israel and other states in support of their cause.

In October 1973, the Egyptians and Syrians launched an attack on Israel known as the Yom Kippur War. With some difficulty the attacks were repulsed. A settlement was mediated by American Secretary of State Henry Kissinger. The situation has remained unstable, however, with both sides resorting to border raids and other forms of violence short of full-scale war.

The government under King Farouk I (1920–1965) did little to alleviate the overriding problem of poverty after the war. In 1952, a group of army officers, including Gamal Abdel Nasser (1918–1970) and Anwar Sadat (1918–1981), plotted against the government, and on July 23 the king was overthrown. Colonel Nasser became premier in April 1954. A treaty with Britain later that year resulted in the withdrawal of all British troops from the Canal Zone.

India under Jawaharlal Nehru (1889–1964) and the Congress Party became a parliamentary democracy. The country made economic progress, but gains were largely negated by a population increase to 600 million from 350 million.

The French in Indochina and Algeria

Following World War II, the French returned to Indochina and attempted to restore their rule there. The opposition nationalist movement was led by the veteran Communist Ho Chi Minh. War broke out between the nationalists and the French forces. In 1954 their army was surrounded at Dienbienphu and forced to surrender. This military disaster prompted a change of government in France.

This new government under Premier Pierre Mendès-France (1907–1982) negotiated French withdrawal at a conference held at Geneva, Switzerland in 1954. Cambodia and Laos became independent and Vietnam was partitioned at the 17th parallel. The North, with its capital at Hanoi, became a Communist state under Ho Chi Minh. The South remained non-Communist. Under the Geneva Accords, elections were to be held in the South to determine the fate of that area. However, the United States chose to intervene and support the regime of Ngo Dinh Diem (1901–1963), and elections were never held. Eventually a second Vietnamese war resulted, with the United States playing the role earlier played by France.

In a referendum, on January 8, 1961, the French people approved of eventual Algerian self-determination. In July 1962 French rule ended in Algeria. There was a mass exodus of Europeans from Algeria, but most Frenchmen were grateful to de Gaulle for ending the long Algerian conflict.

The Dutch and Indonesia

During World War II, the Japanese conquered the Dutch East Indies. At the end of the war, they recognized the independence of the area as Indonesia. When the Dutch attempted to return, four years of bloody fighting ensued against the nationalist forces of Achmed Sukarno (1901–1970). In 1949, the Dutch recognized Indonesian independence. In 1954, the Indonesians dissolved all ties with the Netherlands.

The Cold War after the Death of Stalin

Following Stalin's death in 1953, Russian leaders appeared more willing than Stalin to be conciliatory and to consider peaceful coexistence.

In the U.S. the atmosphere also changed with the election of President Dwight Eisenhower and conciliatory gestures were not always automatically considered appeasement of the Communists. In 1955 a summit conference of Eisenhower, the British and French leaders, and Khrushchev (1894–1971) met at Geneva in an atmosphere more cordial than any since World War II. The "spirit of Geneva" did not last long, however.

After his return to power in France in 1958, General de Gaulle endeavored to make France a leader in European affairs with himself as spokesman for a Europe that he hoped would be a counter to the "dual hegemony" of the U.S. and U.S.S.R. His policies at times were anti-British or anti-American. Despite his prestige as the last great wartime leader, he did not have great success.

A New Era Begins

Josef Stalin died in March 1953. Eventually a little-known party functionary, Nikita Khrushchev, became Communist Party General Secretary in 1954. Khrushchev's policy of relaxing the regime of terror and oppression of the Stalin years became known as "The Thaw," after the title of a novel by Ilya Ehrenburg (1891–1967).

Change occurred in foreign affairs also. Khrushchev visited Belgrade and re-established relations with Tito, admitting that there was more than one road to socialism.

He also visited the United States, met with President Eisenhower, and toured the country. Later, relations became more tense after the U-2 spy plane incident.

Following the loss of face sustained by Russia as a result of the Cuban Missile Crisis and the failure of Khrushchev's domestic agricultural policies, he was forced out of the party leadership and lived in retirement in Moscow until his death in 1971.

After Khrushchev's ouster, the leadership in the Central Committee divided power, making Leonid Brezhnev (1906–1982) party secretary and Aleksei Kosygin chairman of the council of ministers, or premier.

Stalin's successors rehabilitated many of Stalin's victims. They also permitted somewhat greater freedom in literary and artistic matters and even allowed some political criticism. Controls were maintained, however, and sometimes were tightened. Anti-Semitism was also still present, and Soviet Jews were long denied permission to emigrate to Israel.

Brezhnev occupied the top position of power until his death in 1982. He was briefly succeeded by Yuri Andropov (1914–1984) (a former secret police chief) and Konstantin Chenenko (1911–1985), then by Mikhail Gorbachev, who carried out a further relaxation of the internal regime. Gorbachev pushed disarmament and detente in foreign relations, and attempted a wide range of internal reforms known as *perestroika* ("restructuring"). Gorbachev resigned in 1991. Boris Yeltsin assumed control over the collapsing Soviet Union, which would later become known as the Commonwealth of Independent States, with Yeltsin as president.

Economic difficulties associated with a transition to a free economy, the mishandled repression of the Chechnya independence movement, and the forceful dispersal of Yeltsin's parliamentary opponents in 1993 gave ammunition to Yeltsin's opponents. In the 1996 elections, Yeltsin retained office as president, but the poor state of his health, despite successful heart bypass surgery in the fall of 1996, eventually made him step down and yield leadership to Vladimir Putin in late 1999.

Change in Eastern Europe

In the 1980s, the trade union movement known as Solidarity and its leader, Lech Walesa, emerged as a political force, organizing mass protests in 1980–1981 and maintaining almost continuous pressure on the government headed by General Wojciech Jaruzelski. Despite government efforts to maintain strong central control and suppress the opposition, the ruling Communists were forced to recognize the opposition and make concessions. In June 1989, after power had passed to the Polish Parliament, a national election gave Solidarity an overwhelming majority, and Walesa assumed the presidency. By 1993–94, economic problems resulted in a Communist majority and a change of administration, but there was no return to the old Communist dictatorship.

Change in Western Europe

In March 1957, inspired chiefly by Belgian Foreign Minister Paul-Henri Spaak, two treaties were signed in Rome creating a European Atomic Energy Commission (Euratom) and a European Economic Community (the Common Market)—which eventually absorbed Euratom. The EEC was to be a customs union creating a free market area with a common external tariff for member nations. Toward the outside world, the EEC acted as a single bargaining agent for its members in commercial transactions, and it reached a number of agreements with other European and Third World states.

In 1973, the original six were joined by three new members: Britain, Ireland, and Denmark. The name was changed to "European Community." In 1979, there were three more applicants: Spain, Portugal, and Greece. These latter states were less well off and created problems of cheap labor, agricultural products, etc., which delayed their acceptance as members until 1986. With the acceptance of the Maastricht Treaties in 1993, the group's name became the "European Union."

Relations with Northern Ireland proved a burden to successive British governments. The 1922 settlement had left Northern Ireland as a self-governing part of the United Kingdom. Of 1.5 million inhabitants, one-third were Roman Catholic and two-thirds were Protestant. Catholics claimed they were discriminated against and pressed for annexation by the Republic of Ireland. Activity by the Irish Republican Army brought retaliation by Protestant extremists. From 1969 on, there was considerable violence, causing the British to bring in troops to maintain order.

Under Prime Minister Margaret Thatcher in the 1980s, the British economy improved somewhat. London regained some of its former power as a financial center. In recent years, an influx of people from former colonies in Asia, Africa, and the West Indies has caused some racial tensions.

Prime Minister Thatcher was a partisan of free enterprise. She fought inflation with austerity and let economic problems spur British employers and unions to change for greater efficiency. She received a boost in popularity when Britain won a brief war with Argentina over the Falkland Islands. She stressed close ties with the Republican administration of Ronald Reagan in the U.S. A Conservative victory in the 1987 elections made Thatcher the longest-serving prime minister in modern British history.

In 1990, having lost the support of Conservatives in Parliament, Thatcher resigned and was replaced by Chancellor of the Exchequer John Major. Under Major's leadership, Conservatives had to deal with slow economic growth, unemployment, and racial tensions caused by resentment over the influx of immigrants from other parts of the Commonwealth. And there remains the seemingly intractable religious strife in Northern Ireland, with its Protestant-Catholic animosities. Tony Blair, prime minister from 1997 to 2007, has made Northern Ireland peace a priority, with tentative success. He has had more success in achieving closer relations with the European Union.

France under de Gaulle saw a new constitution drafted and approved establishing the Fifth Republic with a much strengthened executive in the form of a president with power to dissolve the legislature and call for elections, to submit important questions to popular referendum, and if necessary to assume emergency powers. De Gaulle used all these powers in his 11 years as president.

In domestic politics, de Gaulle strengthened the power of the president by often using the referendum and bypassing the Assembly. De Gaulle was re-elected in 1965, but people became restless with what amounted to a republican monarch. Labor became restive over inflation and housing while students objected to expenditures on nuclear forces rather than education. In May 1968, student grievances over conditions in the universities caused hundreds of thousands to revolt. They were soon joined by some 10 million workers, who paralyzed the economy. De Gaulle survived by promising educational reform and wage increases. New elections were held in June 1968, and de Gaulle was returned to power. Promised reforms were begun, but in April 1969, he resigned and died about a year later.

De Gaulle's immediate successors were Georges Pompidou (1969–1974) and Valéry Giscard d'Estaing (1974–1981). Both provided France with firm leadership, and continued to follow an independent foreign policy.

In 1981 François Mitterand succeeded Giscard d'Estaing. He inherited a troubled economy. During his first year Mitterand tried to revitalize economic growth, granted wage hikes, reduced the work week, expanded paid vacations, and nationalized 11 large private companies and banks. The aim was to stimulate the economy by expanding worker purchasing power and confiscating the profits of large corporations for public investment. Loans were made abroad to finance this program. When results were poor, these foreign investors were reluctant to grant more credit. Mitterand then reversed his policy and began to cut taxes and social expenditures. By 1984, this had brought down inflation but increased unemployment.

Mitterand lost his Socialist majority in Parliament in 1986, but regained it in 1988. In 1995, an ailing Mitterand indicated he would retire at the end of his term. He died in January 1996. Out of the election of April 1995 emerged a fractured right-of-center bloc that came to coalesce around Jacques Chirac, the mayor of Paris and former two-time prime minister. Following a second-round runoff, Chirac won 52 percent of the vote. Facing a far-right challenger, Jean-Marie Le Pen, in 2002, Chirac won a decisive victory for re-election.

In Germany in November 1966, the Christian Democrats formed a so-called "great coalition" with the Social Democrats under Willy Brandt. Kurt Georg Kiesinger (1904–1988) became chancellor, and Brandt the Socialist took over as foreign minister. Brandt announced his intention to work step by step for better relations with East Germany, but found that in a coalition of two very dissimilar parties he could make no substantial progress.

Problems with the economy and the environment brought an end to Kiesinger's chancellorship and the rule of the Socialists in 1982. An organization called the Greens, which was a loosely organized coalition of environmentalists alienated from society, detracted from Socialist power. In 1982, the German voters turned to the more conservative Christian Democrats again, and Helmut Kohl became chancellor. Kohl served until 1998, when he was replaced by Social Democrat Gerhard Schroeder.

In Italy, the Christian Democrats, who were closely allied with the Roman Catholic Church, dominated the national scene. Their organization, though plagued by corruption, did provide some unity to Italian politics by supplying the prime ministers for numerous coalitions.

Italy advanced economically. Natural gas and some oil was discovered in the north and the Po valley area especially benefited. Unfortunately, business efficiency found no parallel in the government or civil service. Italy suffered from terrorism, kidnappings, and assassinations by extreme radical groups such as the Red Brigades. These agitators hoped to create conditions favorable to the overthrow of the democratic constitution. The most notorious terrorist act was the assassination in 1978 of Aldo Moro (1916–1978), a respected Christian Democratic leader.

In 1983, Bettino Craxi (Socialist) became prime minister at the head of an uneasy coalition that lasted four years—the longest single government in postwar Italian history. By the 1990s Italian industry and its economy had advanced to a point where Italy was a leading center in high-tech industry, fashion, design, and banking, but instability continued to mark Italian politics. Corruption within a system dominated by the Christian Democrats resulted in criminal trials in the 1990s that sent a number of high government officials to prison. In 1993 the electoral system for the Senate was changed from proportional representation to one that gives power to the majority vote-getting party. The 1994 elections for Parliament brought to power the charismatic, conservative Silvio Berlusconi and his *Forzia Italia* ("Let's go, Italy") movement.

In Portugal, Europe's longest right-wing dictatorship came to an end in September 1968, when a stroke incapacitated Antonio Salazar, who died two years later. A former collaborator, Marcelo Caetano (1906–1980), became prime minister, and an era of change began. Censorship was relaxed and some freedom was given to political parties.

In April 1974, the Caetano regime was overthrown and a "junta of national salvation" took over, headed by General Spinola, who later retired and went into exile. Portugal went through a succession of governments. Its African colonies of Mozambique and Angola were finally granted independence in 1975. Portugal joined the Common Market in 1986.

Spain's Francisco Franco, who had been ruler of a fascist regime since the end of the Civil War in 1939, held on until he was close to 70. He then designated the Bourbon prince, Juan Carlos, to be his successor. In 1975, Franco relinquished power and died three weeks later. Juan Carlos proved an able leader and took the country from dictatorship to constitutional monarchy. Basque and Catalan separatist movements, which had caused trouble for so long, were temporarily appeased by the granting of limited local autonomy. Spain also entered the European Community in 1986.

Under the Maastricht Treaties of 1991, all members of the EC began measured steps toward an economic and political union that would ultimately have its own common currency, the euro. In 1996, the 12 member nations of the European Union accounted for one-fifth of world trade.

Today, the European Union comprises 27 European countries, with corresponding common economic, social, and security policies.

Table 3.1 Significant Dates in World History

220 and 476	Fall of Han dynasty and fall of western Roman Empire
622	Flight of Muhammad to Medina (beginning of Islam
1096–1099	The First Crusade
1200–1300	Mongol domination of Asia
1453	Constantinople falls to the Ottomans
1492	Columbus lands in the Americas
1750–1780	Height of the Atlantic slave trade
1789	The French Revolution
1870's	Colonialization of Africa begins
1914–1918	First World War
1939–1945	Second World War
1947	Independence of India and Pakistan
1957	Russia launches Sputnik
1989	The Berlin Wall falls

CHAPTER 4

Government, Civics, and Political Science

FOUNDATIONS OF GOVERNMENT

The purpose or role of a central government was a hotly debated topic between the Federalists and Anti-federalists during the formation of the United States. Indeed, it remains intense today given the debates surrounding, for example, health care reform. But most people can agree that a government's purpose is to provide public services, protect its citizenry, and allow the marketplace to operate to the benefit of the people. In order for the government to provide these basic necessities its citizens must agree to abide by certain decisions the government makes. Theorists call this agreement a social contract. English philosopher Thomas Hobbes (1588-1679), one of the first to theorize on the social contract, wrote that in a natural state, no government existed. People surrendered to the state the power needed to maintain order and this surrender, for Hobbes, was an unbreakable contract. John Locke took the social contract a step further, writing that people were naturally endowed with the right to life, liberty, and property. To preserve their rights, they willingly contracted to give power to a governing authority. When government failed the preserve the rights of the people, the people had the right to break the contract and rebel.

ECONOMIC THEORIES

There are three main economic systems: **capitalism, socialism, and communism;** and, a fourth if we take into account those systems that a mix two of the three main systems. Regardless of the system certain major economic decisions must be made for a system to be successful: what goods and services will be produced, how much should be produced; and who gets the goods and services which are produced.

For capitalism the key emphases is on the freedom of choice and individual incentive for every player in the system. Capitalism has five main characteristics:

1. Private ownership and control of property and economic resources

2. Free enterprise

3. Competition among businesses

4. Freedom of choice

5. The possibility of profits

In socialism the basic means of production and all decisions as to how to use resources, distribute the products and wages, and how to provide social services such as education, health care, and welfare is left to a centralized government. The three main goals of socialism are:

1. The distribution of wealth and economic opportunity equally among people

2. Society's control through government, of all major decisions about production

3. Public ownership of most land of factories, and of other means of production

In communist nations central government planners decide what and how much to produce, and how to distribute goods and services. A communist economy is termed a command economy because decisions are made at the upper levels of government.

CONSTITUTIONAL FOUNDATIONS OF THE UNITED STATES GOVERNMENT

The government of the United States rests on a written framework created in an attempt to strengthen a loose confederation that was in crisis in the 1780s. The Constitution is a basic plan that outlines the structure and functions of the national government. Clearly rooted in Western political thought, it sets limits on government and protects both property and individual rights.

Historical Background

Following the successful revolt of the British colonies in North America against imperial rule, a plan of government was implemented that was consciously weak and ultimately ineffective, the Articles of Confederation. The Articles served as the national government from 1781–1787. The government under the Articles consisted of a unicameral (one house) legislature that was clearly subordinate to the states. Representatives to the Congress were appointed and paid by their respective state legislatures, and their mission was to protect the interests of their home states. Each state, regardless of size, had one vote in Congress, which could request but not require states to provide financial and military support. Key weaknesses of the Articles included: its inability to regulate interstate and foreign trade, its lack of a chief executive and a national court system, and its rule that amendments must be approved by unanimous consent.

Dubbed the "critical period," the 1780s was a decade in the United States marked by internal conflict. The economy deteriorated as individual states printed their own currencies, taxed the products of their neighbors, and ignored foreign trade agreements. Inflation soared, small farmers lost their property, and states engaged in petty squabbles with one another. The discontent of the agrarian population reached crisis proportions in 1786 in rural Massachusetts when Revolutionary War veteran Daniel Shays led a rebellion of farmers against the tax collectors and the banks that were seizing their property. Shays' Rebellion symbolized the inability of the government under the Articles to maintain order. Bostonians subscribed money to raise an army, which successfully suppressed the rebels.

In response to the economic and social disorder and the dangers of foreign intervention, a series of meetings to consider reform of the Articles was held. In 1787, the Constitutional Convention was convened in Philadelphia ostensibly to revise the ineffective Articles. The result was an entirely new plan of government, the Constitution.

Philosophy and Ideology of the Founders

Among the distinguished men assembled at the Constitutional Convention in 1787 were James Madison, who recorded the debate proceedings; George Washington, president of the body; Gouverneur Morris, who wrote the final version of the document; and Alexander Hamilton, one of the authors of the Federalist Papers (1787–1788). This collection of essays, to which Madison and John Jay also contributed, expresses the political philosophy of the Founders and was instrumental in bringing about the ratification of the Constitution.

Clearly the framers of the Constitution were influenced by the ideological heritage of the seventeenth and eighteenth centuries Enlightenment in Western Europe. From Hobbes and Locke came the concept of the social contract. The latter had a marked influence upon Thomas Jefferson, who incorporated Locke's doctrines with respect to equality; government's responsibility to protect the life, liberty, and property of its constituency; and the right of revolution in his Declaration of Independence (1776). The Constitution itself includes Montesquieu's separation of powers and checks and balances. British documents, such as the Magna Carta (1215), the Petition of Right (1628), and the Bill of Rights (1689), all promoting the principle of limited government, were influential in shaping the final form of the Constitution.

Basic Principles of the Constitution

The authors of the Constitution sought to establish a government free from the tyrannies of both monarchs and mobs. Two of the critical principles embedded in the final document, federalism and separation of powers, address this concern.

The federal system established by the Founders divides the powers of government between the states and the national government. Local matters are handled on a local level, and those issues that affect the general populace are the responsibility of the federal government. Such a system is a natural outgrowth of the colonial relationship between the Americans and the mother country of England. American federalism is defined in the Tenth Amendment, which declares, "those powers not delegated to the

United States by the Constitution, nor prohibited by it to the States, are reserved to the States respectively, or to the people." In practice, the system may be confusing in that powers overlap (i.e., welfare). In cases where they conflict, the federal government is supreme.

The principle of separation of powers is codified in Articles I, II, and III of the main body of the Constitution. The national government is divided into three branches which have separate functions (legislative, executive, and judicial). Not entirely independent, each of these branches can check or limit in some way the power of one or both of the others (checks and balances). This system of dividing and checking powers is a vehicle for guarding against the extremes the Founders feared. Following are some examples of checks and balances:

- The legislative branch can check the executive by refusing to confirm appointments.

- The executive can check the legislature by vetoing its bills.

- The judiciary can check both the legislature and the executive by declaring laws unconstitutional.

Additional basic principles embodied in the Constitution include:

- The establishment of a representative government (republic).

- Popular sovereignty or the idea that government derives its power from the people. This concept is expressed in the Preamble which opens with the words, "We the People."

- The enforcement of government with limits ("rule of law").

STRUCTURE AND FUNCTIONS OF THE NATIONAL GOVERNMENT

The national government consists of the three branches outlined in the Constitution as well as a huge bureaucracy comprised of departments, agencies, and commissions.

The Legislative Branch

Legislative power is vested in a bicameral (two-house) Congress which is the subject of Article I of the Constitution. The bicameral structure was the result of a compromise at the Constitutional Convention between the large states, led by Virginia, which presented a plan calling for a strong national government with representation favoring the larger states (Virginia Plan) and the smaller states, which countered with the New Jersey Plan. The latter would have retained much of the structure of the Articles of Confederation including equal representation of the states in Congress. Connecticut offered a solution in the form of the Great Compromise. It called for a two-house legislature with equal representation in the Senate and representation in the House of Representatives based on population.

The expressed or delegated powers of Congress are set forth in Section 8 of Article I. They can be divided into several broad categories including economic, judicial, war, and general peace powers.

Economic powers include:

- to lay and collect taxes

- to borrow money

- to regulate foreign and interstate commerce

- to coin money and regulate its value

- to establish rules concerning bankruptcy

Judicial powers include:

- to establish courts inferior to the Supreme Court

- to provide punishment for counterfeiting

- to define and punish piracies and felonies committed on the high seas

War powers include:

- to declare war

- to raise and support armies

- to provide and maintain a navy

- to provide for organizing, arming, and calling forth the militia

Peace powers include:

- to establish rules on naturalization

- to establish post offices and post roads

- to promote science and the arts by granting patents and copyrights

- to exercise jurisdiction over the seat of the federal government (District of Columbia)

The Constitution includes the so-called "elastic clause" which grants Congress implied powers to implement the delegated powers.

In addition, Congress maintains the power to discipline federal officials through impeachment (formal accusation of wrongdoing) and removal from office.

Article V empowers Congress to propose amendments (changes or additions) to the Constitution. A two-thirds majority in both houses is necessary for passage. An alternate method is to have amendments proposed by the legislatures of two-thirds of the states. In order for an amendment to become part of the Constitution, it must be ratified (formally approved) by three-fourths of the states (through their legislatures or by way of special conventions as in the case of the repeal of Prohibition).

Article I, Section 9 specifically denies certain powers to the national legislature. Congress is prohibited from suspending the right of habeas corpus (writ calling for a party under arrest to be brought before the court where authorities must show cause for detainment) except during war or rebellion. Other prohibitions include: the passage of export taxes, the withdrawal of funds from the treasury without an appropriations law, the passage of ex post facto laws (make past actions punishable that were legal when they occurred), and favored treatment of one state over another with respect to commerce.

The work of the Congress is organized around a committee system. The standing committees are permanent and deal with such matters as agriculture, the armed services, the budget, energy, finance, and foreign policy. Special or select committees are established to deal with specific issues and usually have a limited duration. Conference committees iron out differences between the House and the Senate versions of a bill before it is sent on to the President.

One committee unique to the House of Representatives is the powerful Rules Committee. Thousands of bills are introduced each term, and the Rules Committee acts as a clearing house to weed out those that are unworthy of consideration before the full House. Constitutionally, all revenue-raising bills must originate in the House of Representatives. They are scrutinized by the powerful House Ways and Means Committee.

Committee membership is organized on party lines with seniority being a key factor, although in recent years, length of service has diminished in importance in the determination of chairmanships. The composition of each committee is largely based on the ratio of each party in the Congress as a whole. The party that has a majority is allotted a greater number of members on each committee. The chairman of the standing committees are selected by the leaders of the majority party.

The legislative process is at once cumbersome and time consuming (see Figure 4.1). A bill (proposed law) can be introduced in either house (with the exception of revenue bills, which must originate in the House of Representatives). It is referred to the appropriate committee and then to a subcommittee, which will hold hearings if the members agree that it has merit. The bill is reported back to the full committee, which must decide whether or not to send it to the full chamber to be debated. If the bill passes in the full chamber, it is then sent to the other chamber to begin the process all over again. Any differences between the House and Senate versions of the bill must be resolved in a conference committee before it is sent to the President for consideration. Most of the

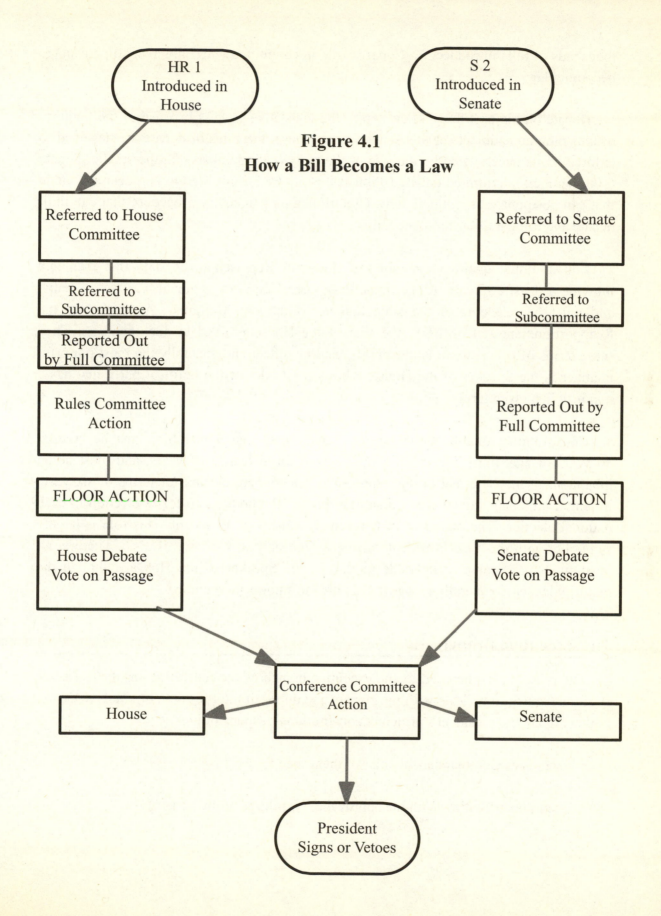

Figure 4.1
How a Bill Becomes a Law

thousands of bills introduced in Congress die in committee with only a small percentage becoming law.

Debate on major bills is a key step in the legislative process because of the tradition of attaching amendments at this stage. In the House, the rules of debate are designed to enforce limits necessitated by the size of the body (435 members). In the smaller Senate (100 members), unlimited debate (filibuster) is allowed. Filibustering is a delaying tactic that can postpone action indefinitely. Cloture is a parliamentary procedure that can limit debate and bring a filibuster to an end.

Constitutional qualifications for the House of Representatives state that members must be at least 25 years of age, must have been U.S. citizens for at least seven years, and must be residents of the state that sends them to Congress. According to the Reapportionment Act of 1929, the size of the House is fixed at 435 members. They serve terms of two years in length. The presiding officer and generally the most powerful member is the Speaker of the House, who is the leader of the political party that has a majority in a given term.

Constitutional qualifications for the Senate state that a member must be at least 30 years of age, must have been a U.S. citizen for at least nine years, and must be an inhabitant of the state that he/she represents. Senators are elected for terms of six years in length on a staggered basis so that one-third of the body is up for re-election in each national election. The president of the Senate is the Vice President. This role is largely symbolic, with the Vice President casting a vote only in the case of a tie. There is no position in the Senate comparable to that of the Speaker of the House, although the majority leader is generally recognized as the most powerful member.

The Executive Branch

The president is the head of the executive branch of the federal government. Article II of the Constitution deals with the powers and duties of the President or chief executive. Following are the president's principal constitutional responsibilities:

- serves as Commander-in-Chief of the armed forces

- negotiates treaties (with the approval of two-thirds of the Senate)

- appoints ambassadors, judges, and other high officials (with the consent of the Senate)

- grants pardons and reprieves for those convicted of federal crimes (except in impeachment cases)

- seeks counsel of department heads (Cabinet members)

- recommends legislation

- meets with representatives of foreign states

- sees that the laws are faithfully executed

Despite the attempts by the Founders to set clear limits on the power of the chief executive, the importance of the presidency has grown dramatically over the years. Recent trends to reassert the pre-eminence of the Congress notwithstanding, the president remains the most visible and powerful single member of the federal government and the only one (with the exception of the vice president) elected to represent all the people. He shapes foreign policy with his diplomatic and treaty-making powers and largely determines domestic policy. Presidents also possess the power to veto legislation. A presidential veto may be overridden by a two-thirds vote in both houses, but such a majority is not easy to build, particularly in the face of the chief executive's opposition. A pocket veto occurs when the president neither signs nor rejects a bill, and the Congress adjourns within ten days of his receipt of the legislation. The fact that the president is the head of a vast federal bureaucracy is another indication of the power of the office.

Although the Constitution makes no mention of a formal Cabinet as such, since the days of George Washington, chief executives have relied on department heads to aid in the decision-making process. Washington's Cabinet was comprised of the secretaries of state, war, treasury, and an attorney general. Today there are 15 Cabinet departments, with Homeland Security being the most recently created post. Efforts to trim the federal government in the 1990s have resulted in suggestions to streamline and eliminate some Cabinet posts.

The Executive Office of the President is made up of agencies that supervise the daily work of the government. The White House Staff manages the President's schedule and is usually headed by a powerful chief of staff. Arguably the most critical agency of the Executive Office is the Office of Management and Budget, which controls the budget process for the national government. Other key executive agencies include the Council of Economic Advisors and the National Security Council, which advises the President on matters that threaten the safety of the nation and directs the Central Intelligence Agency.

The Constitutional Requirements for the office of president and vice president are as follows: a candidate must be at least 35 years of age, must be a natural-born citizen, and must have resided in the United States for a minimum of 14 years. Article II provides for an Electoral College to elect the president and vice president. Each state has as many votes in the Electoral College as it has members of Congress plus three additional electors from the District of Columbia—making a grand total of 538 electors. The Founding Fathers established the Electoral College to provide an indirect method of choosing the chief executive; as shown in the 2000 election, the Electoral College can still play a decisive role in determining the outcome of presidential elections.

The question of presidential succession has been addressed by both legislation and amendment. The Constitution states that if the President dies or cannot perform his duties, the "powers and duties" of the office shall "devolve" on the Vice President. The Presidential Succession Act (1947) placed the speaker of the house next in line if both the president and the vice president were unable to serve. Until recently, when the vice president assumed the office of President, his former position was left vacant. The Twenty-Fifth Amendment (1967) gives the president the power to appoint a new vice president (with the approval of a majority of both houses of Congress). It also provides for the vice president to serve as Acting President if the chief executive is disabled or otherwise unable to carry out the duties of the office. The Twenty-Second Amendment (1951) says, "No person shall be elected to the office of the President more than twice...." In addition, anyone who has served more than two years while filling out another person's term may not be elected to the presidency more than once.

The Judicial Branch

Article III of the Constitution establishes the Supreme Court but does not define the role of this branch as clearly as it does the legislative and executive branches. Yet our contemporary judicial branch consists of thousands of courts and is in essence a dual system with each state having its own judiciary functioning simultaneously with a complete set of federal courts. The most significant piece of legislation with respect to establishing a network of federal courts was the Judiciary Act of 1789. This law organized the Supreme Court and set up the 13 federal district courts. The district courts have original jurisdiction (to hear cases in the first instance) for federal cases involving both civil and criminal law. Federal cases on appeal are heard in the Courts of Appeal. The decisions of these courts are final, except for those cases that are accepted for review by the Supreme Court.

The Supreme Court today is made of a Chief Justice and eight Associate Justices. They are appointed for life by the President with the approval of the Senate.

In the early history of the United States, the Supreme Court was largely preoccupied with the relationship between the federal government and those of the states. In 1803, the process of judicial review (power to determine the constitutionality of laws and actions of the legislative and executive branches) was established under Chief Justice John Marshall in the case of *Marbury v. Madison*. This power has become the foundation of the American judicial system and underscores the deep significance of the courts in determining the course of United States history.

The Supreme Court chooses cases for review based on whether or not they address substantial federal issues. If four of the nine justices vote to consider a case, then it will be added to the agenda. In such cases, writs of certiorari (orders calling up the records from a lower court) are issued. The justices are given detailed briefs and hear oral arguments. Reaching a decision is a complicated process. The justices scrutinize the case with reference to the Constitution and also consider previous decisions in similar cases (precedent). When all of the justices agree, the opinion issued is unanimous. In the case of a split decision, a majority opinion is written by one of the justices in agreement. Sometimes a justice will agree with the majority but for a different principle, in which case he/she can write a concurring opinion explaining the different point of view. Justices who do not vote with the majority may choose to write dissenting opinions to air their conflicting arguments.

In addition to the Supreme Court, the federal District Courts, and the Courts of Appeal, several special courts at the federal level have been created by Congress. The U.S. Tax Court handles conflicts between citizens and the Internal Revenue Service. The Court of Claims was designed to hear cases in which citizens bring suit against the U.S.

government. Other special courts include the Court of International Trade, the Court of Customs, and the Court of Military Appeals.

The Federal Bureaucracy

In addition to the President's Cabinet and the Executive Office, a series of independent agencies makes up the federal bureaucracy, the so-called "fourth branch" of the national government. Most of these agencies were established to protect consumers and to regulate industries engaged in interstate trade. Others were set up to oversee government programs. From the time of the establishment of the Interstate Commerce Commission in 1887, these departments grew in number and influence. Late in the 1970s, the trend began to reverse, as some agencies were cut back and others eliminated altogether.

Among the most important of these powerful agencies are the regulatory commissions. The President appoints their administrators with the approval of the Senate. Unlike Cabinet secretaries and other high appointees, they cannot be dismissed by the chief executive. This system protects the independent status of the agencies. Following are examples of some of the major regulatory agencies and their functions.

Table 4.1 Regulatory Commission

Agency	Regulatory Functions
Interstate Commerce Commission	Monitors surface transportation and some pipelines
Federal Reserve Board	Supervises the banking system, sets interest rates, and controls the money supply
Federal Trade Commission	Protects consumers by looking into false advertising and antitrust violations
Federal Communications Commission	Polices the airwaves by licensing radio and television stations and regulating cable and telephone companies
Securities and Exchange Commission	Protects investors by monitoring the sale of stocks and bonds
National Labor Relations Board	Oversees labor and management practices
Consumer Product Safety Commission	Sets standards of safety for manufactured products
Nuclear Regulatory Commission	Licenses and inspects nuclear power plants

Another category of the "fourth branch" of government is made up of the independent executive agencies. These were created by Congress and resemble Cabinet departments, but they do not enjoy Cabinet status. Nonetheless they are powerful entities. Some of the key executive agencies include the Civil Rights Commission, the Environmental Protection Agency, and the National Aeronautics and Space Administration. Their names are indicative of their functions. The top level executives of these agencies are appointed by the President with the approval of the Senate.

Some of the independent agencies are actually government corporations. These are commercial enterprises created by Congress to perform a variety of necessary services. Their roots can be traced back to the First Bank of the United States established in 1791 by Secretary of the Treasury Alexander Hamilton. The Federal Deposit Insurance Corporation (FDIC), which insures bank deposits, is a more recent example. Under Franklin Roosevelt's New Deal, the Tennessee Valley Authority (TVA) was authorized to revive a depressed region of the nation. Today it oversees the generation of electric power throughout a vast region and maintains flood control programs as well. The largest of the government corporations and the most familiar to the general public is the United States Postal Service. The original Post Office Department was established in 1775 by the Second Continental Congress, and it enjoyed Cabinet status. It was reorganized in 1970 in hopes that it would eventually become self-supporting.

The large and powerful federal bureaucracy shapes and administers government policy. It is inherently political despite sporadic efforts throughout the years to maintain the integrity of the bureaucratic staff. Dating back to the administrations of Andrew Jackson, the practice of handing out government jobs in return for political favors (spoils system) had been the rule. The Civil Service Act (the Pendleton Act) was passed in 1883 in an attempt to reform the spoils system. Federal workers were to be recruited on the basis of merit determined by a competitive examination. Veterans were given preferential status. The Civil Service system was reorganized in the 1970s with the creation of the Office of Personnel Management. The OPM is charged with recruiting, training, and promoting government workers. Merit is the stated objective when hiring federal employees. A controversial policy of the OPM is affirmative action, a program to help groups discriminated against in the job market to find employment.

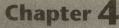

Political Beliefs and Characteristics of Citizens

The population of the United States, with its diverse components, is difficult to characterize with respect to political beliefs and attitudes. The process by which individuals form their political allegiances is called political socialization. Several factors (cleavages) are relevant to the formation of political opinions, including family, race, gender, class, religion, education, and region. Following are some generalizations as to the impact of these cleavages on an individual's political identification and activity.

Family – affiliation with a political party is commonly passed from one generation to another.

Race – African Americans tend to be more liberal than whites on economic, social, and public policy issues.

Gender – women tend to be more liberal than men.

Class – citizens from the middle and upper classes tend to be more politically active than those from the lower socioeconomic brackets. Low income voters tend to identify more with the liberal agenda.

Religion – Protestants tend to be more conservative than Catholics and Jews. Evangelical Protestants seem to be most conservative on ethical and moral issues.

Education – graduate-level education seems to have a liberalizing effect that remains potent after schooling is completed.

Region – Southerners tend to be most conservative, mid-westerners more liberal, and those living on the East and West coasts the most liberal of all.

Despite the categorization of Americans as either liberals or conservatives, most studies indicate that they do not follow clearly delineated ideologies (firm and consistent beliefs with respect to political, economic, and social issues). The terms *liberal* and *conservative* with reference to the political beliefs of Americans are difficult to define in precise terms. Liberals tend to favor change and to view government as a tool for improving the quality of life. Conservatives, on the other hand, are more inclined to view both change and government with suspicion. They emphasize individual initiative and local solutions to problems. A puzzling reversal is seen in the attitudes of liberals and conservatives when confronting moral issues such as abortion and school prayer. Here conservatives see a role for government in ensuring the moral climate of the nation while liberals stress the importance of individual choice.

Political Institutions and Special Interests

Civic culture in the United States is dominated by the two major political parties and is heavily influenced by the activities of interest groups and the mass media. These latter forces, both directly and indirectly, are largely responsible for molding and swaying public opinion.

Political Parties

A political party is an organization that seeks to influence government by electing candidates to public office. The party provides a label for candidates, recruits and campaigns, and tries to organize and control the legislative and executive branches of government through a set of leaders.

The Constitution does not mention political parties, and the Founders in general were opposed to them. Yet they developed simultaneously with the organization of the new government in 1789. It was the initial conflict over the interpretation of the powers assigned to the new government by the Constitution that gave rise to the first organized American political parties.

The Federalist Party evolved around the policies of Washington's Secretary of the Treasury, Alexander Hamilton. He and his supporters favored a "loose construction" approach to the interpretation of the Constitution. They advocated a strong federal government with the power to assume any duties and responsibilities not prohibited to it by the text of the document. They generally supported programs designed to benefit banking and commercial interests, and in foreign policy, the Federalists were pro-British.

The Democratic or Jeffersonian Republicans formed in opposition to the Federalists. They rallied around Washington's Secretary of State, Thomas Jefferson. The Jeffersonians took a "strict constructionist" approach, interpreting the Constitution in a narrow, limited sense. Sympathetic to the needs of the "common man," the Democratic-Republicans were mistrustful of powerful centralized government. They saw the small farmers, shopkeepers, and laborers as the backbone of the nation. In the area of foreign affairs, the

Democratic-Republicans were pro-French. The present-day Democratic Party traces its roots to the Jeffersonians.

By the 1820s, the Democrats had splintered into factions led by Andrew Jackson (the Democrats) and John Quincy Adams (National Republicans). The Jacksonians continued with Jefferson's tradition of supporting policies designed to enhance the power of the common man. Their support was largely agrarian. The National Republicans, like their Federalist predecessors, represented the interests of bankers, merchants, and some large planters. Eventually a new party, the Whigs, was organized from the remnants of the old Federalists and the National Republicans. The Whigs were prominent during the 1840s, but like their Democratic rivals, they fragmented during the 1850s over the divisive slavery issue. The modern Republican Party was born in 1854 as Whigs and anti-slavery Democrats came together to halt the spread of slavery. The Republicans built a constituency around the interests of business, farmers, workers, and the newly emancipated slaves in the post–Civil War era.

Political parties exert a variety of functions essential to the democratic tradition in the United States. Nominating candidates for local, state, and national office is their most visible activity. At the national level, this function has been diluted somewhat by the popularity of primary elections allowing voters to express their preference for candidates. Raucous conventions where party bosses chose obscure "dark horse" candidates in "smoke filled rooms" are largely a thing of the past.

Political parties stimulate interest in public issues by highlighting their own strengths and maximizing the flaws of the opposition. They also provide a framework for keeping the machinery of government operating, most notably in their control of Congress and its organization, which is strictly along party lines.

American political parties appear in theory to be highly organized. The geographic size of the country coupled with the federal system of government keep the parties in a state of relative decentralization. At the local level, the fundamental unit of organization is the precinct. At this level, there is usually a captain or committee to handle such routine chores as registering voters, distributing party literature, organizing "grass-roots" meetings, and getting out the vote on election day.

State central committees are critical to the parties' fund-raising activities. They also organize the state party conventions. There is great variety from state to state regarding the composition and selection of the state committees, which often formulate policies independent from those of the national committee.

In presidential election years, the national party committees are most visible. They plan the national nominating convention, write the party platforms (summaries of positions on major issues), raise money to finance political activities, and carry out the election campaigns. Representatives from each state serve on the national committees, and the presidential nominee chooses the individual to serve as the party chairperson.

Although the two-party system is firmly established in the United States, over the years, "third parties" have left their marks. The national nominating conventions were introduced in the 1830s by the Anti-Masonic Party and were soon adopted by the Democrats and the Whigs. The Prohibition Party opposed the use of alcohol and worked for the adoption of the Eighteenth Amendment. In the 1890s, the Populist Party championed the causes of the farmers and workers and impacted the mainstream parties with its reform agenda. Among the Populist innovations were the initiative petition (a mechanism allowing voters to put proposed legislation on the ballot) and the referendum (allowing voters to approve or reject laws passed by their legislatures). The Progressive or Bull Moose Party was a splinter party (one that breaks away from an established party, in this case the Republican Party) built around the personality of Theodore Roosevelt. Another party formed around the personality of a forceful individual was the 1992 Reform Party of H. Ross Perot. Perot failed capture any electoral votes but garnered 19 percent of the popular tally.

Elections

In comparison to citizens in other democratic systems, Americans elect a large number of public officials. Elections in the United States are largely regulated by state law. The Constitution does assign to Congress the responsibility for determining "the times, places, and manner of holding elections for Senators and Representatives." Article II establishes the Electoral College for presidential elections and specifies that they shall be held on the same day throughout the nation. Several of the Amendments deal with election procedures, voter qualifications, and suffrage (the right to vote) for target groups (former slaves, women, and those 18 years of age and older). Nonetheless, the principal responsibility for arranging and supervising elections rests with the states.

The actual election process consists of two phases: nominating the candidates and choosing the final officials. Primary elections screen and select the final party candidates.

Closed primaries allow voters registered (legal procedure that must be completed before an individual can vote) in one of the political parties to express their preferences for the final candidate from among the field of hopefuls in that party. Open primaries allow voters to select their party affiliations on site. Some states allow "crossover" voting which permits voters registered in one party to vote for candidates in the other party. This practice can lead to the tactic of voting for the weakest choice in the opposition party to give an advantage in the final election to the candidate and the party the voter actually supports.

In national elections (those held in November of each even-numbered year to choose national officeholders), the campaign traditionally begins after Labor Day. Off-year elections are those in which only members of Congress are chosen and no presidential contest is held. In both presidential and off-year elections, candidates follow exhausting schedules and spend huge sums on media advertising. Their activities usually dominate the national and local news coverage, and debates are common forums for airing their differences. Funding for political campaigns comes from a variety of sources including the candidates' own resources, private supporters, political action committees (PACs), and the federal government. In the election reform drive of the 1970s, the Federal Election Commission was created to ensure that laws concerning campaign financing are followed.

The cost of the elections themselves is borne by the state and local governments which must prepare ballots, designate polling places, and pay workers who participate in administering the elections. Registrars of voters oversee the preparation of ballots, the establishment of polling places, and the tallying of the votes. In a close election, the loser may request a recount. Some states require them in closely contested races.

Voter Behavior

In recent years, attention has focused on the problem of voter apathy. Despite efforts to extend suffrage to all segments of the adult population, participation in the electoral process has been on the decline. Several theories have been advanced to explain this trend. There is widespread belief that Americans are dissatisfied with their government and mistrust all elected officials. Therefore, they refuse to participate in the electoral process. Some citizens do not vote in a given election, not because they are "turned-off" to the system, but because they are ill, homeless, away on business, or otherwise preoccupied on Election Day. College students and others away from their legal residences find registration and the use of absentee ballots cumbersome and inconvenient. Efforts were made in the 1990s to streamline the registration process with such legislation as the "motor-voter" bill that makes it possible for citizens to register at their local registries of motor vehicles.

While most attempts to explain voter apathy focus on negatives such as citizen apathy, some analysts disagree. They see disinterest in the ballot as a sign that the majority of Americans are happy with the system and feel no sense of urgency to participate in the political process.

Political participation is not limited to voting in elections. Working for candidates, attending rallies, contacting elected officials and sharing opinions about issues, writing letters to newspapers, marching in protest, and joining in community activities are all forms of political participation. While voter turnout has decreased in recent years, other forms of participation seem to be on the increase.

Interest Groups

American officials and political leaders are continually subjected to pressure from a variety of interest groups seeking to influence their actions. Such groups arise from bonds among individuals who share common concerns. Interest groups may be loosely organized (informal), with no clear structure or regulations. A good example of such an informal or ad hoc interest group was the "March of the Poor" on Washington, D.C., in 1963 to focus Congress's attention on the needs of the "underclass" in America. A group of neighbors united in opposition to development of a new shopping mall that threatens a wetland is an example of this type of group. Other interest groups are much more formal and permanent in nature. They may have suites of offices and large numbers of employees. Their political objectives are usually clearly defined. Labor unions, professional and public-interest groups, and single issue organizations fall into this category. The National Rifle Association and the National Right to Life Organization are examples of single-issue pressure groups.

Interest groups employ a variety of tactics to accomplish their goals. Most commonly, they lobby (influence the passage or defeat of legislation) elected officials, particularly members of Congress. Lobbyists provide legislators with reports and statistics to persuade them of the legitimacy of their respective positions. They may present expert testimony at public hearings and influence the media to portray their causes in a favorable light. Lobbyists are required to register in Washington and to make their positions public. They are barred from presenting false and misleading information and from bribing public officials. Regulatory legislation cannot, however, curb all the abuses inherent to a system of organized persuasion.

One particularly controversial brand of pressure group is the political action committee (PAC). PACs were formed in the 1970s in an attempt to circumvent legislation limiting contributions to political campaigns. Critics see these interest groups as another means of diluting the influence individual voters may have on their elected officials. Some politicians refuse to accept PAC money.

Public Opinion

Public opinion refers to the attitudes and preferences expressed by a significant number of individuals about an issue that involves the government or the society at large. It does not necessarily represent the sentiments of all or even most of the citizenry. Nonetheless, it is an important component of a democratic society.

In today's technological society, the influence of the mass media on public opinion cannot be over-emphasized. The print and broadcast media can reach large numbers of people cheaply and efficiently, but the electronic media in particular have been criticized for over-simplifying complicated issues and reducing coverage of major events to brief sound bites. Both the print and broadcast media claim to present news in a fair and objective format, but both conservatives and liberals claim that coverage is slanted. Paid political advertising is another vehicle for molding public opinion. In this case, objectivity is neither expected nor attempted, as candidates and interest groups employ "hard-sell" techniques to persuade voters to support their causes.

Measuring the effects of the media on public opinion is difficult, as is gauging where the public stands on a given issue at a particular point in time. Public opinion polls have been designed to these ends. Pollsters usually address a random sample and try to capture a cross-section of the population. Their questions are designed to elicit responses that do not mirror the biases of the interviewer or the polling organization. Results are tabulated and analyzed, and generalizations are presented to the media.

Although polls are more accurate today than in the past, they are still subject to criticism for oversimplifying complicated issues and encouraging pat answers to complex problems. Public opinion is constantly in a state of flux, and what may be a valid report today is passé tomorrow. Another criticism is that interviewees may not be entirely candid, particularly with respect to sensitive issues. They may answer as they think they should but not necessarily with full honesty.

A type of election poll that has been the target of sharp criticism is the exit poll in which interviewers question subjects about their votes as they leave the polling places. These polls may be accurate, but if the media present the results while voting is still in progress, the outcome may be affected. Predicting the winners before voters throughout the country have had the opportunity to cast their ballots in a national election robs a segment of the electorate of the sense that its participation is of any consequence. In the 2000 election, exit polls led to confusion as Florida results were projected prematurely; the television networks vowed to be more careful.

Civil Rights and Individual Liberties

Civil rights are those legal claims that individuals have to protect themselves from discrimination at the hands of both the government and other citizens. They include the right to vote, equality before the law, and access to public facilities. Individual or civil liberties protect the sanctity of the person from arbitrary governmental interference. In this category belong the fundamental freedoms of speech, religion, press, and rights such as due process (government must act fairly and follow established procedures, as in legal proceedings).

The origin of the concept of fundamental rights and freedoms can be traced to the British constitutional heritage and to the theorists of the Enlightenment. Jefferson's Declaration of Independence contains several references to the crown's failure to uphold the civil rights that British subjects had come to value and expect. When fashioning the Constitution, the Founding Fathers included passages regarding the protection of civil liberties, such as the provision in Article I for maintaining the right of habeas corpus. One of the criticisms of the Constitution lodged by its opponents was that it did not go far enough in safeguarding individual rights. During the first session of Congress in 1789, the first ten amendments (the Bill of Rights) were adopted and sent to the states for ratification. These amendments contain many of the protections that define the ideals of American life. The Bill of Rights was meant to limit the power of the federal government to restrict the freedom of individual citizens. The Fourteenth Amendment of 1868 prohibits states from denying civil rights and individual liberties to their residents. The Supreme Court is charged with interpreting the law, particularly as it applies to civil rights and individual liberties cases. Not until the *Gitlow* case in 1925 did the Supreme Court begin to exercise this function with respect to state enforcement of the Bill of Rights. States are now expected to conform to the federal standard of civil rights.

The Amendment that is most closely identified with individual liberty in the United States is the First Amendment, which protects freedom of religion, speech, press, assembly, and petition. The First Amendment sets forth the principle of separation of Church and State with its "free exercise" and "establishment" clauses. These have led the Supreme Court to rule against such practices as school prayer (*Engel v. Vitale*, 1962) and Bible reading in public schools (*Abington Township v. Schempp,* 1963).

The Fourth Amendment, which outlawed "unreasonable searches and seizures," mandates that warrants be granted only "upon probable cause," and affirms the "right of the people to be secure in their persons," is fundamental to the Court's interpretation of due process and the rights of the accused. The Fifth Amendment, which calls for a grand jury, outlawed double jeopardy (trying a person who has been acquitted of a charge for a second time) and states that a person may not be compelled to be a witness against himself, is also the basis for Supreme Court rulings that protect the accused. "Cruel and unusual punishments" are banned by the Eighth Amendment. This clause has been invoked by opponents of capital punishment to justify their position, but the Supreme Court has ruled that the death penalty can be applied if states are judicious and use equal standards in sentencing to death those convicted of capital crimes.

In the twentieth century, a major concern for litigation and review by the Supreme Court has been in the area of civil rights for minorities, particularly African Americans. When civil rights organizations such as the NAACP brought a series of cases before the courts under the "equal protection clause" of the Fourteenth Amendment, they began to enjoy some victories. Earlier when the Supreme Court enforced its "separate but equal" doctrine in the 1896 case *Plessy v. Ferguson*, it did not apply the equal protection standard and allowed segregation to be maintained. The Court reversed itself in 1954 in the landmark case *Brown v. Board of Education,* which ruled that separate but equal was unconstitutional. This ruling led to an end to most de jure (legally enforced) segregation, but de facto (exists in fact) segregation persisted, largely due to housing patterns and racial and ethnic enclaves in urban neighborhoods.

Landmark Supreme Court Cases

In addition to the previously cited Supreme Court rulings in civil rights and individual liberties cases, the following landmark decisions are notable for their relevance to the concepts of civil rights and individual freedoms:

Dred Scott v. Sanford (1857) – ruled that as a slave Scott had no right to sue for his freedom and further that Congressional prohibitions against slavery in U.S. territories were unlawful.

Near v. Minnesota (1931) – states were barred from using the concept of prior restraint (outlawing something before it has taken place) to discourage the publication of objectionable material except during wartime or in the cases of obscenity or incitement to violence.

West Virginia Board of Education v. Barnette (1943) – overturned an earlier decision and ruled that compulsory saluting of the flag was unconstitutional.

Korematsu v. United States (1944) – upheld the legality of the forced evacuation of persons of Japanese ancestry during World War II as a wartime necessity.

Mapp v. Ohio (1961) – extended the Supreme Court's exclusionary rule, which bars at trial the introduction of evidence that has not been legally obtained to states. The Court has modified this ruling, particularly with reference to drug cases, so that evidence that might not initially have been obtained legally, but which would eventually have turned up in lawful procedures, can be introduced.

Gideon v. Wainwright (1963) – ruled that courts must provide legal counsel to poor defendants in all felony cases. A later ruling extended this right to all defendants facing possible prison sentences.

Escobedo v. Illinois (1964) – extended the right to counsel to include consultation prior to interrogation by authorities.

Miranda v. Arizona (1966) – mandated that all suspects be informed of their due process rights before questioning by police.

Tinker v. Des Moines School District (1969) – defined the wearing of black armbands in school in protest against the Vietnam War as "symbolic speech" protected by the First Amendment.

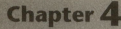

New York Times v. United States (1971) – allowed, under the First Amendment's freedom of the press protection, the publication of the controversial Pentagon Papers during the Vietnam War.

Roe v. Wade (1973) – legalized abortion so long as a fetus is not viable (able to survive outside the womb).

Bakke v. Regents of the University of California (1978) – declared the university's quota system to be unconstitutional while upholding the legitimacy of affirmative action policies in which institutions consider race and gender as factors when determining admissions.

Hazelwood School District v. Kuhlmeier (1988) – ruled that freedom of the press does not extend to student publications that might be construed as sponsored by the school.

COMPARATIVE GOVERNMENT AND POLITICS

This subfield of government and politics includes two principal areas of scholarship and information: the theoretical frameworks for the government structures, functions, and political cultures of nations and a comparative analysis of the political systems of a series of targeted nations or societies.

Theoretical Frameworks for Government Structures, Functions, and Political Culture

Environmental Factors

In order to understand the political institutions and civic life of any nation, several environmental factors need to be considered. Such questions as the size, location, geographic features, economic strength, level of industrialization, and cultural diversity of a society must be explored. Both the domestic and international contexts need to be examined as well as the level of dependence on or independence from the world community. The location of the United States in the Western Hemisphere, separated from both Europe and Asia by vast expanses of ocean, is a critical component in the development of its relatively independent political culture. Conversely, the location of Eastern European countries in the shadow of the post-World War II Soviet Union led to political dependence. The cultural diversity and traditional hostilities of the Balkan peoples are key elements in the political and military volatility of the region. Industrialization and economic stability are conditions that are commonly conducive to a highly developed political system.

The age and historical traditions of a nation have a great impact on its current political culture. France's contemporary unitary form of government can be viewed as an evolutionary manifestation of earlier traditions that centralized power in divine right monarchs and ambitious emperors. Legitimacy (acceptance by citizens) is quite another prospect in such places as Somalia and Haiti with their unstable political histories and economic vulnerability.

Government Structures and Functions

How a government is organized, its mechanisms for carrying out its mission, the scope of that mission, and how its structures and functions compare with other governments are prime considerations in comparative government.

The geographic distribution of authority and responsibility is a key variable. Confederations, such as the United States under the Articles of Confederation, have weak central governments and delegate principal authority to smaller units such as the states. Federal systems, on the other hand, divide sovereignty between a central government and those of their separate states. Brazil, India, and the United States are contemporary examples of federal republics. Highly centralized, unitary forms of government concentrate power and authority at the top, as in France and Japan.

Separation of governmental powers is another aspect of structure useful in comparing political systems. Authoritarian governments center power in a single or collective executive, with the legislative and judicial bodies having little input. The former Soviet Union is an example. Great Britain typifies the parliamentary form of government. Here legislative and executive combine, with a prime minister and cabinet selected from within the legislative body. They maintain power only so long as the legislative assembly supports their major policies. The democratic presidential system of the United States clearly separates the legislative, executive, and judicial structures. The branches, particularly the executive and the legislative, must cooperate, however, in order for policy to be consistent and for government operations to be carried out smoothly.

A third aspect of governmental structure and function involves the limits placed on the power to govern. This facet of politics closely reflects the theoretical and ideological roots of a system. Constitutional systems limit the powers of government through written and/or unwritten sources. Law, custom, and precedent combine to protect individuals from the unchecked power of a central authority. The United States and Great Britain have constitutional governments. Authoritarian regimes, such as those found in China and the former Soviet Union, do not limit the power of the central authority over the lives of individuals. Those in control impose their values and their will on the society-at-large regardless of popular sentiments. Authoritarianism is associated with fascism, Nazism, and totalitarianism in general.

Political Culture, Parties, Participation, and Mechanisms for Change

Understanding a nation's political culture is key to analyzing the theoretical foundations, structure, and functions of its government. It can be defined as the aggregate values a society shares about how politics and government should operate. Some societies function from a consensus framework, while other political cultures are more conflicted. The Soviet Union's political culture after World War II, as contrasted with the situation there in the early 1990s, illustrates the difference between consensual and conflicted societies. The vehicles for transmitting the political culture and the social cleavages that characterize that culture will impact its system of governing and its legitimacy in the minds of its citizenry. Analysis of the extent to which citizens support their political systems is an important component of comparative government.

The methods citizens employ to have an impact upon their political system and the ease of their access to the power structure are the types of questions comparative politics examines. Do elections offer a choice between candidates with diverse programs and contrasting agendas, as is often the case in the United States, or do they present citizens the opportunity to show their support for the government in a one party system such as in China? The number, nature, and power of political parties are additional factors for analysis with respect to how the demands and concerns of citizens in various nations are represented and met. The presence and proliferation of other interest groups, such as labor unions and environmental activists, provide additional clues as to the values and methods of a political culture.

Beyond voting in elections and joining and supporting political parties and interest groups, citizen participation can take other forms. Contacting politicians, lobbying for legislation, and demonstrating in the streets are common vehicles for involvement in the political life of a nation. The degree to which such expressions are encouraged and tolerated by government officials is another facet of political culture that varies from society to society.

Comparative politics and government as a field is concerned with mechanisms for change in different nations. Can citizens effect reform through ballots, protest, public opinion polls, or revolts? The underlying factors precipitating the need for change are relevant to an understanding of the overall process.

INTERNATIONAL RELATIONS

The Theoretical Framework

The study of how nations interact with one another can be approached from a variety of perspectives including the following:

- A **traditional analysis** uses the descriptive process and focuses on such topics as global issues, international institutions, and the foreign policies of individual nation-states.

- The **strategists' approach** zeroes in on war and deterrence. Scholars in this camp may employ game theory to analyze negotiations, the effectiveness of weapons systems, and the likelihood of limited versus all-out war in a given crisis situation.

- The **middle range theorists** analyze specific components of international relations, such as the politics of arms races, the escalation of international crises, and the role of prejudice and attitudes toward other cultures in precipitating war and peace.

- A **world politics approach** takes into consideration such factors as economics, ethics, law, and trade agreements and stresses the significance of international organizations and the complexities of interactions among nations.

The grand theory of international relations is presented by Hans J. Morgenthau in *Politics Among Nations* (1948). He argues for realism in the study of interactions on the international stage. Morgenthau suggests that an analysis of relations among nations reveals such recurring themes as "interest defined as power" and striving for equilibrium/ balance of power as a means of maintaining peace.

The idealists assume that human nature is essentially good; hence, people and nations are capable of cooperation and avoiding armed conflict. They highlight global organizations, international law, disarmament, and the reform of institutions that lead to war.

An analysis of international politics can be conducted at various levels by looking at the actions of individual statesmen, the interests of individual nations, and/or the mechanics of a whole system of international players. In studying the rise of nazism and its role in precipitating World War II, the individual approach would focus on Hitler, the state approach would treat the German preoccupation with racial superiority and the need for expansion, and the systemic approach would highlight how German military campaigns upset the balance of power and triggered unlikely alliances, such as the linking of the democratic Britain and the United States with the totalitarian Soviet Union in a common effort to restore equilibrium.

Foreign Policy Perspectives

International relations as a discipline is inextricably linked to the field of foreign policy. Foreign policy involves the objectives nations seek to gain with reference to other nations and the procedures in which they engage in order to achieve their objectives. The principal foreign policy goals of sovereign states or other political entities may include some or all of the following: independence, national security, economic advancement, encouraging their political values beyond their own borders, gaining respect and prestige, and promoting stability and international peace.

The foreign policy process involves the stages a government goes through in formulating policy and arriving at decisions with respect to courses of action. A variety of models have been identified in reference to the process of creating foreign policy. The primary players (nations, world organizations, multinational corporations, and non-state ethnic entities such as the Palestine Liberation Organization) are often referred to as actors.

The **unitary/rational actor model** assumes that all nations or primary players share similar goals and approach foreign policy issues in like fashion. The actions players take, according to this theory, are influenced by the actions of other players rather than by what may be taking place internally. The rational component in this model is based on the assumption that actors will respond on the world stage by making the best choice after measured consideration of possible alternatives. Maximizing goals and achieving specific objectives motivate the rational actor's course of action.

The **bureaucratic model** assumes that, due to the many large organizations involved in formulating foreign policy, particularly in powerful nation-states, final decisions are the result of struggle among the bureaucratic actors. In the United States, the bureaucratic actors include the Departments of State and Defense, as well as the National Security Council, the Central Intelligence Agency, the Environmental Protection Agency, the Department of Commerce, and/or any other agencies and departments whose agendas might be impacted by a foreign policy decision. While the bureaucratic model is beneficial in that it assumes the consideration of multiple points of view, the downside is that inter-agency competition and compromise often drive the final decision.

A third model assumes that foreign policy results from the intermingling of a variety of political factors including national leaders, bureaucratic organizations, legislative bodies, political parties, interest groups, and public opinion.

The implementation of foreign policy depends upon the tools a nation or primary player has at its disposal. The major instruments of foreign policy include diplomacy, military strength/actions, and economic initiatives.

Diplomacy involves communicating with other primary players through official representatives. It might include attending conferences and summit meetings, negotiating treaties and settlements, and exchanging official communications. Diplomacy is an indispensable tool in the successful conduct of an entity's foreign policy.

The extent to which a player may rely on the military tool depends upon its technological strength, its readiness, and the support of both its domestic population and the international community. President George H. W. Bush's decision to engage in a military conflict with Iraq's Saddam Hussein in 1991, after Iraq's invasion of Kuwait, largely rested on positive assessments of those factors. Sometimes the buildup of military capabilities is in itself a powerful foreign policy tool and thus a deterrent to armed conflict—as was the case in the Cold War between the United States and the Soviet Union.

Economic development and the ability to employ economic initiatives to achieve foreign policy objectives are effective means by which a principal player can interact on the international scene. The Marshall Plan, through which the United States provided economic aid to a ravaged Europe after World War II, could be viewed as a tool to block Soviet expansion as well as a humanitarian gesture. It was a tool to resurrect the devastated economies of Europe which had been major trading partners and purchasers of U.S. exports before the war. Membership in an economic community such as OPEC (Organization of Petroleum Exporting Countries) or the EU (European Union) can drive the foreign policy of both member nations and those affected by their decisions.

The Modern Global System

International systems today evidence many of the global forces and foreign policy mechanisms formulated in Western Europe in the eighteenth and nineteenth centuries. Largely due to the influence of Western imperialism and colonialism, the less developed countries of modern times have, to a great extent, embraced ideological and foreign policy values that originated in Europe during the formative centuries. Such concepts as political autonomy, nationalism, economic advancement through technology and industrialization, and gaining respect and prestige in the international community move the foreign policies of major powers and many less developed countries as well.

Historical Context of the Modern Global System

The modern global system or network of relationships among nations owes its origins to the emergence of the nation-state. It is generally recognized that the Peace of Westphalia (1648), which concluded the Thirty Years' War in Europe and ended the authority of the Roman Catholic popes to exert their political dominance over secular leaders, gave birth to the concept of the modern nation-state. The old feudal order in Europe that allowed the Holy Roman Emperor to extend his influence over the territories governed by local princes was replaced by a new one in which distinct geographic and political entities interacted under a new set of principles. These allowed the nation-states to conduct business with each other, such as negotiating treaties and settling border disputes, without interference from a higher authority. Hence, the concept of sovereignty evolved.

The eighteenth century in Europe was notable for its relatively even distribution of power among the nation-states. With respect to military strength and international prestige, such nations as England, France, Austria, Prussia, and Russia were on the same scale. Some of the former major powers, such as Spain, the Netherlands, and Portugal, occupied a secondary status. Both the major and secondary players created alliances and competed with each other for control of territories beyond their borders.

Alignments, based primarily on economic and colonial considerations, shifted without upsetting the global system. Royal families intermarried and professional soldiers worked for the states that gave them the best benefits without great regard for political allegiances.

Military conflicts in the eighteenth century tended to be conservative with the concept of the balance of power at play. Mercenaries and professionals controlled the action mindful of strategic maneuvers to bring about victory. Wiping out the enemy was not the principal goal. Major upheavals were avoided through the formation of alliances and a high regard for the authority of monarchs and the Christian Church. The eighteenth century has been dubbed the "golden age of diplomacy" because it was an era of relative stability in which moderation and shared cultural values on the part of the decision-makers were the rule.

Structural changes in the process and implementation of international relations occurred in the nineteenth and twentieth centuries due to major political, technological, and ideological developments.

The nation-state of the eighteenth century was a relatively new phenomenon. Statesmen of the era traded territory with little consideration of ethnic loyalties. This style of diplomacy was irrevocably altered by the French Revolution and the Napoleonic Wars that saw nationality emerge as a rallying point for conducting wars and for raising the citizens' armies necessary to succeed in military conflicts. The trend was exacerbated in the mid-nineteenth century by the European drive for unification of distinct ethnic groups and the creation of the Italian and German nation-states. The twentieth century has seen a particularly impassioned link between nationalism and war.

The scientific and industrial revolutions of the eighteenth century gave rise to advancements in military technology in the nineteenth and twentieth centuries that dramatically altered the concept and the conduct of war. Replacing the eighteenth century conservative, play-by-the-rules approach was a new, fiercely violent brand of warfare that increasingly involved civilian casualties and aimed at utter destruction of the enemy. The World Wars of the twentieth century called for mass mobilization of civilians as well as of the military, prompting leaders to whip up nationalistic sentiments. The development of nuclear weapons in the mid-twentieth century rendered total war largely unfeasible. Nuclear arms buildups, with the goal of deterrent capabilities (the means to retaliate so swiftly and effectively that an enemy will avoid conflict) was viewed by the superpowers as the only safety net.

Another factor molding the structural changes in international relations that surfaced in the nineteenth and twentieth centuries was the ideological component. Again the French Revolution, anchored in the ideology of "liberty, equality, and fraternity," is viewed as the harbinger of future trends. Those conservative forces valuing legitimacy and monarchy fought the forces of the Revolution and Napoleon to preserve tradition against the rising tide of republican nationalism. In the twentieth century, with its binding "isms"—Communism, democratic republicanism, liberalism, Nazism, socialism—competing for dominance, ideological conflicts have become more pronounced.

The Contemporary Global System

The values of the contemporary system are rooted in the currents of eighteenth and nineteenth century Europe, transplanted to the rest of the world through colonialism and imperialism. The forces of nationalism, belief in technological progress, and ideological motivations, as well as the desire for international respect and prestige, are evident worldwide. Principal players in Africa, Asia, Latin America, and the Middle East as often as not dominate the diplomatic arena.

The contemporary scene in international relations is comprised of a number of entities beyond the nation-state. These include: non-state actors or principal players, nonterritorial transnational organizations, and nonterritorial intergovernmental or multinational organizations.

Contemporary nation-states are legal entities occupying well-defined geographic areas and organized under a common set of governmental institutions. They are recognized by other members of the international community as sovereign and independent states.

Non-state actors or principal players are movements or parties that function as independent states. They lack sovereignty, but they may actually wield more power than some less developed nation-states. The Palestine Liberation Organization (PLO) is an example of a non-state actor that conducts its own foreign policy, purchases armaments, and has committed acts of terror with grave consequences for the contemporary international community. The Irish Republican Army (IRA) is another example of a non-state actor that has employed systematic acts of terror to achieve political ends.

Nonterritorial transnational organizations are institutions such as the Catholic Church that conduct activities throughout the world but whose aims are largely nonpolitical. A relatively new nonterritorial transnational organization is the multi-national corporation (MNC), such as General Motors, Hitachi, or British Petroleum. These giant business entities have bases in a number of countries and exist primarily for economic profit. Despite their apparent nonpolitical agendas, multinational corporations can greatly impact foreign policy, as in the case of the United Fruit Company's suspect complicity in the overthrow of the government of Guatemala in the 1950s. Initially the MNC was largely an American innovation, but in recent years, Asian players, particularly the Japanese, have proliferated, changing the makeup of the scene.

An intergovernmental organization, such as the United Nations, NATO, or the European Union (EU), is made up of nation-states and can wield significant power on the international scene. While NATO is primarily a military intergovernmental organization and the EU is mainly economic, the UN is really a multipurpose entity. While its primary mission is to promote world peace, the UN engages in a variety of social, cultural, economic, health, and humanitarian activities.

The contemporary global system tends to classify nation-states based on power, wealth, and prestige in the international community. Such labels as "superpower," "secondary power," "middle power," "small power," and the like tend to be confusing because they are not based on a single set of criteria or a shared set of standards. Some countries may be strong militarily, as was Iraq prior to the Persian Gulf War, yet lack the wealth and prestige in the international community to classify them as super or secondary powers. Others like Japan may have little in the way of military capabilities, but wide influence due to economic preeminence.

The structure of the contemporary global system during the Cold War was distinctly bipolar, with the United States and the Soviet Union assuming diplomatic, ideological, and military leadership for the international community. With the breakup of the Soviet Union and the reorganization of the Eastern bloc countries has come the disintegration of the bipolar system. Since the 1970s, when tensions between the United States and the Soviet Union eased, a multipolar system, in which new alignments are flexible and more easily drawn, has been emerging. President George H. W. Bush spoke of the New World Order at the end of the Cold War. This concept involves alliances that transcend the old bipolar scheme with its emphasis on ideology and military superiority and calls for multinational cooperation as seen in the Persian Gulf War. It also assumes greater non-military, transnational cooperation in scientific research and humanitarian projects. The multipolar system is less cohesive than the bipolar system of the recent past and the orders of the distant past, such as the hierarchical system (one unit dominates) of the

Holy Roman Empire or the diffuse system (power and influence are distributed among a large number of units) of eighteenth-century Europe.

A set of fundamental rules has long governed international relations and, though often ignored, is still held as the standard today. These rules include territorial integrity, sovereignty, and the legal equality of nation-states. However, in an age of covert operations, mass media, multinational corporations, and shifting territorial boundaries, these traditional rules of international conduct are subject to both violation and revision.

INTERNATIONAL LAW

The present system of international law is rooted in the fundamental rules of global relations: territorial integrity, sovereignty, and legal equality of nation-states. It embodies a set of basic principles mandating what countries may or may not do and under what conditions the rules should be applied.

Historical Context

Despite evidence that the legal and ethical norms of modern international law may have guided interactions among political entities in non-Western pre-industrial systems, contemporary international law emanates from the Western legal traditions of Greece, Rome, and modern Europe. The development of the European nation-state gave rise to a system of legal rights and responsibilities in the international sphere that enlarged upon the religious-based code of the feudal era. In medieval Europe, the church's emphasis on hierarchical obligations, duty, and obedience to authority helped shape the notion of the "just war." Hugo Grotius (1583–1645), Dutch scholar and statesman, codified the laws of war and peace and has been called the "father of international law."

A new era was launched in 1648, with the Peace of Westphalia, that promulgated the idea of the treaty as the basis of international law. Multilateral treaties dominated the eighteenth century, while Britain, with its unparalleled sea power, established and enforced maritime law. By the nineteenth century, advances in military technology rendered the old standard of the "just war" obsolete. Deterrents, rather than legal and ethical principles, provided the means to a relatively stable world order. The concept of neutrality evolved during this period, defining the rights and responsibilities of both warring and neutral nations. These restraints helped prevent smaller conflicts from erupting into world wars.

Contemporary International Law

In the twentieth century, international law has retreated theoretically from the tradition of using force as a legitimate tool for settling international conflicts. The Covenant of the League of Nations (1920), the Kellogg-Briand Pact (1929), and the United Nations Charter (1945) all emphasize peaceful relations among nations, but the use of force continues to be employed to achieve political ends. The International Court of Justice, the judicial arm of the United Nations and its predecessor, the Permanent Court of International Justice represent concerted efforts to replace armed conflict with the rule of law. Unfortunately, the World Court has proven to be an ineffective organ. Nation-states are reluctant to submit vital questions to the Court, and there is a lack of consensus as to the norms to be applied. Members of the United Nations are members of the Court, but they are not compelled to submit their international disputes for consideration.

The UN Charter seeks to humanize the international scene in its admonition that all member nations assist victims of aggression. This approach negates the old idea of neutrality. It further dismisses the tradition of war as a legitimate tool for resolution of disputes between nation-states of equal legal status. Aggressive conflicts can be categorized as crimes against humanity, and individuals may be held personally accountable for launching them.

The concept of international law has been criticized on several fronts. The rise of multiculturalism, with its emphasis on multiple perspectives, has called into question the relevance of applying Western legal traditions to the global community. International law has been seen as an instrument of the powerful nations in pursuit of their aims at the expense of weaker nations. Strong nation-states are in a position to both enforce international law and to violate it without fear of reprisal. These observations have led some to conclude that international law is primarily an instrument to maintain the status quo.

International law can be effective if parties involved see some mutual self-advantage in compliance. Fear of reprisal is another factor influencing nations to observe the tenets of international law. Diplomatic advantage and enhanced global prestige may follow a nation's decisions to abide by international law. It can be argued that international law is valuable in that it seeks to impose order on a potentially chaotic system and sets expectations that, while not always met, are positive and affirming.

CHAPTER 5

Geography

Geography is the study of the earth's surface, including such aspects as its climate, topography, vegetation, and population.

THE SPATIAL PERSPECTIVE

The geographer's craft is all about space—not outer space, but physical space. Geographers look at space and investigate patterns—a geographer might look at the space of your bedroom and ask several questions: How are things distributed? What processes operate in that space? How does this space relate to other nearby spaces? Such a way of identifying, explaining, and predicting the human and physical patterns in space and the interconnectedness of various spaces are known to geographers as the **spatial perspective**. The field of geography has several subfields that branch from two main fields: human (cultural) geography and physical geography. Human geography takes as its subject humans and the cultures they create relative to their space. Physical geography looks at the planet earth—its water, air, animals, and land (i.e., all that is part of the four spheres—the atmosphere, biosphere, hydrosphere, and lithosphere).

The five themes of geography created in 1984 by the *National Council for Geographic Education and the Association of American Geographers* were to facilitate and organize the teaching of geography in the K-12 classroom. These themes have been supplanted by the **National Geography Standards,** which we will discuss, but the original five continue to provide an effective way of organizing your understanding the field of geography.

THE FIVE THEMES OF GEOGRAPHY

Location

Most geographic study begins with learning the location of places. Location can be **absolute** or **relative**. *Absolute Location* refers to a position on the global grid. Technically, a location is absolute when it has only one possible reference point. That is why latitude and longitude work; only one place is 85 degrees north, 37 degrees west on the planet.

Your home address is another absolute location. There is only one 28 North Main Street in Williamsport, Pennsylvania. In addition to absolute location, anything can have a **relative location**, or its location as described in relation to places around it. The relative location of Nashville, Tennessee, could be described as being "south of Louisville, Kentucky," for example. "Hillsboro High School is located 9 miles southwest of McGavock High School" is another example of a relative location. While a site's absolute location will not vary, 28 North Main Street in Williamsport, Pa., will always be 28 North Street, in Williamsport, the site relative to the Joe's Corner Grocery store may change, if Joe's Corner Grocery becomes Slidell's Barber Shop, for instance.

The global grid is an invisible map of latitude and longitude lines. Lines of **latitude** measured in degrees that run north and south from the equator, which lies at 0 degrees latitude. The North Pole is 90 degrees north latitude, while the South Pole is 90 degrees south latitude. Lines of latitude never intersect, so geographers often call lines of latitude parallels. Because lines of latitude encircle the earth and never intersect, the circumferences of lines of latitude decrease as they move away from the equator in both directions. Therefore, the equator has the largest circumference of all the lines of latitude. Latitude exerts a large amount of control over any given area's climate—probably the single most important factor. Latitude dictates the intensity and duration of sun exposure to an area. When an area is closer to the sun, the days are longer and the sun's rays are stronger. This heats the climate.

Lines of longitude are measured in degrees east and west of one line of longitude known as the prime meridian, which runs through Greenwich, England, and is located at 0 degrees longitude. The line of longitude on the opposite side of the prime meridian is known as the International Date Line. The International Date Line is aligned with the 180-degree longitude line for some latitudes but not for others. This reflects the political influence on time zones. For example, the International Date Line was moved to put all of Russia ahead of Greenwich Mean Time (which is discussed later in this section).

Figure 5.1   Lines of Latitude and Longitude

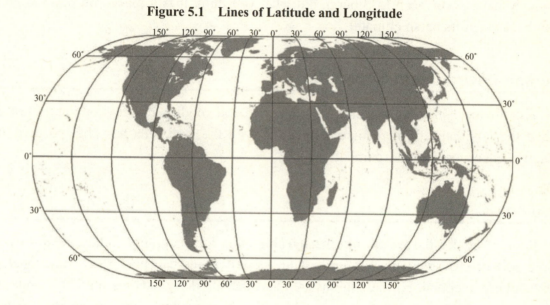

Place

The fourth geographic theme is **place**, which is a unique combination of physical and cultural attributes that give each location on the earth its individual "stamp." Place describes the human and physical characteristics of a location. Physical characteristics include a description of such things as the mountains, rivers, beaches, topography, and animal and plant life of a place. Human characteristics include the human-designed cultural features of a place, from land use and architecture to forms of livelihood and religion to food and folkways to transportation and communication networks.

Human components of place include religion, language, politics, and artwork, whereas the physical attributes include climate, terrain, and natural resources. The combination of these two parts of place, the human and physical, are what differentiate each location from another, almost like fingerprints.

Humans also develop a **sense of place**, which is a person's perception of the human and physical attributes of a location that give it a unique identity in our minds. For example, you probably remember a set of smells, sounds, and images from your ninth-grade English classroom. Think of how that sense of place differs from the total set of memories you have of your childhood bedroom or a favorite vacation spot. People can even develop a sense of place for a location they have never visited—through movies, television, and interactions with others who have traveled or heard of the places. You probably have never been to Siberia, but I bet you think it is a place you never want to visit because of its harsh climate!

Human-Environment Interaction

This theme considers how humans adapt to and modify the environment. Humans shape the landscape through their interaction with the land; this has both positive and negative effects on the environment.

Region

Region divides the world into manageable units for geographic study. Regions have some sort of characteristic that unifies the area. Regions can be formal, functional, or vernacular/perceptual. Formal regions are those that are designated by official boundaries, such as cities, states, counties, and countries. For the most part, they are clearly indicated and publicly known. Functional regions are defined by their connections. For example, the circulation area for a major city area is the functional region of that paper. Vernacular regions are perceived regions, such as "The South," "The Midwest," or the "Middle East"; they have no formal boundaries but are understood in our **mental maps** of the world.

Formal regions (sometimes referred to as uniform regions) are areas that have common (or uniform) cultural or physical features. A country is a formal region, or an area of places linked by a shared government. A climate region is a formal region because it links places that share a climate. A map showing where Christianity is practiced is showing a formal region, or a group of places sharing that religion.

A **functional region** (sometimes referred to as a nodal region) is a group of places linked together by some function's influence on them. Often the influencing function diffuses, or spreads, from a central node, or originating point. Functional regions are created through the movement of some phenomenon, like a disease, or a perceived interaction among places, like pizza delivery routes. For example, a functional region might appear on a map of Delta Airlines' flights from Atlanta, Georgia. A mapmaker would plot all the places to which Delta travels from its hub in Atlanta—the node. Then the mapmaker would draw a boundary enclosing all those places into one functional region. The area affected by the spread of a flu epidemic is a functional region. A functional region could even show the transmission of a rumor from its source to all the people who hear it. Remember, functional regions are defined by the places affected by the movement of some phenomenon from its source or node of other places.

The third type of region is a **perceptual (or vernacular) region.** The boundaries of a perceptual region are determined by people's beliefs, not a scientifically measurable process. For example, the space in which the "cool kids" sit at lunch would be a perceptual region because its boundaries are totally determined by the region maker's perception of who is cool and who is not—something that could be debated by any other person in the room. Another example of a perceptual region is the South in the United States. People differ in their perceptions of which places are considered part of the South.

Movement

Humans move…a lot! In addition, ideas, fads, goods, resources, and communication all travel distances. The fifth theme studies **movement** and migration across the planet. Geographers analyze the movement occurring in a space—movement of information, people, goods, and other phenomena. Geographers also evaluate how places interact through movement, a process known as **spatial interaction**. Although everything is theoretically linked to everything else, nearer things are usually related more to each other than to faraway things. Thus, the extent of spatial interaction often depends on distance.

In evaluating movement and spatial interaction, geographers often evaluate the **friction of distance**, which is the degree to which distance interferes with some interaction. For example, the friction of distance for a working-class Ohio man wanting to visit a dentist in Ethiopia is quite high, meaning that the distance gets in the way of this interaction occurring. However, the friction of distance has been reduced in many aspects of life with improved transportation and communication infrastructures.

Today, the friction of distance is not as much of a problem for a business in Kentucky to sell something to a business in Taiwan, for example. Businesses can now communicate over the Internet, buying and selling their goods in transactions that would have taken months to complete just 30 years ago. This increasing sense of accessibility and connectivity seems to bring humans in distant places closer together, a phenomenon known as **space–time compression**. Note that space–time compression is reducing perceived distance, which is the friction of distance thought by humans, not the actual distance on the land.

Related to space–time compression is the effect of **distance decay**, in which the interaction between two places declines as the distance between the two places increases. Imagine putting a magnet on your desk and putting an iron nail on it. The farther you pull the iron nail away from the magnet, the less of a pull effect the magnet has on the nail, right? It is the same with distance decay; as the distance between two entities increases, the effect of their interaction decreases.

However, improved transportation and communication technologies have reduced the effect of distance decay on most human interactions. In 1850 on any given day, a person living in Atlanta probably never interacted with someone from 30 miles outside the city. Now a person in Atlanta can interact with people from all over the world via the Internet and improved transportation.

New Standards of Geographic Education

The **National Geography Standards** were published in 1994 to guide geographic education in the United States. The eighteen standards shed light on what the geographically informed person should know and understand. The hope is that every student in America would become a geographically informed person through implementation of these standards in the classroom.

The World in Spatial Terms

1. How to use maps and other geographic representations, tools, and technologies to acquire, process, and report information.

2. How to use mental maps to organize information about people, places, and environments.

3. How to analyze the spatial organization of people, places, and environments on Earth's surface.

Places and Regions

4. The physical and human characteristics of places.

5. That people create regions to interpret Earth's complexity.

6. How culture and experience influence people's perception of places and regions.

Physical Systems

7. The physical processes that shape the patterns of Earth's surface.

8. The characteristics and spatial distribution of ecosystems on Earth's surface.

Human Systems

9. The characteristics, distribution, and migration of human populations on Earth's surface.

10. The characteristics, distributions, and complexity of Earth's cultural mosaics.

11. The patterns and networks of economic interdependence on Earth's surface.

12. The process, patterns, and functions of human settlement.

13. How forces of cooperation and conflict among people influence the division and control of Earth's surface.

Environment and Society

14. How human actions modify the physical environment.

15. How physical systems affect human systems.

16. The changes that occur in the meaning, use, distribution, and importance of resources.

The Uses of Geography

17. How to apply geography to interpret the past.

18. To apply geography to interpret the present and plan for the future.

MAPS AND MAPMAKING

A **map** is a two-dimensional model of the earth or a portion of its surface. The process of mapmaking is called **cartography**. All maps include a somewhat simplified view of the earth's surface. **Simplification** is when a cartographer gets rid of unnecessary details and focuses on the information needing to be displayed on the map. When designing a map of Europe for high school students to use to help them memorize the names of countries and capitals, a mapmaker would present a simplified map of Europe's political states and boundaries, eliminating details such as vegetation or climate. Another example of simplification involves a cartographer designing a map of London's underground subway for tourists. Such a cartographer might eliminate unnecessary details such as unrelated buildings and streets from their maps because tourists do not need these details to understand London's subway tracks. Tourists are simply interested in getting on and off the correct subway stops.

Distortion and Map Properties

It is impossible to take the earth's round surface and put it onto a flat surface without some form of **distortion**, or error, resulting from the "flattening" process. Think of distortion as caused by a process similar to trying to flatten an orange peel. Sorry to inform you of this, but all the maps you have memorized are wrong. As it is often said, "All maps lie flat, and all flat maps lie." Yes, that's right; every map is, in some way, wrong. The globe is the most accurate representation of the earth.

Each map has **four main map properties**: shape, size (area), distance, and direction. *Shape* refers to the geometric shapes of the objects on the map. *Size* (area) refers to the relative amount of space taken up on the map by the landforms or objects on the map. *Distance* refers to the represented distance between objects on the map. *Direction* refers to the degree of accuracy representing the **cardinal directions**—north, south, east, and west—and their **intermediate directions**—northwest, northeast, southwest, and southeast. Less accurate are the **relative directions** that people commonly use to describe a location, such as *right, left, up,* and *down,* among many others.

All four properties cannot be accurately represented, so a cartographer must choose which of the properties to distort. Cartographers make this decision by considering the map's purpose. When designing a map for navigational purposes, the cartographer would keep direction and distance accurate; size (area) and shape are not as important.

The Process of Mapmaking: Projection

In making a flat map of the round earth, geographers use geometric shapes. They can choose a cylinder, cone, or flat plane to touch to the earth and construct a map. To visualize this process, imagine that the globe has a light in it and is in a dark room. When the chosen geometric shape, such as a flat plane, is placed on the globe, the globe reflects onto this geometric shape, forming a flat image, or projection, of the round earth. The resulting projection reflects the geometric surface used in constructing it.

The projection is distorted in some way, however, depending on the geometric shape used to make the map. Geographers have different labels for maps that reflect the different properties distorted by the maps:

- **Equal-area (or equivalent) projections:** maps that maintain area but distort other properties

- **Conformal (or orthomorphic) projections:** maps that maintain shape but distort other properties (it is impossible to have a projection that is both conformal and equal area)

- **Azimuthal projections:** maps that maintain direction but distort other properties

- **Equidistant projections:** maps that maintain distance but distort other properties

The Mercator projection, described in more detail in the next section, is a conformal projection created using a cylindrical surface, and the Albers projection was created using a conic surface. Azimuthal projections are flat-plane-constructed maps of each hemisphere. Great-circle routes are apparent on azimuthal projections.

Uses of Projections

Consider the different maps you have seen in your lifetime. You probably have used a **Robinson projection** in your social studies class to memorize points on the world map because the Robinson projection shows the world according to slight distortion of all four properties, rather than getting just one correct and drastically distorting others. Before the Robinson projection was invented, social studies teachers often used the **Mercator projection**. Though the Mercator projection shows the shapes of the continents and landforms accurately, it drastically distorts the size (area) of the continents. For example, Greenland is almost as large as Africa on the Mercator. Moreover, schools in the former Soviet Union used the Mercator projection to teach its children because the map made the USSR look larger than its enemies. A geographer created the **Peter projection** to show relative sizes of the earth's continents accurately (equal area), but because it distorts shape, it is not conformal.

TYPES OF MAPS

Most maps include a compass which indicates which way is north, south, east and west. They also include a scale so you can estimate distances. Different maps include:

- **Climate maps** provide information about precipitation (rain and snow) of a region. Cartographers, or mapmakers, use colors to show different climate or precipitation zones.

- **Economic or resource maps** feature the type of natural resources or economic activity that dominates an area. Cartographers use symbols to show the locations of natural resources or economic activities. For example, oranges on a map of Florida tell you that oranges are grown there.

Figure 5.2   Economic Resource Map

Source: Pennsylvannia Department of Natural Resources
http://www.dcnr.state.pa.us/topgeo/econresource/inex.aspx

- **Physical** maps illustrate the physical features of an area, such as the mountains, rivers and lakes. Colors are used to show relief—differences in land elevations. Green is typically used at lower elevations; orange or brown indicate higher elevations and blue indicates a body of water.

- **Political maps** indicate state and national boundaries and capital and major cities. A capital city is usually marked with a star within a circle.

- **Road maps** show major along with some minor highways, as well as roads, airports, railroad tracks, cities and other points of interest in an area.

- **Topographic maps**, such as the one in Figure 5.3, include contour lines to show the shape and elevation of an area. Lines that are close together indicate steep terrain, and lines that are far apart indicate flat terrain.

Figure 5.3 Topographical Map

Geographers examine how people shape their world—how they settle the land, form community and how they permanently change the landscape. The various branches of geography taken as one give the geographer the tools to understand the vastness of the earth.

Physical geography is a branch of geography concerned with the natural features of the earth's surface. Physical geography concentrates on such areas as land formation, water, weather, and climate. **Population geography** is a form of geography that deals with the relationships between geography and population patterns, including birth and death rates. **Political geography** deals with the effect of geography on politics, especially on national boundaries and relations between states. **Economic geography** is a study of the interaction between the earth's landscape and the economic activity of the human population.

A GEOGRAPHIC TOUR

Geographers examine how people shape their world—how they settle the land, form community and how people permanently change the landscape. The various branches of geography taken as one give the geographer the tools to understand the vastness of the earth.

Physical geography is a branch of geography concerned with the natural features of the earth's surface. Physical geography concentrates on such areas as land formation, water, weather, and climate. **Population geography** is a form of geography that deals with the relationships between geography and population patterns, including birth and death rates. **Political geography** deals with the effect of geography on politics, especially on national boundaries and relations between states. **Economic geography** is a study of the interaction between the earth's landscape and the economic activity of the human population.

Figure 5.4 Continents and Oceans of the World

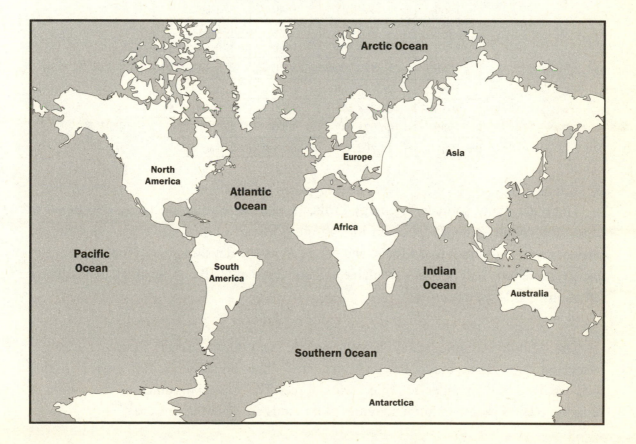

The United States

The United States is a relatively young country made up of immigrants from all over the world.

Table 5.1 — U.S. City Populations

San Diego, California	1,266,731
Omaha, Nebraska	424,482
Baltimore, Maryland	637,455
Houston, Texas	2,208,180
Boston, Massachusetts	599,351
New York, New York	8,274,527

Source: United States Census Bureau, July 2007

Table 5.2 – Population of the United States

Year	Population	Year	Population
1860	31,443,321	1940	132,164,569
1870	38,558,371	1950	151,325,798
1880	50,189,209	1960	179,323,175
1890	62,979,766	1970	203,302,031
1900	76,212,168	1980	226,547,082
1910	92,228,496	1990	248,790,925
1920	106,021,537	2000	282,171,936
1930	123,202,624	2008 (est.)	304,059,724

There are many sources of energy in the United States that are being developed to lessen the country's dependence on foreign oil. Some of these sources are solar energy, nuclear energy, gasohol, fossil fuels, and others. With the development of these sources of energy, more jobs will be made available and our economy will not be afflicted by adverse situations in oil-rich countries.

The Middle Atlantic states, which include New York, West Virginia, Delaware, Maryland, New Jersey, and Pennsylvania, are a hub of activity. This area is highly industrialized and includes a skilled work force. The financial center of the nation is found in New York and cultural activities of all kinds are found in this area.

The states of North Dakota, South Dakota, Nebraska, Kansas, Minnesota, Iowa, Missouri, Wisconsin, Illinois, Michigan, Indiana, and Ohio make up the Plains states. This area is also referred to as the Midwest Region of the United States. It is known as a great agricultural region. Some of the crops grown are wheat, corn, and oats.

The Plains states are highly industrialized. Their location near waterways and the close proximity to coal and iron deposits have made it relatively easy for industries to develop. Skilled laborers are available and are necessary to work in manufacturing plants.

The South includes the following states: Texas, Oklahoma, Louisiana, Arkansas, Mississippi, Alabama, Florida, Georgia, South Carolina, North Carolina, Tennessee, Kentucky, and Virginia. This area is known for its relatively mild weather and good, rich soil. Agriculture and oil are two of the most important industries in the South. Some of the crops grown are cotton, corn, tobacco, peanuts, and rice. Cattle raising is also very important in some of these states. Five of these states border on the Gulf of Mexico.

Texas is the second-largest state in land area. It is composed of 267,000 square miles and 254 counties. It is broken up into many large physical regions such as piney woods, post oak belt, plains, rolling prairie, high plains, valley, coastal prairie, and West Texas. The estimated population of Texas in 2008 was 24.3 million. Texas is, without a doubt, one of the most geographically varied states in the United States.

The Pacific states include Washington, Oregon, and California. California has the largest population of any state in the United States. It is known for its agriculture and leads all other states in this regard. Oregon and Washington also are known for farming. All three states also have very developed industries.

Some of the major cities located in the Pacific states are Seattle, Spokane, Portland, Olympia, San Francisco, Los Angeles, Salem, and San Diego. There are many interesting places to visit in this area and thus tourism is a major industry.

The Mountain states are Montana, Idaho, Wyoming, Nevada, Utah, Colorado, Arizona, and New Mexico. These states are sparsely populated, even though the combined square mileage is over 800,000. The Rocky Mountains stretch through this area, and most people feel they are a beautiful sight to behold.

The New England states include Maine, Massachusetts, New Hampshire, Vermont, Rhode Island, and Connecticut. Territorially, this is a very small region. The total size is about 67,000 square miles. The main industries in this area are fishing, shipping, manufacturing, and dairy farming.

Mexico

Mexico borders the United States on the south and has about 107 million people. The land area is about 762,000 square miles. The capital is Mexico City. Some of the chief crops are coffee, cotton, corn, sugar cane, and rice.

Mexico has an abundance of natural resources, such as oil, gold, silver, and natural gas. Textiles, steel production, tourism, and petroleum are the major industries in Mexico.

Canada

Canada is the United States' neighbor to the north. It includes the second largest territory in the world. The current population is about 32 million people. The capital of Canada is Ottawa.

The United States and Canada are two sprawling countries that make up North America. Each country is an industrial giant and provides a very high standard of living for its population. The population of the United States is about nine or ten times larger than that of Canada.

The United States and Canada have large supplies of natural resources. In the United States, the minerals include coal, copper, gold, nickel, silver, zinc, and others. In Canada, the minerals found are nickel, gold, lead, silver, zinc, and others.

Central America

Central America is the connecting point between North and South America. The countries in Central America have an extremely long coastline. The main industry of this area is agriculture, and most people who live in this area are extremely poor. Bananas, coffee, and corn are some of their chief crops. The seven nations that make up Central

America are Belize, Guatemala, Honduras, El Salvador, Panama, Costa Rica, and Nicaragua.

Table 5.3 — South America

Country	Population	Square Miles
Argentina	38,592,000	1,065,189
Brazil	184,016,000	3,286,470
Chile	16,295,000	≈292,257
Venezuela	27,216,000	≈352,143
Ecuador	13,419,000	≈109,483

Selected South American Countries, 2005 est. (except Ecuador, 2006)

South America

South America, lying entirely in the Western Hemisphere and mostly south of the Equator, has a Pacific shoreline on the west and an Atlantic shoreline east and north. South America connects with Central America and lies to the south and east of the Caribbean Sea and North America. It is the realm closest to Antarctica.

A few physical characteristics dominate the physiography of South America. The Andes Mountains stretch the length of the west coast while the Amazon Basin covers the north central part of the realm. The remaining parts of the realm consist mainly of plateaus.

Roughly half of the area and half of the population of South America are concentrated in Brazil.

The population of South America resides primarily on the periphery of the continent. The interior is only lightly populated. However, parts of the interior are undergoing extensive development with some population shifts.

Historically, the difficult terrain and the large distances separating the various states have limited the interchange between the different states on the continent. More recently, the states have increased their interconnections, particularly economically. Economic integration has become a significant factor throughout the continent, but primarily so in the southern part of the continent.

South America can be easily divided into four distinct regions: the North, the West, the Southern Cone, and Brazil.

The North consists of Colombia, Venezuela, Guyana, French Guiana, and Suriname. Each of the states has a Caribbean orientation both economically and culturally. All the states followed a plantation development model that involved the importation of slaves and contract laborers. Eventually, those immigrants were absorbed into the culture. While Guyana, French Guiana, and Suriname retained the culture from the colonial period, Colombia and Venezuela expanded into farming, ranching, mining, and oil and became much more diversified.

The West includes the Andean states Ecuador, Peru, Bolivia, and Paraguay. In addition to the influence of Andes, these states also share a strong Amerindian heritage.

The South, or Southern Cone, consists of Argentina, Chile, and Uruguay. These states have a strong European influence and little Amerindian influence.

Brazil distinguishes itself in two respects from the rest of South America. First is the influence of Portugal rather than Spain and second is the importance of Africans as opposed to Amerindians in both culture and demography.

Most states exhibit a marked degree of cultural pluralism. While there are a variety of ethnicities that are remnants of the colonial and slave heritage, these groups exist side by side without mixing. This pluralism is often expressed economically as well. Within the predominant economic activity, agriculture, commercial and subsistence farming exist side by side to a greater extent than any place else in the world. This, too, reflects the history of the continent, as commercial farming is associated with the land distribution of European landholders while subsistence farming is associated with the landholdings of indigenous, African, and Asian peoples.

Urban growth throughout the continent continues its rapid rise. Levels of urbanization overall today are equivalent to those in Europe and the United States.

Europe

Europe consists of 39 states and approximately 731 million people, according to the United Nations. On the north, west, and south, it has boundaries facing the Atlantic Ocean and the Mediterranean Sea, as well as a large number of other bodies of water. The eastern boundary is somewhat uncertain, with the line of demarcation lying along the border of Russia or along the Ural Mountains.

The physiography of Europe includes a wide range of topographic, climatic, and soil conditions which have had an impact on the cultural, political, and economic development.

In the south, the coastal areas have hot dry summers that required the development of specially adapted plants. Lacking the richness of natural resources of other regions, the southern region of Europe has nonetheless achieved a continuity of culture that has continuously depended on the exploitation of agriculture. As a result, the region tends to have a lower standard of living than other parts of Europe with the notable exception of Eastern Europe. While not as urbanized as Northern Europe, Southern Europe is actually more populous than Northern Europe.

Eastern Europe encompasses the largest region in Europe as well as the largest range of physiological, cultural, and political characteristics. This is a region of open plains, major rivers, lowlands, highlands, and mountains and valleys that provide key transit corridors. The result is that numerous peoples have converged on the area and kept this rich area in almost continuous conflict. The region is referred to as a shatter belt because of the unrelenting break up of existing orders. The term "balkanization" comes from this region where chronic division and fragmentation occurs.

Northern or Nordic Europe, one of the largest regions in terms of size, is also one of the most poorly endowed regions in terms of natural resources. Cold climates with poor soil and limited mineral wealth combined with long distances over mountainous, remote terrain result in an isolated region, yet one that has succeeded economically as is evidenced by Norway's ranking of fourth richest country based on per capita income.

The British Isles, off the western coast of Europe consist of two main islands, Ireland and Britain as well as numerous small islands. While its isolation from continental Europe has protected it from attack, that isolation has led the United Kingdom to look outward to fulfill its economic needs. The United Kingdom had one of the largest empires in history and has become a hub of banking and industry.

Western Europe is at the heart of Europe. It provides the hub of economic power, which has led to its leadership in economic and political union.

Europe consists of strong regional distinctions in physical and cultural characteristics. The distinctions extend to functional specializations, thus helping to provide for extensive interchange.

The economy of Europe is well developed and depends in large part on manufacturing for its income. While Europe is considered to be overall highly productive and developed, the further east one goes, the lower the level of development.

Being at the western end of the Eurasian landmass, Europe is located in a prime position to facilitate contact with the rest of the world. Location as well as durable power cores provided necessary elements for the creation of wide ranging colonial empires.

Europe has an aging population that enjoys a high standard of living, is highly urbanized, and has a long life expectancy. The aging population coincides with a drop in fertility rates and thus a population decline in some states. Immigration partially offsets the population decline, but it is changing the cultural make up of the states, with some instability resulting.

Unlike most other parts of the world, Europe has made significant progress toward economic integration through the European Union. Political progress, although also a part of the developing and expanding European Union, has come much more slowly.

North Africa

Northern Africa is the northernmost part of Africa, separated from Subsaharan Africa by the Sahara Desert. Northern Africa is almost completely surrounded by water in all other directions, with only a small connection to Asia at the Sinai Peninsula of Egypt.

Northern Africa is bordered by the Atlantic Ocean to the west, the Red Sea to the east, and the Mediterranean Sea to the north. The states of Algeria, Egypt, Libya, Morocco, Sudan, Tunisia, and Western Sahara make up the region. The dominant physical feature of Northern Africa is the Sahara Desert, which covers more than 90% of the region. The other physical feature of note is the Atlas Mountains, which extend across much of Morocco, northern Algeria and Tunisia. The Atlas Mountains are part of the mountain system, which also runs through much of Southern Europe. The mountains become a steppe landscape as they transition into the Sahara Desert.

Farming has been the traditional economic base of the region, with Atlas Mountain valleys, the Nile valley and delta, and the Mediterranean coast providing good agricultural land. Cereals, rice, cotton, cedar, and cork are important crops. Olives, figs, dates, and citrus fruits are also grown here. The Nile Valley, being fertile and providing its own source of water, is particularly fertile, while elsewhere irrigation is essential to agricultural production. In the 20th century, the economies of Algeria and Libya were transformed by the discovery of oil and natural gas. Morocco depends on phosphates, agriculture and tourism for its economy. Egypt and Tunisia also depend on tourism. Egypt, also has a varied industrial base, importing technology to develop its electronics and engineering industries.

The population of North Africa can be divided along the main geographic regions of North Africa: the Maghreb (northwest), the Nile Valley (northeast), and the Sahara (south).

Subsaharan Africa

Subsaharan Africa is the whole of the African continent south of the Sahara Desert. It is bordered to the north by the Sahara, the largest desert in the world, the Atlantic Ocean to the west, the Indian Ocean to the east, and the Atlantic and Indian Oceans meeting to border Africa to the south. Despite being geographically part of Subsaharan Africa, the Horn of Africa and large parts of Sudan show a strong Middle Eastern influence.

The landforms of Subsaharan Africa include rainforests, grasslands, and a few mountain ranges. Equatorial Africa, including the Sahel (a transitional zone just north of the equator between the Sahara and the tropical savanna), is covered by tropical rain forests while farther south there are grassy flat highlands leading to coastal plains. While Northern Africa has the Atlas Mountains, the Ruwenzri on the Uganda-Zaire border is the main mountain range in the Subsaharan region. Kilimanjaro, part of the Ruwenzri and Africa's highest mountain, is a dormant volcano. Further to the east is the Great Rift Valley, which contains several lakes. In addition to these landforms, Africa has some of the world's longest rivers, including the Nile, Niger, Zaire, and Zambezi. While there are many great lakes and large river systems, Africa has few natural sea harbors.

Subsaharan Africa is culturally rich and diverse with approximately 50 independent states and hundreds of ethnic groups. The large number of states is a legacy of the colonial occupation of Africa by European states. When African states were given their independence, state boundaries were drawn with little thought given to natural geographic boundaries. The result has been great instability that exists to the present day. Governmental fraud, mismanagement, and poor leadership as well as the highest number of refugees and displaced persons in the world compound the instability. In addition to the political instability, health and nutritional conditions in the region are poor. Many diseases remain uncontrolled, malnutrition is rampant, and the AIDS pandemic, which had its genesis in Africa, is a significant health crisis.

Despite the wide variety of cultures, most people in Subsaharan Africa depend on farming to earn a living. This is true despite the fact that Subsaharan Africa is rich in natural resources. States such as Angola and Nigeria have oil reserves, while South Africa is known for diamonds. The patterns of resource exploitation and transportation still follow those established during the colonial period. Thus, the people of the region have little access to and largely do not benefit from the wealth of raw materials they possess.

Russia

Russia, the largest state in terms of territory, spans most of the northern part of Eurasia. It is almost twice as large as the next biggest state, Canada. It is also the largest and most populous state that lies the farthest north in the world. Russia's climate is largely continental because of its large size and compactness. Most of its land is more than 200 miles from the sea, and the center is approximately 1,600 miles from the sea. Furthermore, Russia's mountain ranges, which are mostly to the south and the east, block moderating temperatures from the Indian and Pacific Oceans.

Despite its large size, comparatively speaking, Russia's population of approximately 143 million people is not very large. Most of that population lives west of the Ural Mountains and that population is very heterogeneous. Russia is a patchwork of many different ethnic groups, which formed the original basis for the 21 internal republics. As such, Russia is multicultural with a multifaceted political geography.

Despite having 80% of its land mass east of the Ural Mountains, most of the development, population, and infrastructure lie west of the Urals. The largest cities with the attendant industrial and transportation structure as well as the most productive farmland exist on the western 20% of Russia. What development does exist east of the Urals follows a narrow corridor near the southern border that reaches the Sea of Japan at Vladivostok. This corridor coincides with the Trans-Siberian Railway, which was built to reach one of the few seaports that is usable all year. Despite the fact that Russia is large, it is almost completely encircled by land within Eurasia.

While having extensive industrial development (at least regionally), Russia also holds the greatest mineral resource reserves in the world. The country is the most abundant in mineral fuels. It may contain up to half of the world's coal reserves and an even larger percentage of petroleum reserves. While Russia is blessed with plentiful resources, they are located in remote areas with extreme climates. For example, deposits of coal are scattered throughout the region, but the largest deposits are located in central and eastern Siberia, making them difficult to reach and expensive to mine.

Despite the wealth of natural resources, Russia has never been an exporter of manufactured goods, with the exception of weapons. Scarcity and low quality have limited the availability of Russian consumer goods outside of Russia (and, in many cases, inside as well).

With the collapse of Soviet Communism in the late 20th century, regions that have been associated with both Russia and the Soviet Union have begun to look outside of the Russian Federation for political, economic, and cultural connections.

South Asia

South Asia is a clearly demarcated realm bounded by deserts in the west, the Himalayas to the north, mountains and dense forests to the east, and ocean to the south. Despite containing over 20 percent of the world's population, South Asia consists of only seven states: Bangladesh, Bhutan, India, the Maldives, Nepal, Pakistan, and Sri Lanka.

The realm of South Asia is the most populous and densest in the world. The region has been beset by political instability and is the site of frequent military conflicts including wars between India and Pakistan, both of whom possess nuclear weapons.

The bulk of the region's territory is on the Indian subcontinent. Sections of all the states in the realm lie within the subcontinent on the Indian tectonic plate.

The climate varies considerably from area to area being influenced by altitude, proximity to the coast, and seasonal monsoons. The south is hot in summer and subject to vast quantities of rain during monsoon periods. The north is also hot in summer, but cools during winter. As the elevation increases in mountainous areas, the weather is colder and snow falls at higher altitudes in the Himalayas. However, on the plains at the foot of the Himalayas, the temperatures are much more moderate, as the mountains block the bitter winds that make Siberia so cold.

Despite the temperature variations, the climate of the region is called a monsoon climate. The weather is humid during the summer and dry during winter, resulting in two seasons rather than four: wet and dry. In the south, the climate is tropical monsoon while the north has a temperate monsoon climate. The impact of the monsoon climate can be seen on agriculture in the prevalence of jute, tea, rice, and other vegetables being grown in this region.

With more than half its population engaged in subsistence agriculture, it follows that South Asia has a high rate of poverty. Average incomes are low as are levels of education. Moreover, the low income and education levels contribute to poor overall health for the region. All of these factors paint a grim picture of economic prospects.

Sitting on only three percent of the land mass of the world, yet possessing over 22 percent of its population, South Asia has a high population density that will only continue to get worse as it also has one of the highest population growth rates. India, with over 1 billion people, is the world's largest federal republic. Despite having a representative government, economic gains for the majority of the population are limited.

With more than 2,000 ethnic groups, South Asia is one of the most ethnically diverse realms. Ethnic groups range in size from hundreds of millions to small tribal groups.

Throughout its history South Asia has been invaded and settled by many ethnic groups. The fusion of the cultures of these different ethnic groups over the centuries has resulted in the creation of a common culture, traditions and beliefs such as the religions of Hinduism, Jainism, Buddhism, and Sikhism. As a consequence, they share many similar cultural practices, festivals, and traditions.

Religion continues to play a major role in South Asia. Hindus in India, Muslims in Bangladesh and Pakistan, and Buddhists in Sri Lanka display fundamentalist and nationalist tendencies that exacerbate already tendentious religious relationships.

British colonialism created a politically unified South Asia. However, when Britain granted its South Asian colony independence, it split into numerous states along mainly cultural/religious lines. Political friction, particularly between India and Pakistan, remains a constant problem. The cultural and religious differences that contribute to conflict combine with ongoing border disputes between India and Pakistan and India and China to create a potentially disastrous situation, as all three countries possess nuclear weapons.

East Asia

East Asia consists of four states and two other political entities. China, Japan, South Korea, and Mongolia are states, while Taiwan and North Korea cannot be classified as states because they lack general recognition by the states of the world. Taiwan, while considering itself independent, is viewed by the People's Republic of China as a temporarily insubordinate or wayward province. North Korea's political status is uncertain. It is not a full member of the United Nations and there are doubts as to whether the division of Korea into North and South is permanent.

Economics

6

Studying economics requires a specific way of looking at how things work in the world. The approach has three main components: economic methods, macroeconomics, and microeconomics. **Adam Smith** (1723–1790) is considered by most to be the founder of the field of economics. Smith was a Scottish economist whose writing can be said to have inaugurated the modern era of economic analysis. **The Wealth of Nations** published in 1776, can be read as an analysis of a market economy. It was Smith's belief that a market economy was a superior form of organization from the standpoint of both economic progress and human liberty. Smith acknowledged that self-interest was a dominant motivating force in a market economy, yet this self-interest was ultimately consistent with the public interest. Market participants were guided by an **invisible hand** to act in ways that promoted the public interest. Firms may only be concerned with profits, but profits are only earned by firms that satisfy consumer demand and keep costs down. Since his work was published, many others have furthered the study of economics, though they certainly have not always agreed with Smith. In fact, four general—and differing—viewpoints have evolved regarding the workings of markets: Classical, Keynesian, Monetary, and Neo-classical.

Most contemporary definitions of economics involve the notions of **choice and scarcity** and their relationship to one another. Perhaps the earliest of these is by Lionell Robbins in 1935: "Economics is a science which studies human behavior as a relationship between ends and scarce means which have alternative uses." Virtually all textbooks have definitions that are derived from this definition, though the exact wording differs from author to author, the standard definition is something like this: "Economics is the social science that examines how people choose to use limited or scarce resources in attempting to satisfy their unlimited wants."

Microeconomics, the study of the individual parts that make up the economy, includes households, business firms, and government agencies, with particular emphasis placed on how these units make decisions and the consequences of these decisions. **Macroeconomics**, the study of the economy as a whole, considers inflation unemployment and economic growth.

FUNDAMENTAL CONCEPTS IN ECONOMICS

Scarcity—Human wants and needs (for goods, services, leisure, etc.) exceed the ability of the economy to satisfy those wants and needs. This is true for the economy as a whole as well as each individual in the economy. In other words, there is never enough to go around. Individuals never have enough money to buy all they want. Business firms cannot pay completely satisfactory wages without cutting into profits, and vice versa. Government never has enough money to fund all worthwhile projects.

Opportunity Cost—The reality of scarcity implies that individuals, businesses, and governments must make choices, selecting some opportunities while foregoing others. Buying a car may mean foregoing a vacation; acquiring a new copy machine may mean canceling the company picnic; paying higher welfare benefits may require terminating a weapons system. The opportunity cost of a choice is the value of the best alternative choice sacrificed.

Individualism—Economic analysis emphasizes individual action. Most economic theories attempt to model the behavior of "typical" individuals. All groups, such as "society," business firms, or unions, are analyzed as a collection of individuals each acting in a particular way. In a sense, the preceding sentence represents an ideal. Not all economic theory achieves this goal.

Rational Behavior—Individuals are assumed to act rationally. This is the most misunderstood term in economics. It does not necessarily mean people are cold, calculating, and greedy. Rather, it means that given a person's goals and knowledge, people take actions likely to achieve those goals and avoid actions likely to detract from those goals. A greedy person acts rationally if she spends on herself and does not give to charity. She is irrational if she does the opposite. An altruistic person acts rationally if she gives her money to the needy and does not spend it on herself. Irrational behavior is the opposite.

Marginal Analysis—Economists assume that people make choices by weighing the costs and benefits of particular actions.

Specialization and Division of Labor—This is a strategy for producing goods and services. Division of labor means that different members of a team of producers are given responsibility for different aspects of a production plan. Specialization means that producers become quite apt at those aspects of production they concentrate on. Specialization and division of labor is alleged to lead to efficiency which facilitates economic growth and development.

THE ECONOMIC PROBLEM

Universal Economic Goals

Allocative (Economic) Efficiency—A society achieves allocative efficiency if it produces the types and quantities of goods and services that most satisfies its people. Failure to do so wastes resources.

Technical Efficiency—A society achieves technical efficiency when it is producing the greatest quantity of goods and services possible from its resources. Failure to do so is also a waste of resources.

Equity—A society wants the distribution of goods and services to conform with its notions of "fairness."

Standards of Equity—Equity is not necessarily synonymous with equality. There is no objective standard of equity, and all societies have different notions of what constitutes equity. Three widely held standards are:

• **Contributory standard**—Under a contributory standard, people are entitled to a share of goods and services based on what they contribute to society. Those making larger contributions receive correspondingly larger shares. The measurement of contribution and what to do about those who contribute very little or are unable to contribute (i.e., the disabled) are continuing issues.

- **Needs standard**—Under a needs standard, a person's contribution to society is irrelevant. Goods and services are distributed based on the needs of different households. Measuring need and inducing people to contribute to society when goods and services are guaranteed are continuing issues.

- **Equality Standard**—Under an equality standard, every person is entitled to an equal share of goods and services, simply because they are a human being. Some of the ongoing issues with this theory are how to allow for needs and how to induce individuals to maximize their productivity when the reward is the same for everyone. Economists remain divided over whether the goals of equity and efficiency (allocative and technical) are complementary or in conflict.

Universality of the Problem of Scarcity

Goods and Services—Goods and Services refers to anything that satisfies human needs, wants, or desires. Goods are tangible items, such as food, cars, and clothing. Services are intangible items, such as education, health care, and leisure. The consumption of goods and services is a source of happiness, well-being, satisfaction, or utility.

Resources (Factors of Production)—Resources refers to anything that can be used to produce goods and services. A commonly used classification scheme places all resources into one of six categories:

Land—All natural resources, whether on the land, under the land, in the water, or in the air; e.g., fertile agricultural land, iron ore deposits, tuna fish, corn seeds, and quail.

Labor—The work effort of human beings.

Capital—Productive implements made by human beings, e.g., factories, machinery, and tools.

Entrepreneurship—A specialized form of labor. Entrepreneurship is creative labor. It refers to the ability to detect new business opportunities and bring them to fruition. Entrepreneurs also manage the other factors of production.

Technology—The practical application of scientific knowledge. Technology is typically combined with the other factors to make them more productive.

Scarcity—Economists assume that human wants and needs are virtually limitless while acknowledging that the resources to satisfy those needs are limited. Consequently, society is never able to produce enough goods and services to satisfy everybody, or most anyone, completely. Alternatively, resources are scarce relative to human needs and desires.

Scarcity and Economic Choice

Economics is always about limits. We are, by the very nature of our existence, limited to the resources provided by the planet. Our wants and needs, however, are not limited, and therein lies the rub! The result is **scarcity,** the fundamental reality of economics. Because of scarcity, humankind must engage in **production choices**. The primary question is: *Which of our needs and wants do we satisfy, and which go unfulfilled?* Answering this question forces people to make choices, and therefore trade-offs. Economists help us to understand these choices and the variety of possibilities that we face. Economists employ models that help us to focus on specific relationships that exist in the production and consumption of goods and services These models employ the scientific method, in that they apply logical analysis based on economic principles to predict and explain outcomes, as well as suggest policies.

Trade-offs and Opportunity Cost

Another basic observation of economics is that the economic choices we make result in trade-offs that can be measured. As those trade-offs are measured, we realize that various combinations of goods and services can be produced. However, as we produce more of one good, we incur a cost, in the form of lost production of an alternative good or service. The **Production Possibilities Frontier Curve**, the **Law of Diminishing Marginal Returns**, and the **Law of Increasing Opportunity** Cost help us to understand this axiom. Together, these realities govern the behavior of the supplier in the free market system.

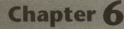

Production Possibilities Curve

The Production Possibilities Curve is a model of the economy used to illustrate the problems associated with scarcity. It shows the maximum feasible combinations of two goods or services that society can produce, assuming all resources are used in their most productive manner.

Assumptions of the Model

1. Society is only capable of producing two goods (guns and butter).

2. At a given point in time, society has a fixed quantity of resources.

3. All resources are used in their most productive manner.

Table 6.1 illustrates selected combinations of the two goods that can be produced given these assumptions.

Table 6.1 Selected Combinations of Guns and Butter

POINT	GUNS	BUTTER
A	0	16
B	4	14
C	7	12
D	9	9
E	10	5
F	11	0

Technical Efficiency—Figure 6.1 is a graphical modal of the table. All points on the curve are points of technical efficiency. By definition, technical efficiency is achieved when more of one good cannot be produced without producing less of the other good. Find point D on the curve. Any move to a point with more guns (i.e., point E) will necessitate a reduction in butter production. Any move to a point with more butter (such as point C) will necessitate a reduction in guns production. Any point inside the curve (such as point G) represents technical inefficiency. Either inefficient production methods are being used or resources are not fully employed. A movement from G to the curve will allow more of one or both goods to be produced without any reduction in the quantity of the other good. Points outside the curve (such as H) are technically infeasible given society's current stock of resources and technological knowledge.

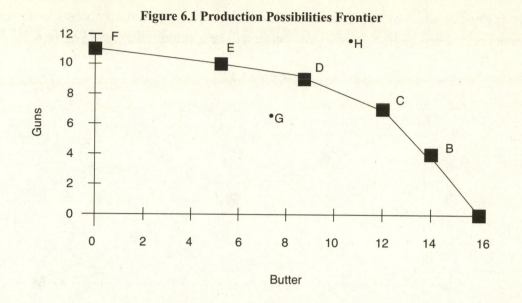

Figure 6.1 Production Possibilities Frontier

Opportunity Cost—Consider a move from D to E. Society gets one more unit of guns, but must sacrifice four units of butter. The four units of butter is the opportunity cost of the gun—one gun costs four butters.

Law of Increasing Costs—Starting from point A and moving up along the curve, note that the opportunity cost of guns increases. From point A to B, two butters are sacrificed to get four guns (one gun costs one half butter); from point B to C, two butters are sacrificed to get three guns (one gun costs two thirds butter); from C to D, three butters are sacrificed for two guns (one gun costs one and one half butter); from D to E, one gun costs four butter; and from E to F, one gun costs five butters.

The law of increasing costs says that as more of a good or service is produced, its opportunity cost will rise. It is a consequence of resources being specialized in particular uses. Some resources are particularly good in gun production and not so good for butter production, and vice versa.

At the commencement of gun production, the resources shifted out of butter will be those least productive in butter (and most productive in guns). Consequently, gun production will rise with little cost in terms of butter. As more resources are diverted, those more productive in butter will be affected, and the opportunity cost will rise. This is what gives the production possibilities curve its characteristic convex shape.

If resources are not specialized in particular uses, opportunity costs will remain constant and the production possibilities curve will be a straight line (see Figure 6.2).

Figure 6.2

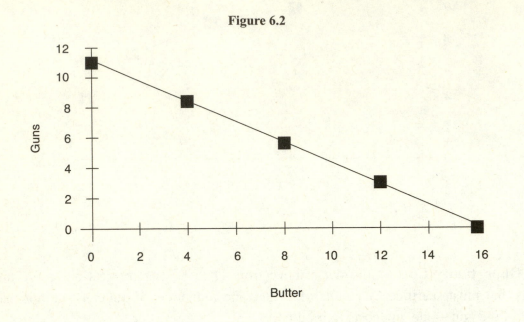

Figure 6.3–Production Possibilities Curve and Economic Growth

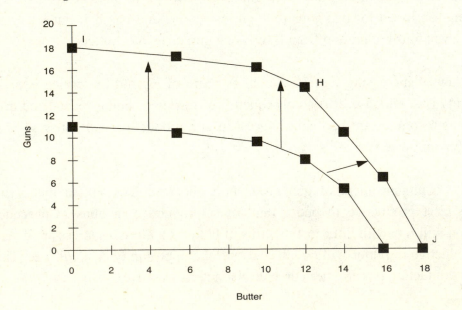

Allocative Efficiency—Allocative efficiency will be represented by the point on the curve that best satisfies society's needs and wants. It cannot be located without additional knowledge of society's likes and dislikes. A complicating factor is that the allocatively efficient point is not independent of society's distribution of income and wealth.

Economic Growth—Society's production of goods and services is limited by its resources. Economic growth, then, requires that society increases the amount of resources it has or makes those resources more productive through the application of technology. Graphically, economic growth is represented by an outward shift of the curve to IJ (see Figure 6.3 on previous page). Economic growth will make more combinations of goods and services feasible, but will not end the problem of scarcity.

DEMAND AND SUPPLY

Demand

Demand is a schedule or a graph showing the relationship between the price of a product and the amount consumers are willing and able to buy, ceteris paribus. The schedule or graph does not necessarily show what consumers actually buy at each price. **The Law of Demand** says there is an inverse relationship between price and quantity demanded; people will be willing and able to buy more if the product gets cheaper.

Ceteris Paribus

All hypothetical relationships between variables in economics include a stated or implied assumption *ceteris paribus*. The term means "all other factors held constant." As we will see, there are many factors affecting the amount of a product people are willing and able to buy. The demand schedule shows the relationship between price and quantity demanded, holding all the other factors constant. This allows us to investigate the independent effect that price changes have on quantity demanded without worrying about the influence the other factors are having.

Demand Schedule—Assume the product is widgets. Let Qd be quantity demanded and P be price.

Table 6.2 Demand Schedule

Qd	P
48.0	1.00
47.5	1.25
47.0	1.50
46.5	1.75
46.0	2.00

Figure 6.4–Graph of Demand Schedule

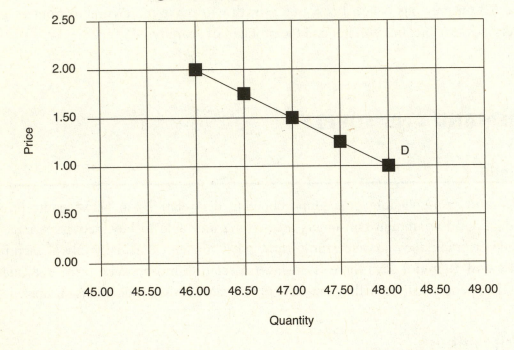

Supply

Supply is a schedule or a graph showing the relationship between the price of a product and the amount producers are willing and able to supply, *ceteris paribus*. The schedule or graph does not necessarily show what producers actually sell at each price. There is generally a positive relationship between price and quantity supplied, reflecting higher costs associated with greater production.

Supply Schedule—Assume the product is widgets. Let Q_s be quantity supplied.

Table 6.3 Supply Schedule

Qs	P
46.0	1.00
46.5	1.25
47.0	1.50
47.5	1.75
48.0	2.00

Figure 6.5–Graph of Supply Schedule

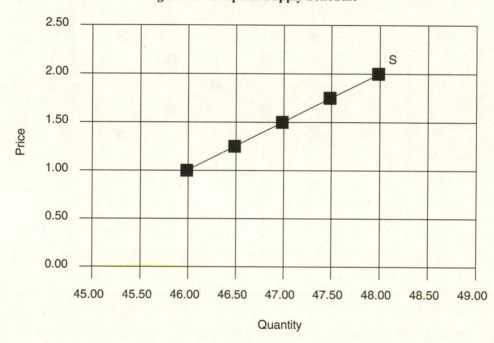

Market Equilibrium

The intersection of the demand and supply curves indicates the equilibrium price and quantity in the market (see Figure 6.6). The word *equilibrium* is synonymous with stable. The price and quantity in a market will frequently not be equal to the equilibrium, but if that is the case then the market will be adjusting, and, hence, not stable.

If the price of the product is $2.00, then the quantity supplied of the product (48) will be greater than the quantity demanded (46). There will be a surplus in the market of 48 – 46 = 2. The unsold product will force producers to lower their prices. A reduction in price will reduce the quantity supplied while increasing quantity demanded until the surplus disappears. Two dollars is not an equilibrium because the market is forced to adjust.

If the price of the product is $1.00, then the quantity supplied of the product (46) will be less than the quantity demanded (48). There will be a shortage in the market of 48 − 46 = 2. Unsatisfied customers will cause the price of the product to be bid up. The higher price will cause the quantity supplied to increase while decreasing the quantity demanded until the shortage disappears. One dollar is not an equilibrium because the market is forced to adjust.

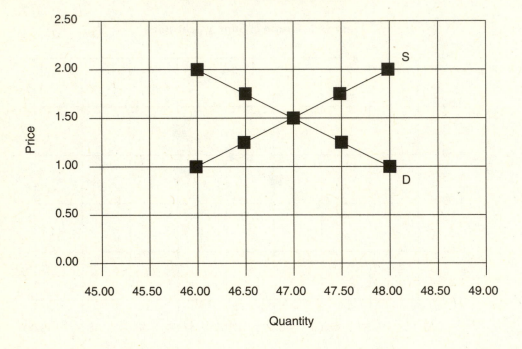

Figure 6.6–Market Equilibrium

If the price of the product is $1.50, then the quantity demanded (47) is just equal to the quantity supplied (47). Producers can sell all they want. Buyers can buy all they want. Since everyone is satisfied, there is no reason for the price to change. Hence, $1.50 is an equilibrium price and 47 is an equilibrium quantity.

ECONOMIC SYSTEMS

Types of Systems

Every society must have some method for making the basic economic decisions.

Tradition—Traditional systems largely rely on custom to determine production and distribution questions. While not static, traditional systems are slow to change and are not well-equipped to propel a society into sustained growth. Traditional systems are found in many of the poorer Third World countries.

Command—Command economies rely on a central authority to make decisions. The central authority may be a dictator or a democratically constituted government.

Market—It is easier to describe what a market system is not than what it is. In a pure market system, there is no central authority and custom plays very little role. Every consumer makes buying decisions based on his or her own needs and desires and income. Individual self-interest rules. Every producer decides for him- or herself what goods or services to produce, what price to charge, what resources to employ, and what production methods to use. Producers are motivated solely by profit considerations. There is vigorous competition in every market.

Mixed—A mixed economy contains elements of each of the three systems defined above. All real world economies are mixed economies, although the mixture of tradition, command, and market differs greatly. The U.S. economy has traditionally placed great emphasis on the market, although there is a large and active government (command) sector. The Soviet economy placed main reliance on government to direct economic activity, but there was a small market sector.

Capitalism—The key characteristic of a capitalistic economy is that productive resources are owned by private individuals.

Socialism—The key characteristic of a socialist economy is that productive resources are owned collectively by society. Alternatively, productive resources are under the control of government.

Circular Flow

The Circular Flow is a model of economic relationships in a capitalistic market economy. Households, the owners of all productive resources, supply resources to firms through the resource markets, receiving monetary payments in return. Firms use the resources purchased (or rented, as the case may be) to produce goods and services, which are then sold to households and other businesses in the product markets. Household income not spent (consumed) may be saved in the Financial Markets. Firms may borrow from the financial markets to finance capital expansion (investment). Firm saving and household borrowing are not shown.

Figure 6.7–The Circular Flow

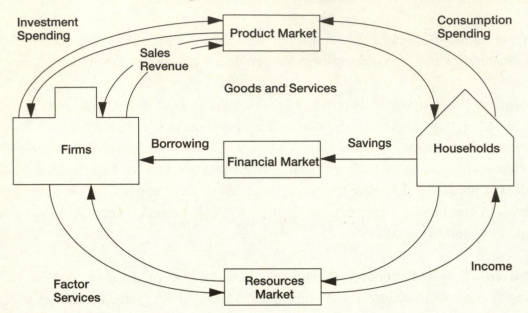

HOW A MARKET ECONOMY WORKS

Although the description of a market economy may suggest that chaos is the order of the day, economists believe that if certain conditions are met, a market economy is easily capable of achieving the major economic goals.

How a Market Economy Achieves Allocation Efficiency—Market forces will lead firms to produce the mix of goods most desired. Unforeseen events can be responded to in a rational manner.

Change in Tastes

Assume a change in consumer tastes from beef to chicken (see Figure 6.8). An increase in demand in the chicken market will be accompanied by a decrease in demand in the beef market. The higher price of chicken will attract more resources into the market and lead to an increase in the quantity supplied. The lower price of beef will induce a reduction in the quantity supplied and the exit of resources to other industries.

Note that the change in the level of output of both goods occurred because it was in the economic self-interest of firms to do so. Greater demand in the chicken market increased the profitability of chicken; lower demand in the beef market decreased the profitability of beef. Chicken and beef producers responded to society's desires not out of a sense of public spiritedness, but out of self-interest.

Figure 6.8–Changes in Tastes

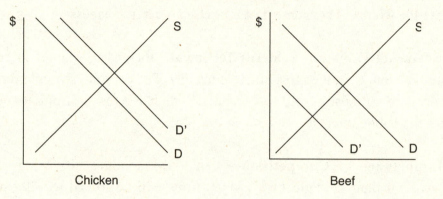

Scarcity

An unexpected freeze in Florida will cause a shift in the supply curve of orange juice, driving up its price, and causing consumers to cut back their purchases (see Figure 6.9). The higher price of orange juice will increase the demand for substitute products like apple juice, causing an increase in the quantity supplied of apple juice to take the place of orange juice.

Figure 6.9–Freeze in Florida

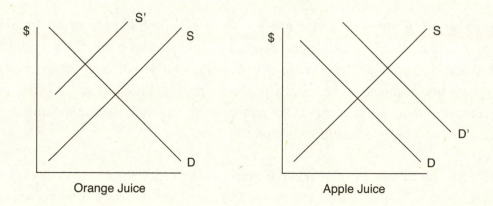

As above, the reaction of market participants reflected their evaluation of their own self-interest. Consumers reduced their quantity demanded of orange juice because it was now more expensive. Apple juice producers expanded production because now it was more profitable.

Consumer Sovereignty—"The Consumer is King." Consumer sovereignty means that consumers determine what is produced in the economy. In a market economy, business must cater to the whims of consumer tastes or else go out of business.

How a Market Economy Achieves Technical Efficiency—Market forces will lead firms to produce output in the most efficient manner. The constant struggle for profits will stimulate firms to cut costs. Note that technical efficiency results from attention to self-interest, not the public interest.

The Importance of Competition—A market economy thrives on competition between firms. In their struggle for survival, firms will be forced to cater to consumer demand (leading to allocative efficiency) and force production costs down as far as possible (leading to technical efficiency).

How a Market Economy Achieves Full Employment—Full employment of resources is thought to be the normal state of affairs in a market economy. Resource surpluses will force down the resource's price, leading quickly to re-employment.

How a Market Economy Achieves Growth—Competition between firms for the consumer's dollar will force a constant search for better products and methods of production. The resulting technological change will lead to optimal growth.

The Market Economy and Equity—This is a problematic area for a market economy. Certainly there are financial rewards for those who produce the products that win consumer acceptance. There are losses for those who do not. Yet winners in a market economy are not necessarily the most virtuous of people, they just sell a better product. While consumer demand determines the pattern of production, those consumers with the most income exert the greatest influence on the pattern.

The Role of Prices in a Market Economy—In order for an economy to operate efficiently, there must be information and incentives. There must be information on what goods and services are in demand, which resources are scarce, and so on. There must be an incentive to produce the goods and services desired, conserve on scarce resources, and so on. Both information and incentives are provided by prices. High prices indicate goods and services in demand; low prices indicate goods and services that have lost favor. High prices indicate scarce resources; low prices indicate plentiful. Firms responding "properly" to high prices will earn profits; firms responding "properly" to low prices will avoid losses. Firms exploiting cheap resources will earn profits; firms conserving on expensive resources will avoid losses.

Prices always provide accurate information and appropriate incentives. Since traditional and command economies downplay the role of prices, they have a much more difficult time achieving allocational and technical efficiency.

Figure 6.10

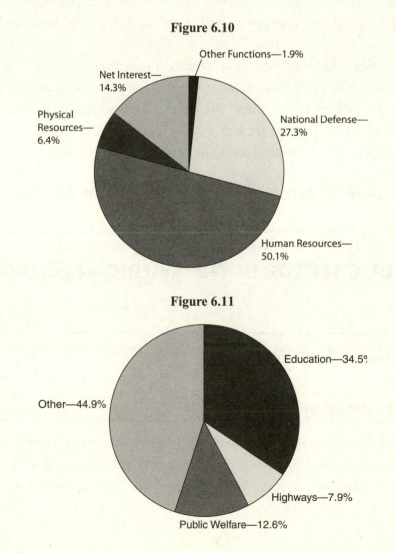

Other Functions—1.9%
Net Interest—14.3%
Physical Resources—6.4%
National Defense—27.3%
Human Resources—50.1%

Figure 6.11

Education—34.5%
Other—44.9%
Highways—7.9%
Public Welfare—12.6%

Conditions that Must be Met for a Market Economy to Achieve Allocative and Technical Efficiency

A market economy will automatically produce the optimum quantity of every good or service at the lowest possible cost if four conditions are met:

Adequate Information—Consumers must be well-enough informed about prices, quality and availability of products, and other matters that they can make intelligent spending decisions. Workers must be well-enough informed about wages and working conditions that they can choose wisely among job opportunities. Other segments of the economy must be similarly well-informed.

Competition—There must be vigorous competition in every market. Monopolistic elements will reduce output, raise prices, and allow inefficiency in particular markets.

No Externalities—Externalities exist when a transaction between a buyer and seller affects an innocent third party. An example would be if *A* buys a product from *B* that *B* produced under conditions that polluted the air that others breathe. (Not all externalities result in damage to society. Some are beneficial.) Where externalities are present, there is the possibility of over- or under-production of particular goods and services.

No Public Goods—The market is unlikely to produce the appropriate quantity of public goods.

THE PUBLIC SECTOR IN THE AMERICAN ECONOMY

Public Sector

The Public Sector refers to the activities of government.

Government Spending

Government Expenditures on Goods and Services versus Transfer Payments—Government spending can be usefully broken down into two categories. One category is spending on goods and services. When government buys a battleship, a hammer, or the Space Shuttle, it is acquiring goods. When government pays the salary of a soldier, teacher or bureaucrat, it is getting a service in return. The second category is transfer payments. Transfers are money or in-kind items given to individuals or businesses for which the government receives no equivalent good or service in return. Examples would be social security payments, welfare, or unemployment compensation.

GROSS NATIONAL PRODUCT

Measuring GNP

Gross National Product—Gross National Product (or GNP) is a measure of the dollar value of final goods and services produced by the economy over a given period of time, usually one year. It is the most comprehensive indicator of the economy's health available, although it is not a measure of society's overall well-being.

Final Goods and Services—Final goods and services are those sold to their ultimate users.

Intermediate Goods and Services—Intermediate goods and services are those in an intermediate stage of processing. They are purchased by firms for immediate resale, such as the frozen orange juice a grocery store buys from the processor for resale to consumers or they are purchased for further processing and then resale, such as the crude oil a refinery buys to refine into gasoline and other petroleum products.

GNP in the Circular Flow—Assume a simple economy composed of three business firms and one household. Firm A manufactures computer chips. It takes silicon from the environment (assumed to be so plentiful as to be a free good) and combines it with resources purchased or rented from the household. The resulting chips are sold to Firm B, a manufacturer of computers. Firm B takes the chips and combines them with the resources purchased from the household to produce computers which it sells to firm C, a retail computer store. The store uses resources obtained from the household to resell the computers to the household, which is the ultimate user.

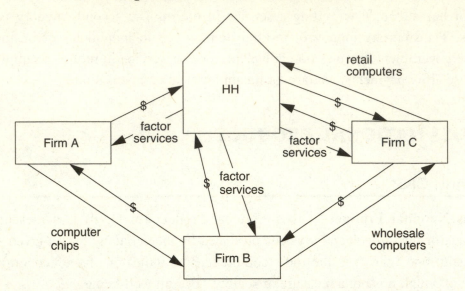

Figure 6.12–GNP in the Circular Flow

Table 6.4 traces the transactions that take place in the economy during the course of a year.

Table 6.4 Transactions of Three Firms over Three Years

FIRM	COST OF INTERMEDIATE GOODS PURCHASED	RESOURCES PURCHASED	COST OF GOODS SOLD	VALUE-ADDED
A	0	50	50	50
B	50	75	125	75
C	125	40	165	40

There are three ways to measure GNP.

1. **Expenditures on Final Goods and Services**—In the example, computer chips and wholesale computers are intermediate goods while retail computers are a final good. Since the household spent $165 on retail computers, this is a direct measure of GNP.

2. **Sum of Value-Added for All Firms**—
Value-Added (VA) = Cost of Goods Sold – Cost of Intermediate Goods Purchased

VA measures the value of the processing and resale activities that the firm performs on the intermediate goods and services it purchases. Adding value-added for all firms in the economy will give GNP. It follows because the value of final goods and services produced results from the contributions of all firms at all stages of the production process.

3. **Gross National Income**—Where does the term "value-added" come from? It comes from the services performed by the resources the firms hires. Therefore, value-added for each firm is just equal to the payments made for resources allowing us to total the incomes earned by all households to get GNP. This measure is frequently given the name Gross National Income (or GNI).

Trends in GNP—GNP rose from $91.3 billion in 1939 to $4,864.3 billion in 1988, although the rise was far from smooth and steady (see Figure 6.13).

Figure 6.13–Trends in GNP

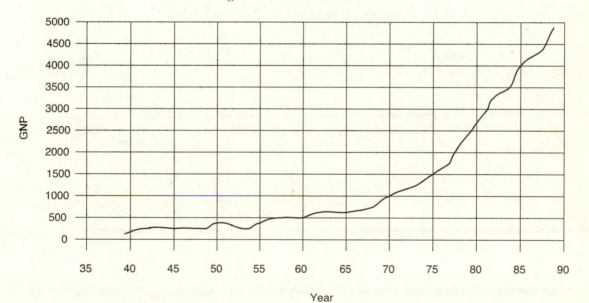

MACROECONOMIC PROBLEMS OF THE AMERICAN ECONOMY

The Business Cycle

Business Cycles—Business cycles are the alternating periods of prosperity and recession that seem to characterize all market-oriented economies.

Four Phases of the Cycle—Every business cycle consists of four phases. The peak is the high point of business activity. It occurs at a specific point in time. The contraction is a period of declining business activity. It occurs over a period of time. The trough is the low point in business activity. It, too, occurs at a specific point in time. The expansion is a period of growing business activity. It takes place over a period of time.

Although the word "cycle" implies a certain uniformity, that is misleading. Each business cycle differs from every other in terms of duration of contractions and expansions, and height of peak and depth of trough.

Figure 6.14–Phases of the Business Cycle

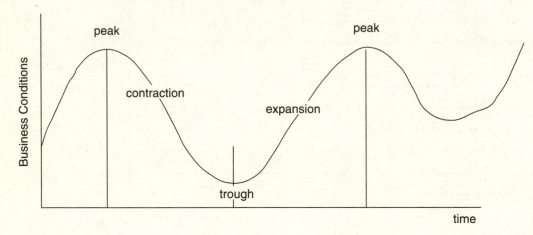

Seasonal Fluctuations—Seasonal fluctuations are changes in economic variables that reflect the season of the year. For example, every summer ice cream sales soar. They decrease during winter. Every December, toy sales increase dramatically. They fall back during January.

Secular Trends—A secular trend is the long run direction of movement of a variable. For example, our economy has become dramatically richer over the past century. We can say that there was a secular upward trend in real GNP. Of course, growth was not steady. There were periods of faster than average followed by slower than average growth, which accounts for business cycles.

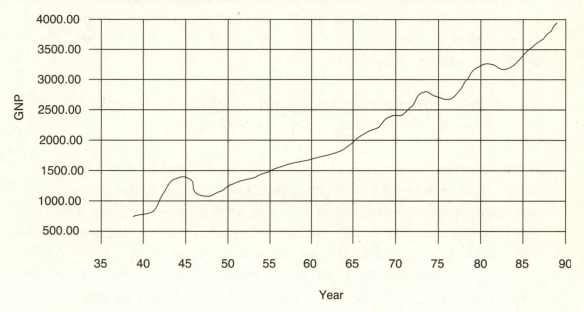

Figure 6.15–Secular Trend and Cycle in Real GNP, 1939–88

MONEY AND BANKING

What Money Is and Does

Money is anything that is generally acceptable in exchange for goods and services and in payment of debts. Suppose you had something you wanted to sell. Few would be willing to part with their product for a commodity like a loaf of bread, a chicken, or an automobile hubcap. All would be willing to exchange their product for coins, currency, or a check. Therefore, these latter items are money because they are generally acceptable. Everybody is willing to accept them in exchange for what they want to sell.

Functions of Money—Money performs four particular functions:

1. **Medium of Exchange**—Money is used to facilitate exchanges of goods and services. Money makes buying and selling easier. Assume we had an economy where nothing was money. Such an economy is known as a **barter economy**. In a barter economy goods and services exchange

directly for other goods and services. If you want an axe that someone is selling, you must find an item that person wants to trade for it. Barter requires a **double coincidence of wants**, each party must want what the other party has. If that condition does not hold, then exchange cannot take place, and valuable resources can be wasted in putting together trades. With money this problem never arises because **everyone always wants money**. Consequently, the resources used to facilitate exchanges can be put to more productive use.

2. **Unit of Value**—We use our monetary unit as the standard measure of value. We say a shirt is worth $25.00, not 14 chickens.

3. **Store of Value**—Money is one of the forms wealth can be stored in. Alternatives include stocks and bonds, real estate, gold, great paintings, and many others. One advantage of storing wealth in money form is that money is the most liquid of all assets. **Liquidity** refers to the ease with which an asset can be transformed into spendable form. Money is already in spendable form. The disadvantage of holding wealth in money form is that money typically pays a lower return than other assets.

4. **Standard of Deferred Payment**—Money is used in transactions involving payments to be made at a future date. An example would be building contracts where full payment is made only when the project is completed. This function of money is implicit in the three already discussed.

What Serves as Money?—Virtually anything can and has served as money. Gold, silver, shells, boulders, cheap metal, paper, and electronic impulses stored in computers are examples of the varied forms money has taken. The only requirement is that the item be generally acceptable. Money does **not** have to have intrinsic value (see below). Typically, the items that have served as money have had the following additional characteristics:

• durability

• divisibility

- homogeneity (uniformity or standardization)

- portability (high value-to-weight and value-to-volume)

- relative stability of supply

- optimal scarcity

What Makes Money Valuable?—Money is valuable if it can be used for or exchanged for something useful. Money's lack of intrinsic value means it cannot be used for anything useful. Why can it be exchanged for something useful? Sellers accept money because they know they can use it anywhere else in the country to buy goods and services and pay off debts. If they could not do that, they would not want it. What this means is that the substance that is used for money need not be valuable, and that money need not be backed by anything valuable. Such is the case. Our money is not backed by gold, silver, or anything else. It is just cheap metal, cheap paper, and electronic impulses stored in computers. Gold can be put to better use filling teeth!

The United States' Money Supply

While there are many different definitions of the money supply available, the two most commonly used are M1 and M2.

M1—M1 consists of currency, demand deposits, other checkable deposits, and traveler's checks.

Figure 6.16 Composition of M1 as of December 1989

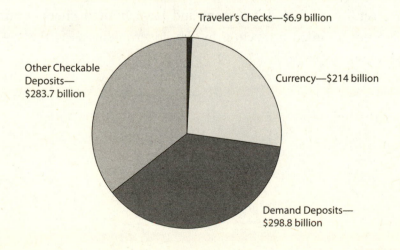

Traveler's Checks—$6.9 billion

Other Checkable Deposits— $283.7 billion

Currency—$214 billion

Demand Deposits— $298.8 billion

Currency—coins and paper money.

Demand deposits—These are checking accounts held in commercial banks. Funds can be transferred from person to person by means of a check. Demand deposits are considered money because checks are generally acceptable.

Other checkable deposits—This category, includes all other financial institution deposits upon which checks can be written. Among these are NOW accounts, ATS accounts, and credit union share drafts.

Traveler's checks—Most traveler's checks are generally acceptable throughout much of the world.

M2—M2 includes all of M1 plus savings deposits, small-denomination time deposits, money-market mutual funds and deposit accounts, overnight repurchase agreements (known as repos), and Eurodollars.

Savings Deposits—These are the common passbook savings accounts. They do not provide check-writing privileges.

Small Denomination time deposits—Better known as certificates of deposits, or CDs. They typically do not provide check-writing privileges.

Money market mutual funds and deposit accounts—Both mutual funds and deposit accounts are investment funds. Large numbers of people pool their money to allow for diversification and professional investment management. Mutual funds are managed by private financial companies. Deposit accounts are managed by commercial banks. Investors earn a return on their investment and have limited check-writing privileges. Mutual funds are not afforded protection by the government, as is the case with FDIC-insured bank accounts.

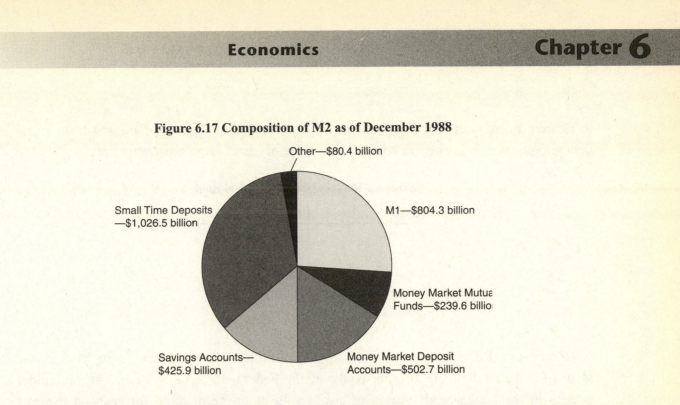

Figure 6.17 Composition of M2 as of December 1988

Other—$80.4 billion

M1—$804.3 billion

Small Time Deposits —$1,026.5 billion

Money Market Mutual Funds—$239.6 billion

Savings Accounts— $425.9 billion

Money Market Deposit Accounts—$502.7 billion

Overnight Repurchase Agreements and Eurodollars—Overnight repos essentially are short-term (literally, overnight) loans. A corporation with excess cash may arrange to purchase a security from a bank with the stipulation that the bank will buy the security back the next day at a slightly higher price. The corporation receives a return on its money, and the bank gets access to funds. Eurodollars are dollar-denominated demand deposits held in banks outside the United States (not just in Europe). From the standpoint of M2, deposits held in Caribbean branches of Federal Reserve member banks are relevant. These deposits are easily accessed by U.S. residents. While both instruments are important in financial affairs, they are negligible in the totality of M2.

A significant proportion of M2 cannot be used as a medium of exchange. Why, then, are the items considered money? First, each of these items is highly liquid. Second, studies indicate that people's economic behavior is not very sensitive to their relative holdings of the various assets in question (see Figure 6.17).

The Financial System

Financial Intermediaries—Financial intermediaries are organizations such as commercial banks, savings and loan institutions, credit unions, and insurance companies. They play an important role in facilitating the saving and investment process which helps the economy grow. Savers typically look to place their money where the combination of return, liquidity, and safety is best. Through the various types of deposits they offer, financial intermediaries compete for the saved funds. The money so obtained is used to finance borrowing. Through their ability to obtain large pools of money from many depositors, intermediaries are able to service the needs of large borrowers.

Table 6.5 Balance Sheet of Typical Bank

Assets	Liabilities
Reserves	Demand Deposits
Loans	Savings Deposits
Securities	Time Deposits
Property	Other Deposits
Other Assets	Net Worth

Reserves—Reserves are a bank's money holdings. Most reserves are held in the form of demand deposits at other banks or the Federal Reserve System. The remainder is cash in the bank's vault. Reserves are held to meet the demand for cash on the part of depositors and to honor checks drawn upon the bank. The amount of reserves a bank must hold is based on the **required reserve ratio**. Set by the Federal Reserve System, the required reserve ratio is a number from 0 to 1.00 and determines the level of reserve holdings relative to the bank's deposits.

Required Reserves—Required reserves are the amount a bank is legally obligated to hold. Required reserves are calculated by multiplying the required reserve ratio by the amount of deposits.

$$\text{Required Reserves} = \text{Required Reserve Ratio} \times \text{Deposits}$$

The required reserve ratio does not make banks safe. In the absence of a requirement, most banks would voluntarily hold adequate reserves to be "safe." In fact, the level of reserves banks are required to hold is probably higher than what they need to be safe. The main purpose of the requirement is to give the Federal Reserve System some control over the banks.

Excess Reserves—Excess reserves are the difference between the amount of reserves a bank holds and what it is required to hold. All banks hold excess reserves at all times for reasons of financial prudence; however, greater excess reserves will be held during periods of financial uncertainty.

$$\text{Excess Reserves} = \text{Reserves} - \text{Required Reserves}$$

Why Can Banks Hold "Fractional" Reserves?—All banks constantly operate with reserve holdings only a fraction of deposit liabilities. This is known as **fractional reserve banking**. If all depositors tried to withdraw their money simultaneously, banks would not be able to honor the demands. Fortunately, this is unlikely to happen because people like to hold deposits because they are safe and convenient. On a normal business day, some withdrawals are made, but these are counterbalanced by new deposits. Reserve holdings need only be a small fraction of deposits for prudent operation.

MONETARY POLICY

The Federal Reserve System

The Federal Reserve System (known as the "Fed") is the central bank of the United States. Its responsibilities are to oversee the stability of the banking system and conduct monetary policy to the end of fighting inflation and unemployment and stimulating economic growth.

Structure—The Fed has an unusual structure. It consists of a Board of Governors, 12 regional banks, money subregional banks, and commercial banks that opt for membership in the system. Although it was created by an Act of Congress (in 1913), nominally the Fed is privately owned by the member banks. Members of the Board of Governors are appointed by the President and confirmed by the Senate for 14 year terms. The Chair of the Board is appointed by the President and confirmed by the Senate for a four year term. The Fed's budget is overseen by a committee of Congress, and it must report to Congress about its operations at least twice a year. To a large extent, the Fed can be considered an independent agency of the government.

The Fed's virtual independence has led to a continuing controversy. Is it wise to give the power to influence the state of the economy to an entity that is not directly accountable to the people? The "pro" side claims the Fed's independence puts it "above" politics and leads to decisions more in the "public interest." The "con" side says that in a democracy, the people should be given a voice in all decisions that affect them.

Functions—The major functions of the Fed are as follows:Bank

- **Regulation**—The Fed has been given the responsibility of examining member banks to determine if they are financially strong and in conformity with the banking regulations. The Fed also approves mergers.

- **Clearing Interbank Payments**—The Fed performs a service for member banks in operating the check clearing function. Banks receiving deposit checks drawn on other banks can present them to the Fed. The Fed will credit the receiving bank's reserve account, reduce the paying bank's reserve account, and send the check back to the paying bank. Banks do not universally avail themselves of this service. Local banks will frequently cooperate and establish their own check clearing process for local checks

- **Lender of Last Resort**—One of the original motivations for establishing the Fed was to have a bank that could act as a "lender of last resort."

    Bank panics refer to situations where depositors lose faith in their bank and try to withdraw their money. Given the fractional reserve nature of modern banking, under which banks, by law, must set aside a fixed percent of their total deposits as reserves with the Fed, it is impossible for all depositors to withdraw their money simultaneously. The inability of depositors to withdraw their money from any one bank has the potential of scaring other depositors and starting a "run on the banks." By standing ready to loan reserves to banks experiencing difficulties, the Fed helps reduce the danger of panics.

    Federal Deposit Insurance was established during the New Deal era. Federal Deposit Insurance provides government guarantees for bank deposits should a bank fail. Both commercial banks and savings and loans are insured. Panics were much more common in the days before the Fed and the Federal Deposit Insurance Corporation, but are not unknown today. Witness the situations with savings and loan institutions in Ohio and Maryland (institutions which *lacked* federal insurance) within the last several years.

- **Monetary Policy**—The Fed's monetary policy actions affect prices, employment, and economic growth by influencing the availability and cost of money and credit in the economy. This in turn influences consumers' and businesses' willingness to spend money on goods and services. The Fed uses three monetary policy tools to influence the availability and cost of money and credit: **open market operations**, the **reserve requirements (ratio)** and the **discount rate**.

Open Market Operations—Open market operations refers to the Fed's buying or selling of U.S. Government bonds in the open market. The purpose is to influence the amount of reserves in the banking system, and, consequently, the banking system's ability to extend credit and create money.

a. **To expand the economy**—The Fed would buy bonds in the open market. If $50 million in bonds was purchased directly from commercial banks, the banks' balance sheet would change as follows:

All Commercial Banks

R + 50 million	
Bonds –50 million	

Banks are now holding an additional $50 million in excess reserves which they can use to extend additional credit. To induce borrowers, banks are likely to lower interest rates and credit standards. As loans are made, the money supply will expand. The additional credit will stimulate additional spending, primarily for investment goods.

The $50 million in bonds could be purchased directly from private individuals. The private individuals would then deposit the proceeds in their bank accounts. After the money was deposited, the balance sheet of all commercial banks would look as follows:

All Commercial Banks

R + 50 million	DD + 50 million

As above, the banks are now holding excess reserves which they can use to extend credit. Lower interest rates, a greater money supply, and a higher level of total expenditure will result.

b. **To contract the economy**—The Fed would sell bonds in the open market. If it sold $20 million in bonds directly to the commercial banks, the banks' balance sheet would change as follows:

All Commercial Banks

R	+ 50 million	
Bonds	−50 million	

Banks are now deficient in reserves. They need to reduce their demand deposit liabilities, and will do so by calling in loans and making new credit more difficult to get. Interest rates will rise, credit requirements will be tightened, and the money supply will fall. Total spending in the economy will be reduced.

If the Fed sells the $20 million in bonds directly to private individuals, payment will be made with checks drawn against the private individuals' bank accounts. The banks' balance sheet will change as follows:

All Commercial Banks

R	− 20 million	DD	− 20 million

Again, banks are deficient in reserves. They are forced to reduce credit availability, which will raise interest rates, reduce the money supply, and lead to a drop in total spending.

Bonds are a financial instrument frequently used by government and business as a way to borrow money. Every bond comes with a par value (often $1,000), a date to maturity (ranging from 90 days to 30 years), a coupon (a promise to pay a certain amount of money each year to the bondholder until maturity), and a promise to repay the par value on the maturity date. The issuing government or business sells the bonds in the bond market for a price determined by supply and demand. The money received from the sale represents the principal of the loan, the annual coupon payment is the interest on the loan, and the principal is repaid at the date of maturity. There is also a secondary market in bonds.

Assume a bond carries a coupon of $100 and is sold for $1,000. Then the annual yield to the purchaser is roughly 10% ($100/$1,000). If the same bond was sold for $950, the yield would be roughly 10.5% ($100/$950). If the same bond was sold for $1,050, the yield would roughly be 9.5% ($100/$1,050). Note the inverse relationship between bond yield and price. Also note that the actual yield formulas are considerably more complicated than those used.

Reserve Ratio—The Fed can set the legal reserve ratio for both member and non-member banks. The purpose is to influence the level of excess reserves in the banking system, and consequently, the banking system's ability to extend credit and create money.

a. **To expand the economy**—The Fed would reduce the reserve requirement. Assume the reserve requirement is 8%, and all banks are "all loaned up."

If the Fed reduces the reserve requirement to 6%, required reserves fall to $30 million, and there are immediately $10 million in excess reserves. Banks will lower the interest rates they charge and credit requirements in an attempt to make more loans. As the loans are granted, the economy's money supply and total spending will rise.

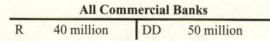

All Commercial Banks

R	40 million	DD	50 million

b. **To contract the economy**—The Fed would raise the reserve requirement. Assume the reserve requirement is 8%, and all banks are "all loaned up."

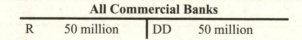

All Commercial Banks

R	50 million	DD	50 million

If the Fed raises the reserve requirement to 10%, required reserves rise to $50 million, and banks are immediately $10 million deficient in reserves. Banks will raise the interest rates they charge and credit requirements to reduce the amount of money borrowed. They may also call in loans. As the loans are reduced, the economy's money supply and total spending will fall.

Discount Rate—One of the responsibilities of the Fed is to act as a "lender of last resort." Member banks needing reserves can borrow from the Fed. The interest rate the Fed charges on these loans is called the **discount rate**. By changing the discount rate, the Fed can influence the amount member banks try to borrow, and, consequently, the banking system's ability to extend credit and create money.

a. **To expand the economy**—The Fed would lower the discount rate. A lower discount rate would make it less "painful" for member banks to borrow from the Fed. Consequently, they will be more willing to lend money and hold a low level of excess reserves. A lower discount rate would lead to lower interest rates and credit requirements, a higher money supply, and greater total spending in the economy.

b. **To contract the economy**—The Fed would raise the discount rate. A higher discount rate would make it more "painful" for member banks to borrow from the Fed. Consequently, they will be less willing to lend money and more likely to hold a high level of excess reserves. A higher discount rate would lead to higher interest rates and more stringent credit requirements, a lower money supply, and lower total spending in the economy.

Table 6.5—Monetary Policy Summary Table

TOOL	ACTION	EFFECT ON INTEREST RATES	EFFECT ON MONEY SUPPLY	EFFECT ON TOTAL SPENDING	EFFECT ON GNP
Open Market	buy	lower	raise	raise	raise
Operations	sell	raise	lower	lower	lower
Reserve	raise	raise	lower	lower	lower
Ratio	lower	lower	raise	raise	raise
Discount	raise	raise	lower	lower	lower
Rate	lower	lower	raise	raise	raise

IMPACT OF THE GLOBAL ECONOMY

Remember that one of the components of AE is net foreign trade (X_n). World trade has increased globally and is an increasingly significant portion of the U.S. economy. The volume of world trade has increased tremendously since the end of World War II. The United States plays a major role in shaping this trade. Adam Smith's book *The Wealth of Nations* points out the advantages of specialization and international trade. They both increase productive efficiency and allow greater total output than would otherwise be possible. Production possibilities tables allow us to quantify the efficiency gains of specialization. This is known as the *principle of comparative advantage*.

NAFTA and GATT

Three major international agreements have furthered the movement toward a global economy: the 1958 EU, the 1993 NAFTA, and the 1995 Uruguay GATT. The European Union ("common market") comprises 15 European nations. The EU has formed a powerful trade bloc, reducing or eliminating tariffs among its members while at the same time establishing tariffs on g/s from outside. Some U.S. firms have argued that this bloc makes it difficult for them to compete within the EU. One of the most recent, controversial, and significant accomplishments of the EU was the establishment of a common currency, the *euro*.

Somewhat in response to the growing power of the EU, was the 1993 North American Free Trade Agreement, forming a major trade bloc of Canada, Mexico, and the United States. This trade agreement, which is to be phased in by 2008, established a free-trade zone designed to reduce and eventually eliminate tariffs and other trade barriers among the signatories. Recently, Latin American nations have expressed an interest in expanding the benefits of NAFTA to all of Central and South America.

The 1995 General Agreement on Tariffs and Trade (GATT) established the World Trade Organization (WTO) as a permanent successor to the less formal GATT negotiations. China's recent entrance into the WTO has broadened the reach of the organization to more than 140 nations. Although in some ways incomplete, the WTO provides for some standardization on significant trade issues such as protectionist quotas, subsidies, and trademark, patent, or copyright infringement. Structural resolution of trade disputes is possible in WTO institutions, with approved tariff punishment for violators.

Both the NAFTA and the GATT have proponents as well as critics. Critics are concerned that firms will be able to circumvent U.S. laws that protect workers and the environment. Are labor unions, worker safety laws, minimum wage laws, and environmental protection rules effective if firms can shift production to nations that are weak in these areas? Proponents counter that most of the world's trade is among advanced industrial nations that have well-established worker and environmental protection laws. Adherents argue that as the free flow of g/s raises the output and disposable income levels in poorer nations, the increase in living standards will engender stronger laws, thereby spreading free market benefits across the world.

The new rules have created intense competition between firms. The tendency of firms to survive competition through merger and acquisition has hastened the formation of new multinational companies. These multinationals, as the name implies, produce and distribute g/s globally.

Comparative Advantage

The principle of comparative advantage is based on the law of increasing opportunity costs. Opportunity costs reflect the differing levels of inputs and technology present within a country. When two nations are compared as to efficiency of production of certain goods, we can see which total output is the greatest, resulting in the lowest cost. Even though one nation may enjoy absolute advantage over another in the production of goods, it serves both nations' best interests to seek the lower domestic opportunity cost for the less productive nation.

Financing International Trade

A major stumbling block to trade between nations is the involvement of different national currencies. An American firm exporting a g/s to a Brazilian does not want to be paid in Brazilian *riales,* because that currency cannot be spent in the United States. So, the importer must exchange its currency for U.S. dollars. This service is provided (for a fee) by major banks that have created currency exchanges.

U.S. exports cause an increased demand by Brazilians for U.S. dollars. The increased foreign demand for the U.S. dollar increases the supply of the foreign currency in exchange markets. U.S. imports would increase the demand for the foreign currency and would increase the supply of U.S. dollars in exchange markets.

Balance of Payments

The balance of payments account refers to the sum of a country's transactions with other countries and is summarized in three main accounts: current, capital, and financial account balances. Today, most economists combine the capital and financial accounts (as they are similar in content) into the financial account.

The current account primarily tracks the import and export of goods and services, but also includes net international transfer payments and net international factor income. If a nation imports more than it exports, it has an unfavorable balance of trade/current account deficit. If a nation exports more than it imports, it has a favorable balance of trade/current account surplus. The current account is exports – imports + net investment income (net interest and dividends paid by foreigners to Americans) + net transfers (foreign aid, money sent to Americans or their families living overseas). This account is often termed the "balance of trade" and the U.S. has run deficits in this account for decades. This trade deficit results because the U.S. imports more than it exports.

The economic impact of trade deficits is an oft-debated topic. Is it good or bad for an economy? If a nation imports more than it exports, a net job increase in the foreign nation is created. If there is unemployment at home, it is difficult to justify this "exporting of jobs" (a view of some towards NAFTA and WTO reducing trade barriers). If the demand for foreign goods and services must be paid for in the foreign currency, this causes a depreciation of the net importer's currency (discussed later) that at some point may reverse the trade imbalance. On the positive side a net importer is able to live outside their domestic PPF curve. Also, if the foreign worker's wages are lower, this represents a deflationary effect.

The financial account records trade in assets such as gold, government securities, banking liabilities (deposits/loans), corporate securities, and fixed assets such as real estate. The official reserves account consists of the foreign currencies held by a nation's central bank. These reserves are increased or decreased in reaction to the balance of the current and capital account. If the balance is negative, a deficit is noted; if the balance is positive, a benefit is noted. Whether a deficit or surplus is good or bad depends on how the issue is resolved. The implications of trade deficits or surpluses can be complicated.

The 2003 U.S. Balance of Payments

In 2003, the United States exported $714 billion of merchandise and imported $1,263 billion, for a merchandise trade deficit of $549 billion. Service exports, however, were $305 billion and service imports were $246 billion, for a surplus of approximately $59 billion. The trade deficit on goods and services, therefore, was $490 billion. U.S. interest payments to other countries and U.S. interest income from abroad were $250 billion and $272 billion, respectively. There was also a net outflow of $68 billion in unilateral transfers. Therefore, the current account showed an overall deficit of $536 billion.

Capital account transactions yielded a net outflow of $3.1 billion. For the financial account, U.S. investors acquired $277 billion of assets abroad and foreign investors acquired $857 billion of assets in the United States, yielding a net financial and capital account surplus of $580 billion. That surplus, minus a statistical discrepancy of $34 billion, balanced the $536 billion current account deficit.

This is an example of a capital inflow. It allows the United States to run a trade deficit without any impact on the dollar's international value (without the capital inflow the dollar would depreciate). There are many reasons why investors and foreign governments would do this. Some examples are:

1. Investors prefer to save in the U.S. for security reasons.

2. The interest yield may be higher than domestic rates.

3. Capital appreciation is at a higher rate (a U.S. company's growth or profits may be attractive).

4. A country may want to prevent its currency from appreciating.

Currency Exchange Rates

There are two major types of currency exchange formats: floating and fixed, although a managed float is an available option also. At the end of World War II, 44 nations met and created the Bretton Woods system. The U.S. dollar served as the focal point of this system because the U.S. dollar became the reserve currency of the system. Countries bought and sold dollars to maintain their exchange rates. The value of the U.S. dollar was fixed at $35 per ounce of gold and was convertible on demand for foreigners holding U.S. dollars. The dollar became as good as gold.

Two new organizations were also created at **the Bretton Woods Conference**, the **International Monetary Fund** (IMF) and the World Bank. The IMF was created to supervise the exchange-rate practices of member nations. It also was intended to lend money to nations that were unable to meet their payment obligations (that is, to do "bailouts"). IMF funds come from fees charged to the 178 member nations. The World Bank, funded through the sale of bonds, loans money to developing nations for economic development. The Bretton Woods system dissolved in 1971 as the U.S. dollar came under devaluation pressure and gold drained from the nation's reserves. In March 1973, a managed, floating exchange rate was established by the major industrial countries. Central banks of various nations have at times intervened to alter their nation's currency value. An example of this occurred in 1995 when the Fed and U.S. Treasury bought German marks and Japanese yen to increase the value of the dollar, which they thought had fallen excessively. The managed float has withstood severe economic upheaval, such as the OPEC oil crisis in 1973. Some nations, to maintain a more stable domestic currency, have "pegged" the value of their currency to a fixed rate with the U.S. dollar or another industrial nation's currency. An independent floating exchange rate would be subject to the laws of supply and demand in the currency marketplace.

DEVELOPING NATIONS' ECONOMIES

Many economists will tell you that for the economy to work for one country it must work (somewhat) well for all countries. Economic growth in developing nations is confronted with four entrenched obstacles:

- traditional attitudes and beliefs,

- continued rapid population growth,

- a misuse of resources (including capital flight-the legal or illegal export of currency or money capital from a nation by that nations' leaders), and

- trade restrictions.

Just one example highlights the attendant problems associated with rapid economic growth. Indonesia suffers from a lack of a national identity, massive government corruption and bureaucracies, reliance on a single product, and government interference in trade.

THE BRAVE NEW WORLD BROUGHT ABOUT BY TECHNOLOGY

The New Economy

It is still early but many economists are predicting that the technological revolution will be as significant to human society as the Industrial Revolution. For the twenty-first century, innovation and knowledge are the most important factors driving economic growth and the new knowledge economy. Along with the global transportation infrastructure, network-based information systems have been a factor in the growth of international business and corporations. Although studies have yet to show a relationship between the deployment of information systems and higher productivity, it is widely believed that such a relationship exists. In addition to investing in other information systems, a large and growing number of organizations have embraced electronic commerce over the Internet.

As the use of information systems has become pervasive in advanced economies and societies at large, several ethical and social issues have moved into the forefront:

- individual privacy—the right to control personal information. Electronic commerce presents a particular challenge to privacy, as personal information is routinely collected and disseminated in a largely unregulated manner. Preventing abusive invasions of privacy is complicated by the lack of an international legal standard;

- intellectual property rights—computer software, books, music and movies are protected by copyright laws, but newer ways of regulating the illegal copying using a combination of technical safeguards and the law are resulting in antipiracy encryption, watermarks, and innovative ways to stop piracy.

- universal access and free speech—the emergence of a digital divide between countries, and social and ethnic groups is one of the most challenging facets of the new economy. Access to information is imperative for an economy based on knowledge and information. Information systems can expand participation by ordinary citizens in government through electronic elections, referendums, and polls and also provide electronic access to government services and information permitting, for instance, electronic filing of taxes, direct deposit of government checks, and distant viewing of current and historical government documents and photographs.

- information security and accuracy—the security and accuracy of health and insurance records, credit information, and government files is a necessity to assuring wide-spread public use. It remains for society to harness the power of information systems by strengthening legal, social, and technological controls.

- and, quality of life—in the workplace, information systems can be deployed to eliminate tedious tasks and give workers greater autonomy, or they can be used to eliminate jobs and subject the remaining workforce to pervasive electronic surveillance. At home, consumers use the Internet to comparison shop for everything from manufactured goods to financial services or even to participate in on-line auctions but with the added costs of contending with spam (unsolicited e-mail), intercepted credit card numbers, and malicious computer viruses.

Behavioral Sciences

THE BEHAVIORAL OR SOCIAL SCIENCES

The social sciences are concerned with social life—psychology, with its emphasis on individual behavior and mental processes; economics, with its emphasis on the production, distribution, and consumption of goods and services; political science, with its emphasis on political philosophy and forms of government; and anthropology, with its current emphasis on both primitive and modern culture. What then distinguishes sociology from these other social sciences? In sociology the "social," however it is defined, is the immediate concern.

The Theory: Inductive or Deductive

A theory describes and/or explains the relationship between two or more observations. **Deductive theory** proceeds from general ideas, knowledge, or understanding of the social world from which specific hypotheses are logically deduced and tested. **Inductive theory** proceeds from concrete observations from which general conclusions are inferred through a process of reasoning.

More recent sociology includes three such approaches: **interpretative**, which includes the perspectives of symbolic interaction, dramaturgy, and ethnomethodology; **conflict theory**; and **structural functionalism**.

SOCIOLOGY

Interpretative sociology studies the processes whereby human beings attach meaning to their lives. Derived from the work of Mead and Blumer, symbolic interaction is focused on the process of social interaction and on the meanings that are constructed and reconstructed in that process. Human beings are viewed as shaping their actions based upon both the real and anticipated responses of others. Thus defined by an ongoing process of negotiation, social life is considered far from stable.

Actors are thought to be continually engaged in the process of interpreting, defining, and evaluating their own and others' actions, a process that defies explanation in law-like terms or in terms of sociological theories proceeding deductively. Thus, out of the **symbolic interactionist** school of thought, the social construction of reality—the familiar notion that human beings shape their world and are shaped by social interaction—was conceived (Berger & Luckman, 1967).

Focused on the details of everyday life, the dramaturgical approach of Erving Goffman conceives social interaction as a series of episodes or human dramas in which we are more or less aware of playing roles and, thereby, engaging in impression management. We are actors seeking 1) to manipulate our audience, or control the reaction of other people in our immediate presence by presenting a certain image of ourselves; 2) to protect or hide our true selves, or who we really are offstage through "onstage," "frontstage," and "backstage" behavior; and 3) to amplify the rules of conduct that circumscribe our daily encounters.

Conflict Theory

The **conflict paradigm** views society as being characterized by conflict and inequality. It is concerned with questions such as whose interests are expressed within existing social arrangements, and who benefits or suffers from such arrangements?

Sociologists viewing the social world from a conflict perspective question how factors such as race, sex, social class, and age are associated with an unequal distribution of socially valued goods and rewards (i.e., money, education, and power). Generally associated with the work of Coser, Dahrendorf, and Mills, modern conflict theory sees conflict between groups or within social organizations, and not merely class conflict (Marx), as a fact of life of any society. Conflict may have positive as well as disturbing effects (Coser). Conflict includes disagreement over who gets what, as well as tension, hostility, competition, and controversy within and between social groups over values and purposes.

Structural Functionalism

Inspired by the writings of Emile Durkheim and Herbert Spencer, functionalism (or structural functionalism) originally took as its logical starting point a society conceived as a social system of interrelated parts, and therefore analogous to a living organism where each part contributes to the overall stability of the whole. Society, then, is seen as a complex system whose components work with one another.

The components of a society are interdependent, with each one serving a function necessary for the survival of the system as a whole. Sociologists viewing the social world from a structural-functional perspective may identify components of society and explore the functions these structures may perform for the larger system.

Social Research

The term **research methods** refers both to a strategy or plan for carrying out research and the means of carrying out the strategy. Some sociologists favor **quantitative methods**. Following the example of the natural sciences, they make use of statistical and other mathematical techniques of quantification or measurement in their efforts to describe and interpret their observations. Others favor **qualitative methods**, relying on personal observation and description of social life in order to explain behavior. Conceding that their methods entail the loss of precision, they argue that their method achieves a deeper grasp of the texture of social life. Thus, Max Weber developed the method of *verstehen*.

Verstehen is understanding as a means of characterizing and interpreting or explaining. This is done through applying reason to the external and inner context of specific social situations, such as the origins of Western capitalism.

Survey Research

Sociologists most often use the **survey method** of observation in their research. Subjects are asked about their opinions, beliefs, or behavior, such as how they have behaved in the past or how they intend to behave in the future, in a series of questions. The information is collected from the respondents of the survey directly by means of an interview, or indirectly by means of a self-administered written form of a questionnaire that the respondents fill out themselves. Interviews may be conducted in person, by phone, or even by electronic means of communication.

The interview may be structured such that respondents are asked a series of questions in which they are given a limited choice between several possible responses on each question, unstructured where respondents are asked questions to which they can respond freely in their own words, or may involve the use of a combination of both open-ended and close-ended questions. The researcher may be interested in determining or gauging the general characteristics of a population or in collecting information about some event from the persons involved.

A survey can be mainly **descriptive** or **explanatory**. In the latter case, researchers may be interested in understanding either causal or correlational relationships between variables. Variables can either be **independent** or **dependent**. An independent variable is one that influences another variable, while the dependent variable is the one being influenced by another variable (the cause and effect, respectively). In order to assess the relationship between two variables, controls may need to be applied. A control is a technique of differentiating between factors that may or may not influence the relationship between variables. Relationships between two variables can either be **correlational** or **causal**. A correlational relationship exists when a change in one variable coincides with, but doesn't cause a change in another. A causal relationship exists when a change in one variable causes or forces a change in the other.

How, then, is survey research carried out? First a population is selected. All members can be approached in the case of a relatively small population or in the case of an event that requires collecting information from certain key persons that were involved. If the population is relatively large, a sample will be selected for study from the entire population. A **representative sample** is one that accurately reflects the population from which it is drawn. A **random sample** is one where every member of the population has the same chance of being chosen for study, as in throwing the names of everyone in a hat, mixing them up, and selecting as many as are thought necessary to achieve representativeness. **Systematic sampling** is a type of sample in which the nth unit in a list is selected for inclusion in the sample. For example, every fiftieth resident listed in a phone book of a given area will be selected. In this way, every member of the population is guaranteed the same chance of being selected for study.

Stratified sampling uses the differences that already exist in a population, such as between males and females, as the basis for selecting a sample. Knowing the percentage of the population that falls into a particular category, the researcher then randomly selects a number of persons to be studied from each category in the same proportion as exists in the population.

Experimentation

Sociologists can and sometimes do conduct experiments. In the broadest sense, experimentation involves the observation, measurement, or calculation of the consequences of an action. Typically, the social science researcher selects a group of subjects to be studied (the experimental group), exposes them to a particular condition, and then measures the results. The researcher usually measures the results against that of a control group (a similar population upon which the action has not been performed). Experiments are used to test theories and the hypotheses drawn from them. In one type of experiment, researchers create a situation in which they test the extent of the relationship that presumably exists between an independent and a dependent variable, by means of controlling a third.

Experiments may be carried out in a laboratory or in the field. Field experiments are carried out in natural settings. One of the most famous field experiments of social science was conducted in the 1930s at the Hawthorne Plant of the Western Electric Company in Chicago. This research led Elton May to identify what has come to be known as the Hawthorne effect, which showed that the mere presence of a researcher affects the subject's behavior.

Observation

Observation is a technique that provides firsthand experience of real situations. **Unobtrusive observation** is observation from a distance, without being involved in the group or activity being studied. Unobtrusive observation may be observing subjects from afar (e.g., watching children play in a schoolyard) or observing subjects more closely (e.g., watching children play in a classroom from behind a one-way mirror).

Often referred to as field research, **participant observation** is observation by a researcher who is (or appears to be) a member of the group or a participant in the activity he/she is studying. Participant observers may or may not conceal their identities as researchers. They may conceal their identities as researchers so as not to influence their subjects who, not knowing they are being observed, will act naturally. On the other hand, they may disclose their identities as researchers and seek to minimize their influence by not allowing themselves to get too involved with subjects while they are establishing a rapport.

Secondary Analysis

Secondary analysis refers to the analysis of existing sources of information. In the hope of discovering something new, the researcher examines old records and documents, including archives and official statistics provided by the government. Thus, by using available data, the researcher avoids having to gather information from scratch, and by analyzing old records and documents, the researcher can acquire an understanding of relations between people in the past.

Content analysis refers to the techniques employed to describe the contents of the materials. They may be quantitative—using such techniques as percentages, rates, or averages to describe how the contents vary, e.g., arithmetic means, modes, or medians, or qualitative—using concepts and employing reason to capture the contents of the materials observed.

The Stages of Research

Research is a process that includes:

1. Defining the problem—the questions, issues, or topic with which one is concerned.

2. Identifying and reviewing the literature or relevant literature bearing upon the problem.

3. Formulating a hypothesis—a tentative statement about what one expects to observe, e.g., the prediction of a relationship between variables or the prediction that a certain relation between people will be obtained.

4. Selecting and implementing a research design to test one's hypothesis—the plan for collecting and analyzing information.

5. Drawing a conclusion—determining whether or not one's hypothesis is confirmed and presenting one's findings in an organized way that both describes and, wherever possible, explains what one has observed.

SOCIALIZATION

Socialization is the process through which we learn or are trained to be members of society, to take part in new social situations, or to participate in social groupings. In other words, it is the prescriptive term in sociology for the process of being "social."

Generally, sociologists consider the process of socialization to be based on social interaction, the ways in which we behave toward and respond to one another. Not all sociologists agree on what is formed by such reciprocal or mutual action. Does interaction imply society, social groups, social structure, or that human beings make the perpetuation and transformation of a particular culture possible? Sociologists tend to differ in their opinion of what is learned, produced, reproduced, or altered in the process of socialization: 1) in their orientation toward society, social groups, social structure, or man-made culture; and 2) in their conception of the part, if any, human biology and individual psychology play in socialization.

Primary and Secondary Forms of Socialization

Sociologists hold the view that the individual cannot develop in the absence of the social environment—the groups within which interaction takes place and socialization occurs. Within this context, **primary socialization** refers to the initial socialization that a child receives through which he or she becomes a member of society (i.e., learns and comes to share the social heritage or culture of a society through the groups into which he or she is born). **Secondary socialization** refers to the subsequent experience of socialization into new sectors of society by an already socialized person.

Personality

Focused on society, socialization is the process through which personality is acquired, marked by the fairly consistent patterns shown in the thoughts, feelings, and activities representative of the individual. Socialization is the essential link between the individual and the social realms, without which neither is thought to be capable of surviving.

Socialization not only makes it possible for society to reproduce itself, but for society's continuity to be assured across generations as well as within generations in the personalities that are its product. This is the biological and "historical" continuity of individual and social circumstances of the life course of birth, childhood, maturity, old age, and death, and in the cultural continuity in society up to the present.

Assuming that the content of socialization varies from one person to the next as a consequence of being subject to the influence of various cultures and subcultures including race, class, region, religion, and groups in society, then every person would be different. Most of the differences would be a product of socialization, with the remainder the result of the random impact of relatively different social and cultural environments.

The socialization process is thought to explain both the similarities in personality and social behavior of the members of society and the differences that exist in society between one person and the next. It does not matter then that the two factors of nature and nurture are intimately related and cannot be separated, which is the view of most social scientists. Hence, the part that human biology plays in socialization (i.e., of nature in nurture) cannot be accurately measured. Heredity represents a basic potential, the outlines and limits of which are biologically fixed, because the socialization process is thought to be all important to the development of personality, the uniqueness, the similarities, and the differences of which are relative to society and, thereby, to the groups to which people belong.

Consistent with a view held by modern psychologists, it is argued that any instincts (unlearned, inherited behavior patterns that human beings once had) have been lost in the course of human evolution. There is no human nature outside of what culture makes of us. Hence, the concern that children raised in isolation or in institutions, who have little or no opportunity to develop the sorts of emotional ties with adults that make socialization possible, will be devoid of personality and will lack the social skills necessary to face even the simplest of life's challenges.

The process of becoming human in the sense of being able to participate in society is understood to be the process of socialization. The self at the core of personality, the individual's conscious experience of having a separate unique identity, is thought to be a social product objectively created and transformed throughout a person's life by interaction with others.

Agents of Socialization

The various agents of socialization are the individuals, groups, and institutions that supply the structure through which socialization takes place in modern societies.

Family

Generally considered the most basic social institution, the **family** is a union that is sanctioned by the state and often by a religious institution such as a church. As such, the family provides continuity in such areas as language, personality traits, religion, and class. The family is generally believed to be the most important agent of socialization in a child's social world, until schooling begins. Although the school and peer group become central to social experience as the child grows older, the family remains central throughout the entire life course.

School

As the social unit devoted to providing an education, the school provides continuity both in cognitive skills and in the indoctrination of values. Many subject areas of knowledge that may or may not be available at home, or that the modern home is ill-equipped to provide, are also provided by the school. Unlike the family, which is based on personal relationships, in school the child's social experiences broaden to include people of a variety of different social backgrounds. It is here where children learn the importance society gives to race and gender.

Peer Groups

As a primary group whose members are roughly equal in status, **peer groups** (such as play groups) provide continuity in lifestyles. Although first peer groups generally consist of a young child's neighborhood playmates, as the child meets new people at school and becomes involved in other activities, his peer group expands. It is in the peer group where the child, free of direct supervision from adults, comes to define him or herself as independent from his family. During adolescence the peer group becomes particularly important to the child and sometimes proves to be a more influential agent of socialization than the family.

Mass Media

Instrumental in making communication with large numbers of people possible, mass media provides continuity as far as knowledge or public information about the people, the events, and changes occurring in society and the threat they sometimes pose to the existing social order. Among the various kinds of mass media are books, radio, television, and motion pictures.

Resocialization and the Role of Total Institution

Resocialization refers to the process of discarding behavioral practices and adopting new ones as part of a transition in life. For example, when one becomes a parent for the first time, he or she may have to perform new duties. Resocialization such as this occurs throughout our lives. Resocialization, however, can be a much more dramatic process, especially when it takes place in a **total institution**, such as a place of residence to where persons are confined for a period of time and cut off from the rest of society. This type of resocialization involves a fundamental break with the past to allow for the rebuilding of personality and the learning of norms and values of a new, unfamiliar social environment. The environment of a total institution is deliberately controlled in order to achieve this end. Some examples of total institutions include mental hospitals, the military, and prisons.

MAJOR FIGURES IN SOCIOLOGY

Sigmund Freud

An Austrian physician and the founder of psychoanalysis, Sigmund Freud considered biological drives to be the primary source of human activity. Activated by the pleasure principle to demand immediate and complete gratification of biological needs, the id represents these unconscious strivings without specific direction or purpose, which must be repressed and subsequently channeled in socially acceptable directions. Otherwise, without socialization the human being would be a violent, amoral, predatory animal, and organized social life would be impossible. According to Freud it is through the processes or mechanisms of identification and repression (the holding back and the hiding of one's own feelings) that the human personality is formed—which is comprised of the id, the ego, and the superego. The ego represents the most conscious aspect of personality. Defining opportunities, the goals one strives toward, and what is "real," the ego controls and checks the id. Operating according to the pleasure principle, the ego deals with the world in terms of what is possible, providing limits and direction.

Charles Horton Cooley

An economist turned social psychologist, Charles Horton Cooley (1864–1924) theorized that the self-concept, which is formed in childhood, is reevaluated every time the person enters a new social situation. There are three stages in the process of self-formation, which Cooley referred to as "the **looking-glass self**": 1) we imagine how we appear to others; 2) we wonder whether others see us in the same way as we see ourselves, and in order to find out, we observe how others react to us; and 3) we develop a conception of ourselves that is based on the judgments of others. Thus, we acquire a conception of ourselves from the "looking glass" or mirror of the reactions of others.

George Herbert Mead

An American philosopher and social psychologist, George Herbert Mead (1863–1931) is best known for his evolutionary social theory of the genesis of the mind and self. Mead's basic thesis—that a single act can best be understood as a segment of a larger social act or communicative transaction between two or more persons—made social psychology central to his philosophical approach. To describe the process whereby mind and self evolve through a continuous adjustment of the individual to himself and to others, Mead used several concepts: the "Me" is the image one forms of one's self from the standpoint of a "generalized others" and the "I" is the individual's reaction to a situation as he sees it from his unique standpoint.

Mead pointed out that one outcome of socialization is the ability to anticipate the reactions of others and to adjust our behavior accordingly. We do this, Mead argues, by role taking or learning to model the behavior of significant others, such as our parents. For example, playing "house" allows children to view the world from their parents' perspective.

Erving Goffman

Like other sociologists, Erving Goffman (1922–1983) considered the self to be a reflection of others—the cluster of roles or expectations of the people with whom one is involved at that point in the life course. It is the product of a series of encounters in which we manage the impression that others receive to convince others that we are who we claim to be. In every role we undertake, there is a virtual self waiting to be carried out. Goffman used the term **role-distance** to describe the gap that exists between who we are and who we portray ourselves to be.

Jean Piaget

Based on experiments with children playing and responding to questions, Swiss psychologist Jean Piaget (1896–1980) proposed a theory of **cognitive development** that describes the changes that occur over time in the ways children think, understand, and evaluate a situation. Piaget not only stressed the part that social life plays in becoming conscious of one's own mind, but more broadly speaking, he also observed that cognitive development does not occur automatically. A given stage of cognitive development cannot be reached unless the individual is confronted with real life experiences that foster such development. In the **sensorimotor stage**, infants are unable to differentiate themselves from their environment. They are unaware that their actions produce results, and they lack the understanding that objects exist separate from the direct and immediate experience of touching, looking, sucking, and listening.

Through sensory experience and physical contact with their environment, the infant begins to experience his surroundings differently. The world becomes a relatively stable place, no longer simply the sifting chaos it is first perceived to be. In the **preoperational stage** the child begins to use language and other symbols. Not only do they begin to attach meaning to the world, they also are able to differentiate fantasy from reality.

In the **concrete operational stage**, children make great strides in their use of logic to understand the world and how it operates. They begin to think in logical terms, to make the connection between cause and effect, and are capable of attaching meaning or significance to a particular event. Although they cannot conceive of an idea beyond the concrete situation or event, they have begun to imagine themselves in the position of another and thus to grasp a situation from the other's point of view. In effect it is during this stage of cognitive development that the foundation for engaging in more complex activities with others (such as role taking) is laid. Finally, in the **formal operational stage** the child develops the capacity for thinking in highly abstract terms of metaphors and hypotheses which may or may not be based in reality.

Erik Erikson

Departing from Freud's emphasis on childhood and instinct, Erik Erikson delineated eight stages of psychosocial development in which ego identity, that sense of continuity and sameness in the conception one has of one's self that does not change over time or situation, ego development, the potential for change and growth that exists over the course of a person's life, and the social environment are involved. They are:

Stage 1—the nurturing stage, in which a child's sense of either basic trust or mistrust are established.

Stage 2—there emerges the feeling of autonomy or feelings of doubt and shame from not being able to handle the situations one encounters in life.

Stage 3—the child develops either a sense of initiative and self-confidence or feelings of guilt depending on how successful they are in exploring their environment and in dealing with their peers.

Stage 4—the focus shifts from family to school where the child develops a conception of being either industrious or inferior.

Stage 5—failure to establish a clear and firm sense of one's self results in the person's becoming confused about their identity.

Stage 6—one meets or fails to meet the challenge presented by young adulthood of forming stable relationships, the outcome being "intimacy or isolation and loneliness."

Stage 7—a person's contribution to the well-being of others through citizenship, work, and family becomes self-generative, and hence, their fulfilling of the primary tasks of mature adulthood is complete.

Stage 8—the developmental challenge posed by the knowledge that one is reaching the end is to find a sense of continuity and meaning and hence, to break the sense of isolation and self-absorption that the thought of one's impending death produces, thereby yielding to despair.

Lawrence Kohlberg

Inspired by the work of Piaget to conduct a series of longitudinal and cross-cultural studies extending over several decades, Lawrence Kohlberg concluded that given the proper experience and stimulation, children go through a sequence of six stages of moral reasoning. At the earliest stage (between ages four and ten), a child's sense of good and bad is connected with the fear of being punished for disobeying those in positions of power. During adolescence, a child's conformity to the rules is connected with the belief that the existing social order must ultimately be the right and true order and therefore ought to be followed.

Finally, there are several factors that serve as a guide to action and self-judgment among older children and young adults. These individuals have reached the highest of two stages of moral development, and are able to consider the welfare of the community, the rights of the individual, and such universal ethical principles as justice, equality, and individual dignity. Kohlberg has been criticized for basing his model of human development on the male experience, having assumed that women and girls are incapable of reaching the higher stages of moral reasoning.

Carol Gilligan

Taking Kohlberg to task on this point, Carol Gilligan found that women bring a different set of values to their judgments of right and wrong. For instance, males approached the moral problem of whether or not it is wrong to steal to save a life in terms of the ethic of ultimate ends. However, females approached the same problem from the standpoint of an ethic of responsibility by wondering what the consequences of the moral decision to steal or not to steal would be for the entire family—the goal being to find the best solution for everyone involved.

In effect, these different approaches to resolving the problem can be explained by the different roles women have in our society as compared with men. Thus, Gilligan concludes there is no essential difference between the inner workings of the psyches of boys and girls.

SOCIAL INTERACTION

Defining Social Interaction

Consistent with Weber's view of society, every culture has a structure that can be described and analyzed. This structure represents the multitude of shared values, shared beliefs, and common expectations of a particular culture around which people have organized their lives, and leads to a certain degree of predictability in human affairs.

Social Structure, Society, and Social Systems

Consistent with a view of society as a continuing number of people living in the same region in a relatively permanent unit, **social structure** is the way in which people's relations in society are arranged to form a network. These networks are relatively organized in the sense that there is thought to be some degree of structure and system to the patterns of social interaction of which any society is composed.

Contrary, then, to the latter definition, "society" here does not represent a whole. The structure is thought to be composed of similar elements of statuses (position in a society or in a group), roles (the behavior of a person occupying a particular position), groups (a number of people interacting with one another in ways that form a pattern and who are united by the feeling of being bound together and by "a consciousness of kind"), and institutions (organized systems of social relationships that emerge in response to the basic problems or needs of every society).

In terms of society constituting more than one system, social structure consists of the patterns of interaction formed by the enactment of culture (the map for living in a society). The social structure is thought to be composed of multiple systems or institutions—each considered a total system unto itself—in addition to several other types of components. It is argued that there are certain elements that are necessary to both individual and collective survival. When these elements become organized into institutional spheres, they form a society's economic system, political structure, family system, educational processes, and belief system.

Besides being determined by the social context of statuses and roles, behavior is also thought to be largely determined by the definition of the situation (the process whereby we define, explain, and evaluate the social context of the situation we find ourselves in before deciding the behavior and attitudes that are appropriate). Each system forms an arrangement or structure of statuses and roles existing apart from their occupants.

Status

Status may refer to a position in society and/or in a group.

Ascribed Status

An **ascribed status** is automatically and involuntarily conferred on individuals without any effort or choice made on their part. Being a Native American, a woman, a son, or a widower are examples of ascribed statuses.

Achieved Status

The opposite status, one that is assumed largely through one's own doings or efforts, is referred to as **achieved status**. Examples of achieved statuses include being a husband, a rock star, an "A" student, and an engineering major.

Master Status

Master status is the status with which a person is most identified. It is the most important status that a person holds, not only because it affects almost every aspect of the person's life, but also because of its general symbolic value. People take for granted that a person holding the position possesses other traits associated with it.

Status Set

Status set consists of all the statuses that a person occupies. All of us occupy a number of statuses simultaneously. A woman may be a mother to her children, a wife to her husband, a professor to her students, and a colleague to her co-workers. The statuses of mother, wife, professor, and colleague together form the status set of this woman.

Roles

Role refers to what a person does (i.e., the part they play or how one is expected to behave) by virtue of occupying a particular status or position.

Every status and role is accompanied by a set of norms or role expectations describing behavioral expectations, or the limits of what people occupying the position are expected to do and of how they are expected to do it. There are thought to be marked differences and, thus, extensive variations in how a particular role is played out, depending on differences in how those holding a particular position define their role. In effect, group differences and the conflicts they generate are thought to continually transform the system and structure.

Role Strain

Role strain refers to the situation where different and conflicting expectations exist with regard to a particular status. For example, a professor may enjoy his students and may socialize outside of class with them. At the same time, though, he is responsible for ascertaining that their performance is up to par and that they attend class regularly. To achieve this end, he may have to distance himself from his students.

Role Conflict

Role conflict occurs when a person occupies multiple statuses that contradict one another. For example, a single mother, who is the primary breadwinner, who plays on her church's softball team, and who is the den mother to her son's Boy Scout troop, may have conflicting roles corresponding to many of these statuses. This single mother may find that her volunteering duties conflict with her parenting and breadwinning duties.

GROUPS AND ORGANIZATIONS

Social Groups and Relationships

Strictly speaking, a **group** is an assembly of people or things. However, not all people who are assembled together are thought to constitute human or social groupings. The members of a group are considered united generally through interaction, more specifically by the relationships they share, or in particular by the quality or specific character of the relationship between the individuals of which it is composed. In theory, any specific group represents no more than a relationship of "individual" persons.

Associations and Communal Relationships

An **association** is a type of relationship formed on the basis of an accommodation of interests or on the basis of an agreement. In either case, the basis of the rational judgment of common interest or of agreement is ultimate value or practical wisdom. A **communal relationship** is one formed on the basis of a subjective feeling of the parties "that they belong together" whether the feeling is personal or is linked with tradition. In practice, however, most actual associations and communities incorporate aspects of both types of relationships.

Social Groups

There are various types of social groups, from formally structured organizations to those that happen by chance. Sociologists have always been interested in types of social groups and the overall and individual characteristics of their members.

Peer Group

A peer group may be defined "as an association of self-selected equals" formed around common interests, sensibilities, preferences, and beliefs. By offering members friendship, a sense of belonging, and acceptance, peer groups compete with the family for the loyalty of their members. Peer groups serve to segregate their members from others on the basis of their age, sex, or generation. A peer group, as a type of social group, therefore consists of those whose ages, interests, and social positions or statuses are relatively equivalent and who are closely associated with one another.

Family

By contrast, the family serves to emotionally bind members of all ages, sexes, and various generations. As such, the family is plagued by issues surrounding succession. Particularly in a vacillating period of social change, the conflict between the family and peer group becomes more pronounced, caused by the widening of the cultural gap that separates different generations who may even speak a different language. For example, urbanism (which allowed for sustained contact between age-mates) paved the way not only toward age-grading (the sensitivity toward chronological age gradations characteristic of modern culture), but also toward the age-graded sociability that is characteristic of our times.

Aggregates and Social Categories

Unlike an **aggregate**, which consists of a number of people who happen to be in the same place at the same time, or a **social category**, which consists of a number of people with certain characteristics in common, a **social group** consists of a collection of people interacting with one another in an orderly fashion.

In a social group, there is an interdependence among the various members which forges a feeling of belonging and a sense that the behavior of each person is relevant to each other. Thus, whether or not the membership of a social group is stable or changing, all such group relationships are thought to have two elements in common: 1) members are mutually aware of one another, and 2) members are mutually responsive to one another, with actions therefore determined by or shaped in the group context.

Social groups have been classified in many different ways—according to the group's size; nature of the interaction or the quality of the relationship that exists; whether or not membership is voluntary; whether or not a person belongs to and identifies with the group; or according to the group's purpose or composition.

Primary and Secondary Groups

Charles Horton Cooley (1864–1924) distinguished between primary groups and secondary groups. In a **primary group**, the interaction is direct, the common bonds are close and intimate, and the relationships among members are warm, intimate, and personal. In **secondary groups**, the interaction is anonymous, the bonds are impersonal, the duration of time of the group is short, and the relationships involve few emotional ties.

Characteristics of Groups

Through the years, sociologists have developed various theories about groups. The following sections offer a sampling of these theories.

Gemeinschaft and Gesellschaft

Ferdinand Tönnies (1853–1936) distinguished between *gemeinschaft* (community) and *gesellschaft* (society). By **gemeinschaft**, Tönnies was referring to those small communities characterized by tradition and united by the belief in common ancestry or by geographic proximity in relationships largely of the primary group sort. **Gesellschaft** refers to contractual relationships of a voluntary nature of limited duration and quality, based on rational self-interest, and formed for the explicit purpose of achieving a particular goal.

Dyad and Triad

Focused on discovering the various and relatively stable forms of social relationship within which interaction takes place, George Simmel (1858–1918) made the distinction between the **dyad** of two people in which either member's departure destroys the group, and the **triad** of three, the addition of a third person sometimes serving as a mediator or nonpartisan party. An example of a triad with a mediator to close the circle is parents who strengthen their mutual love and union by conceiving a child. A nonpartisan-based triad is typified by a mediator who seeks harmony among colliding parties or who, as an arbitrator, seeks to balance competing claims.

Group Size and Other General Structural Properties

Small groups, as the name suggests, have so few members as to allow them to relate as whole persons. The smallest group consists of only two persons. Robert Bales developed the technique of **interaction process analysis**, that is, a technique of observing and immediately classifying in predetermined ways the ongoing activity in small groups.

Also, J. L. Moreno developed the technique of **sociometry**, a technique focused on establishing the direction of the interaction in small groups. An example of this technique is assessing who is interacting with whom by asking such questions as "Who is your best friend in the group?" or "Who would you most like to work with on an important project?"

In addition to size, some of the other general structural properties and related social processes affecting the functioning of social groups are 1) the extent of association (for instance, it has been suggested that the more people associate, the more common values and norms they share and the greater the tendency to get along) and 2) the social network of persons that together comprises all the relationships in which they are involved and groups to which they belong.

Interaction Processes

Also involved in the interaction processes (the ways role partners agree on goals, negotiate reaching them, and distribute resources) are such factors as:

1) the differentiation between the characteristics of the role structure with task or instrumental roles. Instrumental roles are oriented toward specific goals and expressive roles, which are instrumental in expressing and releasing group tension.

2) front stage (public) and backstage (free of public scrutiny) behavior.

3) principles of exchange (characteristic of market relationships in which people bargain for the goods and services they desire).

4) competition between individuals and groups over scarce resources in which the parties not only agree to adhere to certain rules of the game but also believe they are necessary or fair.

5) cooperation (an agreement to share resources for the purpose of achieving a common goal).

6) compromise (an agreement to relinquish certain claims in the interest of achieving more modest goals).

7) conflict (the attempt by one party to destroy, undermine, or harm another) and such related methods of reducing or temporarily eliminating conflict as coaptation (the case of dissenters being absorbed into the dominant group), mediation (the effort to resolve a conflict through the use of a third party), and the ritualized release of hostility under carefully controlled circumstances such as the Olympic games.

In-Group and Out-Group

Other types of social groups include **in-groups** which, unlike **out-groups** (those groups toward which a person feels a sense of competition or opposition), are those to which "we" belong.

Reference Group

Reference groups are social groups that provide the standards in terms of which we evaluate ourselves. For example, if a college student is worried about how her family will react to her grades, she is using her family as a reference group. Similarly, if a lawyer is worried about how the other partners of his firm will react to a recent case he lost, the lawyer is using his colleagues as a reference group.

Group Conformity and Groupthink

Research on groups has illustrated the power of group pressure to shape human behavior. **Group conformity** refers to individuals' compliance with group goals, in spite of the fact that group goals may be in conflict with individual goals. In an attempt to be accepted or "fit in," individuals may engage in behaviors they normally would not.

Groupthink, a related phenomenon, occurs when group members begin to think similarly and conform to one another's views. The danger in this is that decisions may be made from a narrow view. Rather than exploring various sides of an issue, group members seeking conformity may adopt a limited view.

Group Leadership

Leadership is an element of all groups. A leader is a person who initiates the behavior of others by directing, organizing, influencing, or controlling what members do and how they think.

Instrumental and Expressive Leaders

Group research has found two different types of leaders: instrumental (task-oriented leaders who organize the group in the pursuit of its goals) and expressive (social-emotional leaders who achieve harmony and solidarity among group members by offering emotional support).

Authoritarian, Democratic, and Laissez-faire Styles of Leadership

Among the various styles of leadership are the authoritarian leader who gives orders, the democratic leader who seeks a consensus on the course of action to be taken, and the laissez-faire leader who mainly lets the group be—doing little if anything to provide direction or organization.

Organizations

In the sense in which sociologists use the term, an **organization** represents a specific type of social relationship or arrangement between persons that is either closed to outsiders or that limits their admission. Regulations are enforced by a person or by a number of persons in authority active in enforcing the order governing the organization.

Formal Organization

In the latter sense, a **formal organization**, which represents a type of group or structural pattern within which behavior is carried out in a society, is characterized by 1) formality, 2) a hierarchy of ranked positions, 3) large size, 4) a rather complex division of labor, and 5) continuity beyond its membership.

DEVIANCE

Defining Deviance

Strictly speaking, **deviance** represents a departure from a norm. Although deviance is usually associated with criminal activity or mental illness, it also includes behavior that stands out as being more ambitious, industrious, heroic, or righteous than the rest—behavior which is generally not expected nor very frequently found.

However, sociologists have primarily concerned themselves with deviant behavior that violates or is contrary to the rules of acceptable and appropriate behavior of a group or society. This becomes evident in the strong negative reaction, or ridicule, generated by the members of the group.

Sociologists have tended to differ in their understanding of deviance. The question is whether or not deviance represents more than a violation of a norm and, if so, what this contrary behavior is thought to ultimately represent.

Deviance and Stigma

Consistent with an orientation toward society as a whole, the one characteristic shared by those with a deviant reputation is stigma. A **stigma** is the mark of social disgrace that sets the deviant apart from other members of society who regard themselves as "normal." In most instances, people escape having their deviant behavior discovered. Because they are not stigmatized or marked deviant, they think of themselves as being relatively normal.

Deviance is seen as relative to the time, place, and context of a group or society in which it is observed. In addition, it is also relative to the social status of the person doing the defining, and to whether or not that person is in a position to label the behavior as "deviant."

Conformity, Social Order, and Social Control

Even if most people have violated significant social norms at some point in their lives, the majority of people at any given moment are thought to be conforming to those norms that are important to a society's continued existence. It is because of this that social order exists.

It is believed that a social order depends on its members generally knowing and doing what is expected of them. They have common values and guidelines to which they generally adhere. These norms prescribe the behavior that is appropriate to a situation as it is given or commonly construed at the time. In other words, a social order presumably cannot exist without an effective system of social control. Social control is best defined as a series of measures that serve as a general guarantee of people conforming to norms.

Through the process of socialization, social control is achieved. The success of this process is demonstrated by the fact that most people usually do what is expected out of sheer habit, and without question. When socialization cannot guarantee sufficient conformity through the informal, as well as the formal and organized ways of rewarding conformity and punishing nonconformity, there becomes a need for negative sanctions. Negative sanctions indicate that social control has failed and that deviance has occurred.

Deviance represents a residual category of behavior unlike that which is generally found. This behavior, unless adequately checked, may threaten the effectiveness of the system of social control and the social order. Ultimately some deviance is necessary so that the boundaries of permissible behavior may be defined. The major function of deviance is to reassure people that the system of social control is working effectively.

Deviance and Social Groups

Consistent with an orientation to social groups and the process through which conformity to norms is structured or organized in them, deviance represents an unusual departure from an established group rule of acceptable conduct. These norms denote a negotiated world of meanings; these are rules that shape what individuals perceive and how they behave, thereby eliminating the uncertainty that exists in the absence of such behavior guidelines. The acknowledgment of such a departure assures members that they are "normal." Members can feel that their own behavior falls within the usual parameters of what is and what is not acceptable in the group, while ridiculing those whose observed behavior departs from the expected.

In this way, the social order, which depends upon people doing what others expect of them, is more or less guaranteed. Those who usually behave in socially approved ways are provided with a reason for continuing to do what is expected and are momentarily relieved of their anxiety about the unusual occurring too soon again. Those who have departed from a norm have a reason to avoid behaving in ways that are unacceptable to group members.

Given the many different groups that make up a society, and the competing values and the diversity of interests they represent, social order is never guaranteed or certain without there being value systems. These value systems enjoy such wide acceptance in society that even those groups that represent opposing interests find them to be consistent with, or suited to, their own concerns.

In the competition or struggle between groups, those with the most to lose or gain in terms of immediate self-interest, or those who feel most strongly about their cause, may succeed in defining and shaping the standards of right and wrong that become the group's norms. But they may never succeed in altering the meaning that represents the core values or culture of a society.

As previously noted, the latter are acquired during primary socialization and are thought to be a product of unique circumstances. Thus, deviant behavior is not essentially different from that of conformity.

Both roles are socially constructed relative to the culture of the society in which they thrive. Therefore, the processes and actions that are defined as deviant in our society are merely those that fall outside the canon of processes and actions that are defined as conformist.

These "deviant" actions are those that powerful people, those in a position to both define and enforce social norms, find threatening. Because this sector of society agrees with, supports, and serves to define the status quo, anything that threatens this sector is then labeled deviant. In this way, deviance is defined by its opposite rather than any inherent threat it may pose.

Particularly in complex societies, some norms are thought to be more important than others in that they involve behavior necessary to a group's continuity, survival, or well-being. This is evidenced by the severity of the sanctions associated with them. Whether or not norms are proscriptive ("thou shalt not") or prescriptive ("thou shalt"), they all are thought to be relatively arbitrary in principle. Their definition changes over time and from one society to the next but never so much as to be inconsistent with a society's core values.

Functions of Deviance

In terms of the group, deviance serves several functions. Consistent with Durkheim's viewpoint, deviance serves to unify the group by identifying the limits of acceptable behavior and thus identifying who are insiders and who are outsiders. Deviance also serves as a safety valve that allows people to express discontent with existing norms without threatening the social order. Principled challenges to norms are possible.

Social control refers to the ways of getting people to conform to norms. Such techniques, which include persuasion, teaching, and force, may be planned or unplanned, and may be informal (involving the approval or disapproval of significant others) or formal (involving those in positions responsible for enforcing norms). In this context, **primary deviance** is the term used to refer to behavior violating a norm, while **secondary deviance** refers to the behavior that results from the social response to such deviance.

It is in connection with secondary deviance that stigma symbolizes a moral blemish or undesirable label that tends to be extended to other undesirable traits. Deviant subcultures represent peer groups that support deviance by providing social networks to deviants.

Biological Explanations of Deviance

In 1875 Cesare Lombroso published the results of his work comparing the body measurements of institutionalized criminals, non-criminals, and primitive human beings. He had concluded that deviant behavior is inherited and that the body measurements of criminals bore a greater resemblance to apes than to non-criminals.

William Sheldon (1941) based his work on the earlier work of Ernst Kretschmer (1925). He classified people according to their body types. He concluded that a relationship exists between body type, psychological state, and criminal behavior (with short and fat endomorphs being prone to manic depression and alcoholism; thin and small ectomorphs being prone to schizophrenia; and muscular and large boned mesomorphs being prone to criminal behavior, alcoholism, and manic depression).

Such studies attempting to link criminal behavior and body type have not always produced consistent results. More recently efforts have been made to link deviant behavior with an "abnormal" (XYY) chromosomal pattern found among inmates of prisons and mental hospitals. This pattern is unlike the usual male XY pattern or female XX pattern. Researchers also have been studying the relationship between the brain and body chemistry, diet, and behavior.

Psychological Explanations of Deviance

Psychologists have attributed antisocial or deviant behavior to the unconscious making itself known to a superego that lacks the strength to overcome the id. This way of thinking was influenced by Freud and others who sought to trace personality and behavior to early childhood learning experiences and the manner in which the repression of the powerful biological drives of the id takes place. The unconscious is that part of the mind where unpleasant, or perhaps even antisocial, memories of experiences are stored.

Such research has supported the use of personality tests to identify troublemakers and delinquents, to assess the guilt or innocence of those suspected of committing a crime, and to ferret out problems before they occur.

Sociological Explanations of Deviance

Sociological explanations of deviance fall into two categories. The first category includes those sociologists who assume that most people conform most of the time as a consequence of adequate socialization. They treat deviance as a special category of behavior and the deviant as deserving of special consideration. They ask why every society has known deviance. They want to know why people become deviant. They wonder why social control mechanisms are applied as a means of limiting and punishing clear violations of significant social norms.

Sociologists also tend to locate the source of deviance outside the individual person. They look within the social structure or in a social process of labeling. Labeling focuses on the process through which persons come to be defined as deviant. It also focuses on the means through which deviant behavior is created through the interaction taking place between those committing acts in violation of group's norms and those responding to such violations.

Robert Merton (1957) expanded upon Durkheim's understanding of deviance as the product of a structural circumstance of disorganization in the individual and in society. Both Merton and Durkheim saw this as a result of weak, inconsistent, or even nonexistent social norms. Merton concluded that in American society, for example, there is a disjunction between means and ends, such as the emphasis on wealth and success without many legitimate means to achieve them. Those individuals without such opportunities attempt to bridge this gap in a number of ways:

1. The "conformist" seeks to continue the acceptance of the goals and means offered for their attainment.

2. The "innovator" may continue to accept the goals while seeking new, and in many cases, illegitimate revenues for the attainment of these goals.

3. The "ritualist" may make the means into an end by rejecting the culturally prescribed goals as being out of his reach. This person is in favor of an overemphasis upon the means of achieving these goals. An example of this would be the bureaucrat who is more concerned with adhering to the rules and with keeping his job, than with his own personal achievement.

4. The "retreater" rejects both the means and ends offered by society by dropping into drug use, mental illness, alcoholism, and homelessness.

5. The "rebel" rejects both the means and ends while seeking to replace both with alternatives, thereby changing the way society as a whole is structured.

In his theory of differential association, Edwin Sutherland (1939) concluded that criminal behavior is learned through social interaction in primary groups. His theory states that it is in the primary group where a person acquires knowledge of the techniques used in committing crimes. This primary group also provides reasons for conforming to or violating rules of permissive or not permissive behavior in a given situation, as well as an understanding of what motivates criminal activity. It is claimed that becoming a criminal means that the definitions favorably outweigh those unfavorable to violating the law. Moreover, the kinds of differential associations favoring criminal activity occur frequently, are long lasting and intense, and take place earlier rather than later in life.

SOCIAL STRATIFICATION

Defining Social Stratification

All sociologists agree that societies are stratified, or arranged along many levels. Where they begin to differ is on the question of what, if anything, the layers represent beyond the distinctions made among differing degrees of power, wealth, and social prestige.

Stratification and inequality are consistent with an orientation toward society; it is claimed that all societies make distinctions between people. There are some distinctions that always receive differential treatment—as between old and young, or male and female. There are other distinctions that may or may not receive differential treatment depending upon a given society's values. The usual result of a society treating people differently on the basis of their age, sex, race, religion, sexual orientation, or education is social inequality. This inequality can take the form of an unfair distribution of wealth, prestige, or power.

Social stratification represents the structured inequality characterized by groups of people with differential access to the rewards of society because of their relative position in the social hierarchy. Thus, a fundamental task of sociology is the determination of why stratified societies are so prevalent. Because almost the entire human population lives in stratified societies, sociologists must try to decide whether stratification is inevitable, and if so, what the effects of social inequality might be.

Sociologists have found that those in the same social stratum generally share the same **life chances** or opportunities. They seem to benefit or suffer equally from whatever advantages or disadvantages society has to offer.

Consistent with an orientation toward **social structure**, **stratification systems** serve to rank some people (whether individuals or groups) as more deserving of power, wealth, and prestige than others.

The inevitable result of this stratification is a **social hierarchy** of ranked statuses in which people function. These statuses may be either ascribed or achieved. An ascribed social position is either received at birth or involuntarily placed upon an individual later in life. An achieved social position is usually assumed voluntarily, and generally reflects personal ability or effort. Individuals in a society are treated differently depending on where their social position stands in the overall social hierarchy.

Social mobility refers to the ability of a given individual or group to move through the social strata. Structural mobility refers to factors at the societal level that affect mobility rates. For example, the number and types of available jobs, dependent on changes in the economic system, have a profound effect on social mobility. In addition, the number of people available to fill those jobs will fluctuate depending on current birthrates and the changing birthrates of previous generations.

Social mobility may be either relative or absolute. An example of relative mobility would be an entire occupational structure being upgraded so that only the content of the work changes, not relative position in the social hierarchy from one generation to the next. An example of absolute mobility would be when a son's education, occupational prestige, and income exceeds that of his father.

Systems of Stratification

A system of stratification refers to the institutions and ideas that permit or limit the distribution of prestige, status, and opportunities in life. Based on the degree of significance attached to certain values in a particular society at a particular time, and the extent to which a particular group monopolizes the areas in which the values are available as evidenced by the development or decline of institutions, stratification may have several sources. These sources include race, ethnicity, gender, age, and sexual orientation—which at times have served as the basis for assigning inferior or superior status to an entire population.

Race and Ethnicity

As sociologists use the term, **race** is more than a biologically complex phenomenon in that it involves the attribution of hereditary differences to human populations that are genetically distinct. The more than 6 billion people living in the world today display an array of physical characteristics—hair color, skin color, eye color and shape, height, weight, facial features, etc. That we categorize people into "races" is a social phenomenon rather than a biological one. In fact, the biological term for race is meaningless. Society, not biology, categorizes people into "races."

Ethnicity refers to a population known and identified on the basis of their common language, national heritage, and/or biological inheritance. Although race primarily refers to differences in physical characteristics, ethnic differences are culturally learned and not genetically inherited.

Gender

Gender stratification refers to those differences between men and women that have been acquired or learned and, hence, to the different roles and positions assigned to males and females in a society. Gender encompasses differences in hairstyle, in the types and styles of clothing worn, and in family and occupational roles. Across societies women have been systematically denied certain rights and opportunities based on assumptions regarding their abilities. This inferior status of women has often been legitimized through a sexist ideology (a belief system assuming that innate characteristics translate into one gender being superior to another) which is passed on across generations via culture.

Age

Age stratification refers to the ways in which people are differentially treated depending on their age. This form of stratification is concerned with the attitudes and behaviors we associate with age, and to the different roles and statuses we assign to people depending upon their age.

Sexual Orientation

Stratification on the basis of sexual orientation or affection refers to the ways in which individuals are differentially treated on the basis of their sexual preferences. In some societies, the results of this stratification are relatively benign. However, results of this stratification have also taken the form of criminalization of same-sex unions, as well as discrimination in housing, employment, and social status. Many societies forbid homosexual marriages, thereby systematically excluding homosexual couples from the social and economic benefits of marriage. In addition, this exclusion from major social institutions has often translated into a perceived social condonation of discrimination against homosexuals.

Davis and Moore—A Functionalist View of Social Stratification

In their classic presentation of the functionalist view of stratification, Kingsley Davis and Wilbert Moore (1945) argue that some stratification is necessary. Not everyone has the same abilities. At any given time, some members of a society will have more of the qualities that are needed and desired than others. Also some roles will be more essential to the society's functioning effectively than others. Thus, in order to attract the appropriate people with the requisite talents and skills to the more demanding, often stressful, roles that are not only essential to a society's functioning effectively but that also involve prolonged training and sacrifice, a society must offer greater rewards and higher status. In this way, inequality (the unequal distribution of social rewards) is considered functional for society in that it guarantees that those most able will be in the most demanding positions. Social stratification, in other words, is inevitable.

Marx, Weber, and Modern Conflict Theory

Marx attributed inequalities of wealth, power, and prestige to the economic situation that class structures present. Thus, the elimination of classes would serve to put an end to inequality, to the exploitation of man by man, and to the basic conflict of interest between the haves and the have nots. According to Marx, the elimination of class structure would also enable men and women to regain their humanity through the creation of a genuine or true community "where individuals gain their freedom in and through their association."

By contrast, Weber distinguished between class, status situation, and parties as a step toward explaining the origins of the different economic, social, political, and religious situations of society that he saw in India, China, ancient Greece, and Rome, and in the West extending from Great Britain to Russia. By class he meant economic situation as defined by wealth, property, and other opportunities for income. A status situation consisted of every aspect of a person's situation in life that is caused by a positive or negative social assessment of status. Parties were groups oriented toward acquiring social power, i.e., opportunities to realize their common goals despite resistance.

Focused on the origins of man-made culture, Weber often found such differences to be a source of conflict and change that he could not foresee ending. He discovered various systems of stratification. Some were modes of organization based on caste, where social mobility is not permitted by religious sanctions. Others were based on class, including the feudal system of medieval society that was based on vassalage, or reciprocal obligations of loyalty and service between lord and knight or lord and serfs.

Modern conflict theory continues to struggle with the question of the bases of conflict. Believing that Marx placed too much emphasis on class, Ralf Dahrendorf (1959) focused on the struggle among such groups as unions and employers. Randall Collins continues to focus on the way that different groups seek to maintain their social position by acquiring educational credentials that they then use to secure jobs and other advantages. And still others see the conflict over ideological hegemony, including beliefs, attitudes, and ideals, as being the decisive element distinguishing the higher from the lower strata.

ANTHROPOLOGY

Anthropology is the study of human behavior in all places and at all times. It combines humanistic, scientific, biological, historical, psychological, and social views of human behavior. Anthropology is divided into two broad subfields:

Physical Anthropology is the study of the biological, physiological, anatomical, and genetic characteristics of both ancient and modern human populations. Physical anthropologists study the evolutionary development of the human species by a comparative analysis of both fossil and living primates. They study the mechanics of evolutionary change through an analysis of genetic variation in human populations.

Cultural Anthropology is the study of learned behavior in human societies. Most cultural anthropologists specialize in one or two geographic areas. They may also specialize in selected aspects of culture (e.g., politics, medicine, religion) in the context of the larger social whole. Cultural anthropology is further subdivided as follows:

Archaeology is the study of the cultures of prehistoric peoples. It also includes the study of modern societies, but from the evidence of their material remains rather than from direct interviews with or observations of the people under study.

Ethnography is the systematic description of a human society, usually based on first-hand fieldwork. All generalizations about human behavior are based on the descriptive evidence of ethnography.

Ethnology is the interpretive explanation of human behavior, based on ethnography.

Social Anthropology is the study of human groups, with a particular emphasis on social structure (social relations, family dynamics, social control mechanisms, economic exchange).

Linguistics is the study of how language works as a medium of communication among humans. Language is the vehicle through which all culture is learned and transmitted.

Defining Characteristics of Anthropology

Holism is the belief that the experiences of a human group are unified and patterned. No one aspect of human behavior can be understood in isolation from all the rest.

Culture is the organized sum of everything a people produces, does, and thinks about—all of which they learn as members of a particular social group. A people's culture develops over time as they adapt to their environment.

Comparative Method is the belief that generalizations about human behavior can only be made on the basis of data collected from the widest possible range of cultures, both contemporary and historical.

Relativism is the belief that we cannot make value judgments about a culture based on standards appropriate to another culture. When such judgments are made on the basis of one's own culturally derived values, it is said that we are making **ethnocentric** judgments.

Fieldwork is the study of cultures in their natural settings, the communities in which people live, work, and interact on a regular basis.

Anthropologists attempt to live for an extended period of time among the people they study. They are both **participants** in and **observers** of the culture of the group.

THE FAMILY

When anthropologists study the relationships of marriage and family, they use a shorthand notation system whose symbols allow for the quick diagramming of relationships that would otherwise take extensive narrative description. All kinship diagrams are drawn from the point of view of a single person at a time. This person, whether a male or a female, is known as **Ego**. Ego is usually shaded or marked in some other way to note his or her special place. All relationships on a kinship diagram are read in relation to Ego.

The woman married to Ego is called a "wife" in our kinship system. She is, of course, also a "mother" to the two children shown on the diagram, and she is probably also somebody else's daughter, sister, or aunt. But in terms of this diagram, we identify her relationship to Ego alone.

Marriage establishes the basic unit of family relationship—the nuclear family. The **nuclear family** serves four fundamental functions:

- to regularize sexual relationships between certain men and women;

- to bear and nurture new members of the community;

- to organize and institutionalize a sexual division of labor and to regulate the transfer of property; and

- to establish the members of the family within a larger network of kin.

Although the role of the family as a social institution has been somewhat de-emphasized in urban, industrial societies, it is still an institution of overwhelming importance.

1. There is no known human society lacking in a family organization.

2. There is no known human society in which the family is not the primary focus of socialization and the model for all later social relationships, no matter how widespread they may become.

Because the family is so basic to every person's social identity, it is the social institution most frequently seen in an ethnocentric light. We must keep in mind that although "the family" is universal, its structure and organization vary widely from culture to culture.

There are two types of nuclear family:

- That into which a person is born is the **nuclear family of orientation**, in which Ego's statuses are those of child and sibling.

- That which is established upon marriage is the **nuclear family of procreation**, in which Ego's statuses are those of spouse and parent.

Our society is quite unusual in its emphasis on the nuclear family. It is much more common for social organization to be based on more extended family groups. One way to extend the family is by extending the marital bond (to create what are called **composite conjugal families**, or **polygamous** unions), which may occur in two ways:

1. **Polygyny**, the simultaneous marriage of one man to two or more women; if the women happen to be sisters, the union is technically called **sororal polygyny**.

2. **Polyandry**, the simultaneous marriage of a woman to two or more men; this is a rare pattern, and only occurs when the men in question are brothers.

A family in which children, upon marriage, bring their spouses to live in the parental households, such that all their children in turn are raised together, is known as a **joint family**.

After marriage, the most important question is where the newly joined couple will live. The decision is rarely allowed to be based on whim. It is, like marriage itself, patterned by rules and expectations:

- **Virilocal** residence—the couple settles in the vicinity of the husband's kin.

- **Patrilocal** residence—they settle in the actual household of the husband's father.

- **Uxorilocal** residence—they settle in the vicinity of the bride's kin.

- **Matrilocal** residence—they settle in the actual household of the bride's mother.

- **Ambilocal** residence—they settle in the vicinity of either the husband's or the bride's kin.

- **Avunculocal** residence—they settle in the household of the groom's mother's brother.

- **Neolocal** residence—they settle in a new locale, without reference to the location of either family.

KINSHIP-BASED SOCIAL GROUPS

Kinship groups are determined by culture, not by biology. The kinship group represents the culture's fundamental beliefs about how people should behave toward one another. (Keep in mind that in most traditional societies, everyone one encounters is either a relative, or a stranger to be treated with distrust.) In any given kinship system, certain statuses are singled out as being of unique importance; they are given **descriptive** kinship terms — terms that apply to no other category of relative. For example, in our kinship system, mother, father, brother, sister, son, and daughter are all descriptive kin terms because they describe unique relationships. (We may, of course, have more than one brother or sister, but all of them are people who stand in the same unique "biological" or adoptive relationship to us. We may also use the terms "brother" and "sister" to address members of certain religious orders, or to refer to members of one's political party, but these are metaphoric usages outside the kinship system.) This practice emphasizes the special role of the nuclear family in our society.

All other terms, however, are formed by lumping people of various relationships together into a single category, and labelling them with **classificatory** terms. In English, for example, **cousin** is a classificatory term because it lumps people of both sexes, of all generations, and people related either through blood or marriage. Such a term is indicative of the social reality that, for most Americans, relatives outside the nuclear family are remote and do not need to be distinguished by special labels.

Kinship terms therefore designate categories of social status and suggest expected behaviors linking persons. It is for this reason that anthropologists have spent a great deal of effort in studying systems of **kinship terminology**.

Kinship terminology systems are based on one or more of the following principles:

- differences in generational level (e.g., father/son),

- differences in age level within the same generation (e.g., elder brother/ younger brother),

- differences between lineal (those in the direct line of descent) and collateral (those outside the direct line of descent) relations (e.g., father/uncle),

- differences in sex of relations (e.g., brother/sister),

- differences in sex of the speaker (e.g., male Ego's brother/female Ego's brother),

- differences in sex of the person through whom relationship is established (e.g., father's brother/mother's brother),

- differences between "blood" relatives and relatives through marriage (e.g., mother/mother-in-law), and

- differences in status or life condition of the person through whom the relationship is established (e.g., son of a living sister/son of a deceased sister).

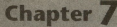
PSYCHOLOGY

Psychology is the science of behavior. Its goal is to measure, predict, and explain behavior. Some psychologists also describe psychology as the study of experience, or an organism's "internal" activities. Other psychologists believe that "experience" cannot be systematically studied. There are many varied approaches to the study of behavior, making psychology a rich and complex field.

Over time, psychology has acquired many definitions. Psychology was once considered to be the study of the mind. Researchers have come to agree that the mind is neither entirely open to study, nor very well defined. The mind can only be observed through the behavior it causes, but what this "mind" is and how it "causes" behavior has never been clearly defined. To make the discipline more objective and scientific, psychologists redefined psychology as the study of human behavior.

Behavior refers to any action or reaction of a living organism which can be observed. Psychologists study all levels of behavior. Some psychologists focus on the biology of behavior, such as the actions of nerve cells, genetics, or sweat glands. Other psychologists study higher level behaviors, such as aggression, prejudice, or problem solving.

The key to the definition of behavior is that behavior is observable. Behavior refers to overt movement, activity, or action. Some behaviors are more observable than others. For instance, any bystander can see aggressive behavior on a city street. However, more subtle behavior, such as the change in brain waves during sleep may require special equipment to be observed.

Psychologists do not want merely to describe behavior: they wish to predict and understand it. To do this, they have set forth four fundamental factors of behavior: the organism, motivation, knowledge, and competence.

The **organism** refers to the biological characteristics of a living biological entity, including the creature's nervous system, endocrine system, biological history, and heredity. **Motivation** entails the states which cause behavior. These are the immediate forces that act to energize, direct, sustain, and stop a behavior. The term is vague, but motivation generally includes the organism's internal state—e.g., "tired" or "confused"—and the behavior related to this state—e.g., searching for a warm den. Some psychologists include the goal of a behavior (rest) in their descriptions of motivation, though others deny that behavior has a goal. The term **cogni-**

tion refers to "knowledge," that is, what and how the organism thinks, knows, and remembers. For example, a contestant on a television game show who must choose which of three boxes she wants for a prize may base her decision on how big each box is, how much she trusts the game show host, and so on. Her guesses at the location of the prize, her reasoning about the estimation of the size of the boxes, and her memory of the host's past performance all make up her cognition. She does not know what is actually in the boxes. The contents of the boxes are not part of her cognition. **Competence** means the skills and abilities of an organism. How well can it perform a certain task? Does a rat have the physical ability to jump to the top of its cage? Does the a colege student have the skill at fast writing and the physical stamina to finish her term paper on time? These are questions of competence.

Psychology is not as simple as it may first appear. Psychologists today study many other scientific fields such as biology, physics, chemistry, and linguistics, as well as other social sciences like sociology, anthropology, economics, and political science. To evaluate behavior, a psychologist should be familiar with all of these areas.

Major Schools of Thought

By the late 1800s, psychology had become empirical and left the realm of mere fanciful philosophy forever. In organizing and explaining their observations, psychologists created eight major schools of thought: structuralism, functionalism, gestalt, and biological, cognitive, humanistic, and psychoanalytic theories. There are many other branches of psychological study: social, educational, developmental, and so on. These are merely the theories which have had the greatest impact on psychology as a whole.

Structuralism, the first theoretical school in psychology, derived from Wundt's work. Wundt believed that the science of psychology should study the conscious mind. Influenced by the physical scientists of his time, Wundt embraced the atomic theory of matter. This theory stated that all complex substances could be separated and analyzed into component elements. Wundt wished to divide the mind into mental elements. This approach came to be called structuralism.

To analyze mental elements, Wundt used an experimental method called introspection. Subjects reported the contents of their own minds as objectively as possible, usually in connection with stimuli such as light, sound, or odors. The subjects' verbal reports were analyzed to see the number and types of "mental elements" they contained. Subjects were specially trained to give elaborate reports.

The major drawback of structuralism was that it focused on the internal structure and activity of the mind, rather than overt, objectively observable behavior. Subjective reports of the mind's activities are easily manipulated by both the subject and the experimenter, and they are unreliable. Psychologists today are still concerned with internal activities, but are primarily interested in how these activities influence behavior.

While structuralist psychologists were busy asking their subjects to describe mental images, **functionalists** examined behavior from a different point of view. While structuralists were concerned with what the mind is, functionalists were asking what the mind does, and why. Functionalists were inspired by Darwin's theory of evolution; they believed that all behavior and mental processes help organisms to adapt to a changing environment. They expanded their studies beyond perception to include questions of learning, motivation, and problem solving. Functionalist William James (1842–1910) coined the phrase "stream of consciousness" to describe the way the mind experiences perception and thought as a constant flow of sensation.

Functionalists did not reject the structuralists' introspection, but they preferred to observe both the stream of consciousness and behavior. The functionalists' most important contribution to psychology was the introduction of the concept of learning, and thus adaptation to the environment, to psychological study. The most influential proponents of functionalism were William James and John Dewey (1859–1952), a philosopher and educator who played a substantial role in the development of educational psychology.

Soon, psychologists tired of introspection's dainty ways. **Behaviorism**, as developed by John B. Watson (1878–1958), swept the United States at the turn of the century. Watson rejected the idea of the "mind," stating that this structure not only could not be objectively studied, but did not even exist! Instead, Watson presented behavior as consisting of the stimulus, a "black box" which processed the stimuli, and the response the "black box" produced. Nothing could be said about the "black box" apart from the behavior it regulated. Watson also disregarded introspection, asserting that only observations of outward behavior could provide valid psychological data. He stated that the major component of psychological study should be the identification of relationships between stimuli (environment) and responses (behavior).

While structuralists believed that the mind could be divided into mental/experiential elements, behaviorists believed that all behavior could be broken down into a collection of conditioned responses. These conditioned responses (CRs) were simple learned responses to stimuli. All human behavior was supposed to be the result of learning. According to this theory, everyone could become lawyers, murderers, or trapeze artists, if only they were given the correct training.

Behaviorists have also studied animal behavior extensively. Many held that there was no difference between human and animal behavior, and several tried to formulate general theories of behavior based on animal experiments. Leaders of this school, prominent in the late 1930s and 1940s, include Edward C. Tolman (1886–1959), Clark L. Hull (1884–1952), and Edwin R. Guthrie (1886–1959).

Behaviorism is still an active, vibrant branch of psychology. Its rigorous experimentation and emphasis on actual behavior has proved useful, especially in treating difficult groups such as institutionalized and mentally retarded patients.

Gestalt psychology, though, survives only as a name for a collection of theories. Like functionalism and behaviorism, gestalt psychology was a reaction to structuralism. It was founded in Germany in 1912 by Max Wertheimer (1880–1943). The word "gestalt" has no exact equivalent in English, but its meaning is similar to "form" or "organization." Gestalt psychologists emphasized the organizational processes in behavior, rather than the content of behavior. Like the structuralists, gestalt psychologists mainly focused on problems of perception.

Unlike the reductionist structuralists and functionalists, gestaltists believed that behavior and experiences consisted of patterns and organized sets. Like many physical scientists, gestalt psychologists believed the whole is more than the sum of its parts. A series of lines shows a picture, jumbled notes become a song; the mind constantly organizes perception into unified wholes.

Gestalt psychologists stressed **phenomenology**, or the study of natural, unanalyzed perception, as the basis for behavior. They instructed untrained subjects to introspect without structuralist elaboration on their experience. However, they studied other problems as well, particularly those involving learning, thought, and problem solving. Wolfgang Kohler (1887–1967) argued that learning and problem solving were organizational processes like perception. He described the "moment of insight," when an individual realizes the solution to a problem suddenly crystallizes as a whole gestalt out of reasoning, intuition, etc.

Many of the gestaltists' observations about perception are still being explored. Today's cognitive psychologists draw heavily on their ideas, particularly when dealing with questions of vision and information processing. How much information does a person need before she can figure out what she is seeing? What are the most important, salient parts of an object which let a person identify the whole? What kinds of information does a robot need to tell the difference between a rubber ball and an orange? These sorts of questions keep gestalt concerns alive.

Biological, cognitive, humanistic, and psychoanalytic psychologists are most active today. **Biological psychologists** explore the effect that changes in an organism's physical body or environment have on behavior, and the interaction between behavior and the brain. They do not study the mind, or soul, or most "internal" experiences. Biological psychologists concentrate on physical techniques, and hence find physical results.

The term biological psychology covers a wide range of study. Their topics include genetics, the nervous system, and the endocrine system. Biological psychologists' research may involve dissecting the brain of a human or animal who suffered a behavior disorder, experimenting with drug treatments for mental illness, measuring brain waves during sleep, or investigating the effects of biological factors on eating and drinking, sexual behavior, aggression, speech disorders, dyslexia, or learning.

Major contributors to biological psychology include Ivan Pavlov (1849–1936), who conditioned dogs to salivate when they heard a bell ring; Eric Kandel, who pioneered the use of the sea slug Aplysia to study motor neurons; and Norman Geschwind, who revolutionized studies of the neural basis of dyslexia.

Cognitive psychology is heir to the early experiential psychologists. It is concerned with the processes of thinking and memory, as well as attention, imagery, creativity, problem solving, and language use. In contrast to the behaviorists, cognitive psychologists discuss the mental processes which determine what humans can perceive, or communicate, as well as how they think. Cognitive psychologists also use animals, particularly in memory research.

In the 1950s, several events led to the rise of interest in the mind, after decades of neglect. Psychologists realized that behaviorism, while a useful approach, had taught them nothing about the "black box" of mental processing. Scientists like Norbert Wiener (1894–1964) began work on cybernetics, the study of automatic control systems like thermostats and computers, asking, "How does a thinking machine process information?" Noam Chomsky published his theories on language as a system with infinite, non-learned possibilities generated by rules. New technology and logic gave psychologists the power to explore realms that were considered too subjective by the dominant behaviorists. Many cognitive psychologists use computers to simulate human memory, language use, and visual perception.

Humanistic psychology also arose in the 1950s, with a completely different focus. According to the humanistic psychologists, behaviorism concentrated on scientific fact, to the exclusion of human experience, and psychoanalysis (described below) concentrated too much on human frailty. Humanistic psychologists sought to begin a psychology of mental health, not illness, by studying healthy, creative people.

Humanistic psychology grew out of two main influences: phenomenology, the idea that behavior is based on subjective perception, and **existentialism**, which states that humans' basic existential anxiety is fear of death. Both approaches concentrated on the individual's point of view. Humanistic psychologists had little use for statistics; the focus was to understand each person's struggle to exist.

Psychoanalytic theories have an important place in psychology. Sigmund Freud (1856–1939), the father of psychoanalysis, is perhaps the most famous psychologist in the world, as well as the most challenged. Though current psychodynamic theories of personality originated in his work, subsequent psychoanalysts have moved far beyond the scope of his theories.

In the nineteenth century, psychiatry did not offer either explanations of or treatment for mental illness. Freud developed his method of treatment and a theory of personality through empirical (observational) and experimental techniques. Freud developed a treatment called **psychoanalysis**, where patients work with a therapist to explore the sources of their illness in their own past, stressing early experience and unconscious, "repressed" memories. Freud's primary tool for investigation was the **case study**, which included both his commentary and a patient's autobiographical material, dream analysis, and free association.

Neo-Freudians revised Freud's theories to provide for more cogent views of women's development, learning throughout life, interpersonal influences on personality, and social interaction. Important writers included Eric Erikson, Karen Horney (1885–1952), Carl Jung (1875–1961), and Alfred Adler (1870–1937).

Though psychoanalytic theory has its limitations, particularly with regard to biologically-based illnesses like schizophrenia, it is the most influential of psychological fields to date. Without it, clinical psychology as we know it would not exist.

Types of Studies

Psychology is a science, and many different research methods are used to study the behavior of subjects—the humans or animals who are observed.

Naturalistic observation is the systematic observation of an event or phenomenon in the environment as it occurs naturally. The researcher does not manipulate the phenomenon. Laboratory investigation often interferes with the natural occurrence of a phenomenon. Therefore, psychologists may prefer to witness it in its natural environment. For example, social behavior in monkeys may differ in a safe laboratory from that exhibited in the more perilous wild world.

When psychologists wish to manipulate conditions, they perform experiments. Some event, treatment, or condition is changed, controlled, or recorded by the psychologist: this factor is called the independent variable. The change in the organism—behavioral or biological—is recorded by the psychologist. This change is the dependent variable. By observing the change in the organism correlated with the change in conditions, the psychologist can infer the change in environment changed the organism's behavior. However, correlation is not causation. A social scientist must beware that the change in the dependent variable, behavior, is truly due to a change in the independent variable and not some other factor. Generally, psychologists perform their experiments in laboratories or other controlled settings, such as schools, prisons, or hospitals, where conditions are much the same for all subjects.

Surveys are another method of psychological investigation. Individuals are asked to reply to a series of questions or to rate items. The purpose is not to test abilities, but to discover beliefs, opinions, and attitudes. Psychologists may take answers to survey questions and see how they match with respondents' characteristics—age, gender, social class, and so on.

Three types of studies are typically used to examine human subjects: **longitudinal**, **cross-sectional**, and **case studies**. In longitudinal studies, psychologists study their subjects over a long period of time to observe changes in their behavior. Cross-sectional studies take a group of subjects and examine their behavior at one point in time. Case studies, or case histories, are commonly used in clinical psychology and medical research. A single individual is studied intensely to examine a problem or issue relevant to that person. Sigmund Freud favored case studies in his research.

Reliability and Validity

To be applicable to the general population, any test a psychologist administers must be standardized. The results must be reproducible, and must measure what the psychologist wishes to measure. These concerns are termed **reliability** and **validity**.

In psychology, reliability refers to how consistently individuals score on a test. Reliability measures the extent to which differences between individuals' scores show true difference in characteristics, and not "error variance," or the proportion of the score due to errors in test construction. With a reliability value for a test, a psychologist can predict the range of error in a single individual's score. For example, SAT tests generally have an error variance of 10 points: your score may vary 10 points in either direction from your "true score."

The question of validity is whether a test measures what the examiner wants it to measure. Specifically, **construct validity** is the extent to which a test measures something—a theoretical construct. **Criterion-related validity** refers to how effective a test is in predicting an individual's behavior in other, specified situations. For example, if a student does well on the SAT, does that student also have high grades now? Will that student do well in college? If that student's teacher hears that she did poorly on the math SAT, the teacher may expect that the student will do badly in math in school, and grade her more harshly. This is known as criterion contamination, when results on a test bias an individual's score on another test.

SOCIAL PSYCHOLOGY

Social psychology focuses on the psychology of the individual in society. Social psychologists may draw from sociology and cultural anthropology, though their primary interest is still the psychological level of thought and action. Using the scientific method and objective study, social psychologists have produced a body of knowledge about the underlying psychological processes in social interactions.

Within social psychology, there are two major schools of thought. **Cognitive theorists** concentrate on an individual's internal processes and thoughts. They believe that a human being organizes and processes experience, and that her "world view" greatly influences her social behavior. **Behaviorists**, on the other hand, put more emphasis on external events and tend to believe that people react to events that occur around them.

Attitudes and Attributions

An **attitude** is a person's beliefs about an object or a situation. An attitude both precedes behavior and causes behavior toward an object. The average adult probably has thousands of attitudes of which he is not aware. Attitudes usually occur in clusters or sets around a particular issue or situation—for example, taxes or abortion—supporting and reinforcing each other. A **value**, on the other hand, is a person's enduring belief about how she should act, and what goals are appropriate or desirable. Values direct behavior on a long-term basis. Examples of values (from Rokeach's Value Survey) are pleasure, wisdom, and a sense of accomplishment. A person generally holds many more attitudes than values.

Attitudes are generally formed through imitation, classical conditioning, or operant conditioning. Learning often occurs by imitation without obvious reinforcement. Hence, children often take on their parents' behavior and attitudes. In a study of Bennington College students, Theodore Newcomb found that incoming freshmen held conservative political attitudes, like those of their reference group—their parents. By graduation, though, they had acquired significantly more liberal attitudes, like those of their new reference group: classmates. One example of attitudes acquired by classical conditioning is the connotation of words. If you give a person a neutral word and immediately follow it with a word that evokes a strong negative or positive reaction, this will eventually cause the same type of reaction to the previously neutral word. In operant conditioning, a subject emits a behavior. If the behavior is reinforced, it will likely reoccur; if it is punished, it will not recur as often. If your child says, "I want to be a fireman!" and you respond with a smile and an assurance that she'll be just like Mommy then, the child will continue to have a positive attitude about firefighters. If, on the other hand, you scowl and admonish her for even considering such a thing, you have punished her response, and the chances are that she will develop negative attitudes about the firefighting profession and all emergency-rescue careers.

Though it may seem that the principles of attitude acquisition are simple, the actual process is quite complex. An adult's attitudes are quite difficult to trace to their source. This is complicated by the fact that attitudes can change, even quite significantly, in the course of a person's lifetime. There is much yet to be learned about attitudes and their acquisition.

Persuasion refers to a type of social influence that involves attitude change. Persuasion is not necessarily the result of conscious communication: a person can be persuaded that a street is dangerous if he sees a person being mugged there. In general, though, three factors affect how persuasive a particular communication is, i.e., how effective it is at changing attitudes. These factors are the source of the communication (who says it), the nature of the communication (how it is said), and the characteristics of the audience. All these factors can also be applied to print and broadcast media, not just face-to-face persuasion.

The first aspect of the source that the audience examines is credibility. People tend to believe people who appear to be experts or seem trustworthy. To the average person, it makes a lot of sense to be influenced by someone with these characteristics. Often, visual impressions are the only items a person can base impressions on, and these are what are used to infer credibility, whether of a TV news anchor, an auto mechanic, or a teacher. Trustworthiness, on the other hand, can be improved by arguing there is nothing to lose, arguing against one's (apparent) self-interest, and appearing not to be trying to influence people or change their minds.

The concern for the nature of communication is the emotional approach vs. the reasonable (or logical) approach. Research results generally indicate that a shocking (emotional-based) approach is usually more effective in communication and persuasion than the logical approach.

As for the audience, individuals with low self-esteem are quicker to be convinced if the speaker appears credible or takes an emotional approach, while high self-esteem listeners are in higher conflict when presented with less-than-reliable information from a medium-credibility speaker. The speaker's prior experience with the audience is another crucial factor, as are educational level and previous contact with the issue being discussed.

Prejudice is an attitude. It is generally a negative attitude held toward a particular group and any member of that group. Prejudice is translated into behavior through discrimination, which refers to any action that results from prejudiced points of view. **Ethnocentrism** is a special form of prejudice where a person holds positive prejudices about her own ethnic group and negative prejudices about all other ethnic groups.

It is possible for individuals to be quite prejudiced and still not discriminate. Civil rights laws, for example, have reduced a great deal of the more obvious discrimination. However, some evidence exists that the prejudicial attitudes of Americans have been influenced by civil rights law. For instance, in 1964, most Americans were opposed to the Civil Rights Act, but today over 75 percent of the public favors integration.

When discrimination decreases and prejudice remains, discrimination may begin to take more subtle forms, such as not being included in informal discussions with other managers at work, being assigned the more routine tasks of a project, and being listened to through the filter of prejudiced attitudes—"he's not too bright," "she's too emotional," and so forth.

Although prejudice is a complex topic and difficult to analyze on an individual level, psychologists hypothesize that there are four basic causes of prejudice. The first cause of prejudice is **economic** and **political competition**. This view states that when any resource is limited, majority groups will vie for resources and thus form prejudices against the competing group for their own personal gain and advantage. Research has demonstrated a clear link between the level of discrimination and prejudice against a certain group in an area and the scarcity of jobs in that area.

The second causal factor of prejudice is **personality needs**. After World War II, researchers began to search for a prejudiced personality type. The major piece of research in this area, by Adorno et al., is titled *The Authoritarian Personality*. Adorno developed the F (fascist) Scale for authoritarianism. These researchers established a relationship between the strictness of parental upbringing and authoritarianism and a correlational relationship between authoritarianism, prejudice, and ethnocentrism. Yet they did not determine what causes prejudice, only what personality traits accompany it.

The third cause of prejudice is the **displacement of aggression**. This is referred to as a "scapegoat" theory of prejudice. Here, aggression (described further below) that cannot be otherwise expressed is displaced onto socially acceptable victims.

The fourth cause of prejudice is **conformity to preexisting prejudices** within the society or subgroup. Researchers note that while there seems to be a large difference between the amount of anti-black prejudice in the North and the South, neither group is distinguishable on the basis of how they score on the Authoritarian test. The problem appears to be caused by socially acceptable beliefs in each region. As Elliot Aronson has noted, historical events in the South set the stage for greater prejudice against blacks, but it is conformity which keeps it going.

There are four other factors which contribute to the construction and continuation of prejudice. People tend to be prejudiced against the group which is directly under them on the socio-economic scale. The four additional contributions are 1) people need to feel superior to someone, 2) people most strongly feel competition for jobs from the next lower level, 3) people from the lower socio-economic levels are more frustrated and therefore more aggressive (see below), and 4) a lack of education increases the likelihood that they will simplify their world by the consistent use of stereotyping.

There are ways of reducing prejudice. One unsuccessful manner of reducing prejudice is to provide information contrary to people's beliefs. Unfortunately, people tend to pay attention only to information which agrees with their beliefs. However, if people of different backgrounds are brought together in **equal-status contact**, people tend to change their behavior and their attitudes towards other groups. Unfortunately, forced busing and desegregation efforts often bring people together in unequal status, defying their purpose. Finally, one very successful way to reduce prejudice is through **interdependence**, where all participants must work together with a mixed group. Social psychologists are currently trying to apply this method to educational settings.

Attributes and Stereotypes

An **attribute** is a perceived characteristic of some object or person. In attribution, people infer that some individual has certain characteristics. If a person infers that people possess certain characteristics because of their gender, race, or religion, that person is attributing a **stereotype** to that group. Stereotyping is not necessarily an intentional act of insult; very often it is merely used as a means of simplifying the complex world. However, if a stereotype narrows a person's views of actual interpersonal differences, prejudiced attitudes can result.

Attribution theory contends that individuals have a tendency to attribute a cause to any recently viewed behaviors. This attribution is essentially a specialized sort of stereotyping. When viewing an event, the observer uses the information available to her at the time to infer causality. Although there are many factors which affect what inference will be made, the major contributors are a person's beliefs, e.g., stereotypes or prejudices. The process of attribution based on a person's prejudices can be described as a "vicious circle." A person's prejudices affect her attributions, and her misdirected attributions then serve to reinforce and intensify her prejudice.

CONFORMITY AND OBEDIENCE

Conformity is a change in behavior or belief caused by real or imagined social pressure. For example, a teenager who goes to school in formal clothes will quickly observe that every other person her age is wearing blue jeans. No one may say a word about her dress, yet she observes that others are acting differently and may imagine that they are discussing her clothing. The next day, in blue jeans, she conforms. Conformity is generally divided into three subtypes: compliance, identification, and internalization.

Compliance is a change in external behavior, as opposed to a real attitude change, termed "private acceptance." Compliance is generally exhibited by individuals attempting to gain a reward or punishment. This behavior generally ceases once the reward or punishment is either not available or avoidable, respectively.

Identification results from the individual's desire to be like some other person, the person she is identifying with. Such behavior is self-satisfying, and does not require reward or threat of punishment. The individual loosely adopts the beliefs and opinions of the person she identifies with, a fact which differentiates identification from compliance.

Internalization occurs when the individual adopts the groups beliefs as his own. This process is a deeply rooted social response based on the desire to be right. The reward here is intrinsic. Identification is usually the method which introduces a belief to an individual, but once it is internalized it becomes an independent belief, and is highly resistant to change.

The most famous psychological demonstration of conformity was a series of experiments by Solomon Asch. Asch asked subjects to choose which of three lines on a card was the same length as line X, a line on a separate card. Each subject was on a panel with other "subjects" (Asch's confederates) who all initially gave the same wrong answer. Approximately 35 percent of the real subjects chose to give the obviously incorrect, but conforming, response. Since there were no explicit rewards or punishments, the reason for conformity could be that in the face of such "overwhelming" opposition the subjects doubted their own perceptions or agreed with the confederates to gain group acceptance (or avoid group rejection). Asch and his colleagues have repeated this study many times, varying the conditions in attempts to determine what variables play a causal role in decreasing or increasing conformity.

Obedience also involves conforming to others' expectations. Yet in obedience, an authority's demands are clearly expressed; the individual must consciously choose whether or not to obey. The study of obedience became especially important after World War II, when psychologists were eager to investigate just how and why the Nazis committed their death-camp atrocities.

While investigating obedience, Stanley Milgram discovered that the average middle-class American male would, under the direction of a legitimate authority figure, give severe shocks to other people in an experimental setting. Briefly, in his experiments two men were told that they would be taking part in an experiment on the effects of punishment on learning. One man was chosen as the learner (who was actually a confederate in the experiment), the other as the teacher. The learner was taken into an adjoining room and strapped into a chair. The experimenter read the instructions to the learner about a word list he was to learn so that the teacher-subject could hear. The teacher was placed in front of a generator which could administer shocks from 15 to 450 volts to the learner. Under the shock levels were descriptions of the effects of the shock from "slight shock" to "danger, severe shock." The learning session would begin: the first time the learner would give an incorrect answer, a mild shock was given, and with each subsequent wrong answer stronger and stronger shocks were administered. Even amidst cries from the learner of "Let me out, I've got a heart condition," the teacher would continue administering the shock, though more and more reluctantly.

Out of the 40 males who took part in the initial experiments, 26, or 65 percent, went all the way to the maximum shock of 450 volts. This alarming finding has been replicated many times. It demonstrates how much ordinary people will comply with the orders of a legitimate authority even to the point of committing cruel and harmful actions. On a television interview, Milgram stated that he would have no trouble staffing a Nazi-style concentration camp with guards from any middle-sized American town. This is not due to American anti-Semitism, but because of the evidence of his experiments regarding the power of legitimate authorities to evoke obedience.

GROUP DYNAMICS

People tend to act differently when they are in a group. A few of the differences are outlined above in the Asch experiment. In general, a group's primary purpose is to achieve some definite goal. To accomplish the goal, the group establishes **positions**, or places, where people fit into a group's hierarchy. Individuals themselves choose to fill **roles**, the set of different behaviors an individual displays in connection with a given social position. There are certain behaviors associated with the role of mother, employer, student, secretary, and teacher, for example. Most people have many roles which must be filled each day. However, people who occupy the same type of position may play very different roles. Three different roles are possible in any given position in a group. The **task-oriented** role requires that a person be concerned directly with accomplishing the goal of the group. The **maintenance** role requires that the individual playing it be more concerned with the group morale. The final type of role is the **self-oriented** role; the person who takes this role cares mainly for herself, and may even attempt to undermine the group's goals if they interfere with her personal desires or needs.

If a group is large enough—say, the size of New York City—social influence may move the person away from socially acceptable behavior. **Deindividuation** is a state where a person feels a lessened sense of personal identity and a decreased concern about what people think of him. This state, which probably results from feelings of anonymity, lessened responsibility and arousal, can lead to anti-social behavior. Philip Zimbardo once left an apparently abandoned car with the license plates removed and the hood raised in two cities, New York (pop. 8 million) and Palo Alto, CA (pop. 100,000). In New York, within 10 minutes a man, woman, and a nine-year-old child came by and immediately began to remove parts of the car. Within 24 hours, the car was completely ransacked. The vandals were not gangs, but most often well-dressed adults. In Palo Alto, the car remained untouched after 72 hours, except for one passerby who politely put the hood down when it began to rain. Zimbardo took this result as supporting the hypothesis that the anonymity of a large city gives rise to antisocial behavior. The chances of a person being recognized by someone in a city with a population of 8 million is much less than in a city with a population of 100,000.

Yet groups can also improve performance. In **social facilitation**, the mere presence of other people such as an audience or coworkers can increase individual performance. In the 1890s, Norman Triplett became interested in the fact that cyclists rode faster in groups than alone, while in the 1930s, John Dashiell discovered that though people respond more frequently in the presence of others, their rate of errors also increased. Robert Zajonc (1965) theorized that the presence of other people produces an increase in a person's arousal level and enhances strong responses. However, if responses are poorly learned or weak, responses will suffer. This theory helps explain why stage fright may paralyze young actors and galvanize more experienced thespians into grand performances.

Altruism and Bystander Intervention

Altruism and the "bystander effect" are two opposite responses to situations where another person needs help. In **altruism**, a person will risk his own health or well-being to help another. Yet if a large group of people witnesses an event where someone desperately needs assistance, each individual person is less likely to intervene than if she were alone. This phenomenon is called the **bystander effect**.

Latane and Darley produced the most famous experiments on bystander intervention. In their study, male subjects heard someone fall, apparently uninjured, in the room next door. Whether subjects tried to help and how long they took to do so were the main dependent variables in the experiment. Subjects were placed in one of four conditions: alone, with a friend, with another subject who was a stranger, and with a confederate in the experiment who had been instructed to remain passive at the sounds of injury. In the alone situation, subjects responded to the need for help 91 percent of the time, while with the passive confederate, subjects responded only 7 percent of the time. With pairs of strangers, at least one of the subjects responded in 40 percent of the pairs, while in the group of two friends, at least one person intervened in 70 percent of the pairs. This finding can be explained through **social influence** or **diffusion of responsibility**. The former option suggests that people are susceptible to the apparent reactions of other people present. The subject may not feel the situation is serious or merely be concerned and confused by the confederate's passivity. In diffusion of responsibility, when other people are present, each person's total sense of responsibility (and justification for responding to emergencies) may diminish.

AGGRESSION

In animals, many types of aggression are specific to certain species and are clearly controlled by brain structures and hormone levels, such as maternal aggression in rats. In humans, sex steroid hormones called **androgens** have been conclusively linked to an increase in aggressive behavior. However, it is not clear whether high levels of androgens produce aggression, or high levels of aggression result in the production of testosterone; there is evidence for both conclusions. Mazur and Lamb (1980) found that men who lost tennis matches had lower levels of testosterone (an androgen) an hour later, while the men who won had higher levels.

According to social psychologists, three different **distinctions** should be used when discussing aggressive behavior. The first distinction is between **harmful and nonharmful behavior**, which is judged by the outcome of the behavior. The second distinction involves the **intent of the aggressor**, as hitting a person accidentally is not considered aggressive. Finally, there is a distinction between aggression necessary to achieve a goal (as in professional boxing), called **instrumental aggression**, and aggression which is an end in itself (as in common street fighting), called **hostile aggression**. Interpersonal aggression occurs most often between friends, relatives, and acquaintances, and is much less often associated with crime than most people think.

Many social psychologists believe that aggression is a learned behavior, like other behaviors. Albert Bandura's work on modeling, or learning through imitation, was designed to explain aggressive tendencies in children. Aggression, like attitudes, may also be conditioned. The frustration-aggression hypothesis states that frustration toward the accomplishment of some goal produces aggression. For example, if you are trying to buy a soda in a convenience store, but the clerk will not serve you because he is busy talking on the telephone, that clerk is frustrating you with regard to buying the soda. If the source of frustration is available and unthreatening, the aggression will be displaced onto that person: you may yell at the talkative clerk. Otherwise, the aggression will be displaced onto someone or something else, called a "scapegoat."

However, some psychologists believe that aggression is an inborn tendency. The only reason, according to these theories, that we are not involved in more wars than we currently are is that humans use their intelligence to vent their aggression, and therefore do not always express aggression physically. Konrad Lorenz applied Darwin's "survival of the fittest" theory to aggression, arguing that aggression is necessary for the continued existence of the species. However, he based his argument on the observation of animals, not humans. Others, including Freud, believe the catharsis theory. This theory states that aggression is a means of releasing inner tension. If this tension were to remain unreleased, mental illness would result. Research does not support this theory, though, and has actually shown the opposite to be true.

ORGANIZATIONAL PSYCHOLOGY

Organizational psychology studies human behavior in an industrial or organizational environment. It can be divided into two important subfields: **industrial psychology** and **human factors psychology**. Human factors psychology is concerned specifically with how people receive information through their senses, store this information, and process it when making decisions.

The differences in these two areas is best understood by examining the jobs of industrial psychologists and human factors engineers. The industrial psychologist helps to improve safety programs and works with engineers on the human aspects of equipment design. She assists the office of public relations in its interactions with consumers and the local community. Industrial psychologists also engage in programs dealing with workers' mental health, and assist management in finding ways to reduce absenteeism and grievances. The industrial psychologist may draw up a plan for the executive development of newly hired college graduates on one day and discuss problems of aging employees the next.

The role of a human factors engineer, on the other hand, is concerned with contriving, designing, and producing structures and machines useful to humans. He applies his knowledge of the mechanical, electrical, chemical, or other properties of matter to the task of creating all kinds of functional devices—safety pins and automobiles, mousetraps and missiles. Since the ultimate users of these machines are humans, human characteristics must be considered in their construction. Human muscular frailty dictated the need for and design of such devices as the lever, pulley, screw, and hand tools of all sorts (though these simple machines were not designed by human factors engineers). The L-shaped desk for the secretary was designed to bring an enlarged work space within easy reach. The task which confronts the human factors engineer is to describe humans' special abilities and limitations so that design engineers can effectively include the human operator in their man-made system. This requires knowledge about sensation and perception, psychomotor behavior, and cognitive processes as well as knowledge about the properties of the material world. It is because of the need for this special knowledge about human behavior that this type of engineer is also considered a psychologist.

Praxis Social Studies
Assessment 0081

Practice Test 1

This test is also on CD-ROM in our special interactive TestWare® for the PRAXIS II Social Studies Assessment: 0081. It is highly recommended that you first take this exam on computer. You will then have the additional study features and benefits of enforced timed conditions and instantaneous, accurate scoring.

1. (A) (B) (C) (D)	34. (A) (B) (C) (D)	67. (A) (B) (C) (D)	100. (A) (B) (C) (D)
2. (A) (B) (C) (D)	35. (A) (B) (C) (D)	68. (A) (B) (C) (D)	101. (A) (B) (C) (D)
3. (A) (B) (C) (D)	36. (A) (B) (C) (D)	69. (A) (B) (C) (D)	102. (A) (B) (C) (D)
4. (A) (B) (C) (D)	37. (A) (B) (C) (D)	70. (A) (B) (C) (D)	103. (A) (B) (C) (D)
5. (A) (B) (C) (D)	38. (A) (B) (C) (D)	71. (A) (B) (C) (D)	104. (A) (B) (C) (D)
6. (A) (B) (C) (D)	39. (A) (B) (C) (D)	72. (A) (B) (C) (D)	105. (A) (B) (C) (D)
7. (A) (B) (C) (D)	40. (A) (B) (C) (D)	73. (A) (B) (C) (D)	106. (A) (B) (C) (D)
8. (A) (B) (C) (D)	41. (A) (B) (C) (D)	74. (A) (B) (C) (D)	107. (A) (B) (C) (D)
9. (A) (B) (C) (D)	42. (A) (B) (C) (D)	75. (A) (B) (C) (D)	108. (A) (B) (C) (D)
10. (A) (B) (C) (D)	43. (A) (B) (C) (D)	76. (A) (B) (C) (D)	109. (A) (B) (C) (D)
11. (A) (B) (C) (D)	44. (A) (B) (C) (D)	77. (A) (B) (C) (D)	110. (A) (B) (C) (D)
12. (A) (B) (C) (D)	45. (A) (B) (C) (D)	78. (A) (B) (C) (D)	111. (A) (B) (C) (D)
13. (A) (B) (C) (D)	46. (A) (B) (C) (D)	79. (A) (B) (C) (D)	112. (A) (B) (C) (D)
14. (A) (B) (C) (D)	47. (A) (B) (C) (D)	80. (A) (B) (C) (D)	113. (A) (B) (C) (D)
15. (A) (B) (C) (D)	48. (A) (B) (C) (D)	81. (A) (B) (C) (D)	114. (A) (B) (C) (D)
16. (A) (B) (C) (D)	49. (A) (B) (C) (D)	82. (A) (B) (C) (D)	115. (A) (B) (C) (D)
17. (A) (B) (C) (D)	50. (A) (B) (C) (D)	83. (A) (B) (C) (D)	116. (A) (B) (C) (D)
18. (A) (B) (C) (D)	51. (A) (B) (C) (D)	84. (A) (B) (C) (D)	117. (A) (B) (C) (D)
19. (A) (B) (C) (D)	52. (A) (B) (C) (D)	85. (A) (B) (C) (D)	118. (A) (B) (C) (D)
20. (A) (B) (C) (D)	53. (A) (B) (C) (D)	86. (A) (B) (C) (D)	119. (A) (B) (C) (D)
21. (A) (B) (C) (D)	54. (A) (B) (C) (D)	87. (A) (B) (C) (D)	120. (A) (B) (C) (D)
22. (A) (B) (C) (D)	55. (A) (B) (C) (D)	88. (A) (B) (C) (D)	121. (A) (B) (C) (D)
23. (A) (B) (C) (D)	56. (A) (B) (C) (D)	89. (A) (B) (C) (D)	122. (A) (B) (C) (D)
24. (A) (B) (C) (D)	57. (A) (B) (C) (D)	90. (A) (B) (C) (D)	123. (A) (B) (C) (D)
25. (A) (B) (C) (D)	58. (A) (B) (C) (D)	91. (A) (B) (C) (D)	124. (A) (B) (C) (D)
26. (A) (B) (C) (D)	59. (A) (B) (C) (D)	92. (A) (B) (C) (D)	125. (A) (B) (C) (D)
27. (A) (B) (C) (D)	60. (A) (B) (C) (D)	93. (A) (B) (C) (D)	126. (A) (B) (C) (D)
28. (A) (B) (C) (D)	61. (A) (B) (C) (D)	94. (A) (B) (C) (D)	127. (A) (B) (C) (D)
29. (A) (B) (C) (D)	62. (A) (B) (C) (D)	95. (A) (B) (C) (D)	128. (A) (B) (C) (D)
30. (A) (B) (C) (D)	63. (A) (B) (C) (D)	96. (A) (B) (C) (D)	129. (A) (B) (C) (D)
31. (A) (B) (C) (D)	64. (A) (B) (C) (D)	97. (A) (B) (C) (D)	130. (A) (B) (C) (D)
32. (A) (B) (C) (D)	65. (A) (B) (C) (D)	98. (A) (B) (C) (D)	
33. (A) (B) (C) (D)	66. (A) (B) (C) (D)	99. (A) (B) (C) (D)	

Directions: Each of the questions or statements is followed by four suggested answers or completions. Select the one that is best in each case.

Historical Population, 1994

Persons/sq km
- <2
- 2-10
- 11-40
- 41-100
- 101-500
- >500

1. In 1994, which continent had the least amount of people per square mile?

   (A) South America
   (B) North America
   (C) Australia
   (D) Asia

2. Which of the following is NOT true of mental maps?

   (A) Unnecessary details are left out
   (B) Includes an awareness that the destination or object exists
   (C) May include reference points
   (D) Applies reference points known by the population in general and is not specific to one person

3. Which contemporary conflict is an example of *irredentism*?

   (A) Kashmir
   (B) Kurds
   (C) Basques
   (D) Roma

4. From examining this *Resident Population of the United States* table on the next page, we can make the following observations about the resident population in the U.S. EXCEPT:

   (A) None of the states had a decrease in population from 1990–2000.
   (B) The U.S. population continued its trend of shifting its population from west to south.

Table T1. Resident Population of the United States, April 1, 2000 and April 1, 1990

Area	April 1, 2000	April 1, 1990	Numeric Change	Percent Change	State Rank as of April 1, 2000	State Rank as of April 1, 1990
Alabama	4,447,100	4,040,587	406,513	10.1	23	22
Alaska	626,932	550,043	76,889	14.0	48	49
Arizona	5,130,632	3,665,228	1,465,404	40.0	20	24
Arkansas	2,673,400	2,350,725	322,675	13.7	33	33
California	33,871,648	29,760,021	4,111,627	13.8	1	1
Colorado	4,301,261	3,294,394	1,006,867	30.6	24	26
Connecticut	3,405,565	3,287,116	118,449	3.6	29	27
Delaware	783,600	666,168	117,432	17.6	45	46
District of Columbia	572,059	606,900	-34,841	-5.7	(NA)	(NA)
Florida	15,982,378	12,937,926	3,044,452	23.5	4	4
Georgia	8,186,453	6,478,216	1,708,237	26.4	10	11
Hawaii	1,211,537	1,108,229	103,308	9.3	42	41
Idaho	1,293,953	1,006,749	287,204	28.5	39	42
Illinois	12,419,293	11,430,602	988,691	8.6	5	6
Indiana	6,080,485	5,544,159	536,326	9.7	14	14
Iowa	2,926,324	2,776,755	149,569	5.4	30	30
Kansas	2,688,418	2,477,574	210,844	8.5	32	32
Kentucky	4,041,769	3,685,296	356,473	9.7	25	23
Louisiana	4,468,976	4,219,973	249,003	5.9	22	21
Maine	1,274,923	1,227,928	46,995	3.8	40	38
Maryland	5,296,486	4,781,468	515,018	10.8	19	19
Massachusetts	6,349,097	6,016,425	332,672	5.5	13	13
Michigan	9,938,444	9,295,297	643,147	6.9	8	8
Minnesota	4,919,479	4,375,099	544,380	12.4	21	20
Mississippi	2,844,658	2,573,216	271,442	10.5	31	31
Missouri	5,595,211	5,117,073	478,138	9.3	17	15
Montana	902,195	799,065	103,130	12.9	44	44
Nebraska	1,711,263	1,578,385	132,878	8.4	38	36
Nevada	1,998,257	1,201,833	796,424	66.3	35	39
New Hampshire	1,235,786	1,109,252	126,534	11.4	41	40
New Jersey	8,414,350	7,730,188	684,162	8.9	9	9
New Mexico	1,819,046	1,515,069	303,977	20.1	36	37
New York	18,976,457	17,990,455	986,002	5.5	3	2
North Carolina	8,049,313	6,628,637	1,420,676	21.4	11	10
North Dakota	642,200	638,800	3,400	0.5	47	47
Ohio	11,353,140	10,847,115	506,025	4.7	7	7
Oklahoma	3,450,654	3,145,585	305,069	9.7	27	28
Oregon	3,421,399	2,842,321	579,078	20.4	28	29
Pennsylvania	12,281,054	11,881,643	399,411	3.4	6	5
Rhode Island	1,048,319	1,003,464	44,855	4.5	43	43
South Carolina	4,012,012	3,486,703	525,309	15.1	26	25
South Dakota	754,844	696,004	58,840	8.5	46	45
Tennessee	5,689,283	4,877,185	812,098	16.7	16	17
Texas	20,851,820	16,986,510	3,865,310	22.8	2	3
Utah	2,233,169	1,722,850	510,319	29.6	34	35
Vermont	608,827	562,758	46,069	8.2	49	48
Virginia	7,078,515	6,187,358	891,157	14.4	12	12
Washington	5,894,121	4,866,692	1,027,429	21.1	15	18
West Virginia	1,808,344	1,793,477	14,867	0.8	37	34
Wisconsin	5,363,675	4,891,769	471,906	9.6	18	16
Wyoming	493,782	453,588	40,194	8.9	50	50
Total Resident Population[1]	281,421,906	248,709,873	32,712,033	13.2	(NA)	(NA)
Northeast	53,594,378	50,809,229	2,785,149	5.5	(NA)	(NA)
Midwest	64,392,776	59,668,632	4,724,144	7.9	(NA)	(NA)
South	100,236,820	85,445,930	14,790,890	17.3	(NA)	(NA)
West	63,197,932	52,786,082	10,411,850	19.7	(NA)	(NA)
Puerto Rico	3,808,610	3,522,037	286,573	8.1	(NA)	(NA)
Total Resident Population Including Puerto Rico	285,230,516	252,231,910	32,998,606	13.1	(NA)	(NA)

[1] Includes the population of the 50 states and the District of Columbia.

Source: U.S. Department of Commerce, U.S. Census Bureau

NA: Not Applicable

(C) The states with the largest percent increase are located in the West.

(D) The states with the largest percent increase are located in the South.

5. The biosphere consists of these three interrelated parts:

(A) parts of the troposphere, hydrosphere, and geosphere where life does not exist

(B) troposphere, hydrosphere, and lithosphere where life exists

(C) troposphere, atmosphere, where life does not exist, and geosphere

(D) geosphere, where life does not exist, atmosphere, and lithosphere

6. Of the following people, who is BEST known for the Montgomery bus boycott?

(A) Martin Luther

(B) Ella Baker

(C) Rosa Parks

(D) Bobby Seale

7. Which of the following is NOT true of ecosystems?

(A) Everything in an ecosystem is interconnected.

(B) Any intrusion in an ecosystem has repercussions elsewhere in the system.

(C) Ecosystems can only exist on a large scale that allows each ecosystem to act independently of one another.

(D) Ecosystems are communities of life forms within a physical environment.

8. Which of the following are examples of human influence on the ecosystem?

I. Cutting of forests has resulted in erosion and flooding

II. Untreated sewage and runoffs lead to water pollution.

III. Nuclear plant waste leading to thermal pollution.

IV. Farming has exposed soil to the weather, promoting erosion and the loss of topsoil.

(A) I, II, and III only

(B) II, III, and IV only

(C) I, III, and IV only

(D) I, II, III, and IV

9. Which of these natural resources is nonrenewable?

(A) Water

(B) Coal

(C) Trees

(D) Animals

10. When one area of urban land generates more rent than others, what is the likely pattern that results in terms of land use?

(A) Use of the land always increases.

(B) Buyers who can pay the highest rent will be able to buy the land that generates the highest return.

(C) The land use will likely not produce a high return.

(D) Production efforts will largely decrease.

11. What sort of migration factor is best defined as conditions in a place that are perceived to be detrimental to a migrant's well-being or security?

(A) Counter-migration factor

(B) Hierarchical migration factor

(C) Push factors

(D) Pull factors

12. Which of the following is NOT one of the chief accomplishments of genetically modified crops, like soybeans, corn, transgenic cotton, and canola?

(A) Herbicide resistance

(B) Insect resistance

(C) Increases in productivity

(D) Increase in cost of crops

13. Which of the following is NOT part of the definition of the term "globalization"?

(A) The elements of the highly integrated global economy

(B) The ancient tradition of buying and selling across great distances

(C) How regional economies, societies, and cultures have become integrated through a global network of political ideas through communication, transportation, and trade

(D) The internet

Use the map below to answer questions 14 through 16.

14. Based on the information in the legend, which city is the state capital?

(A) Tampa
(B) Tallahassee
(C) Orlando
(D) Miami

15. According to the map, the northernmost city on the west coast of Florida is

(A) St. Petersburg.
(B) Naples.

(C) Pensacola.
(D) Tallahassee.

16. What bodies of water are noted on the map?

(A) Lake Okeechobee and the Suwannee River

(B) Tampa Bay and the Florida Keys

(C) Gulf of Mexico, Atlantic Ocean, Lake Okeechobee, and the Suwannee River

(D) Everglades National Park

17. The figure below tells us what about the Four Stages of Demographic Transition?

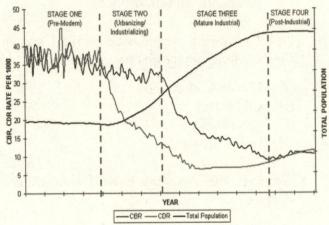

I. That Stage One is characterized by a balance between birth and death rates.

II. That Stage Two had a decline in death rates largely due to factors like an improvement in food supply and public health.

III. That Stage Four is characterized by stability

IV. That over time, the birth rate and death rate are about the same.

(A) I, IV & III only
(B) IV only
(C) II, III & IV only
(D) I, II & III only

18. Use the map below to answer the question.

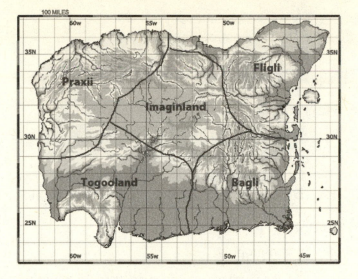

    Which of the following is NOT a problem of Imaginland being landlocked?

    (A) Cannot trade with overseas markets
    (B) Has to arrange to use a foreign country's ports
    (C) Little control over transport outside of its borders
    (D) Not able to provide air flight

19. If a country wants to prevent its exchange rate from rising, the government could

    (A) buy its own currency.
    (B) sell its own currency.
    (C) buy bonds.
    (D) sell treasury bonds.

20. Economics focuses on three basic questions. Which of the following is NOT one of them?

    (A) What to produce?
    (B) For whom to produce?
    (C) How to produce?
    (D) Who profits from the sale of goods and services?

21. If I decide to relax over the summer and play golf instead of teaching at Juvenile Jail, which is open year-round, economics calls the money I do not earn

    (A) 25 percent of my pay.
    (B) the cost of a vacation.
    (C) the opportunity cost.
    (D) the payment for playtime.

22. The essence of a market economy is

    (A) excellent planning.
    (B) freedom.
    (C) capitalism.
    (D) supply and demand.

23. A market economy relies on _____ to allocate resources.

    (A) government
    (B) good planning
    (C) market forces
    (D) small businesses

24. An example of a country with a planned economy is

    (A) Germany.
    (B) France.
    (C) China.
    (D) Australia.

25. Resources that are readily abundant are considered

    (A) free goods.
    (B) worthless.
    (C) priceless.
    (D) scarce.

26. Which of the following is NOT an example of a scarce resource?

    (A) Oil
    (B) Coal
    (C) Clean water
    (D) Carbon dioxide

27. Scarcity is maintained by

    (A) demand.
    (B) supply.
    (C) diamond cartels.
    (D) business owners.

28. What are considered the factors of production in economics?

    (A) Location, location, location
    (B) Land, labor, capital, and entrepreneurship
    (C) Land, money, and labor
    (D) Money, motivation, and action

29. Quotas, license fees, and subsidies are part of

    (A) a market economy.
    (B) a communist society.
    (C) the free enterprise system.
    (D) a planned economy.

30. Macroeconomics studies the elements of economics on the

    (A) business level.
    (B) national level.
    (C) family level.
    (D) government level.

31. Microeconomics is the study of the economic behavior of

    (A) small economic groups such as firms and families.
    (B) the nation.
    (C) the individual.
    (D) the government.

32. Which of the following businesses has the highest barrier to entry?

    (A) Lemonade stand
    (B) Sporting goods shop
    (C) Farm
    (D) Automobile factory

33. Which is the best way to describe the GNP?

    (A) Greater national production
    (B) Total national production
    (C) Total goods and services
    (D) Government natural production

34. Perfect competition for the most part is

    (A) a theoretical extreme.
    (B) found in the United States.
    (C) the same as oligopoly.
    (D) a primary component of planned economies.

35. In a monopoly,

    (A) consumers can be sure they are paying a fair price.
    (B) the firm is equal to an industry.
    (C) there are multiple sellers protected by government regulation.
    (D) competition drives down prices.

36. Which of the following is an example of *monopolistic competition*?

    (A) The film industry
    (B) Agriculture
    (C) Public education
    (D) The automotive industry

37. An oligopoly is

    (A) a market form in which a market or industry is dominated by a small number of sellers.
    (B) a government with a king or queen.
    (C) a market form with a large number of sellers guaranteeing the lowest price.
    (D) great for consumers.

38. Which of the following documents embodies the ideals of individual freedom so commonly associated with the United States?

    (A) The Declaration of Independence
    (B) The Constitution

(C) The Articles of Confection
(D) Both (A) and (B)

39. What are civil liberties?

(A) fundamental individual rights given to all citizens by law
(B) human rights
(C) natural rights
(D) Both (B) and (C)

40. Which of the following issues did NOT cause conflict among the framers of the Constitution?

(A) Slavery
(B) Power of the president
(C) Large versus small states
(D) Checks and balances

41. Why did the framers of the Constitution design the system of checks and balances?

(A) To maintain parity of power between the branches of government
(B) To minimize foreign intervention
(C) To help maintain the financial stability of the new government
(D) To set the foundation for a national bank

42. Which of the following topics does NOT fall within the scope of political science?

(A) Structure of government
(B) Political institutions
(C) Politics
(D) Social diversity

43. Article 1 of the U.S. Constitution creates

(A) a bicameral legislature.
(B) a unicameral legislature.
(C) the presidency.
(D) the judicial branch.

44. Which of the following statements about the legislative branch is NOT true?

(A) Senate members were originally chosen by the state legislatures.
(B) The House was granted some exclusive powers such as the power to initiate revenue bills and impeach officials.
(C) The Constitution provides that the approval of both houses is necessary for the passage of legislation.
(D) Both the House and the Senate must confirm Supreme Court nominees.

45. Which of the following criteria is NOT a requirement to be the president of the United States?

(A) Over 35 years old
(B) Natural-born U.S. citizen
(C) U.S. resident for at least 14 years
(D) Military service

46. For what length of term are federal judges appointed?

(A) 6 years
(B) 1 year, renewable annually
(C) Life
(D) 10 years

47. Thomas Hobbes views the social contract primarily as a means of

(A) maintaining order to escape the violent chaos of nature.
(B) preventing an absolute ruler from taking power.
(C) continually revising the process of helping the people gain power.
(D) correcting inequality in a society.

48. Which one of these is NOT a metaphor for a type of social power?

    (A) Power of the pen
    (B) Power of the purse
    (C) Power of the sword
    (D) Power of the heavens

49. How does the U.S. Constitution provide for political parties?

    (A) Political parties are considered viable if they are on ballots in two-thirds of the states.
    (B) The United States' bicameral system is set up for two parties.
    (C) Political parties are not mentioned in the Constitution.
    (D) Political parties are mentioned as an area of state authority.

50. Which of the following actions are primarily the responsibilities of the states?

    (A) Ensuring public safety, administering and certifying elections, and recording birth and death certificates
    (B) Regulating interstate commerce as well as television and radio
    (C) Regulating immigration and naturalization
    (D) Providing for national defense and creating money

51. How are local governments chartered?

    (A) A local government is chartered according to its state's constitution.
    (B) Local governments apply to the federal government for a charter.
    (C) States are divided into counties, and local governments are authorized by the counties.
    (D) Local governments simply write a constitution and notify the next largest government entity of their existence.

52. Which of the following best defines *realism* in the context of international relations?

    (A) Nations cooperate for the sake of their common interests.
    (B) Nation-states are the basic governmental unit and there is no authority above individual nations.
    (C) Real authority is found in the United Nations.
    (D) People are the real authority for all governments.

53. Government by the many is called

    (A) democracy.
    (B) oligarchy.
    (C) monarchy.
    (D) liberalism.

54. Which of the following terms is closely related to *autocracy*?

    (A) Democracy
    (B) Capitalism
    (C) Despotism
    (D) Theocracy

55. The modern democratic state in which the people do NOT take a direct role in legislating or governing, but elect representatives to express their views and wants, is called a

    (A) republic.
    (B) liberalist state.
    (C) constitutional monarchy.
    (D) totalitarian state.

56. Which article of the U.S. Bill of Rights states in part that "Congress shall make no law respecting an establishment of religion?"

    (A) Amendment 14
    (B) Amendment 5
    (C) Amendment 1
    (D) Amendment 10

57. Reaganomics is most closely associated with

(A) the "trickle-down" theory.
(B) the "controlled growth" theory.
(C) the "bubble up" theory.
(D) New Deal reform economics.

58. The Reign of Terror ended when

(A) Napoleon took over the Committee on Public Safety.
(B) crowds of Parisians stormed the Bastille and released its prisoners.
(C) members of the Convention, afraid that Robespierre would turn on them, had him arrested.
(D) Marie Antoinette was guillotined.

59. What was the first major stronghold in North America during the period of colonialism?

(A) New Amsterdam
(B) The Massachusetts Bay Colony
(C) Louisiana
(D) New South Wales

60. Which of the following is NOT considered one of the devastating effects of colonialism on the native populations of Africa and the Americas?

(A) Settlement brought European diseases to the populations of other continents.
(B) Mercantile trade flourished in the New World.
(C) Procurement of African slaves became an industry unto itself.
(D) Native American populations were eventually decimated.

61. Which religious group came to America fleeing persecution, but fined, whipped, banished, and imprisoned anyone who did not conform to their beliefs?

(A) Quakers
(B) Amish

(C) Puritans
(D) Roman Catholics

62. Which of the following groups were NOT among the settlers of Jamestown?

(A) Artisans
(B) Soldiers
(C) Surgeons
(D) Slaves

63. Which of the following did NOT characterize northern urban areas from 1820 to 1860?

(A) Lacked adequate taxing power to provide services for all of its residents
(B) Developed elaborate system of municipal services
(C) Creation of transportation lines
(D) Creation of seaport cities

64. What proposal did President Woodrow Wilson make in 1918 that convinced the Germans they would be treated fairly if they surrendered?

(A) The Versailles Proposals
(B) The Fourteen Points
(C) The Balfour Declaration
(D) The "New Freedom" Policy

65. Which of the following New Deal programs was designed to reduce unemployment?

I. The Public Works Administration
II. National Industrial Recovery Act
III. Glass-Steagall Act
IV. The Works Project Administration
V. Social Security Act

(A) I, III, and V only
(B) II and V only
(C) III, IV, and V only
(D) I and IV only

421

66. All of the following played a role in the Cold War EXCEPT

    (A) military coalitions.
    (B) espionage.
    (C) the space race.
    (D) mercantilism.

67. All of the following facilitated the Industrial Revolution in 18th-century Britain EXCEPT

    (A) its navy and merchant fleet, the most powerful and largest in the world, could bring in raw materials and send finished goods around the world.
    (B) colonial markets who would provide raw materials and would buy British manufactured goods.
    (C) foreign investment in Britain helped nurture certain industries.
    (D) Parliament passed laws that supported and protected British business so it could compete successfully against other countries.

68. In 1764, the British for the first time imposed a series of taxes designed specifically to raise revenue from the colonies. What was this series of taxes called?

    (A) The Sugar Act
    (B) The Stamp Act
    (C) The Quartering Act
    (D) The Tea Act

69. Which of the following does NOT apply to the Sons of Liberty?

    (A) Resorted to coercion to force stamp agents to resign their posts
    (B) Were prominent citizens
    (C) Had chapters throughout the colonies
    (D) Publicly proclaimed their membership to all

70. Which of the following is NOT a correct statement regarding the Vietnam War?

    (A) More than 58,000 Americans were killed.
    (B) The war is considered the longest military conflict in U.S. history, lasting from 1959 to 1975.
    (C) The United States fought the North Vietnamese with no assistance from allies.
    (D) More than 3 million Vietnamese were killed.

71. What is the "digital divide"?

    (A) The differences in communities and nations of their access to the Internet and other information and communication technologies during the Information Age
    (B) The disagreement between PC and Apple computer advocates
    (C) The division in society between those who use analog or digital televisions
    (D) The poorer sections of Silicon Valley who felt left out by the economic boom of the Clinton years

72. Which of these were NOT a group that switched its party affiliation to support Roosevelt's New Deal platform in the 1936 election?

    (A) African Americans
    (B) Jews
    (C) Labor Union Members
    (D) Cuban immigrants

73. The Articles of Confederation was the first governing document, or constitution, of the United States. Which of the following was among its major deficiencies?

    (A) It lacked taxing authority for the central government.
    (B) It established only the Senate to represent the citizens.
    (C) The Articles did not establish a president.
    (D) There was no writ of habeas corpus.

74. Which of the following is NOT true of the Federalist Papers?

    (A) They consisted of 85 essays.
    (B) They serve as a primary source for interpretation of the Constitution.
    (C) Each of the essay authors was also a signer of the Declaration of Independence.
    (D) The authors wanted to both influence the vote in favor of ratification and shape future interpretations of the Constitution.

75. Which of the following statements is NOT true with regard to *Manifest Destiny*?

    (A) It was a doctrine used to rationalize U.S. territorial expansion.
    (B) The phrase was coined by the U.S. journalist John L. O'Sullivan.
    (C) It was a doctrine initially used as the rationale for annexing Mexican and Indian land in Texas and the Southwest.
    (D) It was a doctrine used to remove the Spanish from Florida.

76. The Northwest Ordinance of 1787 did which of the following?

    (A) Set out a process by which new states formed by new territories could become part of the United States
    (B) Made it clear that original states would always have more power and authority than new states
    (C) Provided for immediate election of government officials in new territories
    (D) Counted all citizens as equal

77. Which of the following did NOT characterize Reaganomics?

    (A) Based on supply-side economics, tax cuts would create economic growth
    (B) Argued that U.S. economic woes were the result of government intrusion in the free market
    (C) Sought to unshackle the free enterprise system by eliminating handouts, high-taxes, and government itself
    (D) Eliminated tax cuts for the wealthy thinking that the money the government earned from getting rid of tax cuts would "trickle down"

78. Which of the following was NOT a factor during the antebellum period?

    (A) Sectional differences created friction between the North and South.
    (B) Massive foreign immigration from Ireland and Germany greatly increased the size of cities in the North.
    (C) Congress struggled with the issue of whether to allow slavery in the western territories.
    (D) Subsistence agriculture replaced commercial agriculture.

79. Which term describes a mechanism in international relations to prevent any one side from gaining dominance?

    (A) Social Contract
    (B) Balance of Power
    (C) Detente
    (D) Equal representation under the law

80. Which of the following was an almost perfect crop for the lower South, because it was easy to grow and well-suited to the region's climate and soil?

    (A) Corn
    (B) Cotton
    (C) Wheat
    (D) Cattle

81. How many lives were lost during the American Civil War?

    (A) More than 600,000
    (B) Less than 500,000
    (C) About 300,000
    (D) 198,300

82. Which of the following states was NOT among the first seven states to secede from the Union, leading to the Civil War?

   (A) Florida
   (B) Alabama
   (C) North Carolina
   (D) Texas

83. Who was president of the United States when the first states seceded from the Union?

   (A) Abraham Lincoln
   (B) James Buchanan
   (C) Robert E. Lee
   (D) Jefferson Davis

84. Who was the first president of the Confederacy?

   (A) Abraham Lincoln
   (B) James Buchanan
   (C) Robert E. Lee
   (D) Jefferson Davis

85. Which of the following was NOT considered a strength of the Union side during the Civil War?

   (A) The Union had vastly superior sea power.
   (B) Britain never formally recognized the Confederacy.
   (C) The Emancipation Proclamation won popular support for the Union in England and France.
   (D) The Union army had an unlimited supply of funds.

86. After the North defeated the South in the Civil War, politicians faced the task of putting the divided country back together. What legislative action made former slaves citizens?

   (A) The Reconstruction Acts of 1867
   (B) The Fourteenth Amendment
   (C) The Fifteenth Amendment
   (D) Individual state laws

87. The policy promoted by Theodore Roosevelt and most explicitly pursued in Central America was the

   (A) "New Deal" policy.
   (B) "Fair Deal" policy.
   (C) "Big Stick" policy.
   (D) "Square Deal" policy.

88. Rudyard Kipling's "white man's burden" referred to

   (A) the high costs of maintaining colonial rule.
   (B) the difficulties white men faced when dealing with sun exposure while in foreign lands.
   (C) the inequities that capitalism imposes on society
   (D) the white man's duty to help the people of Africa, Asia, and Latin America.

89. Which of the following is NOT one of Lenin's contributions to Marxism?

   (A) His analysis of imperialism
   (B) His analysis of the racial divide in Russia
   (C) His concept of a revolutionary party as a disciplined unit
   (D) His critique of monarchy

90. Whose assassination ignited the final spark that plunged Europe into World War I?

   (A) Tsar Nicholas II
   (B) Tsar Alexander III
   (C) Archduke Franz Ferdinand
   (D) President Garfield

91. Hitler gained support because of all of the following reasons EXCEPT

   (A) he promised an end to Germany's misfortunes by creating a German Reich, or empire, that would endure for thousands of years.
   (B) German's parliamentary system was considered corrupt and ineffective.

(C) key people in the army and big business felt they could control him.

(D) Germans were attracted to his pledge to exterminate European Jewry as a "final solution" to Germany's problems.

92. Whose writings have inspired radical Islamic movements to turn to violence in order to achieve their aims?

(A) Sayyid Qutb
(B) Muhammad Abduh
(C) Qasim Amin
(D) Jamal al-Din al-Afghani

93. Slobodan Milosevic's plan that increased feelings of separatism and launched civil war in Yugoslavia was known as

(A) Croatia.
(B) EEU.
(C) Slavic Unity Movement.
(D) Greater Serbia.

94. What has historically been the most important factor enabling societies to keep abreast of the latest technology?

(A) Setting up a patronage system for scholars within one's own country
(B) Developing an education system focused on improving math scores
(C) Having access to the Internet
(D) Participation in global trade and communications networks

95. The Greeks considered the Trojan War as the first moment in history when

(A) they came together as one people with a common purpose.
(B) their true weaknesses as a military power were exposed.
(C) they were embarrassed by the affluent nature of their society.
(D) they lost their access to the sea.

96. Mary I of England earned the nickname _____ because of her merciless executions.

(A) Mary Queen of Scots
(B) Bloody Mary
(C) Virgin Queen
(D) Defender of the Faith

97. Rome was at first ruled by kings. Then, about 500 BCE, the Roman Republic was established, with two annually elected consuls at its head, guided by a senate. What form of government followed next?

(A) Rome was ruled by the consuls and senate until its ultimate fall.
(B) Rome was ruled by a succession of emperors.
(C) Egypt conquered Rome and Egyptian Pharoahs ruled.
(D) Christianity forced the pope into the ultimate authority.

98. The schism that split the Muslim community initially resulted because of

(A) the use of jihad to expand the community.
(B) tribal warfare between the Quraysh and the Umayyads.
(C) who would be best to lead the Muslim community after the death of the Prophet.
(D) differences in opinion over how to include mawalis in the community.

99. Which of the following is the great emperor from Mali who spent so much money during a visit to Egypt that it caused terrible inflation?

(A) Sundiata
(B) Songhai
(C) Mansa Musa
(D) Timbuktu

100. Mussolini's Italy, Stalin's Soviet Union, and Hitler's Germany are all examples of what type of government?

    (A) Republican
    (B) Communist
    (C) Totalitarian
    (D) Socialist

101. Advocates of nationalism in the nineteenth century believed all of the following EXCEPT

    (A) that the national state must have boundaries.
    (B) that members of their national communities had a common destiny that could best be reached by organizing independent nation-states.
    (C) that religion is the primary means of organizing the nation-state.
    (D) that the nation must be the focus of political unity.

102. What first prompted the emergence of America as a "world power"?

    (A) The Spanish-American War and the acquisition of the Philippines
    (B) The War of 1812
    (C) The American Revolution
    (D) The Emancipation Proclamation

103. After the Battle of Buxor, this limited liability company changed from being a private company to being a regional power with responsibilities of tax collecting, administering justice, and providing security.

    (A) Tata Steel
    (B) The British East India Company
    (C) Halliburton
    (D) Dutch East India Company

104. Which of the following is NOT a similarity that women in the age of the Renaissance and Enlightenment shared across England, Spain, and Mughal India?

    (A) Inherited less than sons or brothers
    (B) Had few rights in the legal sphere
    (C) Lacked the right to initiate divorce
    (D) Legally considered property of their husbands

105. What was the focus of Mayan cities?

    (A) Ceremonial centers
    (B) Governmental headquarters
    (C) Central marketplaces
    (D) Festivals and celebrations

106. Which of the following statements is NOT true of the Silk Road?

    (A) The Silk Road was not a trade route that existed solely for the purpose of trading in silk; many other commodities were also traded.
    (B) The Silk Road followed a single route, allowing for much more security and larger trading posts.
    (C) The movement of people along the Silk Road correlates with the movement of religion and development of languages.
    (D) Gold and ivory and even exotic animals and plants were traded on the Silk Road.

107. Which of the following happened in African society from the forced migration of African males?

    (A) Created a slave market that dealt in untended women
    (B) Increase in polygamy and multiple marriages
    (C) Decreased instances of female infanticide
    (D) Created new, matrilineal societies in Africa.

108. Which war demonstrated to OPEC that it not only shared economic, but also political, co-operation?

    (A) Arab-Israeli War of 1973
    (B) Suez Crisis
    (C) War of 1967
    (D) Iranian Revolution of 1979

109. Which of the following did NOT occur during the Renaissance?

    (A) The revival of learning based on classical sources
    (B) The decline of courtly and papal patronage
    (C) The development of perspective in painting
    (D) Advancements in science

110. Effects of industrialization reflected a change in demographic transition because of all of the following EXCEPT

    (A) that fertility began a marked decline due to contraception practices.
    (B) demographic stability in the long term.
    (C) that there was an increase in female infanticide in rural areas.
    (D) declining birthrates led to lower population growth.

111. Which of the following choices is an incorrect association of historical period and date?

    (A) The Renaissance: an era spanning the fourteenth through the seventeenth century
    (B) The Carolingian Renaissance: a period in the late eighth and ninth centuries
    (C) The Protestant Reformation: a movement in the twelfth century
    (D) The Age of Enlightenment: a time of intellectual and philosophical change in eighteenth-century Europe and America

112. The city-state of Sparta was characterized by

    (A) democratic institutions.
    (B) an emphasis on temple worship.
    (C) an emphasis on warfare.
    (D) dependence upon the sea.

113. The Battle of Salamis was significant because it

    (A) finally exacted revenge for Darius's defeat in Athens.
    (B) made a small force of Spartans martyrs for the Greek cause.
    (C) marked the first time the Spartans and Athenians cooperated in battle.
    (D) stranded the Persian army in Greece without naval support.

114. How did the nature of colonialism change in the seventeenth century?

    (A) European nations became dependent on the trade and resources of their New World colonies.
    (B) Europeans developed a desire to conquer the known world.
    (C) Explorers developed a desire to find the end of the earth.
    (D) Many colonies declared their independence.

115. Which of the following were NOT effects of the Columbian Exchange?

    (A) Diseases like smallpox killed millions of Native Americans.
    (B) The introduction of beasts of burden, like horses, provided Americans with a new source of labor and transportation.
    (C) Nutritional benefits to the population helped people live longer.
    (D) It led to the introduction of antibiotics to the European population.

116. Mehmed the Conqueror's 1453 capture of Constantinople was significant to the history of slavery in that it

    (A) ignited the sale of slaves from the Indies to Europe.
    (B) made Europeans turn to sub-Saharan Africa for slaves.
    (C) introduced the idea of slavery to Europe.
    (D) stopped the use of Balkan boys from being used as slaves for the Ottomans.

117. An analysis of immigration's effect on the Austin, Texas school system's clean water supply and social service programs demonstrates

    (A) the interrelationships between social science disciplines.
    (B) the challenges of a major city.
    (C) a fact of life in modern America.
    (D) the need for immigration legislation.

118. The research method which involves a social scientist living among and interacting with the people being studied is known as

    (A) strategic engagement.
    (B) experimentation.
    (C) content analysis.
    (D) participant observation.

119. What is the definition of *sociology*?

    (A) The science of humankind
    (B) The study of how individuals become members of and move between groups, and how being in different groups affects individuals and the groups in which they participate
    (C) The study of the earth and its features
    (D) The study of the interpretation of the past and how it affects our view of the present

120. Which of the following is NOT an example of a social network?

    (A) A church congregation
    (B) A university
    (C) A family
    (D) A party planner

121. *Ethnography* is

    (A) the study of the cultures of prehistoric peoples.
    (B) the systematic description of a human society.
    (C) the interpretive explanation of human behavior.
    (D) the study of human groups, with a particular emphasis on social culture.

122. Which of the following is NOT an example of a social issue?

    (A) How to address poverty
    (B) Whether birth control is taught in schools
    (C) Whether evolution is taught in schools
    (D) How to balance a checkbook

123. Which scholar below may be best associated with human development?

    (A) Jean Piaget
    (B) Albert Einstein
    (C) John Stewart Gardner
    (D) John Dewey

124. Which of the following is NOT a characteristic of human populations?

    (A) Death
    (B) Marriage and divorce
    (C) Athletic interests
    (D) Migration

125. The War Powers Resolution of 1973 may be invoked by Congress to accomplish which of the following?

    (A) Prevent the president from deploying troops abroad
    (B) Declare war
    (C) Force the extradition of foreign ambassadors caught spying in the United States
    (D) Limit the period for which the president may deploy troops abroad in hostile situations

126. The term *socialization* is used by sociologists, social psychologists, and educators to refer to

    (A) the process of learning one's culture and how to live within it.
    (B) finding a date at a party.
    (C) the ability of people to find friendships or relationships.
    (D) humankind's unique pattern of marriage compared to other mammals.

127. Cultural anthropologists systematically compare similar cultures. What is this process called?

    (A) Social networking
    (B) Cultural mapping
    (C) Ethnology
    (D) Mixed method analysis

128. Which of the following is most closely associated with social psychologists?

    (A) Quantitative research
    (B) Qualitative research
    (C) Talk therapy
    (D) Group therapy

129. The term *multicultural diversity* generally does NOT include

    (A) race.
    (B) culture.
    (C) ethnicity.
    (D) class.

130. In psychology, perception is

    (A) the process of attaining awareness or understanding of sensory information.
    (B) reality.
    (C) one's point of view.
    (D) a social issue.

Praxis Social Studies Assessment 0081

Answer Explanations for Practice Test 1

Question Number	Answer	Category	Question Number	Answer	Category
1	C	Geography	39	A	Political Science
2	D	Geography	40	D	Political Science
3	A	Political Science	41	A	Political Science
4	D	Geography	42	D	Political Science
5	B	Geography	43	A	Political Science
6	C	U.S. History	44	D	Political Science
7	C	Geography	45	D	Political Science
8	D	Geography	46	C	Political Science
9	B	Geography	47	A	Political Science
10	B	Geography	48	D	Political Science
11	C	Geography	49	C	Political Science
12	D	Geography	50	A	Political Science
13	D	Geography	51	A	Political Science
14	B	Geography	52	B	Political Science
15	C	Geography	53	A	Political Science
16	C	Geography	54	C	Political Science
17	D	Geography	55	A	Political Science
18	D	Geography	56	C	Political Science
19	B	Economics	57	A	Economics
20	D	Economics	58	C	World History
21	C	Economics	59	B	U.S. History
22	B	Economics	60	B	U.S. History
23	C	Economics	61	C	U.S. History
24	C	Economics	62	D	U.S. History
25	A	Economics	63	D	U.S. History
26	D	Economics	64	B	U.S. History
27	A	Economics	65	D	U.S. History
28	B	Economics	66	D	U.S. History
29	D	Economics	67	C	World History
30	B	Economics	68	A	U.S. History
31	A	Economics	69	D	U.S. History
32	D	Economics	70	C	U.S. History
33	C	Economics	71	A	U.S. History
34	A	Economics	72	D	U.S. History
35	B	Economics	73	A	U.S. History
36	A	Economics	74	C	U.S. History
37	A	Economics	75	D	U.S. History
38	D	Political Science	76	A	U.S. History

Question Number	Answer	Category
77	D	U.S. History
78	D	U.S. History
79	B	U.S. History
80	B	U.S. History
81	A	U.S. History
82	C	U.S. History
83	B	U.S. History
84	D	U.S. History
85	D	U.S. History
86	B	U.S. History
87	C	U.S. History
88	D	World History
89	B	World History
90	C	World History
91	D	World History
92	A	World History
93	D	World History
94	D	World History
95	A	World History
96	B	World History
97	B	World History
98	C	World History
99	C	World History
100	C	World History
101	C	World History
102	A	World History
103	B	World History
104	C	World History
105	A	World History
106	B	World History
107	B	World History
108	A	World History
109	B	World History
110	D	World History
111	C	World History
112	C	World History
113	D	World History
114	A	World History

Question Number	Answer	Category
115	D	World History
116	B	World History
117	A	Behavioral Sciences
118	D	Behavioral Sciences
119	B	Behavioral Sciences
120	D	Behavioral Sciences
121	B	Behavioral Sciences
122	D	Behavioral Sciences
123	A	Behavioral Sciences
124	C	Behavioral Sciences
125	D	Political Science
126	A	Behavioral Sciences
127	C	Behavioral Sciences
128	A	Behavioral Sciences
129	D	Behavioral Sciences
130	A	Behavioral Sciences

PRACTICE TEST 1 (0081): DETAILED EXPLANATIONS OF ANSWERS

1. (C)

Using the legend to the left of the map, we see that Australia has the least amount of people per square mile.

2. (D)

Mental maps are used whenever individuals think about a place or how to get to a place. They are highly personal and idiosyncratic and usually contain both objective knowledge and subjective projections.

3. (A)

Irredentism (Italian for "unredeemed") is an attempt by existing states to annex territories of another state. The Kurd, Basque, and Roma conflicts are from stateless entities, so therefore they are not examples of irredentism.

4. (D)

By glancing through the source, we can see that none of the states had a decrease in population and that the population continued to shift from west to south, with the west having the largest percentage increase in population. While the South had the largest numeric increase, it did not have the largest percentage.

5. (B)

The biosphere consists of these three interrelated parts:

(1) the troposphere, which is the lowest layer of the earth's atmosphere;

(2) the hydrosphere, which includes all of the waters, both on the surface and subsurface;

(3) lithosphere, which contains all of the soils that support plant life, the minerals that plants and animals use, and the fossil fuels and ores that humans use for energy.

The geosphere is the earth's mantle and core, and is only a part of the biosphere if life is also present.

6. (C)

On December 1, 1955, Rosa Parks, an African-American woman, refused to give up her seat to a white man on a bus in Montgomery, Alabama. Her arrest prompted a city bus boycott by African Americans which by all accounts began the civil rights movement and launched the career of the Reverend Martin Luther King, Jr., as a prominent leader. Ella Baker (B) was a central activist in that movement, working beside Dr. King for over 25 years. Choice (A) is incorrect because Martin Luther was the leader of the Protestant Reformation in the 16th century. Bobby Seale (D) was the founder, chairman and organizer of the Black Panther movement of the 1960s.

7. (C)

Ecosystems can vary in size and shape, and while they can be self-sustaining units of all the organisms and physical features that exist together in a particular area, they are interconnected. When there is a disruption in one part of an ecosystem, it has an effect on the other parts.

8. (D)

Human influence on the ecosystem has been tremendous. Humans have significantly altered natural processes like soil generation, the water cycle, waste removal, energy, and nutrient recycling.

9. (B)

Non-renewable resources are those which are found in fixed amounts and usually are found in the ground. They are not living things, they don't re-grow, and are not renewed quickly, if at all. Non-renewable natural resources take longer than a person's lifetime to be replaced. Examples of non-renewable natural resources are fossil fuels, like natural gas, coal, oil, and minerals.

10. (B)

There tend to be some spatial patterns that result from economic activities. We can look at urban land use to make some generalizations. When a type of land use generates more rent than others, and when land uses compete for a location, the land use that creates the highest return usually will be the one who can occupy the land, as a seller sells land to the people who can produce the highest bid.

11. (C)

Push and pull factors often explain reasons why people migrate. A "push factor" is when migrants feel they are being pushed out of an area because they perceive it to be a place that is detrimental for them to remain. A "pull factor" is

a factor that attracts migrants to come to a new area.

12. (D)

Proponents of genetically modified foods herald the arrival of these improvements because the herbicide- and insect-resistant crops have helped productivity and driven down the cost of producing food. Opponents to genetically modified crops suggest that these developments do more to especially help the big corporate farmers than consumers and are wary of the long-term effects these genetically modified foods may have on society.

13. (D)

The Internet is not part of the definition of globalization, but rather a product of globalization. "Globalization" refers to the increasing interconnection of more and more people and places across the world through social, cultural, political, economic, and environmental processes that have become more international in scale and effect. It is not a new process, as we have had long-distance trade and exchange for thousands of years.

14. (B)

This question about the map may seem simplistic, but it underscores the importance of reading the legend. The map-related questions on the Praxis exam will be simple if you read the legend carefully and use it to interpret the map, rather than relying on your own knowledge.

15. (C)

Note that the question asks for the northernmost city on the west coast.

16. (C)

While (A) includes the bodies of water within Florida's borders, the question asks for the bodies of water on the map.

17. (D)

During the First Stage, birth and death rates are both high, and the population grows slowly. During the Second Stage, there is a rapid increase in population because the death rate drops and births remain high. In the Third Stage, birth rates decline, and the population growth is less rapid. The Fourth Stage is marked by a low rate of births and deaths.

18. (D)

Air flight is not a problem of being landlocked. Landlocked areas typically have all of the problems listed—problems of access, control, and transportation dominate. Modern international conventions and agreements between countries have mitigated some situations. For instance, Bolivia has deals with Chile, Peru, and Argentina to use ports in their countries.

19. (B)

If a country sells its own currency, this would increase supply and keep the price down.

20. (D)

Answers (A), (B), and (C) are the three basic questions that economics seeks to answer. As you read each question on the Praxis exam, be sure to focus on key words such as *not, false, true, always, never, sometimes,* and so on. If you misread a question and thus answer incorrectly, you are just giving valuable score points away.

21. (C)

You may think many things about playing and not working, but economics calls this *opportunity cost.*

22. (B)

The connection between market economy and freedom of choice is discussed in chapter 6.

23. (C)

In a market economy, in which everyone is free to make choices about what they purchase, market forces dictate the allocation of resources.

24. (C)

The economies of Germany, France, and Australia are much like that of the United States. China has planned much of its economy and the leaders of the communist party in China direct economic policy.

25. (A)

Free goods are goods that are not scarce, which eliminates answer (D). Since people are able to use the free goods, the goods are not worthless. Free goods are not priceless, however, due to their abundance. Scarcity drives up prices.

26. (D)

Answers (A), (B), and (C) are considered scarce. Scarcity is based on the idea that a limited supply of goods or services comes up against an ever-increasing demand for it and that, as a result, every effort must be made to ensure its proper utilization and distribution so as to avoid inefficiency. Most goods and services can be defined as scarce since individuals desire more of them than they already possess (scarcity is maintained by demand). Carbon dioxide, however, is not scarce.

27. (A)

As noted in the answer above, scarcity is a by-product of demand—the more demand the less there is of a resource.

28. (B)

Land, labor, capital, and entrepreneurship are the factors of production.

29. (D)

Government intervention such as establishing quotas, collecting license fees, and providing subsidies is a sign of a planned economy. Taxes, however, are not normally considered a part of government intervention.

30. (B)

Macroeconomics studies the elements of economics on the national level. Macroeconomics is possibly the largest subfield in economics and includes output, consumption, investment, government spending, and net exports.

31. (A)

Microeconomics is the study of the economic behavior of small economic groups such as firms and families.

32. (D)

The automotive industry has the highest barrier to entry. Starting a sporting goods shop (B) or a farm (C) may, in some areas, have a relatively high barrier to entry, but it is possible for someone to start either business without too much difficulty. Since school-age children can start a lemonade stand (A), that business has the lowest barrier to entry.

33. (C)

GNP is the gross national product and is defined as the total goods and services produced by the nation in a given year. (B) is only partially correct because services are not specified.

34. (A)

Perfect competition exists in theory. A planned economy's primary component (D) is the control involved in the planning, not competition. An oligopoly (C) is a market form in which a market or industry is dominated by a small number of sellers.

35. (B)

In a monopoly, one firm controls an entire industry, so the firm is the industry. Consumers (A) are at the mercy of the monopoly and there is no competition (D) because there are not multiple sellers (C).

36. (A)

In a market structure in which several or many sellers each produce similar, but slightly differentiated products, monopolistic competition is a very common market form. Each producer can set its price and quantity without affecting the marketplace as a whole.

37. (A)

An oligopoly is a market form in which a market or industry is dominated by a small number of sellers.

38. (D)

Both the Declaration of Independence and the Constitution outline the principles of freedom on which the United States was founded. The Articles of *Confection*, choice (C), does not exist; the Articles of *Confederation* was the Second Continental Congress's first, but failed, attempt to define the new nation's federal government.

39. (A)

The critical word in this question is *civil*, which refers to the law. Human rights (B) include civil liberties, but the term implies other rights not yet recognized by law. Natural rights (C) derive from natural law, not civil law.

40. (D)

While the framers of the Constitution grappled with the issues of slavery, presidential power, and the role of large versus small states, among others, they all agreed that the new nation needed a system of checks and balances to check the innate selfishness of human nature.

41. (A)

The three-branch system of government created a system of checks and balances that would prevent any one branch from becoming too powerful, thus protecting the people from an oppressive government.

42. (D)

Political science studies and analyzes the structure of government and other political institutions, and politics in general.

43. (A)

Our federal system of government includes a bicameral legislature—the Senate and the House of Representatives—established in Article 1 of the Constitution.

44. (D)

Even if you were not aware that the state legislatures originally selected Senate members, you should have realized that both (B) and (C) are true, thus making (D) the only possible answer.

45. (D)

Answer choices (A), (B), and (C) are requirements listed in the Constitution. Military service (D) is not required, although many presidents and presidential candidates have served in the United States military.

46. (C)

Federal judges are appointed for life by the president.

47. (A)

Hobbes believed that if society were left to its natural state, people would act violently because they would be inclined to try to prevent their own deaths and to try to gain the power that they inherently crave. Hobbes argued in *The Leviathan* that people had drawn up a social contract among themselves to give up power to someone who could protect them. So, he believed society was all too willing to give up liberty in return for security and community. For Hobbes, the social contract justified the need for an absolute ruler who would take care of the people.

48.   (D)

Social power is the ability to get someone to act the way we want them to. The "power of the pen" is important in politics because it lets us use our voice to express our ideas and to influence, or manipulate others. The "power of the sword" is based on our ability to act in order to get what we want, regardless of whether or not it would be a good action for the other person. The "power of the purse" comes from our ability to refrain from doing what someone wants us to do.

49.   (C)

The Constitution does not mention political parties. In fact, "factions" with "jealousies and false alarms" were feared to cause damage to the country. Political parties were thought of as searching for profit not providing for the common good.

50.   (A)

Choices (B), (C), and (D) list activities that happen across state borders, so they are federal responsibilities. The actions in (A) are local responsibilities.

51.   (A)

A local government is chartered according to its state's constitution. Just as the policies enacted by the state government must not conflict with federal law, a local government is subject to the legal environment created by the state's constitution and statutes.

52.   (B)

Realism has been one of the dominant forces guiding international relations theory and influencing foreign policy, especially since the end of World War II. Realism is an international theory that holds that nation-states are the basic governmental unit and there is no authority above individual nations.

53.   (A)

This is a gift question. Government by the many is what we have in the United States: a constitutional democracy.

54.   (C)

Another related term for *autocracy*, more commonly used in the past, is *despotism*, or rule by a despot.

55.   (A)

The United States is a republic. The modern democratic state is usually a republic, in which the people do not take a direct role in legislating or governing, but elect representatives to express their views and wants. A democratic government exists when these representatives are freely chosen by the people, whose demands are then recognized by the duly elected government.

56.   (C)

Most people remember Article 1 of the Bill of Rights as the "free speech" article. It states: "Congress shall make no law respecting an establishment of religion, or prohibiting the free exercise thereof; or abridging the freedom of speech, or of the press; or the right of the people peaceably to assemble, and to petition the government for a redress of grievances."

57. (A)

"Reaganomics" was the term coined for President Ronald Reagan's supply-side economic policies. Reagan believed that the way to repair the shattered economy he inherited from the Carter administration was to cut federal spending on domestic programs while at the same time cutting taxes for the wealthy and for corporations. The "supply-side" theory advocated by Reagan asserted that by cutting taxes to businesses and to the rich, money would be freed up for future investments and the creation of new jobs. This investment income would offset the initial loss of tax revenue caused by the tax cuts. Eventually, through the creation of new jobs and investments, the money freed up by tax cuts to the rich would "trickle down" to the middle classes and the poor. While this sounded good on paper, it never worked out quite as well in real life. Yes, the tax cuts did spur investment, but the investments often didn't translate into jobs that paid well. The "trickle-down" was uneven and often quite limited. Many wealthy people pocketed the money rather than investing it. Still, new jobs were created and the nation began an economic expansion that lasted well into the 1990s.

58. (C)

Concerned that foreign threats and internal chaos would end the Revolution, French revolutionaries created the Committee on Public Safety, which became an enforcer of the revolution and killed or arrested anyone who was suspected of being against the revolution. Led by Maximilien Robespierre and the Jacobins, the Committee on Public Safety unleashed what is now referred to as "the Reign of Terror" as it sought to eliminate all enemies of the French Revolution—both real and imagined—and wound up executing about 40,000 people and arresting about 300,000. It ended when Robespierre became a victim of the Reign of Terror when he and his supporters were arrested on July 27, 1794, and beheaded soon after.

59. (B)

Although the Massachusetts Bay Colony was not the first successful settlement in the New World, it was the first major stronghold in North America.

60. (B)

You can use the process of elimination on this question: (A), (C), and (D) were all devastating effects, but the development of trade (B) was a positive outcome of colonialism.

61. (C)

Although the Puritans sought religious freedom in the Americas, they were loath to give that freedom to others who held different beliefs. In order to ensure that Puritanism dominated the colonies, they fined, whipped, banished, and imprisoned anyone who did not conform to their beliefs.

62. (D)

The slave trade had yet to begin during the settlement of Jamestown, so (D) slaves were not among the settlers. Recent historical and archaeological research at the site of Jamestown suggest that at least some of the gentlemen and certainly many of the soldiers, artisans, surgeons, and laborers that accompanied them all made every effort to make the colony succeed.

63. (D)

With few exceptions, southern cities were seaports. Between 1820 and 1860 many inland cities were created in the North, along with transportation lines and manufacturing establishments. Northern cities did service the tremendous influx of people to the cities by developing elaborate systems of municipal services, but they lacked adequate taxing power to provide services for all.

64. (B)

The Fourteen Points were presented in a speech before both houses of Congress and were intended to generate support for Wilson's vision of the postwar world, both at home and also among allies in Europe. President Wilson hoped that the promise of a just peace would be embraced by the populations in enemy nations and generate momentum for ending the war.

65. (D)

Both the Public Works Administration (PWA) and the Works Project Administration (WPA) were instituted to reduce unemployment during the Great Depression and were part of the New Deal programs. Options (A), (B), and (C) are incorrect. While they were all programs of the New Deal, the National Industrial Recovery Act was enacted in 1933 to allow collective bargaining; the Glass-Steagall Act created the FDIC, which today, as in 1933, insures bank deposits to prevent bank failures; and the Social Security Act was passed in 1935 to provide benefits to the disabled and the elderly.

66. (D)

The Cold War was the period of conflict, tension, and competition between the United States and the Soviet Union and their respective allies from the mid-1940s until the early 1990s. Throughout the period, the rivalry between the two superpowers was played out in multiple arenas: military coalitions; ideology, psychology, and espionage; military, industrial, and technological developments, including the space race; costly defense spending; a massive conventional and nuclear arms race; and many proxy wars. Mercantilism was a seventeenth-century economic theory.

67. (C)

The Industrial Revolution began in Britain and helped to make the country enormously powerful in the nineteenth century. Britain had the essential elements that a nation needed to achieve economic success—the factors of production (land, labor, and capital). Many political and economic factors enabled the Industrial Revolution to begin and flourish in Britain. The colonies held by Britain provided both raw materials and markets for British goods. Its powerful navy defended its shipping, political stability at home encouraged commerce, the enclosure movement allowed for efficient farming methods, but also pushed poor farmers out of farming and into cities looking for jobs. Also, private investment in businesses funded experiments for creating better products.

68. (A)

The series of taxes, named the American Revenue Act, became popularly known as the Sugar Act. One of its major components was a high duty on sugar. The act was combined with a greater attempt to enforce the existing tariffs.

69. (D)

One of the American reactions to the Stamp Act was the creation throughout the colonies of secret organizations known as the Sons of Liberty.

70. (C)

The U.S. military had assistance from many allies during the Vietnam War, including troops from Australia, Korea, and the Philippines, among others.

71. (A)

Not all areas of the world have been able to join the Information Age at the same time or the same pace as the United States. The digital divide has created not only a gap among nations, but also within the United States.

72. (D)

The 1936 election established a realignment of voting blocs as Roosevelt's Democratic Party became the nation's majority party in terms of voter registration and easily voted Roosevelt into a second term. Democrats had not been the majority party since 1856. Attracted by Roosevelt's New Deal initiatives overwhelming majorities of African Americans, Jews, non-Irish Catholics, urban residents in general, and labor union members joined traditional Democratic voters (southern whites and Irish Catholics) and threw their support behind Roosevelt.

73. (A)

The Articles of Confederation created a weak federal government that lacked the authority to tax; it also established a one-state, one-vote policy, which the larger states resented.

74. (C)

The Federalist Papers consist of 85 essays outlining how the new government would operate and why this type of government was the best choice for the United States of America. All of the essays were signed "Publius," and though the actual authors of some are under dispute, the general consensus is that Alexander Hamilton wrote 52, James Madison wrote 28, and John Jay contributed the remaining 5. None of the authors signed the Declaration of Independence.

75. (D)

Manifest Destiny was a doctrine used to rationalize U.S. territorial expansion in the 1840s and 1850s. It asserted that expansion of the United States throughout the American continents was both justified and inevitable. The phrase was coined by the U.S. journalist John L. O'Sullivan, and was initially used in regard to Mexican and Indian land in Texas and the Southwest. The concept was invoked later in a dispute with Great Britain over Oregon and in relation to territory controlled by the United States as a result of the Spanish-American War. By the age of Manifest Destiny, Spain was long gone from Florida.

76. (A)

The Northwest Ordinance provided the means by which new states would be created out of the western lands and then admitted into the Union.

77. (D)

Reagan sought to cure the nation's financial woes by turning away from demand economics, centered on consumers stimulating businesses to supply more product, and instead focus on supply-side economics. There were four pillars of his platform:

- to reduce government spending

- to reduce income tax and capital gains tax

• to reduce government regulation

• to control the money supply to reduce inflation

Reagan's "trickle-down economics" referred to cutting business taxes so that it would eventually trickle down to those who do not directly benefit from policy changes.

78. (D)

Between 1790 and 1860—the years known as the antebellum period—commercial agriculture replaced subsistence agriculture in the North, and household production was replaced by factory production. Massive foreign immigration from Ireland and Germany greatly increased the size of cities. In the South, slavery impeded the development of industry and cities and discouraged technological innovation.

79. (B)

Balance of Power is a doctrine to prevent any one nation from becoming too strong so that it would end up having power over all of the other nations.

80. (B)

The perfect crop was cotton, especially for the lower South. It was easy to grow, and its demands were met by the region's climate and soil. Between the cotton South and the wheat North, there was a middle ground in which the main crop was corn.

81. (A)

The American Civil War (1861–1865) was one of the most violent times in the history of the United States. More than 600,000 men gave their lives for their country in this war. This is more American lives lost in one war than in all wars and conflicts combined since this period.

82. (C)

Abraham Lincoln's victory in the presidential election of 1860 was the signal for the secession of South Carolina (December 20, 1860), and that state was followed out of the Union by six other states: Mississippi, Florida, Alabama, Georgia, Louisiana, and Texas.

83. (B)

The outgoing president, James Buchanan, a Northern Democrat who was either truckling to the Southern, pro-slavery wing of his party or sincerely attempting to avert war, pursued a vacillating course.

84. (D)

The new Confederate government was led by President Jefferson Davis.

85. (D)

No nation ever has an unlimited supply of funds. Choices (A), (B), and (C) are true.

86. (B)

The Fourteenth Amendment (1868) provided former slaves with national citizenship. The Reconstruction Acts of 1867 (A) laid out the process for readmitting southern states into the Union, and the Fifteenth Amendment (1870) (D), granted black men the right to vote. These were only the first steps, however, toward reconstructing the fragmented nation.

87.   (C)

Big Stick Diplomacy, as the United States press corps termed it, is based on Theodore Roosevelt's invocation of an African proverb, "speak softly, and carry a big stick, you will go far" to describe his belief that the United States had a moral imperative to keep all other interests out of the Western Hemisphere. Many political cartoons of the day depicted Roosevelt carrying a big stick and keeping the monopolists and European countries in line.

88.   (D)

Rudyard Kipling, a British poet, was born in India when it was a British colony. He believed that the countries of Europe and the United States had a duty to help the people of Africa, Asia, and Latin America. He published a poem in 1899 to encourage the United States to impose colonial rule in the Philippines. He understood the unpopularity of foreign rule, but he asserted that people should "take up the White Man's burden" to civilize inferior, nonwhite races, by bringing them order and enlightenment.

89.   (B)

Race, as it is discussed in the context of the United States, does not have the same meaning in either early 20th-century Russia or in modern Russia. Rather, it is ethnicity that divides Russia's social structure. However, during Lenin's lifetime, Russia was an ethnically homogenous country, so answer option (B) is the correct answer. In Lenin's writings one can find a critique of monarchy (D), and imperialism which is answer option (A). His

concept of a "vanguard" or disciplined revolutionary party is, perhaps, his biggest contribution to Marxist thought.

90.   (C)

The assassination of Archduke Franz Ferdinand, the heir to the throne of Austria-Hungary, and his wife by Gavrilo Princep was the final spark that ignited the conflict that became the Great War in Europe. A system of alliances forged by treaties and events tangled Austria-Hungary with its neighbor Germany against the alliance of Russia, France, and Britain, with Britain's colonies and dominions of Australia, Canada, India, New Zealand, and the Union of South Africa offering military and financial assistance. The United States, Japan, and Italy all joined the Allies at later dates. Although Tsar Nicholas II, answer option (A), was assassinated, the murder took place in 1918, following his abdication, the year before the Russian Revolution, which abolished the monarchy. Tsar Alexander III (option B) is an incorrect answer, since he was the father of Tsar Nicholas II and died of nephritis at the age of 49 in 1894. Answer option (D) is also incorrect. James A. Garfield, the 20th president of the United States, was shot on July 2, 1881, and died of his wounds on September 19, 1881.

91.   (D)

While certainly anti-Semitism was a key element of National Socialist rule, the official goal of the Nazi regime was Jewish emigration. The orchestration of the murder of Jews did not begin until later on.

92.   (A)

Sayyid Qutb's theoretical writings became the basis for many radical Islamic movements, including al-Qaeda, who believed that many of the governments in Muslim countries were corrupted by the West and should be overthrown. Qutb felt that the West was, at its heart, a corrupted culture. His dislike of the West intensified after he spent some time in 1949 studying at Colorado State Teacher's College. He believed that the United States had a culture of greed and despaired over how poorly people of color had been treated throughout U.S. history, and in particular how he was treated as an Arab. He was repulsed with what he saw as the rampant sexuality of American culture and concluded that American culture had little to save it, as women, in his view, were promiscuous vixens, and American men seemed obsessed with sports and allowed their women too much freedom. His writings warned Egypt that its fascination with "modernity" was misguided and that Islam offered liberation from the evils of western society. He advocated jihad and asserted that violent resistance against regimes that claimed to be Muslim, but did not act in accordance with Islamic precepts. He was later accused of plotting against the Egyptian government and was hanged in 1966.

93. (D)

Slobodan Milosevic embraced Serbian nationalism with the dream of an ethnically pure Greater Serbia that launched almost of decade of war in the Balkans during the 1990s. During this period Milosevic purged the Yugoslavian Army of non-Serbs and fomented unrest outside of Serbia in areas that had large numbers of Serbian minorities. In 1991, after Croatia, Serbia, and Macedonia declared their independence, Milosevic encouraged Croatian Serbs to take over large portions of Croatia. In 1992, Bosnian Serbs, supported by Milosevic's military and paramilitary forces, rebelled, beginning a brutal struggle to "purify" Bosnia of its Muslim inhabitants. During the conflict, hundreds of thousands of Bosnians were killed, raped, or sent to concentration camps un-

der Milosevic's planned genocide. In 1998, when ethnic Albanians revolted in Kosovo, Milosevic sent in his military. NATO, fearing another ethnic cleansing, launched two months of air strikes until Milosevic finally agreed to withdraw. In 2001, Milosevic was arrested, handed over to the UN who took him to The Hague for trial on crimes against humanity. He died in February 2004 while his trial was still in progress.

94. (D)

Technological innovations occur because of both need and opportunity. Central to this idea is the development of a global trade and communications network so that countries can have access to new technologies and ideas from other parts of the world. For instance, the relative ease of communication that the Abbasid Empire had between the Mediterranean Sea and the Indus Valley enabled it to have access to resources and technology transfers between those areas of the world. China benefited from having the Silk Road, which facilitated the exchange of goods, ideas, and new technologies. A country that was more isolated had to rely only on its own ideas for technology improvements and, in turn, faced an enormous disadvantage in keeping up with new developments.

95. (A)

Technically, the war wasn't fought by Greeks in the classical sense. It was fought by the Mycenaeans. Nevertheless, the Greeks saw the Trojan War as the first moment in history when they came together as one people with a common purpose.

96. (B)

Bloody Mary is the answer. She was called this because of her persecution of Protestants.

97. (B)

About 500 BCE, the Roman Republic was established, with two annually elected consuls at its head, guided by a senate. The republic eventually weakened, and Rome passed to rule by one man—first Julius Caesar, who was assassinated in 44 BCE, then Augustus, who assumed the title of emperor. Over the next few centuries, a succession of emperors followed.

98. (C)

The Prophet Muhammad did not select anyone to be his successor. As a result, after his death, there were disagreements between those who wanted a member of the Ahl al-Bayt, the family of the Prophet, to rule and those who wanted the ruler to be elected by their peers. A group that supported Muhammad's son-in-law and nephew, Ali, to be the caliph (successor), was known as the Party of Ali, or the Shi'a Ali, known as the Shi'ites. This group claimed that God (Allah) had given Ali and his descendants divine knowledge. The Sunnis, "followers of the way of the Prophet," felt that while they hold Ali in high esteem, do not believe that he and his hereditary line are the chosen successors, and that the leaders of the Muslim community should be chosen by tradition and from a broad base of the people.

99. (C)

Mansa Musa's control over the Sub-Saharan trade routes brought him tremendous wealth. The most celebrated event of Mansa Musa's reign was during his pilgrimage to Mecca in 1324–1325 during which he visited the sultan of Egypt. His entourage included more than 60,000 people and had what today is valued at $100 million. Preceded by 500 slaves, each carrying a six pound staff of gold, he followed with a huge host of retainers, including 100 elephants bearing 100 pounds of gold. He gave so much money to the citizens of Egypt that the value of gold was ruined in Egypt. Musa's extravagance also brought Mali into international prominence and it began to appear on European maps for the first time. Within a century, Europeans began to search West Africa for the source of Mali's riches. His pilgrimage also resulted in transfers of ideas and architecture. Upon his return, Mansa Musa brought along artists and architects who designed mosques, schools, and libraries.

100. (C)

There are political, social, and economic characteristics of totalitarian governments. Politically the state is considered more important than the individuals, a single political party controls the government, and a powerful dictator unites the people and symbolizes the government. Socially the government controls all aspects of daily life, denying citizens basic rights and liberties and using secret police to enforce government policies through terror and violence. Economically, the government controls business and directs the national economy and uses labor and business to fulfill the objectives of the state. Mussolini, Stalin, and Hitler all had totalitarian governments.

101. (C)

While religion does sometimes play a role in nationalist movements, it does not have to.

102. (A)

At the turn of the twentieth century, the United States began to emerge as a world power with expansionist goals. The Spanish-American War and the acquisition of the Philippines launched the beginning of its move away from its earlier isolationist policies.

103. (B)

After the Battle of Buxor, the British East India Company became the diwan of Bengal and assumed responsibility for tax collecting, administering justice, and providing security. The British government became increasingly concerned that its limited liability company was now acting as a government.

104. (C)

Muslim women did have the right to divorce.

105. (A)

The cities the Mayas built were ceremonial centers. A priestly class lived in the cities, but for the most part the Maya population lived in small farming villages. The priestly class would carry out daily religious duties, particularly sacrifices, and the peasants would periodically gather for religious ceremonies and festivals.

106. (B)

The Silk Road did not follow a single route. Crossing Central Asia, it branched off in several directions, passing through different oasis settlements.

107. (B)

The Atlantic slave trade preferred men who could work under difficult labor conditions. Women who were left behind had a difficult time, as there were a disproportionate number of women. As a result, the numbers reinforced ideas of polygamy and multiple marriages. African societies were, quite often, already matrilineal societies.

108. (A)

As a result of the Arab-Israeli War of 1973, the cartel ordered an embargo on oil shipments to Israel's ally, the United States. As a result, the U.S. suffered an oil crisis and the cost of petroleum triggered a global economic downturn. OPEC demonstrated that it could control the developed world by changing the price of oil at will.

109. (B)

The Renaissance saw the rise of courtly and papal patronage, and encompassed the revival of learning based on classical sources, the development of perspective in painting, and advancements in science.

110. (D)

As more women became involved in the workplace and as public discussions for reform turned to birth control, fertility began to decline. Similarly, advances in health care and living conditions resulted in decreased mortality. While in the short term, mortality fell faster than fertility, in the long term, lower birth rates led to lower population growth and demographic stability.

111. (C)

The Protestant Reformation was a movement in the sixteenth century to reform the Christianity of Western Europe.

112. (C)

An emphasis on warfare.

113. (D)

The conflict between the Persians and the Greeks resulted in two separate invasions. During the second invasion, about 10 years after the first, the Persian ruler, Xerxes, sent hundreds of thousands of soldiers and sailors to Greece to avenge his father's unexpected defeat at the Battle of Marathon. Athens and Sparta, two rival city-states merged together to try and fend off the Persians. After trying to slow the Persians down through a heroic stand of only 300 Spartans against the Persians at Thermopylae, the Greeks tried to avenge their defeat and prevent the Persians from getting their supplies after they had ransacked Athens. The Greeks lured Persian ships into the narrow Strait of Salamis near Athens. In what came to be known as the Battle of Salamis, the Persians could not maneuver their huge ships in the strait. Greek warships took advantage of this and sank about 300 Persian vessels, demoralizing what was left of the Persian navy.

114. (A)

Trade was the key motivator for European colonialism. European ships traveled around the world in search of new trading routes and partners to feed burgeoning capitalism in Europe.

115. (D)

There were both positive and negative effects of the Columbian Exchange. Europeans brought plants, food, and animals to the Americas. In return, the Europeans brought back corn, potatoes, tomatoes and other food that both changed the European cuisine and better enabled European nutritional needs to be met. These and other foods traveled to Asia and Africa, no doubt contributing to a great worldwide population growth. On the negative side, Europeans brought diseases, such as smallpox, to the Americas that killed millions of Native Americans. In return, Europeans brought syphilis back to their lands. Antibiotics were not introduced until much later.

116. (B)

With the Ottoman capture of Constantinople in 1453, Europeans sought to find a replacement for white slaves from the Black Sea region and Balkans and turned completely to Africa for slave labor.

117. (A)

Immigration is one of those social issues that can be analyzed using geography, anthropology, or a combination of social studies disciplines.

118. (D)

Participant observation involves a researcher interacting with and observing the personal lives of the research subjects. Strategic engagement (A) is not a method used in social research. Experimentation (B) involves a researcher manipulating an experimental stimulus, usually in a laboratory setting. Content analysis (C) involves the study of communication products such as books, letters, advertising, or television programs.

119. (B)

Sociology, simply defined, is the study of how individuals become members of groups and move between groups, and how being in different groups affects individuals and the groups in which they participate.

120. (D)

Virtually any group can be considered a social network, but a party planner is not a group.

121. (B)

Ethnography is the (B) systematic description of a human society, usually based on first-hand field-work. All generalizations about human behavior are based on the descriptive evidence of ethnography.

122. (D)

Choices (A), (B), and (C) are social issues considered to be outside the control of a single individual and impact society-at-large and that can separate people in a community.

123. (A)

Jean Piaget's stage theory of development continues to influence teaching methodology.

124. (C)

Though many people enjoy and participate in sports and other physical activities, interest in athletics is not considered a characteristic of human populations.

125. (D)

The War Powers Resolution stipulates that the president can deploy troops abroad in situations where hostilities are imminent for only 60 days, unless Congress approves a longer deployment, declares war, or cannot meet because the nation is

under attack. (A) is wrong because the War Powers Resolution does not authorize Congress to prevent the initial deployment of troops abroad by the president. Choice (B) is wrong because the Constitution gives Congress the power to declare war. The usual procedure begins with a request from the president for a declaration of war, which is then adopted by the Congress by joint resolution and signed by the president. The War Powers Resolution did nothing to change this procedure. Choice (C) is wrong because the War Powers Resolution has nothing to do with extradition of foreign ambassadors.

126. (A)

The term *socialization* refers to the process of learning one's culture and how to live within it.

127. (C)

Ethnology is a branch of anthropology that analyzes and studies the similarities and difference among cultures.

128. (A)

Social psychologists are devoted to quantitative, or empirical, research, which provides numerical data that can be analyzed and compared. Qualitative research provides verbal (word-based) rather than numerical data. Social psychology is not associated with talk or group therapy. Its focus is research.

129. (D)

Class is not generally included when discussing multicultural diversity. The term *multicultural diversity* refers to the state of racial, cultural, and ethnic diversity within the demographics of a specified place, usually at the scale of an organization such as a school, business, neighborhood, city, or nation.

130. (A)

In psychology and the cognitive sciences, perception is the process of attaining awareness or understanding of sensory information. It is a task far more complex than was imagined in the 1950s and 1960s, when it was proclaimed that building perceiving machines would take about a decade, but, needless to say, that is still very far from reality.

Praxis Social Studies Assessment 0081

Practice Test 2

This test is also on CD-ROM in our special interactive TestWare® for the PRAXIS II Social Studies Assessment: 0081. It is highly recommended that you first take this exam on computer. You will then have the additional study features and benefits of enforced timed conditions and instantaneous, accurate scoring.

1. Ⓐ Ⓑ Ⓒ Ⓓ
2. Ⓐ Ⓑ Ⓒ Ⓓ
3. Ⓐ Ⓑ Ⓒ Ⓓ
4. Ⓐ Ⓑ Ⓒ Ⓓ
5. Ⓐ Ⓑ Ⓒ Ⓓ
6. Ⓐ Ⓑ Ⓒ Ⓓ
7. Ⓐ Ⓑ Ⓒ Ⓓ
8. Ⓐ Ⓑ Ⓒ Ⓓ
9. Ⓐ Ⓑ Ⓒ Ⓓ
10. Ⓐ Ⓑ Ⓒ Ⓓ
11. Ⓐ Ⓑ Ⓒ Ⓓ
12. Ⓐ Ⓑ Ⓒ Ⓓ
13. Ⓐ Ⓑ Ⓒ Ⓓ
14. Ⓐ Ⓑ Ⓒ Ⓓ
15. Ⓐ Ⓑ Ⓒ Ⓓ
16. Ⓐ Ⓑ Ⓒ Ⓓ
17. Ⓐ Ⓑ Ⓒ Ⓓ
18. Ⓐ Ⓑ Ⓒ Ⓓ
19. Ⓐ Ⓑ Ⓒ Ⓓ
20. Ⓐ Ⓑ Ⓒ Ⓓ
21. Ⓐ Ⓑ Ⓒ Ⓓ
22. Ⓐ Ⓑ Ⓒ Ⓓ
23. Ⓐ Ⓑ Ⓒ Ⓓ
24. Ⓐ Ⓑ Ⓒ Ⓓ
25. Ⓐ Ⓑ Ⓒ Ⓓ
26. Ⓐ Ⓑ Ⓒ Ⓓ
27. Ⓐ Ⓑ Ⓒ Ⓓ
28. Ⓐ Ⓑ Ⓒ Ⓓ
29. Ⓐ Ⓑ Ⓒ Ⓓ
30. Ⓐ Ⓑ Ⓒ Ⓓ
31. Ⓐ Ⓑ Ⓒ Ⓓ
32. Ⓐ Ⓑ Ⓒ Ⓓ
33. Ⓐ Ⓑ Ⓒ Ⓓ

34. Ⓐ Ⓑ Ⓒ Ⓓ
35. Ⓐ Ⓑ Ⓒ Ⓓ
36. Ⓐ Ⓑ Ⓒ Ⓓ
37. Ⓐ Ⓑ Ⓒ Ⓓ
38. Ⓐ Ⓑ Ⓒ Ⓓ
39. Ⓐ Ⓑ Ⓒ Ⓓ
40. Ⓐ Ⓑ Ⓒ Ⓓ
41. Ⓐ Ⓑ Ⓒ Ⓓ
42. Ⓐ Ⓑ Ⓒ Ⓓ
43. Ⓐ Ⓑ Ⓒ Ⓓ
44. Ⓐ Ⓑ Ⓒ Ⓓ
45. Ⓐ Ⓑ Ⓒ Ⓓ
46. Ⓐ Ⓑ Ⓒ Ⓓ
47. Ⓐ Ⓑ Ⓒ Ⓓ
48. Ⓐ Ⓑ Ⓒ Ⓓ
49. Ⓐ Ⓑ Ⓒ Ⓓ
50. Ⓐ Ⓑ Ⓒ Ⓓ
51. Ⓐ Ⓑ Ⓒ Ⓓ
52. Ⓐ Ⓑ Ⓒ Ⓓ
53. Ⓐ Ⓑ Ⓒ Ⓓ
54. Ⓐ Ⓑ Ⓒ Ⓓ
55. Ⓐ Ⓑ Ⓒ Ⓓ
56. Ⓐ Ⓑ Ⓒ Ⓓ
57. Ⓐ Ⓑ Ⓒ Ⓓ
58. Ⓐ Ⓑ Ⓒ Ⓓ
59. Ⓐ Ⓑ Ⓒ Ⓓ
60. Ⓐ Ⓑ Ⓒ Ⓓ
61. Ⓐ Ⓑ Ⓒ Ⓓ
62. Ⓐ Ⓑ Ⓒ Ⓓ
63. Ⓐ Ⓑ Ⓒ Ⓓ
64. Ⓐ Ⓑ Ⓒ Ⓓ
65. Ⓐ Ⓑ Ⓒ Ⓓ
66. Ⓐ Ⓑ Ⓒ Ⓓ

67. Ⓐ Ⓑ Ⓒ Ⓓ
68. Ⓐ Ⓑ Ⓒ Ⓓ
69. Ⓐ Ⓑ Ⓒ Ⓓ
70. Ⓐ Ⓑ Ⓒ Ⓓ
71. Ⓐ Ⓑ Ⓒ Ⓓ
72. Ⓐ Ⓑ Ⓒ Ⓓ
73. Ⓐ Ⓑ Ⓒ Ⓓ
74. Ⓐ Ⓑ Ⓒ Ⓓ
75. Ⓐ Ⓑ Ⓒ Ⓓ
76. Ⓐ Ⓑ Ⓒ Ⓓ
77. Ⓐ Ⓑ Ⓒ Ⓓ
78. Ⓐ Ⓑ Ⓒ Ⓓ
79. Ⓐ Ⓑ Ⓒ Ⓓ
80. Ⓐ Ⓑ Ⓒ Ⓓ
81. Ⓐ Ⓑ Ⓒ Ⓓ
82. Ⓐ Ⓑ Ⓒ Ⓓ
83. Ⓐ Ⓑ Ⓒ Ⓓ
84. Ⓐ Ⓑ Ⓒ Ⓓ
85. Ⓐ Ⓑ Ⓒ Ⓓ
86. Ⓐ Ⓑ Ⓒ Ⓓ
87. Ⓐ Ⓑ Ⓒ Ⓓ
88. Ⓐ Ⓑ Ⓒ Ⓓ
89. Ⓐ Ⓑ Ⓒ Ⓓ
90. Ⓐ Ⓑ Ⓒ Ⓓ
91. Ⓐ Ⓑ Ⓒ Ⓓ
92. Ⓐ Ⓑ Ⓒ Ⓓ
93. Ⓐ Ⓑ Ⓒ Ⓓ
94. Ⓐ Ⓑ Ⓒ Ⓓ
95. Ⓐ Ⓑ Ⓒ Ⓓ
96. Ⓐ Ⓑ Ⓒ Ⓓ
97. Ⓐ Ⓑ Ⓒ Ⓓ
98. Ⓐ Ⓑ Ⓒ Ⓓ
99. Ⓐ Ⓑ Ⓒ Ⓓ

100. Ⓐ Ⓑ Ⓒ Ⓓ
101. Ⓐ Ⓑ Ⓒ Ⓓ
102. Ⓐ Ⓑ Ⓒ Ⓓ
103. Ⓐ Ⓑ Ⓒ Ⓓ
104. Ⓐ Ⓑ Ⓒ Ⓓ
105. Ⓐ Ⓑ Ⓒ Ⓓ
106. Ⓐ Ⓑ Ⓒ Ⓓ
107. Ⓐ Ⓑ Ⓒ Ⓓ
108. Ⓐ Ⓑ Ⓒ Ⓓ
109. Ⓐ Ⓑ Ⓒ Ⓓ
110. Ⓐ Ⓑ Ⓒ Ⓓ
111. Ⓐ Ⓑ Ⓒ Ⓓ
112. Ⓐ Ⓑ Ⓒ Ⓓ
113. Ⓐ Ⓑ Ⓒ Ⓓ
114. Ⓐ Ⓑ Ⓒ Ⓓ
115. Ⓐ Ⓑ Ⓒ Ⓓ
116. Ⓐ Ⓑ Ⓒ Ⓓ
117. Ⓐ Ⓑ Ⓒ Ⓓ
118. Ⓐ Ⓑ Ⓒ Ⓓ
119. Ⓐ Ⓑ Ⓒ Ⓓ
120. Ⓐ Ⓑ Ⓒ Ⓓ
121. Ⓐ Ⓑ Ⓒ Ⓓ
122. Ⓐ Ⓑ Ⓒ Ⓓ
123. Ⓐ Ⓑ Ⓒ Ⓓ
124. Ⓐ Ⓑ Ⓒ Ⓓ
125. Ⓐ Ⓑ Ⓒ Ⓓ
126. Ⓐ Ⓑ Ⓒ Ⓓ
127. Ⓐ Ⓑ Ⓒ Ⓓ
128. Ⓐ Ⓑ Ⓒ Ⓓ
129. Ⓐ Ⓑ Ⓒ Ⓓ
130. Ⓐ Ⓑ Ⓒ Ⓓ

1. Which of the following sets human behavior above all other creatures on earth?

    (A) Use of tools
    (B) Thumbs
    (C) Nursing their young
    (D) Culture

2. Which of the following statements is NOT an accurate statement about the U.S. president's cabinet?

    (A) It includes heads of the 15 executive departments.
    (B) It includes members of the House of Representatives.
    (C) Although not mentioned in the Constitution, the cabinet has been part of American government since the presidency of George Washington.
    (D) Presidents may appoint special advisors to the cabinet.

3. The purpose of grandfather clauses and literacy tests, used in the southern states in the late 1800s and early 1900s, was to prevent

    (A) illiterate whites from voting.
    (B) recent immigrants from voting.
    (C) blacks from running for public office.
    (D) blacks from voting.

4. Which of the following pairings is accurate?

    (A) Franklin D. Roosevelt and the New Deal
    (B) Adolf Hitler and economic prosperity
    (C) Black codes and freedom for slaves
    (D) Charles de Gaulle and the Tehran Conference

5. Which of the following describes a feature of Spanish colonial ventures?

    (A) Promoted and started industries for the natives
    (B) The New World was divided into four viceroyalties.
    (C) Crown control over the colonies was limited and indirect.
    (D) The Spanish Crown claimed sole ownership of all of the precious metals mined in South America.

6. The Boxer Rebellion was

    (A) a rebellion launched by the Society of Righteous and Harmonious Fists who wanted to expel all Westerners from their lands.
    (B) an armed uprising against the British by the Egyptian army from 1879–1882.
    (C) Japanese assaults against Chinese foreigners who had been monopolizing trade in Japan.
    (D) The mutiny of Indian sepoys against the British whose use of animal fat on the Endfield rifle's bullets offended both Hindus and Muslims.

7. Which of the following was a cause of both World War I and World War II?

    (A) Failure of the League of Nations to keep the peace
    (B) Political instability in Eastern Europe
    (C) Secret alliances and agreements among nations
    (D) The fall of the Ottoman Empire

8. The first issue that the Americans and the Soviets had, following World War II, was over the future of which country?

   (A) West Germany
   (B) France
   (C) Poland
   (D) Balkans

9. The Maastricht Treaty of 1991

   (A) ended the Bosnian war.
   (B) dissolved the Soviet Union.
   (C) reunited Germany.
   (D) led to the creation of the euro and the structure of the European Economic Union.

10. What was the pretext that George W. Bush used for invading Iraq?

    (A) Osama bin Laden and Saddam Hussein had conspired together in the 9/11 attacks.
    (B) Saddam Hussein's use of poisonous gas against the Kurds
    (C) Saddam Hussein had WMDs, weapons of mass destruction.
    (D) The fear that the Shi'ite majority in Iraq would launch a civil war against the Sunnis and threaten U.S. oil supplies.

11. The second *fitna*, or Civil War, among the Muslim Community, was heightened after the death of which religious figure?

    (A) Abu Bakr, the first caliph
    (B) the death of the first Abbasid Caliph, al-Saffah
    (C) Husayn, the Prophet Muhammad's grandson
    (D) the disappearance of the twelfth imam

12. Ashoka converted to Buddhism as a result of

    (A) the death of his infant son.
    (B) anger at the division of society into the different varnas as promoted by Hinduism.
    (C) remorse over the widespread deaths his military campaigns caused.
    (D) the death of Buddha which caused him tremendous grief.

13. Trade along the Silk Road during the Han period affected China's culture in all of the following ways EXCEPT that

    (A) it caused China to conquer more land to the west and go into Central Asia in search of "blood-sweating" horses that the Han interpreted as being blessed by heaven.
    (B) it spread Buddhism.
    (C) it elevated the position of traders in Chinese society.
    (D) it created a profitable trade in luxury items.

14. What traditional form of antidemocratic government dominated Europe before the development of the modern totalitarian state?

    (A) Conservative Authoritarianism
    (B) Nationalism
    (C) Liberalism
    (D) Republicanism

15. The liberalism that emerged by the end of the nineteenth century was more concerned with which of the following than with political and social rights?

    (A) The need for gradual change
    (B) States' rights
    (C) Civil rights
    (D) Religious rights

16. Which one of these nations was NOT part of the Iroquois?

    (A) Mohawk
    (B) Cayuga
    (C) Oneida
    (D) Sioux

17. The harem in the Ottoman Topkapi Palace was all of the following EXCEPT:

    (A) a place to educate women who would prove to be good wives for Ottoman elite
    (B) under the control of the Valide Sultan, the Sultan's mother.
    (C) a place where male relatives of the Sultan were kept in the kafas system (Gilded Cage) so that the Sultan could watch over them.
    (D) a place where the women had no money and received no compensation for their work.

18. What were the initial goals of ASEAN, the Association of Southeast Asian Nations, which was established in 1967?

    (A) To accelerate economic development and promote political stability in the region
    (B) To establish a uniform set of currency regulations tying each nation's currency to the dollar
    (C) To promote travel and tourism to the area to European businessmen
    (D) To become a collective bargaining entity in their deals with OPEC

19. During the nineteenth century, about how many Europeans migrated to the Western Hemisphere?

    (A) 25 million
    (B) 15 million
    (C) 5 million
    (D) 50 million

20. The system of government in the United States is _____.

    (A) a republic.
    (B) totalitarian.
    (C) an absolute monarchy.
    (D) a democracy.

21. Which of the following statements does NOT reflect the amendment to the Constitution?

    (A) The Eighth Amendment prohibits the setting of excessive bail.
    (B) The Seventh Amendment establishes the principle of trial by jury.
    (C) The Fourth Amendment prohibits unreasonable searches and seizures.
    (D) The Tenth Amendment guarantees the accused the right to a speedy and public trial.

22. The definition of *discount rate* is the

    (A) interest rate a Federal Reserve bank charges eligible financial institutions to borrow funds on a short-term basis.
    (B) interest rate a Federal Reserve bank charges eligible financial institutions to borrow funds on a long-term basis.
    (C) percentage rate of deposits required by banks.
    (D) interest rate relative to the prime rate.

23. Which of the following statements is MOST LIKELY to be accurate regarding the gross domestic product (GDP)?

    (A) The GDP is the monetary value of all the finished goods and services produced within a country's borders in a specific time period.
    (B) GDP is usually calculated on a three-year average.
    (C) GDP excludes all public consumption and government outlays.
    (D) GDP does not include investments or exports minus imports.

24. The functional distribution of income is the distribution of income

(A) among the four classes of production factors.
(B) among businesses.
(C) among the poor.
(D) among laborers.

25. All of the following are recognized functions of the major political parties EXCEPT

(A) recruiting candidates for public office.
(B) aggregating interests into electoral alliances.
(C) establishing channels of communication between the public and government.
(D) articulating interests.

26. Which of the following allows the modern U.S. federal government to exercise some control over traditional state responsibilities like education and highways?

(A) Nationalism
(B) Federal funds
(C) Political pressure
(D) The federal government has no control over the states.

27. The Constitution specifically gives the responsibility for education to the states. Which of the following is an example of federal intervention in education?

(A) America's Promise
(B) READ 180
(C) No Child Left Behind Act
(D) Phonics

Use the following graph to answer questions 28 through 30.

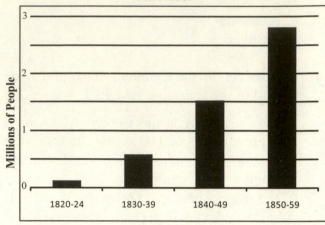

Immigration to the United States
1820-1859

Source: United States Department of Commerce "Historical Statistics, of the United States Colonial Times to 1970"

28. How many people immigrated to the United States from 1830 to 1839?

(A) 50,000
(B) 100,000
(C) 500,000
(D) 1,000,000

29. Which decade shows an influx of 1.5 million immigrants?

(A) 1820s
(B) 1830s
(C) 1840s
(D) 1850s

30. Based on the graph, where did these immigrants come from?

(A) Ireland, due to the potato famine
(B) Eastern Europe
(C) China
(D) The graph does not provide this information.

31. Which of the following government responsibilities is NOT delegated to the states in the Constitution?

    (A) Establishing state-sponsored colleges and universities

    (B) Administering and certifying elections, including elections for federal officials

    (C) Administering publicly funded health, housing, and nutrition programs for low-income and disabled residents

    (D) Commanding the state National Guard when called up to serve in Afghanistan

32. Looking at the figure below, what sort of determinations can we make about population distribution and change?

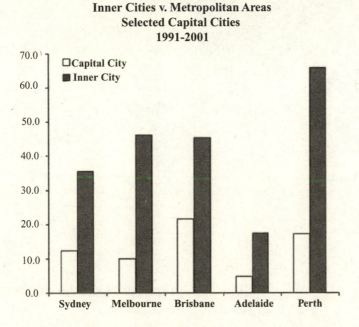

Percentage Change in Population: Inner Cities v. Metropolitan Areas Selected Capital Cities 1991-2001

    (A) The percentage of change has been relatively equal when looking at all five areas.

    (B) The population levels are denser in the inner cities than in the metropolitan area of the capital cities.

    (C) There are more people in the cities than in the capital cities.

    (D) Populations of inner cities have grown at a higher rate than metropolitan, capital areas.

33. *Deviant behavior* is the term used by sociologists to describe behaviors which the dominant group defines as

    (A) violating basic norms.

    (B) uncommonly brave or heroic.

    (C) the standard for others to follow.

    (D) very rare or unusual.

34. The term *Trail of Tears* refers to the

    (A) Mormon migration from Nauvoo, Illinois, to what is now Utah.

    (B) forced migration of the Cherokee tribe from the southern Appalachians to what is now Oklahoma.

    (C) westward migration along the Oregon Trail.

    (D) migration into Kentucky along the Wilderness Road.

35. As students get older and learn more about the world around them, what sort of changes will happen to their mental maps?

    (A) Maps should accumulate more information and become more complex.

    (B) They will find that they rely less and less upon mental maps and more on subjective reasoning.

    (C) As they get older, students place complex maps into a physical context.

    (D) Maps become rigid and do not change.

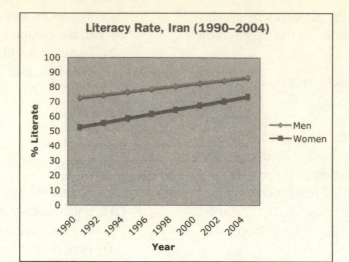

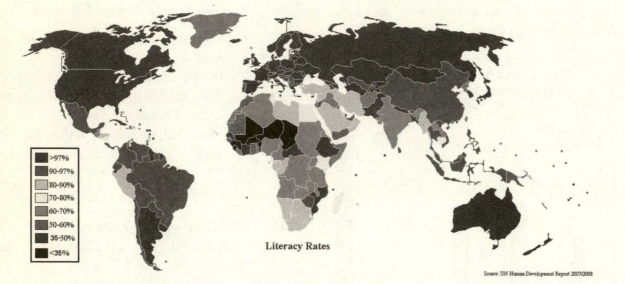

36. If we compare the two images on this page, we can claim all of the following EXCEPT:

    (A) Iran's literacy rate increased from 1990–1994

    (B) Algeria's and Iran's literacy rate is similar

    (C) From 2007–2008, Iran's illiteracy rate ranged from 10–20%

    (D) As women's illiteracy rate rose, so too did men's

37. Which of the following would have the smallest map scale?

    (A) Map of Asia

    (B) Map of Kentucky

    (C) Map of the world

    (D) Map of Nashville, Tennessee

38. The primary reason for trade according to international trade theory is

    (A) a loss of resources.
    (B) the existence of price differentials among nations.
    (C) jobs.
    (D) monopolies.

39. Amnesty International is an example of a(n)

    (A) NGO (nongovernmental organization).
    (B) NGO (national governmental organization).
    (C) court that tries international amnesty cases.
    (D) Committee of the United Nations that promotes peace and human rights.

40. Which of the following was NOT a result of the Industrial Revolution?

    (A) Important developments in transportation, including the steam locomotive, steamship, automobile, airplane
    (B) Important developments in communications, including the telegraph and radio
    (C) Agricultural improvements that made possible the provision of food for a larger non-agricultural population
    (D) The replacement of science in industry with the production line

Trends in Developed and Developing Countries, 1750–2050

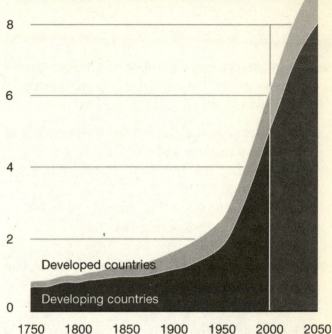

Global population, estimates and projections (billions)

41. If we look at the figure above, *Trends in population, developed and developing countries, 1750–2050 (estimates and projections)*, we see that each day 200,000 more people are added to the world food demand. What is happening with the population?

    (A) It is projected to increase from 6.7 billion (2006) to 9.2 billion by 2050.
    (B) It only took 30 years for the next billion to be added to the population.
    (C) Developed countries have grown more rapidly in the last 50 years than developing countries.
    (D) With the growth of technology, by 2050, it is projected that there will be more people in the developed world than in the developing world.

42. An example of an indirect tax is:

    (A) VAT.
    (B) Income Tax.
    (C) Transfer Tax.
    (D) Inheritance Tax.

43. A relatively large number of Chinese immigrated to the United States in one period in our history. When was that period?

    (A) Between the start of the California gold rush in 1849 and 1882
    (B) During the Industrial Revolution, from 1900 to 1925
    (C) After the Civil War, from 1870 to 1920
    (D) During the Roaring Twenties

44. From a sociological standpoint, what is one difference between Asian immigrants to the United States and those from South America?

    (A) Asians typically have no religion.
    (B) South Americans are used to living in difficult conditions.
    (C) Most South Americans speak Spanish, whereas Asians from different countries do not share a common language.
    (D) Asians and South Americans are basically the same from an immigration point of view.

45. Sir George Carteret and Lord Berkeley settled in what area?

    (A) New York
    (B) New Jersey
    (C) Massachusetts
    (D) Virginia

46. Which of the following was NOT a development in U.S. foreign policy following World War I?

    (A) Selective restrictions were placed on immigration.
    (B) The United States and its people turned inward.

    (C) The United States became a modern middle-class economy.
    (D) Quotas for immigrants were abolished.

47. What was the net result of the Eighteenth Amendment?

    (A) All Americans were eligible to vote.
    (B) Prohibition created major mob activity in the United States.
    (C) The Great Depression was eased.
    (D) Presidents were limited to two terms of four years each.

48. Adolf Hitler became chancellor of Germany in 1933. What was one of his first official acts?

    (A) He began secretly building up Germany's army and weapons.
    (B) He established government policies to ease the effects of the Great Depression.
    (C) He established alliances with Italy and Czechoslovakia.
    (D) He met with France and Britain to work out treaties.

49. What did the Civil Rights Act of 1964 accomplish?

    (A) It prohibited discrimination for reason of color, race, religion, or national origin in places of public accommodation covered by interstate commerce.
    (B) It desegregated public schools for the first time.
    (C) It ensured equal voting rights.
    (D) It dealt with housing and real estate discrimination.

50. Which of the following is a true statement about Martin Luther King, Jr.?

    (A) In 1963, King was named *Time* magazine's Man of the Year.
    (B) All African Americans united behind King.

(C) King was pastor of Ebenezer Baptist Church in Harlem.

(D) King was assassinated on Christmas Day, 1969.

51. The value of a country's total output of goods and services in that country during a year is called its

(A) foreign direct investment.

(B) gross domestic product.

(C) human development index.

(D) inflation rate.

52. The Twenty-sixth Amendment was passed during the Vietnam era. What did it accomplish?

(A) The amendment established age 18 as the legal drinking age throughout the United States.

(B) The amendment ended the draft.

(C) The amendment established age 18 as the legal voting age throughout the United States.

(D) The amendment gave women the right to vote.

53. Which of the following statements about the Han Dynasty is true?

(A) The boundaries established by the Qin and maintained by the Han have more or less defined the nation of China up to the present day.

(B) The Han Dynasty ended before the birth of Christ.

(C) The Han relied on Buddhism as the philosophical basis for government.

(D) China was relatively unsophisticated during the Han Dynasty with little poetry or writings.

54. What does the *IPAT* Equation mean?

(A) Technologies may only increase standard of living.

(B) Shows that growing populations and rising standards of living and the uses of technology all impact the environment.

(C) Rising standards of living put pressure on the population to control their technology.

(D) People in poorer areas have more control over their environment because they use less technology.

55. The stability and balance of ecosystems can be shattered by all but

(A) El Niño.

(B) fire.

(C) humans.

(D) rain.

56. What type of economy relies on market forces to allocate resources and goods, and to determine prices and quantities of each good that will be produced?

(A) Managed

(B) Socialist

(C) Market

(D) Planned

57. Which of the following is NOT one of the four factors of production?

(A) Labor

(B) Capital

(C) Entrepreneurship

(D) Scarcity

58. Which of the following does NOT fall within the scope of political science?

(A) Media

(B) Candidate behavior

(C) Election reform

(D) Education

59. If the federal government wants to influence state governments in an area that the Constitution establishes as a responsibility of the states, what action can it legally take?

    (A) The federal government can use executive privilege.
    (B) The federal political leaders can pressure state leaders.
    (C) The federal government can threaten to withhold money for projects administered by the states unless states comply.
    (D) The states can ignore the federal government.

60. Which philosopher argues that social policy should be established by imagining ourselves "behind the veil of ignorance"?

    (A) Locke
    (B) Rawls
    (C) Gauthier
    (D) Hobbes

61. Which of these is reflective of the unitary/rational actor model of foreign policy?

    (A) Assumes that all nations share similar goals and approach foreign policy issues in like fashion
    (B) Standard operating procedure should rule the day rather than thinking about alternative scenarios
    (C) Decisions are a struggle among bureaucratic actors within a nation.
    (D) Decisions are influenced solely by internal concerns.

62. Which of the following topics does NOT fall within the scope of human-environmental geography?

    (A) Humans adapt to the environment.
    (B) Humans modify the environment.
    (C) Humans depend on the environment.
    (D) Human birth rates.

63. The *IPAT* Equation summarizes the factors that influence the degree of human impact on the environment. What does IPAT stand for?

    (A) I (impact on the environment) is equal to P (population) multiplied by A (affluence or standard of living) multiplied by T (a technology factor).
    (B) I (influence on the environment) is equal to P (percentage of the ecosystem) multiplied by A (amount of action) multiplied by T (technology).
    (C) I (impact on the environment) is equal to P (population) multiplied by A (action) multiplied by T (time).
    (D) I (impact on the government) is equal to P (policy) multiplied by A (attention) multiplied by T (time).

64. Which of the following is NOT a renewable natural resource?

    (A) Air
    (B) Water
    (C) Wind
    (D) Natural Gas

65. Which of the following is NOT a macroeconomic issue?

    (A) Inflation
    (B) A teacher's income
    (C) Unemployment
    (D) Economic growth

66. Free trade is based on the principle of

    (A) balance of payments.
    (B) balance of power.
    (C) economies of scale.
    (D) comparative advantage.

67. The Federal Open Market Committee sets the Federal Reserve's monetary policy, which is carried out where?

    (A) The trading desk of the Federal Reserve Bank of New York
    (B) Washington, D.C., inside the Federal Reserve's office building
    (C) Across the country through brokers
    (D) Boston, Massachusetts

68. Who sets the discount rate for the Federal Reserve?

    (A) A member of the president's cabinet
    (B) The boards of directors of the Federal Reserve Banks
    (C) The chairman of the Federal Reserve
    (D) Alan Greenspan

69. The Federal Reserve sets reserve requirements for all commercial banks, savings banks, savings and loans, credit unions, and U.S. branches and agencies of foreign banks. Depository institutions use their reserve accounts at Federal Reserve Banks for what other purposes?

    (A) To give loans to people who need them
    (B) To set gold reserves
    (C) To insure our money in case of bank failures
    (D) To process check and electronic payments

70. What is the only federal agency to have both consumer protection and competition jurisdiction in broad sectors of the economy?

    (A) The Federal Reserve
    (B) The Federal Open Market Committee
    (C) The Federal Trade Commission
    (D) The Federal Consumer Protection Committee

71. How many judges are on the U.S. Supreme Court?

    (A) Five
    (B) Seven
    (C) Nine
    (D) Eleven

72. Which one of these ideas about the social contract did Rousseau NOT believe in?

    (A) Human society is built on an imperfect social contract.
    (B) People ceded power to a group, not an individual.
    (C) All government may be considered perfect, as it is a reflection of the will of the people who constructed it.
    (D) Hobbes' social contract idea needed to be radically revised.

73. Election primaries are used in the United States to determine presidential candidates. Who decides the rules of the primaries?

    (A) The Congress
    (B) The state chief of elections
    (C) The national committees of each party
    (D) State legislatures

74. Primaries can be opened or closed. What is one feature of a closed primary?

    (A) On the day of the election, each individual is allowed to choose the party primary in which he or she would like to participate.
    (B) Voters must register with a party in advance of the election.
    (C) Candidates are chosen freely by all people.
    (D) Candidates are not able to focus their campaign funds entirely on partisans; instead, they must canvass the entire electorate.

75. What is a covenant?

    (A) An agreement one makes with oneself
    (B) An idea that defines political justice, shapes political behavior, and directs people toward synthesis of their desires so that the two manage political power
    (C) A contract where someone acknowledges that he or she no longer own a piece of property
    (D) A religious community

76. *Sociology* is best defined as the scientific study of

    (A) social problems.
    (B) human personality.
    (C) social interaction.
    (D) human development.

77. When a member of the House of Representatives helps a citizen from his or her district receive some federal aid to which that citizen is entitled, the representative's action is referred to as

    (A) casework.
    (B) pork barrel legislation.
    (C) lobbying.
    (D) filibustering.

78. Which of the following states is NOT a permanent member of the UN Security Council?

    (A) United States
    (B) China
    (C) Germany
    (D) Russian Federation

79. One of the major effects of the Industrial Revolution of the late nineteenth century in the United States was

    (A) an increased emphasis on worker health and safety issues.
    (B) an increased emphasis on speed rather than quality of work.

    (C) an increased emphasis on high-quality, error-free work.
    (D) an increase in the number of small industrial facilities, which could operate more efficiently than larger, more costly industrial plants.

80. Which of the following could be a plausible reason why the French did not enslave the Native Americans?

    (A) They were important allies and helped the French hunt animals.
    (B) The French were mistrustful of the Indians and were nervous about having them live nearby.
    (C) French religion prohibited slavery.
    (D) Indians refused to learn the French language and the French refused to speak any language other than French.

81. Which of the following is NOT true of the Cuban Missile Crisis?

    (A) It was a major incident during the Cold War.
    (B) The crisis began in 1961.
    (C) Russians refer to the event as the "Caribbean Crisis."
    (D) It would never have led to a war.

82. In 1967, where did the nascent counterculture first burst onto the national consciousness?

    (A) At a concert in Woodstock
    (B) On the campus of Kent State
    (C) In the Haight-Ashbury district of San Francisco for a "summer of love"
    (D) At a rally for the Black Panthers

Place the following events in chronological order to answer questions 83 and 84.

    I. President Andrew Johnson is impeached.

    II. Abraham Lincoln issues the Emancipation Proclamation.

    III. James Buchanan is elected president.

    IV. General William Tecumseh Sherman achieves victory in Atlanta.

83. What are the first and last events in chronological order?

    (A) III and I

    (B) II and I

    (C) IV and I

    (D) I and IV

84. What are the middle two events in chronological order?

    (A) III and I

    (B) II and IV

    (C) IV and I

    (D) I and IV

85. Conservatives argued against President Johnson's Great Society because they felt that

    (A) the nation would go into debt if it allowed such things as the Civil Rights Act or Head Start to flourish.

    (B) the programs created a dependency among America's poor.

    (C) there were no problems of poverty and disease that couldn't be solved through increased involvement of government institutions.

    (D) it was really just an American version of the French *mission civilisatrice*.

86. The purpose of the Monroe Doctrine was to

    (A) maintain peace in Africa.

    (B) rebuild Germany after World War II.

    (C) limit European influence in the Western Hemisphere.

    (D) ensure the rights of women during the Industrial Revolution.

87. Who wrote "Common Sense"?

    (A) James Madison

    (B) Thomas Paine

    (C) John Jay

    (D) George Washington

88. What was the purpose of "Common Sense"?

    (A) To encourage citizens to adventure westward

    (B) To encourage Americans to give up slavery

    (C) To argue that the time had come to sever colonial ties with England

    (D) To argue that Americans should befriend Indians, not attack them

89. The most common form of resistance on the part of black American slaves prior to the Civil War was

    (A) violent uprisings in which many persons were killed.

    (B) attempts to escape and reach Canada by means of the "Underground Railroad."

    (C) passive resistance, including breaking tools and slightly slowing the pace of work.

    (D) arson of plantation buildings and cotton gins.

90. All of the following played a role in the Cold War EXCEPT

    (A) military coalitions.

    (B) espionage.

    (C) the space race.

    (D) mercantilism.

91. When looking at urban land use, we need to look at which of the following two elements to gain an understanding of patterns of usage with regard to transportation?

    I.   Nature of land use
    II. Level of spatial accumulation
    III. Nature of people's routine activities
    IV. Nature of institutional activities

    (A) I and IV only
    (B) II and III only
    (C) I and II only
    (D) III and IV only

92. Channelized migration flows may be characterized by which of the following?

    (A) Linked areas that are socially and economically tied to one another
    (B) Must always border each other
    (C) Are marked by the tendency to attract migrants via waterways
    (D) Are always a result of push-pull factors so that migrants tend to go to disparate areas to which they have no cultural, economic, or other affiliated ties

93. Which of the following is NOT an area of interest in sociology?

    (A) Class structure
    (B) Race
    (C) Gender
    (D) Industry

94. Which of the following typically is a view of conservative political ideologies?

    (A) View both change and government with suspicion
    (B) Believe government intervention is necessary because people are inherently out for their own self interests.
    (C) Want central government to resolve local problems in order to have a non-biased judgment
    (D) Governments should set moral standards through legislation

95. *Realpolitik* is associated with which German politician?

    (A) Kaiser Wilhelm II
    (B) Hitler
    (C) Angela Merkel
    (D) Otto von Bismarck

96. Which of the following do historians generally consider the earliest root cause of World War II?

    (A) The Treaty of Versailles
    (B) The rise of Adolf Hitler to power
    (C) The alliance of Adolf Hitler and Benito Mussolini
    (D) Japan's success in China

97. In a floating exchange rate system:

    (A) the balance of payments should be equal.
    (B) there should be a deficit in the balance of payments.
    (C) the total consumption should be more than the total supply.
    (D) the exchange rate should adjust to equate the supply and demand of the currency.

98. Which of the following best defines *wealth*?

    (A) Your total assets
    (B) The ability to do what you want when you want
    (C) The value of assets owned minus the value of liabilities owed at a point in time
    (D) GNP

99. Which of the following best defines *inflation*?

    (A) A general rise in prices measured against a standard level of purchasing power
    (B) The difference between the cost of a good or service now and five years ago
    (C) A government program to keep the economy growing
    (D) The tendency of prices to increase at a reasonable rate

100. Which of the following conditions is NOT considered necessary to a democratic society?

    (A) Free elections
    (B) Capitalism
    (C) Freedom of speech
    (D) Peaceful and orderly transfer of political power

101. Which of the following pairs does NOT follow the pattern of the other three?

    (A) Realism–Liberalism
    (B) Free-market economy–Planned economy
    (C) Quantitative–Qualitative
    (D) House and Senate–Bicameral legislature

102. Which of the following is NOT connected in some way to the settlement of colonial New Hampshire?

    (A) Anne Hutchinson
    (B) Exeter Compact
    (C) John Wheelwright
    (D) George Calvert

103. Ferdinand and Isabella's policies of Spanish nationalism led to the expulsion, from Spain, of large numbers of Spanish

    (A) Protestants.
    (B) Catholics.
    (C) Jews.
    (D) Calvinists.

104. As part of the Untied States' foray into world politics and as part of its path toward becoming a world power, U.S. Secretary of State John Hay issued a series of diplomatic notes between 1899 and 1900 that outlined what became known as the Open Door Policy that dealt with foreign policy in what country?

    (A) India
    (B) Japan
    (C) China
    (D) Thailand

105. The Supreme Court played a huge role in determining the legality and constitutionality of many of the laws that were passed during Reconstruction. Which of the following was NOT a Supreme Court decision related to Reconstruction?

    (A) The Court decided that it was unconstitutional to set up martial law where civil courts were in operation.
    (B) In *Texas v. White*, 1869, the Court upheld President Abraham Lincoln's position that the Union was indivisible and indissoluble.
    (C) The Court decided that the loyalty oaths were wrong and invalidated them.
    (D) The Court ended white control of blacks in the South.

106. Which of the following people was instrumental in the development of the atomic bomb?

    (A) J. Robert Oppenheimer
    (B) Leó Szilárd
    (C) Both (A) and (B)
    (D) Neither (A) nor (B)

107. Which of the following was NOT an objective of the First Continental Congress?

    (A) To remain a part of Britain
    (B) To commission the building of a Continental army
    (C) To compose a statement of colonial rights
    (D) To provide a plan that would convince Britain to restore certain rights

108. Which of the following civil rights leaders had a far different plan than the other three?

    (A) Malcolm X
    (B) Martin Luther King
    (C) Rosa Parks
    (D) James Meredith

109. Which of the following is NOT a correct statement regarding the Vietnam War?

 (A) More than 58,000 Americans were killed.
 (B) The war is considered the longest military conflict in U.S. history, lasting from 1959 to 1975.
 (C) The United States fought the North Vietnamese with no assistance from allies.
 (D) More than 3 million Vietnamese were killed.

110. The United States acquired the Philippines _____.

 (A) after World War I.
 (B) at the end of the Spanish-American War.
 (C) during World War II.
 (D) after the Bay of Pigs invasion.

111. Which country was NOT a participant in the Potsdam Declaration ending World War II?

 (A) United States
 (B) Britain
 (C) China
 (D) France

112. What did the Manhattan Project accomplish?

 (A) It developed ideas for the Second Industrial Revolution.
 (B) It developed the airplane.
 (C) It developed the first nuclear weapon during World War II.
 (D) It developed the Sherman tank.

113. Ellis Island was the main reception facility for immigrants entering the United States in the late nineteenth and early twentieth centuries. Which of the following statements about Ellis Island is true?

 (A) It is within the boundaries of Massachusetts.
 (B) Twelve million immigrants were inspected there.

 (C) It was one of only 10 processing stations opened by the federal government.
 (D) About one-third of all immigrants were denied admission to the United States and sent back to their countries of origin.

114. Which of the following New Deal programs was designed to reduce unemployment?

 I.   The Public Works Administration
 II. National Industrial Recovery Act
 III. Glass-Steagall Act
 IV. The Works Project Administration
 V.   Social Security Act

 (A) I, III, and V only
 (B) II and V only
 (C) III, IV, and V only
 (D) I and IV only

115. Which of the following has chief responsibility for assembling and analyzing the figures in the presidential budget submitted to Congress each year?

 (A) Department of Commerce
 (B) Department of Treasury
 (C) Federal Reserve Board
 (D) Office of Management and Budget

116. The Second Great Awakening was a series of religious revivals in the late 18th and early 19th centuries that sought to help the U.S. achieve its special mission in God's design if sin and evil could be first eliminated. Revivalists specifically sought the end of which "social evils"?

 I.   Dueling
 II. Desecration of the Sabbath
 III. Slavery
 IV. Abortion

 (A) I and II only
 (B) II and III only
 (C) I, II, III only
 (D) I, II, III, IV

117. The three immigrant streams that came to the U.S. had which of the following characteristics?

    (A) The Third Immigrant Stream featured people from Russia, Poland, Portugal, Spain, and Greece.
    (B) The Second Immigrant Stream had immigrants from Latin America, China, and Mexico, which led to the "browning of America."
    (C) The "melting pot" idea came with the introduction of Latin American immigrants to the U.S.
    (D) The First Immigrant Stream came from western and northern Europe where an Anglo-conformity model worked for them.

118. Renaissance Humanism was a threat to the Church because it

    (A) espoused atheism.
    (B) denounced scholasticism.
    (C) denounced neo-Platonism.
    (D) emphasized a return to the original sources of Christianity.

119. The concept of culture includes all of the following EXCEPT

    (A) personal values.
    (B) religious beliefs.
    (C) styles of dress.
    (D) individual intelligence.

120. Which of the following presidents was NOT assassinated?

    (A) Abraham Lincoln
    (B) James A. Garfield
    (C) William McKinley
    (D) William Howard Taft

121. The Presidential Succession Act of 1947 established the line of succession for the president of the United States. Who succeeds the president if the president and vice president are killed or incapacitated at the same time?

    (A) Speaker of the House
    (B) President pro tempore of the Senate
    (C) Secretary of State
    (D) Secretary of the Treasury

122. Which term means a merging of older, farm-centered crop economy with newer patterns of more integrated production and marketing systems?

    (A) Biotechnologies
    (B) Genetically modified crops
    (C) Agribusiness
    (D) Organic farming

123. In a regressive tax system,

    (A) the rate of tax is constant when income increases.
    (B) as income increases, so does the amount of tax.
    (C) as income decreases, the tax rate decreases.
    (D) the marginal rate of tax decreases as income increases.

124. Which of the following countries is a republic like the United States?

    (A) Brazil
    (B) Emirate of Dubai
    (C) Russia, 1721 to 1914
    (D) Cambodia

125. Which of the following is NOT a reason why the World Court has proven to be an ineffective organ?

    (A) Members of the UN are members of the court, but they are not compelled to submit their disputes for consideration.
    (B) Nation-states are reluctant to submit vital questions to the Court.
    (C) Its decisions are not enforced.
    (D) It is situated in The Hague, too far away from the U.S.

126. Which of the following is the BEST choice as the major cause of the Great Depression?

    (A) Military unrest in Europe
    (B) The Cold War
    (C) Extensive stock market speculation
    (D) Weak unions

Use the figure below to answer Question 127.

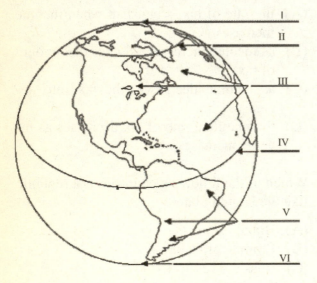

127. All of the following terms identify the correct geographic detail on the figure EXCEPT

    I.   Prime Meridian.
    II.   Arctic Circle.
    III. Northern Hemisphere.
    IV.   Equator.
    V.   Southern Hemisphere.
    VI.   South Pole.

    (A) V.
    (B) III.
    (C) IV.
    (D) I.

128. Which contemporary conflict is an example of *irredentism*?

    (A) Kashmir
    (B) Kurds
    (C) Basques
    (D) Roma

129. Which of the following statements can be said of Emmett Till?

    (A) He was from Chicago and did not understand Mississippi.
    (B) He was arrogant and flaunted his northern roots.
    (C) He was found lynched and hanging from a tree.
    (D) He was a voting rights activist.

130. What does international law have to say about *just wars*?

    (A) The International Court has ruled that there is no concept of a *just war*.
    (B) Does not distinguish between wars of aggression and *just wars*.
    (C) It declares that just wars are legal, but wars of aggression are not.
    (D) All wars are illegal.

Praxis Social Studies Assessment 0081

Answer Explanations for Practice Test 2

Question Number	Answer	Category	Question Number	Answer	Category
1	D	Behavioral Sciences	39	A	World History
2	B	Political Science	40	D	World History
3	D	US History	41	A	Geography
4	A	US History	42	A	Economics
5	B	Political Science	43	A	US History
6	A	Political Science	44	C	Behavioral Sciences
7	B	World History	45	B	US History
8	C	US History	46	D	US History
9	D	US History	47	B	US History
10	C	US History	48	A	World History
11	C	US History	49	A	US History
12	C	US History	50	A	US History
13	C	US History	51	B	Economics
14	A	US History	52	C	US History
15	C	Political Science	53	A	World History
16	D	US History	54	B	Geography
17	D	World History	55	D	Geography
18	A	World History	56	C	Economics
19	D	Economics	57	D	Economics
20	A	US History	58	D	Political Science
21	D	Political Science	59	C	Political Science
22	A	Economics	60	B	US History
23	A	Economics	61	A	Political Science
24	A	Economics	62	D	Geography
25	D	Political Science	63	A	Geography
26	B	Political Science	64	D	Geography
27	C	Political Science	65	B	Economics
28	C	US History	66	D	Economics
29	C	US History	67	A	Economics
30	D	US History	68	B	Economics
31	D	Political Science	69	D	Economics
32	D	Geography	70	C	Economics
33	A	Behavioral Sciences	71	C	Political Science
34	B	US History	72	C	Political Science
35	A	Geography	73	C	US History
36	D	Geography	74	B	Political Science
37	C	Geography	75	B	Political Science
38	B	Economics	76	C	Behavioral Sciences

Question Number	Answer	Category
77	A	Political Science
78	C	World History
79	B	US History
80	A	US History
81	D	US History
82	C	US History
83	A	US History
84	B	US History
85	B	US History
86	C	US History
87	B	US History
88	C	US History
89	C	US History
90	D	US History
91	C	Geography
92	A	Geography
93	D	Behavioral Sciences
94	A	Political Science
95	D	World History
96	A	World History
97	D	Economics
98	C	Economics
99	A	Economics
100	B	World History
101	D	World History
102	D	World History
103	C	World History
104	C	US History
105	D	US History
106	C	US History
107	B	World History
108	A	World History
109	C	World History
110	B	World History
111	D	World History
112	C	US History
113	B	US History
114	D	World History

Question Number	Answer	Category
115	D	Political Science
116	C	US History
117	D	US History
118	D	World History
119	D	Behavioral Sciences
120	D	US History
121	A	Political Science
122	C	Geography
123	D	Economics
124	A	Political Science
125	D	World History
126	C	Geography
127	D	Geography
128	A	World History
129	A	US History
130	B	World History

1.   (D)

Culture sets human behavior above all other creatures on earth.

2.   (B)

The question asks which statement about the cabinet is not accurate. Choice (B) is false, and, therefore, the correct answer. The Constitution states in Article I, section 6, that no person holding any office under the United States may be a member of Congress. Since cabinet positions are offices under the United States, cabinet officials may not be members of Congress. Choices (A) and (D) are true. The cabinet includes the heads of each of the 15 executive departments (State, Treasury, Interior, etc.) as stated in (A). In addition, the president may appoint any other high ranking official whom he wishes to the cabinet, as stated in (D). Choice (C) is true. President Washington was the first to hold cabinet meetings. Every president since Washington has used the cabinet as a tool for managing the federal bureaucracy. So choice (C) is not the correct answer.

3.   (D)

Before the Civil War most blacks in the South were slaves. They were not citizens and had no civil or political rights. After the war, the Fourteenth and Fifteenth Amendments were added to the Constitution. The Fourteenth Amendment extended citizenship to blacks. The Fifteenth Amendment states that the "right of citizens of the United States to vote shall not be denied or abridged by the United States or by any state on account of race, color, or previous condition of servitude." Contrary to what one might assume, blacks did not immediately gain full voting rights. During the 1870s the Supreme Court held that the Fifteenth Amendment did not automatically confer the right to vote on anybody. States could not pass laws to prevent anyone from voting on the basis of race, but they could restrict persons from voting on other grounds. This interpretation of the Fifteenth Amendment allowed southern states to use several techniques to effectively exclude blacks from voting. Since most former slaves were illiterate, prospective voters were often required to pass literacy tests. Poll taxes were also levied, which kept blacks, who were mostly poor, from voting. Since many whites were also poor and illiterate, grandfather clauses were enacted to allow them to bypass the legal restrictions on voting. Grandfather clauses stated that if you or your ancestors had voted before 1867, you could vote without paying a poll tax or passing a literacy test. Choice (D) is correct because the purpose of grandfather clauses and literacy tests was to keep blacks from voting. Choice (A) is wrong because the purpose of the grandfather clause was to allow poor and illiterate whites to escape voting restrictions. Choice (B) is wrong because the intent of the restrictions was to prevent blacks, not immigrants, from voting. In addition, there was little immigration into the South during the time in question. Choice (C) is wrong because the measures were restrictions on the right to vote, not on the right to run for office.

4.   (A)

Franklin D. Roosevelt was the architect of the New Deal, a plan to bring the United States out of the Great Depression. Adolf Hitler rose to power largely due to the economic misery that enveloped post–World War I Germany. Black codes were laws passed by southern states to tie slaves to the land. Charles de Gaulle, president of France during the late 1950s and most of the 1960s, was not at the Tehran Conference; Roosevelt, Winston Churchill, and Josef Stalin were.

5. (B)

As part of the colonial administration, the Spanish Crown divided the New World into four viceroyalties, each with a viceroy and *audencia*, a board of judges who served as a judicial body as well as an advisory council. Crown control over the colonies was direct and those who governed the colonies were responsible directly to the Spanish monarch. The Spanish believed that the colonies existed for the benefit of the Crown. In an effort to promote the mercantilist principle, the development of native industries was discouraged and the Crown claimed the *quinto*, one-fifth of all precious metals mined in South America.

6. (A)

An 1889–1890 anti-foreign uprising among militia units who called themselves the Society of Righteous and Harmonious Fists wanted to rid China of "foreign devils" and their influence. This secret society combined martial arts training, hatred of foreigners, and a belief that they were invulnerable to Western weapons. The foreign press referred to the rebels as *Boxers*. The Boxers killed foreigners, Chinese Christians, and any Chinese who had ties to foreigners. In June of 1890, 140,000 Boxers launched a siege on embassies in Beijing and held the foreigners hostage for 55 days. A combined armed force of 20,000 British, French, Russian, U.S., German, and Japanese troops crushed the movement, forced the Chinese to pay indemnities, and decreed that foreign powers could station troops in their embassies and along routes to the sea.

7. (B)

Some of the reasons why World War I began can be linked to the Austria-Hungarian annexation of Bosnia, Slavic nationalism, and the assassination of Archduke Franz Ferdinand. World War II began as a result of the German occupation of Austria and Czechoslovakia. The League of Nations did not start until after World War I. Secret alliances and secret agreements among nations, while they contributed to World War I, were not really a factor in World War II. The fall of the Ottoman Empire technically occurred after World War I. While the partitioning of the old Ottoman Empire into colonial rule by the British and the French did cause strife and conflict, it was not a cause of World War II.

8. (C)

American-Soviet conflict centered on the postwar fate of Eastern Europe. Stalin, concerned about retaining control over Poland, had asked the U.S. and Great Britain to allow him to keep the territory he had gained in 1939. The Americans, bolstered by a tremendous lobby of Polish-Americans, were reluctant to do so. The fate of Germany had already been decided, and while the Balkans would become an issue, it was not the first issue.

9. (D)

The signing of the Treaty of Maastricht took place in Maastricht, Netherlands, on February 7, 1992. This treaty resulted from European interest in uniting after the collapse of communism in Eastern Europe and German reunification. It also advanced the agenda of the Single European Act (SEA) of 1986 that furthered the idea of the European Political Union by widening EU responsibilities and deepening the integration of European countries through the creation of supranational and intergovernmental structures.

10. (C)

George W. Bush's government asserted that Saddam Hussein had weapons of mass destruction. The claim over who knew what and where remains controversial as some allege that the evidence to go to war was manufactured, altered, or exaggerated to support Bush's desire to get back at Hussein for a failed attempt on his father's life.

11. (C)

The second civil war among the Muslim community started after the death of Caliph Mu'awiya. Many thought that Mu'awiya's son and successor, Yazid was not a good Muslim, and so a rebellion, launched by Husayn, Muhammad's grandson, gained fervor. In 680, Yazid's army and Husayn's small group of supporters met at Karbala, Iraq. Yazid's forces decapitated Husayn and slaughtered most of his forces. The only male survivor was Husayn's child Ali. The Battle at Karbala was known as the martyrdom of Husayn.

12. (C)

Ashoka's reign during the Mauryan Empire (c. 269–232 BCE) spread the empire to its farthest limits. In 261, he conquered Kalinga (the modern state of Orissa) which resulted in a bloody campaign that left over 100,000 dead. Upset with the carnage, he rejected war, adopted non-violence, and converted to Buddhism. He made it part of his duty to spread Buddhist teachings. He initiated a tremendous movement of building 84,000 Buddhist stupas throughout India. He also spread his message to foreign lands and sent out missionaries. One such destination was Central Asia, where Buddhism spread and later made its way to China, Japan, and Korea. Across his empire, Ashoka tried to rule as a moral prince, promoting civic virtue, and the moral welfare of the realm.

13. (C)

Trade over the Silk Road during the Han period created a demand for its most prized product, silk, from areas far to the West. For centuries, the Chinese had known and carefully guarded the secret to making silk, instituting decrees that made it punishable by death if anyone revealed the secrets. Western desire for this magic fabric led to the establishment of overland routes between China and Central Asia. The Silk Road was actually a network of routes that linked China to India, the Middle East, and the Roman Empire. Many of the goods traded along the route were luxury items, which were often small and valuable, and thus highly profitable. Traders also carried ideas along their routes, like Buddhism. One reason Chinese trade with Central Asia increased was that China wanted its swift horses, and horses that were believed to be blessed by heaven because they sweated blood (now known to be caused by a parasite). The social structure in Chinese society placed merchants just above slaves, partly because they were perceived as profiting from other people's work, not their own.

14. (A)

Conservative authoritarian governments, dominated by traditional elites, sought to stymie any change and to keep the status quo. After World War I, conservative authoritarian governments appeared in Eastern Europe, Spain, and Portugal.

15. (C)

By the end of the nineteenth century, liberalism moved away from being just a concern of maintaining the interests of the privileged strata of society and toward a more democratic variety. Liberals during this period looked to government to minimize or correct the problems that accompanied industrialization. They took up issues of slavery, women's rights, universal suffrage, and workers' rights.

16. (D)

The Iroquois were made up of five different nations: Cayuga, Mohawk, Oneida, Onondaga, and Seneca. They lived in eastern North America and relied on materials from the forest for their dwellings. They lived in longhouses and farmed crops such as beans, squash, and maize. The five Iroquois nations joined together to form a joint government called the Iroquois League in which each chief had one vote.

17. (D)

The Ottoman harem was a governmental institution that had rules of conduct and diplomacy. It was also a training ground for women who sought good marriages with Ottoman officials and a place where reproductive politics were managed by the Sultan's mother, the Valide Sultan. Women did receive a salary and some used their money to support philanthropies, and even, at times, to help fund the government when it was short of money.

18. (A)

ASEAN, initially conceived as a bulwark against communism, was established in 1967 by the foreign ministers of Thailand, Malaysia, Singapore, Indonesia, and the Philippines. Its original focus was to accelerate economic development and promote stability in the region. They later focused on economics by signing cooperative agreements with Japan in 1977 and the European Community in 1980, and in 1992 setting up a free-trade zone and cutting tariffs.

19. (D)

Approximately 50 million Europeans migrated to the Western Hemisphere in the nineteenth century, which changed the demographics of the Americas. Some fled the squalid and dangerous factories in Europe, others fled famine, and some left because of persecution. Many of those migrants who came to the United States settled in new industrial centers in Cleveland, New York, and Pittsburgh and contributed to the ability of the U.S. to rapidly industrialize.

20. (A)

While we often talk about the United States as a democracy, it is, in fact, a republic, so (D) would not be correct. A democracy (D) in the classic sense of the word is government by the people, which would be a "direct democracy." An absolute monarchy (C) is a form of government ruled by a king/queen or emperor who holds all power. Totalitarianism (B) is government by a small group of leaders governing under a particular ideology. Such a regime does not tolerate any deviation from its stated ideology. Regime opponents are persecuted, tortured, and detained in concentration camps, and members of ethnic minorities are killed in mass executions (genocide). Historic examples of totalitarian regimes include National Socialism (Germany under Hitler, 1933–1945) and Stalinism. Most modern nation-states are republics (A) where representatives are elected by the public to a governing body, and one where the people elect a head-of-state. A republic also assumes that an independent judiciary balances the governing body and head-of-state.

21. (D)

The right to a speedy and public trial is established in the Sixth Amendment. The Tenth Amendment states: "The powers not delegated to the United States by the Constitution, nor prohibited by it to the states, are reserved to the states respectively, or to the people."

22. (A)

The discount rate is an element of federal monetary policy. This rate affects the cost of money to banks and, subsequently, the cost to borrow by consumers.

23. (A)

The gross domestic product (GDP) is the monetary value of all the finished goods and services produced within a country's borders in a specific time period, though GDP is usually calculated on an annual basis. It includes all of private and public consumption, government outlays, investments, and exports, less imports, that occur within a defined territory.

24. (A)

The functional distribution of income is the distribution of income among the four classes of production factors.

25. (D)

Articulating interests is generally thought of as the special task of interest groups. Parties, on the other hand, bring together or aggregate interests (B) in order to create a working majority to run government. Parties also play a significant role in recruiting candidates (A), and serving as channels of communication (C).

26. (B)

Working with the states, the federal government creates certain laws and programs that are funded federally, but administered by the states. Education, social welfare, assisted housing and nutrition, homeland security, transportation, and emergency response are key areas in which states deliver services using federal funds; such services are thus subject to federal guidelines. (A) refers to a loyalty or pride in one's country of origin. While some political pressure can be asserted by the federal government, it is more finesse than control in many instances.

27. (C)

America's Promise Alliance was founded in 1997 with former Secretary of State Colin Powell as chairman. America's Promise Alliance is a cross-sector partnership of more than 300 corporations and nonprofits. *No Child Left Behind* is federal legislation with massive influence on the states' education programs. READ 180 and Phonics are methods for teaching reading.

28. (C)

The bars represent increments of 500,000. The bar representing the 1830s reaches the first line, equating with 500,000.

29. (C)

The bar representing 1840 to 1849 reaches to the third line, or 1.5 million.

30. (D)

Read the question carefully, specifically the words "Based on the graph." There is no information on the graph to indicate where the people originated. You may know this information from your study of history but the empirical evidence at hand does not give you that information.

31. (D)

The President of the United States is the Commander-in-Chief when the National Guard serves on a national level; otherwise the state commands the Guard.

32. (D)

By reading the graph titles and looking at the vertical and horizontal axes, we can see that populations of inner cities have grown at a higher rate than metropolitan capital areas. None of the other issues are reflected in the graph.

33. (A)

Deviance refers to those behaviors that a group stigmatizes because they are seen as violating basic norms. Rape, child abuse, and incest are examples of behaviors which are seen as deviant by many groups in the United States. Acts that are rare or unusual (D) are not considered deviant if they involve praiseworthy or inoffensive behaviors.

34. (B)

The term *Trail of Tears* is used to describe the forced relocation of the Cherokee tribe from the southern Appalachians to what is now Oklahoma. The migration of Mormons from Nauvoo, Illinois, to the Great Salt Lake in Utah (A), and the westward movements along the Oregon Trail (C) and, much earlier, the Wilderness Road (D) all took place and could at times be as unpleasant as the Cherokees' trek. They were voluntary, however, compared to the Cherokee migration, and therefore did not earn such sad titles as the "Trail of Tears."

35. (A)

As students get older, their mental maps get refined over and over again and represent changing understandings of spatial knowledge as they gain more experience and knowledge, and form more subjective opinions about people and places.

36. (D)

By looking at the legend in the 2007-2008 map, we can see that Iran had a literacy rate of 80-90%, meaning that anywhere from 10-20% of the population was still illiterate.

37. (C)

The smaller the map scale, the larger the area being represented on the map. The largest area from the list of choices is a map of the world.

38. (B)

The existence of price differentials among nations is the primary reason for trade according to international trade theory.

39. (A)

Amnesty International is an example of an NGO (nongovernmental organization).

40. (D)

Science was increasingly used in industry during the Industrial Revolution.

41. (A)

By looking at the graph, we can see that the population increase should climb from 6.7 to 9.2 billion by 2050.

42. **(A)**

An indirect tax is a tax collected by an intermediary from the person who bears the economic burden of the tax. VAT is one example.

43. **(A)**

A relatively large number of Chinese immigrated to the United States between the start of the California gold rush in 1849 and 1882, when federal law stopped their immigration.

44. **(C)**

Asian immigrants do not have a common language. Koreans, Chinese, Japanese, Cambodians, and Vietnamese all speak a different language.

45. **(B)**

In 1664, after obtaining control of Dutch holdings lying between Virginia and New England, the Duke of York made a proprietary grant to Sir George Carteret and Lord Berkeley of the land between the Hudson and the Delaware rivers. These men intended to profit from real estate sales. The new grant was named New Jersey for Carteret, who was governor of the Isle of Jersey.

46. **(D)**

Rather than quotas being abolished after World War I, they were more selectively applied, depending on the country of origin (A). Once the postwar immigration restrictions of the 1920s took effect, the overall total of immigrants to the United States was fixed at approximately 160,000 immigrants a year. The quotas for immigrants from northern and western Europe were set higher to accommodate greater demand; the quotas for immigrants from southern and eastern Europe were very small. In the aftermath of World War I, the United States tried to pretend that the rest of the world did not exist (B). Its people turned inward, and they found that they had plenty to do. In the 1920s, the United States became a modern middle-class economy powered by radios, consumer appliances, automobiles, and suburbs (C).

47. **(B)**

The Eighteenth Amendment made the sale of alcohol illegal, which led to a burgeoning bootlegging industry in which the Mafia played a major role. The amendment was repealed by the Twenty-first Amendment in 1933.

48. **(A)**

Following his ascension to chancellor in January 1933, Adolf Hitler almost immediately began secretly building up Germany's army and weapons stockpile. In 1934, he increased the size of the army, commissioned the construction of warships, and created a German air force. Compulsory military service was also introduced.

49. **(A)**

The Civil Rights Act of 1964 prohibited discrimination for reason of color, race, religion, or national origin in places of public accommodation covered by interstate commerce, that is, restaurants, hotels, motels, and theaters. Besides dealing with the desegregation of public schools, the act, in Title VII, forbade discrimination in employment. Title VII also prohibited discrimination on the basis of sex. In 1965, the Voting Rights Act was passed, placing federal observers at polls to ensure equal voting rights. The Civil Rights Act of 1968 dealt with housing and real estate discrimination.

50.   (A)

In 1963, *Time* magazine named King its Man of the Year; he received the Nobel Peace Prize in 1964. Nevertheless, all African Americans did not unite behind him. Radical African Americans believed King's emphasis on civil disobedience was not the most effective or expedient means of gaining civil rights. Furthermore, as the Black Power movement became stronger and as Malcolm X's message of black nationalism became more accepted by northern urban blacks, King became an increasingly controversial figure. King was co-pastor with his father at Ebenezer Baptist Church, but it was in Atlanta, Georgia, not Harlem as (C) states. King was assassinated on April 4, 1968, while standing on the balcony of a motel. He was 39 years old. A few months later, on June 8, 1968, James Earl Ray was arrested in London, England, and charged with the crime; he pled guilty and was sentenced to 99 years in prison.

51.   (B)

A country's gross domestic product (GDP) shows the total of all of the goods and services counted within a country's domestic borders over the course of a year. Usually, the (GDP) is a helpful measure of the country's overall economic strength. (A) is money invested by firms in countries outside of their home country's borders. (C) is an equation developed by the United Nations to compare development among countries. (D) is a measure of the devaluation of money and currency.

52.   (C)

The Twenty-sixth Amendment was proposed by Congress on March 23, 1971, upon passage by the House of Representatives, the Senate having previously passed an identical resolution on March 10, 1971. It states:

Section 1. The right of citizens of the United States, who are eighteen years of age or older, to vote shall not be denied or abridged by the United States or by any State on account of age.

Section 2. The Congress shall have power to enforce this article by appropriate legislation.

53.   (A)

The Han Dynasty, under whose rule China was reunited, is divided into two major periods: the Western or Former Han (206 BCE–9 CE) and the Eastern or Later Han (25–220 CE). The boundaries established by the Qin and maintained by the Han have more or less defined the nation of China up to the present day. The Western Han capital, Chang'an, in present-day Shaanxi Province, was a monumental urban center laid out on a north-south axis with palaces, residential wards, and two bustling market areas. It was one of the two largest cities in the ancient world (Rome was the other). Poetry, literature, and philosophy flourished during the reign of Emperor Wudi (141–86 BCE). The monumental Shiji written by Sima Qian (145–80 BCE) set the standard for later government-sponsored histories. Among many other things, it recorded information about the various peoples, invariably described as "barbarian," who lived on the empire's borders. Wudi also established Confucianism as the basis for correct official and individual conduct and for the educational curriculum. The reliance of the bureaucracy on members of a highly educated class grounded in Confucian writings and other classics defined China's statecraft for many centuries.

54.   (B)

I=PAT is the formula describing the impact of human activity on the environment—also written as I=P $\times$ A $\times$ T. In words it is the product of population (P) combined with affluence (A) (standard of living), and technology (T) that determines the human impact (I) on the environment.

55. (D)

Ecosystems are rather fragile, as just one disruption to a component can have rippling effects elsewhere. Humans, in particular, have affected ecosystems increasingly as population and energy consumption have increased. Rain is part of the ecosystem.

56. (C)

A market economy relies largely upon market forces to allocate resources and goods, and to determine prices and quantities of each good that will be produced. Capitalist economies are market economies, while managed economies are less so.

57. (D)

Economics is the science that studies and analyzes the production, allocation, and use of goods and services. In economics, the term *resources* encapsulates the four factors of production: labor, capital, land, and entrepreneurship. The supply of these four factors is finite.

58. (D)

Even if you did not know that the media's role in covering and shaping politics is a topic studied and analyzed by political scientists, you would have realized that both choice (B), candidate behavior, and choice (C), election reform, clearly fall under the political science umbrella; thus, choice (D) is the only reasonable answer.

59. (C)

Working with the states, the federal government creates certain laws and programs that are funded federally, but administered by the states. In many cases, the states must also partially fund the programs to qualify for federal funds. Education, social welfare, assisted housing and nutrition, homeland security, transportation, and emergency response are key areas where states deliver services using federal funds and are subject to federal guidelines. This gives the federal government the power to influence the states. For example, in the 1970s the federal government wanted to lower highway speed limits to reduce energy consumption. Rather than simply legislate a lower speed limit, the federal government threatened to withhold money for road projects from states that did not themselves lower the speed limit in their states.

60. (B)

John Rawls believed that the "veil of ignorance" is a better way to determine the morality of a certain issue like slavery based upon the principle that if societal roles were completely re-fashioned and redistributed, and that only from behind the *veil of ignorance* where one would not know what role they would be reassigned, and so only then could valid decisions about the morality of an issue be decided. If we were to take this idea and apply it to slavery, Rawls would argue that if white southerners had not known whether or not they themselves would be enslaved, then perhaps they would have reached a different conclusion about slavery.

61. (A)

The unitary/rational actor model of foreign policy assumes that all nations share similar goals and approach foreign policy issues in like fashion. The actions players take, according to this theory, are influenced by the actions of other players rather than by what may be taking place internally. The rational component in this model is that it is assumed that actors will respond on the world stage by making the best choice after measured consideration of possible alternatives.

62.   (D)

Human environmental geography studies how humans interact with—for example, adapt, modify, and depend on—their environment.

63.   (A)

I=PAT stands for I (impact on the environment) is equal to P (population) multiplied by A (affluence or standard of living) multiplied by T (a technology factor). The IPAT equation reveals that both increasing populations with similar increases in standards of living produce a greater strain on an environment.

64.   (D)

Renewable resources can be replaced in a relatively short time and can be used without depleting the resource. However, non-renewable resources take a very long time to replace, if they can ever be replaced. Such resources may take generations to replace. Examples of non-renewable natural resources are: fossil fuels, oils, natural gas, gold, platinum, and rocks.

65.   (B)

Macroeconomic issues deal with economic issues on a national or international scale, not on the individual scale.

66.   (D)

Free trade is based on the principle of comparative advantage.

67.   (A)

The Federal Open Market Committee (FOMC) sets the Federal Reserve's monetary policy, which is carried out through the trading desk of the Federal Reserve Bank of New York. If the FOMC decides that more money and credit should be available, it directs the trading desk in New York to buy securities from the open market.

68.   (B)

The *discount rate* is the interest rate a Federal Reserve Bank charges eligible financial institutions to borrow funds on a short-term basis. Unlike open market operations, which interact with financial market forces to influence short-term interest rates, the discount rate is set by the boards of directors of the regional Federal Reserve banks, and it is subject to approval by the Board of Governors. Under some circumstances, changes in the discount rate can affect other open market interest rates in the economy. Changes in the discount rate also can have an announcement effect, causing financial markets to respond to a potential change in the direction of monetary policy. A higher discount rate can indicate a more restrictive policy, while a lower rate may be used to signal a more expansive policy.

69.   (D)

Depository institutions use their reserve accounts at Federal Reserve banks not only to satisfy reserve requirements, but also to process many financial transactions through the Federal Reserve, such as check and electronic payments and currency and coin services.

70. (C)

The Federal Trade Commission deals with issues that touch the economic life of every American. It is the only federal agency with both consumer protection and competition jurisdiction in broad sectors of the economy.

71. (C)

The number of justices is determined by Congress rather than the Constitution, and since 1869, the Court has been composed of one chief justice and eight associate justices.

72. (C)

Rousseau believed that all government is inherently flawed, as it creates servitude and inequality. As such, he believed that the social contract needed to be revised, particularly if government failed to protect people, ensure equality, and freedom.

73. (C)

The Democratic National Committee and the Republican National Committee decide how their respective parties will conduct primaries. Each party has its own rules.

74. (B)

The closed primary is often favored by the parties for a number of reasons. First, voters must register with a party in advance of the election. This is favorable for the party because it generates a list of loyal partisans. Closed primaries also ensure that the voters in each party's primary truly support the party and do not mean to undermine its success. The chief criticism of the closed primary is that voters must openly declare partisanship. Consequently, not everyone is involved in the choice of candidates for the general election.

75. (B)

A *covenant* is an agreement between two parties which defines political justice, shapes political behavior, and reconciles two parties toward a synthesis of their desires in order to manage political power.

76. (C)

Sociology studies human interaction, both in small groups and in larger settings, and the results of that interaction, such as groups, organizations, institutions, and nations. Social problems (A) are only a part of the subject matter of sociology. Human personality (B) and human development (D) are more often studied by psychologists.

77. (A)

The term "casework" is used by political scientists to describe the activities of members of Congress on behalf of individual constituents. These activities might include helping an elderly person secure Social Security benefits, or helping a veteran obtain medical services. Most casework is actually done by congressional staff and may take as much as a third of the staff's time. Congresspersons supply this type of assistance for the good public relations it provides. Choice (B) fails because pork barrel legislation is rarely, if ever, intended to help individual citizens. (C) is not the answer because lobbying is an activity directed toward congresspersons, not one done by congresspersons. A lobbyist attempts to get members of Congress to support legislation that will benefit the group which the lobbyist represents. Filibustering (D) is incorrect. It is a technique used in the Senate to postpone a vote on a piece of legislation. The Senate has a tradition of unlimited debate and non-germane debate. This means that a senator may hold the floor for as long as (s)he likes and need not confine his/her remarks to the bill under consideration. Senators opposing a bill might get control of the floor and talk until the supporters agree to withdraw the bill from consideration.

78. (C)

The permanent members of the UN Security Council are China, France, Russian Federation, the United Kingdom, and the United States.

79. (B)

There were many major changes resulting from the rapid industrial development in the United States from 1860 through 1900. The most significant, however, was the attention to speed. First, there was a shift to building larger and larger industrial facilities to accommodate the new machine technologies coming into existence. Small factories could not absorb the cost of much of the machinery and did not produce enough to make the machinery profitable. So, contrary to choice (D), there was an increase in large industrial plants and a relative decline in small factories.

80. (A)

Unlike the Spanish and the Portuguese colonists, the French did not enslave the Native Americans. Instead they were trading partners, with the Native Americans being their main source of furs.

81. (D)

This crisis is generally regarded as the moment when the Cold War came closest to escalating into a nuclear war.

82. (C)

Tens of thousands of young people poured into the Haight-Ashbury district of San Francisco, the heart of America's psychedelic culture, for the "summer of love" when the hippie culture flourished. It was a summer of drugs, music, sexual freedom, creative expression, and politics.

83. (A)

The chronological order of events is III, II, IV, I. James Buchanan was elected president in 1857, prior to Abraham Lincoln, who issued the Emancipation Proclamation in 1863. General Sherman's defeat of Atlanta occurred in 1864, near the end of the Civil War. Andrew Johnson became president after Lincoln's assassination, but was impeached in 1868.

84. (B)

Abraham Lincoln issued the Emancipation Proclamation in 1863 before General Sherman's defeat of Atlanta occurred in 1864, near the end of the Civil War.

85. (B)

Conservatives frowned at the tremendous number of programs that President Johnson's Great Society sought to undertake in their "War on Poverty." Conservatives argued that the programs created a dependency among America's poor.

86. (C)

Expressed during President Monroe's seventh address to Congress in 1823, the Monroe Doctrine was the United States' way of preventing European countries from encroaching on the "backyard." Monroe stated, ". . . that the American continents, by the free and independent condition which they have assumed and maintain, are henceforth not to be considered as subjects for future colonization by any European powers. . ." This policy was the basis for the United States taking the strong stance against Soviet Russia during the Cuban Missile Crisis in 1961.

87.   (B)

"Common Sense," published in January 1776, argued that the time had come to sever colonial ties with England and that it was in the American interest to do so. This pamphlet sold 120,000 copies in the first three months and was instrumental in convincing many colonists that the time had come for independence.

88.   (C)

Published in 1776, "Common Sense" challenged the authority of the British government and the monarchy. The plain language that Thomas Paine used spoke to the common people of America and was the first work to openly ask for independence from Great Britain.

89.   (C)

Blacks most commonly resisted slavery passively, if at all. The Underground Railroad (B), though celebrated in popular history, involved a relatively minute number of slaves. Arson (D) and violent uprising (A), though they did sometimes occur and were the subject of much fear on the part of white Southerners, were also relatively rare.

90.   (D)

The Cold War was the period of conflict, tension, and competition between the United States and the Soviet Union and their respective allies from the mid-1940s until the early 1990s. Throughout the period, the rivalry between the two superpowers was played out in multiple arenas: military coalitions; ideology, psychology, and espionage; military, industrial, and technological developments, including the space race; costly defense spending; a massive conventional and nuclear arms race; and many proxy wars. Mercantilism was a seventeenth centrury economic theory.

91.   (C)

Urban transportation aims at supporting transport demands generated by the diversity of urban activities in a diversity of urban contexts. A key for understanding urban entities thus lies in the analysis of patterns and processes of the transport / land use system. This system is highly complex and involves several relationships between the transport system, spatial interaction, and land use.

Transport system. Considers the set of transport infrastructures and modes that are supporting urban movements of passengers and freight. It generally expresses the level of accessibility.

Spatial interaction. Consider the nature, extent, origins and destinations of the urban movements of passengers and freight. They take into consideration the attributes of the transport system as well as the land use factors that are generating and attracting movements.

Land use. Considers the level of spatial accumulation of activities and their associated levels of mobility requirements. Land use is commonly linked with demographic and economic attributes.

92.   (A)

Channelized migration flows tend to be among areas that are socially and economically tied to one another by past migration patterns, economic trade considerations, or some other sort of affiliation. Examples of channelized migration patterns in the U.S. might be from movements of blacks from south to north, retired people to Florida and Arizona, or European Jews to New York.

93. (D)

You may say that industry involves people and that people are the fundamental focus of sociology, but (D) is the least correct answer. Sociology studies society and human social interaction.

94. (A)

Conservative political ideologies are more inclined to view both government and change with suspicion. They usually emphasize individual initiative and local solutions to problems. Historically conservative political ideologies have argued for less government interference in private moral decisions.

95. (D)

The most famous German politician associated with *realpolitik* was Otto von Bismarck. *Realpolitik* refers to politics or diplomacy based primarily on power and on reality, or rather practical and material factors and considerations, rather than ideological notions or moralistic or ethical premises. Bismarck used this idea to achieve Prussian dominance in Germany by demonstrating a pragmatic view of the real world and doing whatever it took.

96. (A)

When judging the terms of the peace treaties, in particular the Treaty of Versailles, it is important to keep in mind the atmosphere in Europe and the attitude toward Germany in the period just after World War I. Obviously anti-German feeling was strong in 1919. President Woodrow Wilson wanted to secure a peace based on his Fourteen Points. He wanted a peace

that would be based on justice, that would have liberal principles at its core, and that would be maintained by a new international organization (The League of Nations). Wilson did agree that Germany needed to be punished for starting the war, but he wanted the punishment to be fair. Europe took the punishment to the extreme, setting up the next conflict.

97. (D)

In a floating exchange rate system the exchange rate should adjust to equate the supply and demand of the currency.

98. (C)

To determine your wealth, you must consider both your assets and your liabilities.

99. (A)

In mainstream economics, the word *inflation* refers to a general rise in prices measured against a standard level of purchasing power.

100. (B)

Capitalism, an economic and social system, is not a requirement for a democracy. The development of capitalist society may follow the establishment of a democratic state, but a society with many socialist elements can still be a democracy. Free elections (A), freedom of speech (C), and peaceful and orderly transfer of political power (D) are required for a democracy.

101. (D)

In answers (A), (B), and (C), the sets of terms represent opposites. The terms in choice (D) are expressions for the same thing: the House and Senate constitute a bicameral (two-body) legislature.

102. (D)

George Calvert, appointed the first Lord Baltimore by King James I, was an English nobleman who proposed a new colony be established north of Virginia near the Chesapeake Bay. He died, however, before it was established. All the other answer choices are in some way connected to Exeter, a settlement in colonial New Hampshire.

103. (C)

While this question calls for fact retention, it also requires an ability to analyze the implications of each of the other answer choices and to draw on what you already know. The first monarchs of a united Spain, Ferdinand and Isabella, achieved that unity by gaining control of the remaining Muslim sections of southern Spain. In an effort to promote cultural unity and establish a national identity, they defined Spanish nationalism in terms of their understanding of orthodox Catholicism. Those not fitting their definition of orthodoxy were condemned as disloyal or subversive. Two particular groups—Jews, and Muslims who had converted to Christianity but retained Muslim customs or dress—were forced into exile by Spanish authorities.

104. (C)

After the U.S. gained possession of the Philippines, it became more interested in gaining access to the Chinese market. Hay's notes promoted an Open Door Policy with China in which all nations could trade with it. After a group of Chinese militia that the foreign press termed the *Boxers* led an attack on Western embassies, Hay called on countries to respect the integrity of China, but did allow

the U.S. to join a multinational force to put down the rebellion. Hay's concerns with China and other countries in the Caribbean and Central America resulted in increased U.S. interests there in the first decades of the twentieth century.

105. (D)

Though slavery was officially abolished with the ratification of the Thirteenth Amendment in 1865, southern whites continued their control over blacks in the post–Civil War era through the passage of Jim Crow laws, the terror acts of racist groups like the Ku Klux Klan, and the agricultural system of sharecropping, among other means.

106. (C)

The Manhattan Project that developed the atomic bomb was led by J. Robert Oppenheimer, Leó Szilárd, and other scientists. The Manhattan Project eventually hired over 130,000 employees.

107. (B)

The members of the First Continental Congress sought a peaceful resolution of their differences with Britain. They wanted to establish their rights and have them recognized by the government in England. Military conflict was not on their minds at this time.

108. (A)

Malcolm X advocated more confrontational and potentially violent means for achieving civil rights than did leaders like Martin Luther King Jr., Rosa Parks, and James Meredith, who promoted Gandhi's example of civil disobedience as a method for change.

109. (C)

The U.S. military had assistance from many allies during the Vietnam War, including troops from Australia, Korea, and the Philippines, among others.

110. (B)

At the end of the Spanish-American War, the United States acquired the Philippines, and after suppressing an independence movement, it began modernizing the islands, especially in terms of public health measures to stop epidemics that killed hundreds of thousands.

111. (D)

On July 26, 1945, the United States, Britain, and China released the Potsdam Declaration, announcing the terms for Japan's surrender, with the warning, "We will not deviate from them. There are no alternatives. We shall brook no delay."

112. (C)

The Manhattan Project was the project to develop the first nuclear weapon (atomic bomb) during World War II by the United States, the United Kingdom, and Canada. Formally designated as the Manhattan Engineering District (MED), it refers specifically to the period of the project from 1941 to 1946.

113. (B)

Twelve million immigrants were processed at Ellis Island before its closure on November 12, 1954. Ellis Island, located at the mouth of the Hudson River in New York Harbor, was one of 30 processing stations opened by the federal government. It was the major processing station for third-class/ steerage immigrants entering the United States in 1892; it processed 70 percent of all immigrants at the time. Ellis Island is within the boundaries of Jersey City, New Jersey, but is legally part of New York under the 1834 treaty setting the boundary between the two states.

114. (D)

Both the Public Works Administration (PWA) and the Works Project Administration (WPA) were instituted to reduce unemployment during the Great Depression and were part of the New Deal programs. Options (A), (B), and (C) are incorrect. While they are all programs of the New Deal, the National Industrial Recovery Act was enacted in 1933 to allow collective bargaining; the Glass-Steagall Act created the FDIC, which today, as in 1933, insures bank deposits to prevent bank failures; and the Social Security Act passed in 1935 to provide benefits to the disabled and the elderly.

115. (D)

The Office of Management and Budget (OMB) is the chief presidential staff agency. Its primary responsibility is to put together the budget that the president submits to Congress. Each agency and office of the executive branch must have its budget requests cleared by OMB before it gets into the president's budget. The OMB also studies the organization and operations of the executive branch, to ensure that each office and agency is carrying out its appropriate duty, as assigned by law. Choice (A) is incorrect because the Department of Commerce does not help the president to draw up his annual budget. The Department of Commerce was created in 1903 to protect the interests of businesspeople at home and abroad. Choice (B) is incorrect because the Department of Treasury is not involved in drawing up the president's budget. The functions of the Treasury Department include collecting taxes through the Internal Revenue Service (an administrative unit of the Department), administering the public debt, and coining money. Choice (C) is incorrect because the main responsibility of the Federal Reserve Board is the implementation of monetary policy. It has nothing to do with drawing up the president's annual budget.

116. (C)

The Second Great Awakening revivalists felt that Christ would make his second coming after all Americans had been converted and social evils, such as slavery, dueling, and desecration of the Sabbath, were abolished. Abortion was not an issue at that time.

117. (D)

Immigration to the U.S. can largely be divided into three streams:

(1) The First Immigrant Stream came from western and northern Europe where an Anglo-Conformity model worked for them

(2) The Second Immigrant Stream from 1890–1924 featured people from Russia, Poland, Portugal, Spain, and Greece. While their languages were further away from English, they fit into America's "melting pot" and blended in.

(3) The Third Immigrant Stream from 1946 to the present has seenimmigrants from Latin America, China, Mexico, and led to the "browning of America."

118. (D)

Renaissance Humanism was a threat to the Church because it (D) emphasized a return to the original sources of Christianity—the Bible and the writings of the Fathers of the Church. In that light, the humanists tended to ignore or denounce the proceedings of Church councils and pontiffs during the Middle Ages. While many Renaissance Humanists denounced scholasticism, there was no inherent opposition to it and many retained support of the late Medieval philosophy. Renaissance humanism did not espouse atheism nor did it advance an amoral philosophy; it tended to advance a neo-Platonism through the writings of such individuals as Pico della Mirandola and Marsiglio of Padua.

119. (D)

Culture consists of the shared products of human interaction, both material and nonmaterial. An individual's intelligence is the result of personal development and genetic inheritance. Because intelligence may vary greatly among individuals, it is not shared among members of a society.

120. (D)

Four presidents have been killed in office: Abraham Lincoln, James A. Garfield, William McKinley, and John F. Kennedy.

121. (A)

The succession after the vice president is Speaker of the House, president pro tempore of the Senate, secretary of state, and then secretary of the treasury.

122. (C)

Agribusiness is a merging of older, farm-centered crop economy with newer patterns of more integrated production and marketing systems. Depending on the audience, an agribusiness may have a positive or negative connotation. To some, it is a generic term for businesses involved in agriculture. To others, it refers to the idea of corporate farming and contrasted with small, family-run businesses.

123. (D)

In a regressive tax system, the marginal rate of tax falls as income increases.

124. (A)

Choices (B), (C), and (D) are all ruled by a form of monarchy.

125. (D)

The World Court is the judicial arm of the UN and represents a concerted effort to replace armed conflict with the rule of law. Unfortunately, it has proven to be an ineffective organ. Nation-states are reluctant to submit vital questions to the Court, and there is a lack of consensus as to the norms to be applied. Members of the UN are members of the court, but they are not compelled to submit their disputes for consideration.

126. (C)

The stock market crash, which was precipitated by extensive speculation, was one major cause of the Great Depression.

127. (D)

The Prime Meridian is not represented on the figure. Each of the other choices is correctly labeled on the figure.

128. (A)

Irredentism (Italian for "unredeemed") is an attempt by existing states to annex territories of an-other state. The Kurd, Basque, and Roma conflicts are from stateless entities; therefore, they are not examples of irredentism.

129. (A)

On August 24, 1955, 14-year-old Emmett Till was visiting the small town of Money, Mississippi, from his hometown of Chicago. He and his cousin stopped at Bryant's Grocery store to buy some candy. Prior to entering the store, Till pulled out some pictures of his white friends in Chicago, and showed them to some local boys outside of the store. The boys dared Till to talk to Carolyn Bryant, the store clerk. Till went into the store, purchased some candy, and what happened as he was leaving is unclear. Till either said, "Bye, baby" or he whistled at Carolyn Bryant. Apparently Till and his cousin did not understand the magnitude of his act, so they did not tell his uncle, Mose Wright, what had happened. They continued to think nothing of the event as three days passed without incident. However, on the fourth day, early Sunday morning, Roy Bryant, Carolyn's husband, and J.W. Milam, Roy's half-brother, knocked on the door of Wright's home. With a pistol and flashlight in hand, they asked Mose Wright whether three boys from Chicago were staying with him. Wright led them to the room where Till was sleeping, and the men told Till to get dressed. Wright unsuccessfully pleaded with them to just whip Till. As they were leaving, they threatened Wright that if he told anyone they would kill him. Emmett Till was later found severely beaten and shot to death.

130. (B)

A "just war" is the notion that under certain conditions, the use of armed force is justified.

Praxis Social Studies Assessment 0081

Index

N

O

NOTES

NOTES

NOTES

NOTES

NOTES

NOTES